BURYING THE
BLACK SOX

Other Baseball Titles from Potomac Books, Inc.

You Never Forget Your First: Ballplayers Recall Their Big League Debuts,
by Josh Lewin

Forging Genius: The Making of Casey Stengel, by Steven Goldman

Deadball Stars of the American League,
by the Society for American Baseball Research, Edited by David Simon

Deadball Stars of the National League,
by the Society for American Baseball Research, Edited by Tom Jones

The Baseball Rookies Encyclopedia, by David Nemec and Dave Zeman

Wrigley Field: The Unauthorized Biography, by Stuart Shea

Chasing Steinbrenner: Pursuing the Pennant in Boston and Toronto,
by Rob Bradford

Bob Feller: Ace of the Greatest Generation, by John Sickels

Getting in the Game: Inside Baseball's Winter Meetings, by Josh Lewin

Paths to Glory: How Great Baseball Teams Got That Way,
by Mark L. Armour and Daniel R. Levitt

Throwbacks: Old-School Baseball Players in Today's Game,
by George Castle

BURYING THE
BLACK SOX

How Baseball's Cover-Up of the 1919 World Series Fix Almost Succeeded

GENE CARNEY

Potomac Books, Inc.
Washington, D.C.

First Paperback Edition 2007
Copyright © 2006 by Gene Carney.

Published in the United States by Potomac Books, Inc. All rights reserved. No part of
this book may be reproduced in any manner whatsoever without written permission
from the publisher, except in the case of brief quotations embodied in critical articles
and reviews.

Library of Congress Cataloging-in-Publication Data

Carney, Gene, 1946-
  Burying the Black Sox : how baseball's cover-up of the 1919 World Series fix
almost succeeded / Gene Carney.— 1st ed.
     p. cm.
          Includes bibliographical references and index.
          ISBN 978-1-59797-108-9 (paperback : alk. paper)
          1. Baseball—Corrupt practices—United States—History. 2. World Series
(Baseball) (1919) I. Title. 3. Chicago White Sox (Baseball team)—History
          GV875.C58C37 2006
          796.357'64'0977311—dc22

                                        2005017186

Printed in the United States of America on acid-free paper that meets the American
National Standards Institute Z39-48 Standard.

Potomac Books, Inc.
22841 Quicksilver Drive
Dulles, Virginia 20166

First Edition

10 9 8 7 6 5 4 3 2 1

CONTENTS

ACKNOWLEDGMENTS

The Society for American Baseball Research (SABR), especially its internet daily *Digest* (SABR-L), *Lending Library,* publications, regional meetings, free access to the Internet research tool ProQuest, and its incomparable network of baseball experts and friends.

The National Baseball Library and Giamatti Research Center in Cooperstown, especially Gabriel Schechter, Tim Wiles, Claudette Burke, Jim Gates, Jeremy Jones, and Russell Wolinsky.

The Utica Public Library staff, especially Bob Quist, Joan Pellikkan, and Barbara Brookes, for service above and beyond; and the Mid-York Library System. Thanks also to the public libraries of Saratoga, New York, St. Louis, Missouri, Brooklyn, New York, and Cleveland and Columbus, Ohio; the Ohio State and Notre Dame University libraries; and Dawes Memorial Library at Marietta College, Ohio.

Special thanks to Tom Cannon, Bob Hoie, Eliot Asinof, Mike Nola, David Shiner, Rod Nelson, David Fletcher, and Bill Dunstone.

Also Dick Adams, Nic Antoine, Steve Bennett, Charlie Bevis, Mark Braun, Tom Brenn, Bob Broeg, Robert Buege, Bill Burgess, J. Gayle Camarda, Chuck Carey, Ethan Casey, Tama Chute, Michelle Ciccarelli, Merritt Clifton, Scott Collard, William Cook, Warren Corbett, Kathy Dean, Bill Deane, Susan Dellinger, Nicole DiCicco, Rich Domencic, Jim Elfers, Eric Enders, Phil Erwin, David Fleitz, James Floto, Hugh Fullerton V, Steve Gietschier, Daniel Ginsburg, Kevin Grace, Donald Gropman, Daniel E. Harden, Elizabeth Harvey, Roland Hemond, Tim Herlich, William R. Herzog II, Bill Hickman, Stuart Hodesh, Jerome Holtzman, Richard Hunt, Cliff Kachline, Bud Kane, Francis Kinlaw, Kenneth Kinslow, Bill Kirwin, Steve Klein, Ted Knorr, Jeff Kutler, Sean Lahman, Stephanie Leathers, John Leise, Len Levin, Lloyd Lewis, Richard C. Lindberg, Douglas O. Linder, Hildy Linn, Norman Macht, Jim

Mallinson, David Marasco, Arlene Marcley, Adrian Marcewicz, Lesley Martin, Neil Massa, Ken Matinale, Bob Mayer, Andy McCue, William "Biff" McGuire, Bill McMahon, Jeff McMahon, Barry Mednick, Stephen E. Milman, Mark Moore, T. Kent Morgan, Dave D. Mushenheim, Dave G. Mushenheim, Alan M. Nathan, Daniel A. Nathan, David Nevard, Tim Newman, Jim Nitz, Bill Nowlin, Steve Olsen, Royse Parr, Mark Peel, Hayford Peirce, Tom Perry, David Pietrusza, Rebecca Poe, Jacob Pomrenke, Steve Riess, Walter Reuther, Charles Rubin, George Rugg, Jeff Sachse, Eric Sallee, Jim Sandoval, Bill Savage, Dorothy Jane Mills, Lyle Spatz, Steve Steinberg, Patrick J. Stevens, Trey Strecker, Norm Stringer, Jerry Switzer, Bob Timmermann, Cindy Thomson, Rich Thurston, Erik Varon, Mike Veeck, David Q. Voigt, Walter Watts, Paul Wendt, Don Wigal, Gary Wilbur, Allan J. Wood, and John Zajc.

THE ROSTER: WHO WAS WHO IN 1919

Can't Tell the Players Without a Scorecard

THE CHICAGO WHITE SOX
  1B — C. Arnold "Chick" Gandil
  2B — Eddie "Cocky" Collins
  3B — George "Buck" Weaver
  SS — "Swede" Risberg
  IF — Fred McMullin
  LF — "Shoeless Joe" Jackson
  CF — Oscar "Happy" Felsch
  RF — John "Shano" Collins
  RF — "Nemo" Leibold
  C — Ray "Cracker" Schalk
  P — Eddie "Knuckles" Cicotte
  P — Claude "Lefty" Williams
  P — Dickie Kerr
  MGR— William "Kid" Gleason
  OWNER — Charles A. Comiskey

THE CINCINNATI REDS
  1B — Jacob "Jake" Daubert
  2B — Morris "Morrie" Rath
  3B — Henry "Heinie" Groh
  SS — William "Larry" Kopf
  LF — Louis "Pat" Duncan
  CF — Edd "Eddie" Roush
  RF — Alfred "Greasy" Neale
  C — Ivey "Ivy" Wingo

C — "Bedford Bill" Rariden
P — Walter "Dutch" Reuther
P — Horace "Hod" Eller
P — Jimmy Ring
P — Harry "Slim" Sallee
MGR— Pat Moran
OWNER — Garry Herrmann

THE NATIONAL COMMISSION
August "Garry" Herrmann, President
Byron Bancroft "Ban" Johnson, American League
John A. Heydler, National League

POSSIBLE FIXERS
Arnold "The Big Bankroll" Rothstein
Abe "The Little Champ" Attell
David Zelcer ("Bennett")
"Sleepy Bill" Burns
Billy Maharg
Nat Evans ("Brown")
Joseph J. "Sport" Sullivan
Carl Zork

KEY REPORTERS
Hugh S. Fullerton
Ring Lardner
Frank G. Menke
Irving Vaughan

KEY JUDGES
Charles A. McDonald (1920 Grand Jury)
Hugo Friend (1921 Trial)
John J. Gregory (1924 Milwaukee Trial)
Kenesaw Mountain Landis

KEY LAWYERS
William "The Great Mouthpiece" Fallon
Alfred Austrian (White Sox)
Raymond Cannon

CHRONOLOGY OF KEY EVENTS

October 1919

The World Series is played, October 1-9. Cincinnati (NL) defeats Chicago (AL), five games to three.

October 10 — Reporter Hugh Fullerton, quoting Sox owner Charles Comiskey, writes that seven Sox players will not return.

December 1919

Fullerton writes a series of articles for the *New York Evening World*, calling on baseball to investigate the fix rumors.

Spring 1920

Ballplayer Lee Magee sues baseball, claiming that he was "black-listed" after being suspected of crooked play. Magee loses in a trial in June.

August 31, 1920

The Cubs and Phils play a game of little significance to the pennant race. But rumors that a fix was in cause a stir.

September 7, 1920

The Cook County grand jury in Chicago is directed to look into the rumors about the Cubs-Phils game, and the gambling problems of major league baseball.

September 27, 1920

Philadelphia reporter James Isaminger breaks a story from former athlete Billy Maharg about the 1919 Series being fixed.

September 28, 1920

Pitcher Eddie Cicotte confirms to the grand jury that ballplayers and gamblers had plotted to toss the 1919 Series. Shoeless Joe Jackson also testifies to the grand jury. Eight players are indicted, and immediately suspended.

September 29, 1920

Pitcher Lefty Williams appears before the grand jury. Outfielder Happy Felsch talks to reporter Harry Reutlinger.

November 1920

The two major leagues narrowly avoid a schism, and Judge Kenesaw Mountain Landis is named commisioner.

December 1920

Material from the grand jury hearings vanish.

January 1921

Judge Landis begins his term as baseball's first commissioner. He states that the indicted players have been placed on an ineligible list.

March 26, 1921

Thanks to work by AL President Ban Johnson, new indictments are handed up for the banned players and ten gamblers.

June 27, 1921

"The Black Sox Trial" begins in Chicago. It ends August 2, with no one being found guilty of any charges.

August 3, 1921

Judge Landis's edict, permanently banning the players who had been on trial, is issued.

January/February, 1924

In a Milwaukee courtroom, Joe Jackson sues the White Sox for back pay, forcing them to prove that he was not entitled to the salary in his contract.

PREFACE

Before starting this book, try to forget what you have learned about "the Black Sox scandal," that blot which has been on baseball's permanent record for over eighty years. Try to forget that label for the events of 1919, when several gambling syndicates conspired with ballplayers to tip the World Series from the heavily favored Chicago White Sox to the Cincinnati Reds. It happened—that seems certain—but exactly who did exactly what is anything but certain.

Try very hard to pretend that you have never heard the phrase "eight men out." Eliot Asinof's 1963 book, made into a movie in 1988, has a lot of things right. But would *Five Burglars Out* be a fair name for the Watergate scandal? Asinof wrote his version of things without ever seeing the grand jury statements, stolen before the "Black Sox trial" in 1921, but which surfaced again seventy years later; or the pieces of the 1919–20 diary of White Sox secretary Harry Grabiner, which appeared in a book by Bill Veeck in 1965;[1] or the transcripts and other documents from a Milwaukee trial in 1924, in which Shoeless Joe Jackson sued the White Sox for back pay, forcing them to prove that he did something to deserve his banishment from baseball.

Very few writers or historians have seen that last collection, and only two have made any use of it in their publications. Donald Gropman, a sympathetic biographer of Joe Jackson, uses just a select fraction of the trial transcripts in his revised versions of *Say It Ain't So, Joe!* Jerome Holtzman, baseball's official historian, refers to the transcripts fleetingly in just one chapter of his *Baseball, Chicago Style*.[2] So this is the first book to use the Milwaukee trial information to flesh out the whole picture of "the Big Fix," its cover-up, and its uncovering nearly a year later.

The transcripts from the 1924 trial, along with its depositions and exhibits, represent a surviving account of the scandal in the actual words of the participants. Their statements were made under oath and subject to cross-examination by opposing counsel. Lawyer Thomas Cannon: "Cross-examination is often said to be a guarantee of trustworthiness in assessing credibility."[3] The grand jury statements that survive today were not subject to this scrutiny. Further, we know how the evidence in the 1924 trial was evaluated and read by a jury of ten men and two women, some of whom did not even follow baseball.

I do not intend to retell the story that other books such as *Eight Men Out* have already told. However, I need to repeat at least the outline of that story, so readers unfamiliar with the players and events will not be lost.

My main focus will not be on which games were "thrown" by which guilty ballplayers. Those are good questions, but in a sense they are also red herrings. My focus will instead be on the cover-up that very nearly succeeded in preventing the Black Sox scandal from becoming part of baseball and American history. In keeping that focus, I will also try to explain the unique role in these events of Shoeless Joe Jackson.

I shall not attempt to persuade readers one way or the other about Jackson's part in the plot to throw the Series, or about whether he did anything on the field in the Series to earn the $5,000 that he admittedly accepted. I will instead present all the evidence I could find—from books and articles, from Web sites and video documentaries, from interviews and hundreds of conversations. And then, after considering this unprecedented collection of evidence, I will ask readers to make up their own minds.

It is surprising that so many people can get passionate when the topic of "the Big Fix" comes up. Many baseball fans are still upset, even though more than eight decades have separated us from the event. Major League Baseball never really investigated, and the trial of 1921, during which the indicted ballplayers were found not guilty of conspiracy, was in many ways a sham. Most historians agree that Commissioner Landis's edict, barring the accused players from ever playing organized professional baseball, was effective in scrubbing baseball's image clean again. But by failing to give consideration to the different degrees of participation in the fix, and by pretending that banning eight players solved the whole problem, baseball officialdom has perpetuated a cover-up.

It turns out that the more one learns about the events of 1919–20, whatever they are finally called, the more there seems to be learned. Answers spawn fresh questions. It can seem hopeless at times to sort out the actual sequence of events or to give credit (or blame) where it is due. To dig into the events is very much like solving a mystery, with smaller mysteries scattered along the way.

I believe that it is worth the struggle to understand what happened, and why. If baseball reflects America, then in this story we see corporate America, reflected in the White Sox and Major League Baseball, silencing whistle-blowers, keeping real investigators off the trail, controlling the damage and the spin, and finally, when the lid is blown, keeping the focus on eight employees, as if they alone had "guilty knowledge." Baseball survived the scandal; and then along came Babe Ruth, and suddenly baseball fans were hooked on the game again.

The story of the fix and its cover-up is endlessly fascinating, even from this distance in time. There are lessons to be learned about power, its control of the media (back then, this meant the newspapers; radio was still a toddler), and the "conspiracy" among those in power: businessmen, the legal system, law enforcers, politicians, and yes, gamblers. The context of the event is postwar America, when Warren Harding was sweeping to a White House victory with a pledge to return the country to normalcy. But communism was scaring those in power and strikes were shutting down whole industries, while race riots dotted the headlines. Gambling itself was big business, as was baseball, and what had seemed to be a beautiful friendship between the two now threatened to destroy the smaller—baseball.

Not that baseball was a small business in 1919—it was not. As the editors of *The Nation* noted just after the scandal, "The sport has grown to vast dimensions, involving an amount of money and time and emotion that hardly any other institution in the United States can equal." Pitting teams from the country's largest cities against each other, it was fast becoming a national pastime—like gambling. Paul Gardner:

Baseball had for some time [by 1919] been living uneasily in the knowledge that bribes were being offered by gamblers, and that some players were accepting them. The players knew it was going on, and the owners knew it was going on. But more important, the players knew that the owners knew—and they knew that the owners were doing nothing about it for fear of a scandal that might damage organized baseball. Under such conditions it quite obviously did not pay to be honest. Where corruption grows unchecked, cynicism is sure to follow. It was cynicism that enabled the White Sox to accept [the plot] without shock or moral outrage. Fix the World Series? Yeah, why not?[4]

It is time to take a fresh—or a first look—at what happened and why it happened. Casey Stengel was fond of saying, "You can look it up," and I have tried to find and share the sources for everything in this book.

1

THE TRIAL NOBODY NOTICED

John A. Riemer, an employee of Weyenberg Shoe Company, said he saw a baseball game once in a while, but none last year. He read about the players being accused of tossing the 1919 World Series but felt he could decide the Jackson case solely on the evidence.

All John E. Sanderson knew was from the headlines he read in the papers. Mrs. Rose Behling had never seen a ballgame and never heard of the scandal. William Pohlmann had never heard of Oscar "Happy" Felsch, a former big league outfielder who lived in Milwaukee, or the scandal.

They were four of the twelve Milwaukee residents who were summoned to jury duty in the cold January of 1924. To reporter Irving Vaughan, in town to cover the story for the *Chicago Tribune*, the peculiar feature about the jury selected was the absence of their knowledge of baseball. Over eighty years ago, these ten ordinary men and two ordinary women took on the very extraordinary task of unraveling at least part of a mystery that has puzzled millions before and since the trial for which they served. For eighteen days they listened to arguments and questions from lawyers, who were lined up either with Charles A. Comiskey, "the Old Roman," the president of the White Sox (incorporated in Wisconsin), or with a former employee of his, Shoeless Joe Jackson.

Jackson claimed that the Sox had defrauded him when they signed him to a three-year contract before the 1920 season. He said that he never knew—until he was on trial in 1921, accused of conspiring to "throw" the 1919 World Series to the Cincinnati Reds—that the contract he signed included the usual "ten days clause." He said that when team secretary Harry Grabiner came to Savannah and offered him a contract, he was told that there was no ten days clause—told, because he could not read it himself and his wife was not present.

1

With that clause in his contract, the White Sox had the option to terminate him without showing cause, giving only ten days' notice. The clause was fairly standard, but it could be waived, as it was when Sox third baseman Buck Weaver signed a three-year contract before the 1919 season. The team exercised that option when Jackson and the others were indicted in September 1920.

If Jackson could prove in court that he had been misled about the contract, then the White Sox would need to prove that they had had cause for dismissing him. The indicted players had all been tried and found not guilty in 1921, so in the eyes of the law, Jackson would be entitled to two years' back pay, unless the Sox could prove to a jury that he had done something wrong. And not necessarily on the ballfield— if he had conspired to throw a game, that also would be cause for dismissal.

The 1921 Black Sox trial had been a sham. Signed confessions and other material from the grand jury hearing in which the players had been indicted went missing. There were no laws against playing a sport at less than one's best, and conspiracy to defraud was difficult to prove. The evidence against the players amounted to testimony from underworld figures.

But months before the 1921 jury acquitted the accused players and gamblers, baseball's brand new commissioner, Judge Kenesaw Mountain Landis, had gone on record about the chances of the players' ever putting on a uniform again. Immediately after the trial, he rendered another verdict on behalf of baseball: the eight men were *out*.

The 1924 Milwaukee jury had no easy task. Just a few days into the trial, Judge John J. Gregory admitted into evidence the testimony that Joe Jackson had given to the grand jury in 1920, over the objection that it was privileged information. Comiskey's lawyer produced a transcript, perhaps a reconstruction of the testimony that had vanished before the 1921 trial. Alfred Austrian, also Comiskey's lawyer but a witness in the Milwaukee trial, explained, "We got the grand jury records from the state's attorney of Cook County after the [1921] trial."[1] And that was as far as the matter was pursued. Austrian happened to be a collector of manuscripts and first editions; but his acquisition of the grand jury records had nothing to do with his hobby.

The admission of his 1920 testimony created a real problem for Jackson. Why? Because although his testimony was reported in the press as a "confession," in fact, it was an ambiguous and confusing story. He admitted receiving $5,000 from his friend, pitcher Lefty Williams, but he denied doing anything to earn it. He seemed to admit some degree of complicity, but at the same time, he insisted that he played every game to win.

No one had tried to clarify things back in 1920. The lawyer who advised him before he made his grand jury statement, Austrian, was Comiskey's lawyer and was looking out for the team owner's interest. He made sure the illiterate Jackson signed a waiver of immunity so that what he said could and would be used against him. He advised two other players to do the same thing, before delivering them to the grand jury. At the 1921 trial, the three players all took the stand to describe how they had been tricked into signing away their immunity, and they repudiated their 1920 statements. And then, advised by their own lawyers, they said nothing at all at the trial. (It should be noted that at least one player, Buck Weaver, wanted very much to testify to his innocence at the 1921 trial, but the indicted men had become joined together—as it turned out, for all time.)

When the grand jury material surfaced from the briefcase of George Hudnall, Comiskey's defense lawyer, in 1924, and when it was admitted into the trial, there was no story Jackson could tell that could not be contradicted by the earlier testimony. He was perfectly set up for a perjury charge, and that is exactly what happened at the end of the Milwaukee trial. Judge Gregory let the trial run its course, then instructed the jury and let them retire to consider the special verdict. Then he called Jackson to the stand, said that he had perjured himself—either in 1920 or in 1924, it really did not matter—and sent him to jail. He was out on bail a few hours later.

In the Milwaukee trial, Jackson told the story that he told the rest of his life: that he played the Series to win, never plotted with others to throw the Series, and did not know his name was mixed up in the fix until his friend Lefty Williams handed him the money after the Series. Further, he had tried repeatedly to inform the White Sox about what he knew (from Williams), starting the day after the Series ended; each time he had been rebuffed. His recall was not perfect. For example, he was sure that the home run he had hit in the last game of the Series came with two teammates on base; but the bases were empty. It was one of the few things that was easy to prove by looking them up. So it was version against version, causing the jury to assess the credibility of each witness and the plausibility of the accounts that each told.

Comiskey had his own story to tell in Milwaukee. Yes, he heard about the fix the morning before the second game. He at once informed the baseball authorities about his suspicions. He knew which players' names were connected to it a few days after the Series ended. He started an investigation to substantiate the rumors and hearsay, but it was unsuccessful. He signed up the suspected players on advice from his lawyer (all received raises), because he could prove nothing. When the cat was finally out of the bag, he immediately suspended the players. And wasn't it his lawyer who delivered three of them to the grand jury?

Comiskey denied sending his secretary Harry Grabiner to Savannah with instructions to sign Jackson for 1920 and tell him to keep the $5,000 he had received from Williams. Grabiner denied duping Jackson into signing a contract containing the ten days clause. He denied telling Jackson to keep the money.

The twelve Milwaukee jurors had to listen to descriptions of one of the most complicated schemes ever hatched. They heard from Joe Jackson and from Sox outfielder Happy Felsch, and they heard affidavits from pitchers Eddie Cicotte and Lefty Williams and other ballplayers. When they were deposed, Cicotte and Williams had *their* grand jury testimony read at them, too, and they had to deal with that.

The jury heard directly from two of the key gamblers, "Sleepy Bill" Burns and Bill Maharg, who had both helped break open the scandal a few years earlier. They heard from reporters who had seen the games and written about them. And they heard from Charles Comiskey, from his lawyer, Austrian, and from Harry Grabiner. They listened; they watched as each man spoke, trying to sort out who was credible and who was not. They did not need to sort out the whole puzzle because they were focused on just one piece: Joe Jackson.

Throughout the courtroom battle, Jackson was represented by Ray Cannon, a former ballplayer who knew the bigger picture. Baseball's "reserve clause" meant ballplayers had no leverage at all in negotiating contracts. They could accept the terms offered by their team, or find another profession; they could not go elsewhere and play. It would be decades before Curt Flood would name this system slavery, forever changing labor relations within the game.

At this trial, for the first time, there would be new light shed on what Comiskey knew and when he knew it and on exactly what he did or did not do about it. The detective he hired would tell what he found. Hugh Fullerton, a reporter who had crusaded in vain for a full investigation after the Series, would take the stand. His vivid version of the "Say it ain't so, Joe," story, although almost certainly apocryphal, had condemned Jackson; now he would face him in court.

For the first time, Jackson's play in the World Series would be scrutinized. Jurors who knew nothing about the fine points of hitting and fielding would be educated. And if he had played to win, had he done anything crooked *off* the diamond? Had he willingly lent his name to the conspiracy? Or was his name used without his permission— ironically, this was a claim also made by the biggest bankroll of the underworld, Arnold Rothstein.

Finally, the jury would have to weigh the testimony of handwriting experts. Did Jackson sign the 1920 contract in his car, alone with Grabiner? Or was he sitting in his house, with his wife Kate handy to read it to him and to spot that ten days clause? Just as later trials made their followers experts overnight on chains of evidence, DNA testing, or hanging chads, this trial educated the Milwaukee twelve about depths of furrows, nibs, line quality, steel versus fountain pens, blotting, heavier upstrokes, and did you know logwood ink is blacker?

Harry Grabiner testified that he had "never owned a fountain pen." Yet his job was signing players. Had he counted on Jackson, who could not write, to supply the pen?

Judge Gregory gave each side three hours and fifteen minutes for their closing arguments. Then he instructed the jury regarding the special verdict. "An agreement expressly entered into is not necessary. A mere tacit word understood between conspirators to work to a common purpose is all that is essential to a guilty combination." Was Jackson in on the fix, either actively or as a fringe member? Then the jury retired to make its call.

Ten votes out of twelve were needed for Jackson to win his case.

He got eleven. Only one juror believed Comiskey and all his men. The others believed that Grabiner had fooled Jackson. Eleven of twelve believed Jackson had played every game to win. And that he had not received the $5,000 from Williams until the Series was over. And that he had not been in on the conspiracy. And that he deserved his back pay. Jury foreman Sanderson later said he personally believed that Jackson knew where the money he accepted came from. The testimony of the detective convinced him that Comiskey and the team knew Jackson had the money. "To me, this was simply a lawsuit involving breach of contract."

But someone else in the courtroom sided with the lone juror who found for Comiskey. Judge Gregory set aside the verdict of the jury. Then he scolded them. With the righteousness of the judge who banished players without considering their individual cases back in 1921, Gregory ruled that his opinion outweighed that of the jury.

Judge John J. Gregory was not at all a Judge Landis, however. Born and educated through law school in Milwaukee, Gregory was active in Democratic politics. His obituary in the *Milwaukee Journal* described him as a liberal judge, greatly respected by lawyers and litigants. And he was an ardent baseball fan. Thomas Cannon, grandson of the lawyer who pleaded Jackson's case in 1924, thinks Gregory had a strong ethical streak; he once presided over an investigation into ambulance chasing in the legal profession. "I think his sense of right and wrong was offended by Jackson's contrary testimony in the Chicago criminal and the Milwaukee civil trials, both times given under oath."[2]

And what Judge Gregory told the *Milwaukee Journal* after the trial seems to bear that out.

> [Jackson] stands self-accused and self-convicted of perjury. Either his testimony here or his testimony given before the Chicago grand jury was false. I think the false testimony was given here. . . . Mr. Cannon begged the jury to return a verdict for the plaintiff, even if it were only a judgment for $1. This I interpret as a plea for mercy. Such a plea should have been made to the court, not the jury.[3]

Joe Jackson was "jubilant" over the verdict, despite its being immediately overturned. "That doesn't seem as though the jury thought I was lying." Jackson insisted that he had told the truth as he remembered it. "Maybe in some things I was mistaken, but I didn't do no lying—not that I know of."[4]

Judge Gregory:

> I couldn't overlook the conduct of Jackson in this case. I couldn't let it be said that Milwaukee courts overlooked such a flagrant abuse of the oath. No one can commit perjury in the Milwaukee courts and get away with it and I want all the litigants and all members of the bar to understand that.[5]

Happy Felsch also was charged with perjury after testifying in this case.

> While on the witness stand, a nervous and flustered Felsch denied his signatures on, and knowledge of, his 1920 Sox contract and related correspondence, mistakenly thinking he was protecting himself. Cannon was taken aback by Felsch's naïveté,

saying, "If it's your signature, Happy, say so." Even he could not rescue the ballplayer from perjury charges.[6]

Like Jackson, Felsch spent several hours in jail until friends posted bail. Judge Gregory called Felsch's perjury "malicious and vindictive," and the ballplayer faced a possible two-year sentence; Felsch said he misunderstood the questions and any perjury was unintentional. (Eventually Felsch pleaded guilty to false swearing, the perjury count was dropped, and Felsch served one year of probation.)

"The way the Jackson suit ended was nothing less than amazing to the layman," wrote Irving Vaughan. In his view, the judge "severely scored" the jury for failing to take into account what he said was perjured testimony. Vaughan went on to list the ten questions that the jury answered, all in favor of Jackson. "In plain every-day language, the jury found that the White Sox officials perpetrated a fraud when Jackson was signed and that they had knowledge of the crooked work in the series at that time."[7]

"We view the victory obtained by Jackson from a jury of twelve men and women to be so far reaching as to bring about Jackson's ultimate return to organized baseball," Cannon told the press.[8] But this was wishful thinking.

There was a settlement later. The case was not heard again in court. But it has been heard ever since in baseball conversation. And this will continue, even if one day Jackson and Buck Weaver are reinstated to the game. The fire ignited by the fix and the cover-up and the treatment of the eight exiled men seems destined to burn forever.

WELL, ALMOST NOBODY NOTICED

It is not entirely accurate to say that nobody paid attention to the 1924 Milwaukee trial. It was covered in the newspapers, especially in Milwaukee, where it was daily front page news. But the trial and its revelations quickly faded away, so that few baseball fans today who know all about the Black Sox scandal even know that the trial took place.

Three columns by Frank G. Menke appeared in *The Sporting News,* baseball's bible at the time, in the spring of 1924. They were part of a series he had written for King Feature Syndicates, Inc., about the Milwaukee trial that had ended two months earlier. An article by Menke had appeared in *The Sporting News* during the trial, on January 31, in which he gave a detailed account of the events that led to Judge Landis's

elevation to the new post of baseball's commissioner, an event inter-
twined with the maneuverings of Charles Comiskey and American
League president Ban Johnson both before and after the 1919 Series.
Menke traced the "Lasker Plan" to dethrone Johnson and install Landis
to Pittsburgh owner Barney Dreyfuss and Alfred Austrian. So
Menke's interest in the politics of the sport/business of baseball
was evident before his later series on the Milwaukee trial.

Correspondence between Menke and the president of the American League before and during the 1921 Black Sox trial shows that
Menke was also a supporter of Ban Johnson, and his take on the Milwaukee trial has a pro-Johnson and anti-Comiskey flavor.[9] Ban Johnson
was conspicuously absent from the 1924 trial, having been advised about
his participation by Milwaukee lawyer Henry J. Killilea. When it was
reported that the missing grand jury material had surfaced in Milwaukee, Johnson immediately wrote to Killilea and suggested that he ask
Ray Cannon to ask the White Sox who had held the record. (Johnson
thought Rothstein had purchased it "with all evidence" for $10,000, and
he charged Rothstein with that crime in the *Chicago American*.
Rothstein responded by threatening with a libel suit, but never filed
one.) Killilea had followed up on Johnson's suggestion, embarrassing
the White Sox legal team, but the matter was promptly dropped.

In his leadoff piece, April 10, Menke's credentials were listed. His
photo caption read "Student of the Game," and it was noted that Menke
had covered baseball for more than fifteen years. "In this series, Menke
is seeking to write the truth. He has no ax to grind, no personal animus
to get out of his system, but simply believes the public should know the
facts and has set them down under his name." Menke believed the 1924
trial shed new light on the 1919 fix. He was right about that.

Here's how the first installment begins:

What Menke Charges
Exactly one day after the World Series of 1919 had been played,
Joe Jackson walked into the White Sox office, displayed $5,000
in cash, and informed Harry Grabiner, the club secretary, that
he had been given that sum by his fellow players who had
"thrown" the Series to the Reds.

Two days after the Series had been played, Charles A.
Comiskey, president of the White Sox, knew the identity of the
seven White Sox players who had been tools of the crooked
gamblers.

Despite the knowledge which Grabiner had, and the knowledge which Comiskey had, neither man made a determined effort to ferret out the real secret of the World Series crookedness of 1919 and both of the officials permitted all of the crooked men to resume play in the White Sox lineup of 1920. [First baseman Chick Gandil did not sign a contract and did not return to play for the Sox in 1920.]

Menke wrote that the "startling facts" above were established on the witness stand in the Milwaukee trial. "For some strange reason, the real findings which that trial produced, and the amazing admissions made by Comiskey and by Grabiner, were either buried in the general news stories—or, in some way, deleted. They never found their full way into the public print."

Menke thought the trial added "an entirely new chapter" to the tale of "the crooked Series—and its bewildering aftermath." He went on to make these points:

- Comiskey completed his "bluff" by announcing the offer of a $10,000 reward for information—after he knew the Series was crooked, who was in on the fix, and "practically all of the details."
- Comiskey admitted at the trial that he knew the identity of the crooked players two days after the Series but made no attempt to get signed statements from them; that he permitted them to play in 1920; and that he started an "'investigation' merely as a subterfuge to fall back on in case Ban Johnson made a successful investigation."
- Ray J. Cannon proved the above "and many other wierd [*sic*] and strongest [strangest?] things."

Menke's first article ended with the promise that the next chapter would detail the facts produced at the trial and would include Jackson's own story.

His April 17 column, "Menke Writes Another Chapter in White Sox Scandal Investigation," made these points:

- Comiskey knew the truth but "kept it covered" because it would wreck his team.
- Ban Johnson's investigators "uncovered the real truth"— they knew who the guilty players were, and when they told Johnson, he "immediately took it to the office of the D.A. and asked for indict-

ments." (This may not be entirely accurate; it at least oversimplifies what happened.)

- ◆ Comiskey admitted that he signed Jackson after he knew that he "participated in the 1919 World Series spoils. Jackson . . . was always the mystery player of that Series. He outbatted every man on either team . . . fielded flawlessly, and played brilliant, remarkable baseball throughout. . . . It was, therefore, difficult for the public to believe that Jackson, in view of his remarkable record, could have played crooked baseball. Jackson's story, told on the witness stand, and which was not disproved, explains it all. It went this way."

- ◆ Jackson did not know the Series was crooked until after it was over. Lefty Williams gave the money to him, and he took it to Comiskey the next morning. Grabiner told him to take it home. In Savannah, Grabiner again directed Jackson to keep it, because "Cicotte, Williams and the others wrongfully used his name." Grabiner told Jackson he knew who the guilty players were and how much each got.

It is almost surprising that Menke's columns appeared in *The Sporting News* because their editors—reflecting the feeling throughout baseball—did not want to put baseball through another wrenching experience, as the sport suffered in 1920 (with the grand jury revelations) and 1921 (with the trial). In an editorial that appeared on February 14, 1924, as the trial was ending, they wrote, "Taking up one phase of that odorous law suit of Jackson versus Comiskey, we have no patience with those people who are trying to make it appear that Jackson wasn't a blackguard after all; that possibly, while he did take part of the gambler's money, he only double-crossed them and was not a party to the actual selling out of the series."

That Jackson played wonderful ball is "all bunk" to *The Sporting News*. Jackson himself had admitted that he let up in the pinches. Cannon had "not sought to stress Jackson's own crookedness."

It long since was resolved to make no further comment in these columns on the attitude or action or lack of action by Charles A. Comiskey and his various associates with regard to the big cheat of 1919. That is a closed incident, we take it, and the baseball world knows the suppressed part the office end of the White Sox has played in the game since the disclosures.

The Sporting News argued that Comiskey should have "tactfully" settled this case out of court. There had been no new evidence that Jackson was any less guilty than he confessed to be and as "the inside record of his play has indicated" (crooked).

National League president John Heydler said that he was astonished by the "tolerant and even heedless" attitude of people in attendance at the trial. *The Sporting News* noted that the public sometimes makes heroes of crooks. The magnates (club owners) were lucky that the public was tolerant; it might have otherwise risen up against the sport in 1920, "demanding an accounting of its trustees."

The Sporting News said that the trial suggested that Jackson took the money to Comiskey after the Series and was turned away and told to shut up. Their editors were surprised that Grabiner would travel to Savannah to sign Jackson, on terms "calculated to keep his mouth shut." (In fact, Jackson wanted $10,000 per year and was holding out for that; he signed for $8,000, a $2,000 raise.) Mention is made of how an earlier "fix" case was handled. "The public may have gotten their tolerant attitude from the magnates themselves." The magnates "should be very glad of the [public's] lapse of memory."

In his final column, Menke called attention to what had been suggested to the public when the scandal broke in 1920, bypassed when the players were put on trial in 1921, but then confirmed when Comiskey was deposed and then took the stand at the 1924 Milwaukee trial: Comiskey had engineered a cover-up, and it nearly worked. (The fact that Charles Comiskey is in baseball's Hall of Fame is testimony that it *did* work on at least one level.)

In his last article, Menke ticked off point after point: Comiskey knew, two days after the 1919 Series ended, the names of seven players who were involved in the plot (Fred McMullin's came to him later); right after the Series, he accused Gandil of being the ringleader; he made no effort to obtain statements from any of the players in October 1919 or later; he wrote to Jackson after the Series, mentioning that Jackson's name was in the rumors, but never followed up on his invitation to Jackson to come to Chicago and clear things up; he saw Hugh Fullerton's syndicated column saying "seven men will not return" (October 10, 1919) but never discussed it with him (they met three weeks after the Series, about the same time Comiskey hired his detectives).

Menke's view was that the hiring of detectives by Comiskey, to "run down" the crookedness, was "merely a trick by which he could later show the public in case Ban Johnson's" investigation succeeded, that he, too, had tried to find out the truth. Menke relies here on lawyer Cannon's interpretation; in reading the transcripts, I did not find that Comiskey ever actually admitted that his detectives were just for show.

What did come out about his investigation[10] at the Milwaukee trial was that it *was* bogus. The detective's full report, in a letter dated May 11, 1920, was virtually empty. What made this fact even more damaging to Comiskey was that the letter contained the bill—$3,820.71—not the $10,000 Comiskey had claimed to spend "running down" the truth.[11]

Menke's last article did contain a few glaring mistakes. Comiskey did not sign "ringleader" Chick Gandil and permit him to play in 1920. He did send him a contract, but that may have been for show if Comiskey and Gandil agreed right after the series that it was time to part company.

Menke also stated that the jury awarded Jackson the bonus he claimed had been due to him since the 1917 World Series, when, he said, Comiskey had promised $1,500 to each team member if the team won. In a pre-trial deposition, Comiskey had admitted knowledge of the bonus, according to Menke. The jury believed Comiskey had made and broken that promise, but it did not award Jackson any money. The foreman explained that the case was strictly about breach of contract, and there was nothing in writing from 1917. Still, the 11-1 vote for Jackson's credibility, versus Comiskey's and his secretary Grabiner's, is striking.

The Sporting News, not surprisingly, thought the jury was off-base with its calls. They judged the testimony of Comiskey "and his crew" (Austrian and Grabiner) to have been "straight-forward" and believed Grabiner's version of his signing Jackson in Savannah, not the ballplayer's. Yet, given the editors' later inclusion of Menke's searing articles, it is difficult to decide whether *The Sporting News* was being genuine or sarcastic, when it published:

> For such clear and honest statements and no beating around the bush, we find the president of a major league [John Heydler] complimenting and praising Mr. Comiskey for "making the fight alone for honest baseball." We fall over ourselves to add our congratulations, and to apologize for our blindness and prejudice in earlier failure to hail the "Old Roman" as noblest of them all, and his secretary and agent [Harry Grabiner] as a new Messiah come to save the game.

Like the trial, Menke's "exposé" went mostly unnoticed. As sensational as Menke judged his articles to be, *The Sporting News* buried them amongst box scores and other features.[12] This may indicate that the paper wanted to report baseball news, but not make it; and certainly it wanted the stench from the Big Fix to go away and stay away. The Milwaukee trial, covered differently, might have brought about a clamor for Comiskey's resignation. But the Old Roman held on, through the new assault, and kept his franchise. It was tarnished, but it still made a great heirloom.

EXONERATING OR INCRIMINATING?

The transcripts from the Milwaukee trial are a treasure trove of material that will force many assumptions about the Big Fix of 1919 and its aftermath to be reevaluated. To date, Donald Gropman is the only person who has used the transcripts in a significant way, in the revised editions of his book *Say It Ain't So, Joe!* Baseball's official historian, Jerome Holtzman, has a copy of the transcripts and refers to them briefly in the first chapter of *Baseball, Chicago Style.*

Gropman has perhaps the most sympathetic view of Joe Jackson of any biographer. Holtzman may be one of Jackson's greatest antagonists. To Gropman, the transcripts exonerate Jackson; to Holtzman, they incriminate him. Having read the transcripts myself, I must wonder if Holtzman has read them at all. But Gropman may also have done the truth some disservice, by being too selective in his use of them and by not providing the context of some items he quotes. For example, while it is true that Comiskey stated under oath that he believed Jackson played every game to win (standing to lose over $16,000 if he lost the lawsuit), he quickly added that the Sox did not release him for what he did on the ballfield (see p. 223).

Gropman includes as one of his appendices a document prepared by Louis Hegeman, a lawyer who took Jackson's case to Major League Baseball at the request of Hall of Famer Ted Williams. Hegeman cites the transcripts, too, and in one footnote[13] he says that reporter Hugh Fullerton, also, could think of nothing Jackson did wrong in the Series. But I was not able to find that, and I was looking hard and read Fullerton's 1924 testimony several times. It is nice to think Hugh would recant his "Say it ain't so"—but that ain't so; Fullerton was there testifying for the White Sox and his longtime friend, Charles Comiskey.

When I asked Jerome Holtzman about the variance between his take on the transcripts and that of Donald Gropman, he replied that while he had not read Gropman's book, he suspected that Gropman had been selective—picking out only those parts of the transcripts that supported his ideas about Jackson's innocence. He said that there was no need for corroboration of his own interpretation.

In *The Jerome Holtzman Baseball Reader*, there is a column reprinted from Holtzman's Sunday space in the *Chicago Tribune* of June 11, 1989. "Shoeless Was Hardly Blameless" is the title, and Mr. Holtzman was writing almost seven decades after the events he was describing. In the column, Holtzman does *exactly* what he accused Gropman of doing: he cites only those parts of Jackson's grand jury testimony that are incriminating. In fact, he stops precisely where things in that testimony get interesting, where Jackson mentions his attempts to inform his club and then says that he played every game to win. Holtzman calls the testimony "a confession," and that's that.

The full Joe Jackson grand jury Q and A is readily available these days, in several books and at a number of websites. If someone slipped Holtzman a defective copy back in 1989, he's had ample time to locate and read the rest. And he should, because those who believe Jackson guilty need to explain Jackson's saying "No, sir" when asked, "Did you do anything to throw those games?" and "Not a one" to the follow-up question, "Any game in the series?" (Those who believe Jackson *not* guilty also have some explaining to do, of course. But it just is not fair to pretend it's an easy call.)

In *Baseball, Chicago Style*, co-authored by George Vass, Holtzman mentions the Milwaukee trial transcripts. Chapter 1, "Black and Bleak Sox," is just an awful piece of history-writing. Here are some of the errors I spotted. You can look them up.

• Holtzman writes that Gropman "ignores much of the evidence that clearly demonstrates [Jackson] participated in the swindle." How does he know this, if he has not read Gropman's book? In fact, Gropman deals with the hard questions, such as why Jackson took the money, and offers explanations.

• Holtzman writes, "When the confessions were 'lost,' the Cook County Grand Jury dismissed the charges and the players were acquitted." That's right—according to Holtzman, there was no 1921 trial that found the players not guilty of the conspiracy-to-defraud charges. You might think that is a typo, like his calling the "Ninth Man Out," St. Louis Browns second baseman and pal of Swede Risberg, Joe Gedeon, "Joe Gideon."

But I have heard from Jackson student and advocate Mike Nola that Holtzman also said this on a national radio program, with Nola challenging and pointing him to Asinof's book *Eight Men Out* as one of many places to look it up.

- Holtzman cites the Fullerton "Say it ain't so, Joe" story as if it is generally accepted as factual. It is regarded as fictitious by many who have researched the subject.

- Holtzman reprints the only "damning" section of Jackson's grand jury testimony but leaves out the passages that are troublesome for his own beliefs.

- He reports how the returning Sox all got nice raises for 1920, "an aggregate 101 percent pay hike." But he says that the show of generosity happened "after the scandal was exposed" when in fact it did not occur for another seven months. And his 101 percent might be a bit high, as he has utility man McMullin getting a raise from $2,750 to $7,000 (instead of the $3,600 cited in team secretary Harry Grabiner's 1920 diary).[14]

- Holtzman repeats the argument that Jackson must have meant to lose the Series because he was "inept in the clutch" in the first five games and batted .462 the last three games, without noting that this particular logic would make "fixers" of Hall of Famers Eddie Collins and Edd Roush, too.

- He has Jackson making an "admission of guilt" to wire service reporters on September 19, 1920. This is a typo—Jackson was quoted on September 29—but there is also reason to doubt that the words are his. The reporters from the Associated Press and United Press International included statements attributed to Jackson, most likely guessing at what he said before the grand jury. None of the statements about not giving his best effort can be found in the grand jury testimony we can read today.

- Holtzman has Jackson suing in 1924 for back pay for the 1922 and 1923 seasons—it was for 1921 and 1922.

- He cites the *Milwaukee Journal*'s description of the "shock of the people in the courtroom and elsewhere, [when] lawyers for Comiskey produced Jackson's signed grand jury confession [it was a statement, later characterized by some as a confession] in which Jackson admitted his role in the scheme to throw the World Series" (he admitted taking money, but made contradictory statements about his performance). What Holtzman does not say is that the shock was not at Jackson's words, but at the fact that this document appeared out of thin air—after being very conspicuously missing before the 1921 trial. Some believe that Comiskey and underworld kingpin Rothstein teamed up on that disappearing act.

- Holtzman has Hugh Fullerton working for the *Tribune* instead of the *Herald and Examiner* and writes that Hugh predicted after the Series "with uncanny accuracy, that seven of the White Sox players would not be back with the club the next season." That was not uncannily accurate, it was plain wrong—not Hugh's fault because he had put his faith in Comiskey. But the fact is that only Gandil did not return. He has Fullerton's most famous charges appearing in the *New York Evening Mail*, while they appeared in the *New York Evening World*.

To be fair, Holtzman has some very good material in this chapter, too—a chapter that he told me (with some pride in his voice) that he (and not co-author George Vass) wrote. Holtzman comes down hard on Comiskey and his lawyer Austrian, harder than most writers.[15]

But on the whole, Holtzman's work is bleak and black journalism, which begs for a fact-checker. If there is conclusively "incriminating" material in the 1924 transcripts, Holtzman has failed to reveal it in this book—and he told me he has cited the transcripts nowhere else.

Not all of the errors listed above are major, and a few are just typos. But the frequency, nearly one a page, is significant, for someone who holds the position of Major League Baseball's "official historian." And the tone is so plainly slanted that Holtzman simply should let someone else handle the Joe Jackson issue, should current commissioner Bud Selig send it his way.

I have enjoyed reading Jerome Holtzman's books over the years. But he apparently has a blind spot regarding the Black Sox. He is not at all alone. It seems that many people do. And if baseball's official historian seems confused about the facts, what about the average fan, who probably learned most of what he knows of these events from *Eight Men Out*? It is time to pull together the facts that we can find and let all of the evidence speak for itself.

2

THE WORLD SERIES OF 1919

You just never knew when [the White Sox] were going to go out there and beat your brains out or roll over and play dead. Somebody was betting on those games [in 1920], that's a cinch. When they wanted to play, you had a hard time beating them, that's how good they were.
　　　　　　　　　　　　　—Roger Peckinpaugh in *A Donald Honig Reader*

October 1: Cincinnati 9, Chicago 1, at Cincinnati
October 2: Cincinnati 4, Chicago 2, at Cincinnati
October 3: Chicago 3, Cincinnati 0, at Chicago
October 4: Cincinnati 2, Chicago 0, at Chicago
October 6: Cincinnati 5, Chicago 0, at Chicago
October 7: Chicago 5, Cincinnati 4, at Cincinnati
October 8: Chicago 4, Cincinnati 1, at Cincinnati
October 9: Cincinnati 10, Chicago 5, at Chicago

In the record books, the 1919 "fixed" World Series looks like all the other postseason baseball championship matches that have been played. That has puzzled me since I first started looking things up as a kid in the late fifties, in the books that came with my family's subscription to *The Sporting News*. If the White Sox had "thrown" the Series to the Reds, why was this Series even *in* the record books? Surely at least the games that are known or suspected to have been thrown should have an asterisk, or some kind of explanatory footnote. But they do not. The cover-up continues, if in subtle ways.

The World Series in 1919 was eagerly anticipated by fans as a joyful event, capping a season in which baseball soared back into popularity after the 1918 season was cut short by World War I. It was to be a best-of-nine games affair, the first in a three-year experiment.

That the World Series had become a huge event with national interest is demonstrated by this description from 1915:

> The World Series is the great event in contemporary sport. It is great because it appeals to two fundamental characteristics in human nature, viz, a craving after the best, as exemplified in world series games, and a love of wholesome rivalry as shown in the struggle of the two leagues for the championship of the world.[1]

Cincinnati, the National League champion by nine games over the legendary John McGraw's New York Giants in the 140-game season, would host Games One and Two at Redland Field. Their opponent was the Chicago White Sox, winner of the American League flag.

There were the usual reports of betting men trying to get an edge by pumping players or team employees for inside dope. Reds manager Pat Moran: "Some piker-gambler tried to get one of my pitchers oiled up with the hooch a couple days before the Series, but I found out and stopped it."[2]

The World Series, begun in 1903 and played regularly each October since 1905, had emerged as the premier betting event in America. But it can be argued that gambling was the true national pastime, because everybody seemed to be doing it. Daily newspapers published the odds for the World Series—and not just on who would win the Series, as this October 1917 excerpt indicates:

> Even money that Cicotte gives fewer bases on balls than Schupp. Even money Sox win the first game, October 6. Fifteen to one that the Sox win the first four games. Six to five that the Giants don't break even in the first four games. Twelve to five that the Giants don't win three of four games. Twelve to five that the Sox don't take three of four games. *[The Sox and Giants split the first four games.]* Eleven to ten that the Sox steal more bases than the Giants. Even money that Benny Kauff don't get a hit in his first four times at bat. Even money that the first ball pitched is a called strike. Three to one that the first man at bat doesn't hit safely. Two to one that Eddie Collins gets more hits than Herzog.[3]

In other words, the kind of betting frenzy that today we associate more with the Super Bowl or the NCAA college basketball Final Four, gripped America every October. In New York City alone, an estimated two million dollars changed hands in betting on the 1919 World Series, and the *New York Times* called that estimate conservative.

Professional gamblers had been moving into the country of baseball steadily, with the corruption of boxing and horse racing. Just how pervasive their reach was would only be known later, after the Big Fix was uncovered. Suffice it to say that gamblers and players had numerous connections in 1919, and that, in fact, the line between the two groups had become blurred. To this day, it is not clear whether the fix of the 1919 Series was initiated by ballplayers or by gamblers, and it could well have been an idea that occurred to men in both groups at the same time. And fixing a World Series was not even a new idea—but more on that later.

Eliot Asinof has compared the way today's athletes are at risk for drug abuse to the way ballplayers in 1919 were open game for preying gamblers.

> How like the charming, debonair urbane gamblers of old, who used to wine and dine the impressionistic rubes showing them the glamours of the big-league city life, teaching them how to dress, supplying them with desirable women! And if there was a price to pay—a little inside information about a pitcher's sore arm, say, or a slugger's drunken night out, anything that might give a betting man an edge—why not?[4]

As Joe Garagiola is fond of saying, baseball is a funny game. If you assume that "the fix is in" before watching a game, you will see all kinds of suspicious plays. Each error will seem to be intentional. After all, each play involves failure and success: if the batter succeeds and gets on base, the pitcher has failed to get him out. And vice versa. The turning point can come at any time, games can be lost in the first inning or in the final at bat. In baseball, you never know.

But for the moment, let us just take a look at the 1919 World Series as the fans did back then, without wondering if the fix was in or if any ballplayer was playing crooked. Later, we will look at each of the eight players who were "bunched together" in the rumors that surrounded the eight games played in October 1919.

The World Series back then was in the hands of the National Commission, which consisted of the presidents of the two major leagues and a chairman. In 1919, the chairman was Cincinnati Reds owner Garry Herrmann. The commission was not effective, and the owners of the clubs had appointed or elected a joint committee to recommend a new chairman—someone without the conflict of interest that any club owner would have.

On September 21, joint committee member Col. Jacob Ruppert, president of the American League New York team, called on Garry Herrmann to step down from his chair for the next two weeks, or until the 1919 World Series was over. Ruppert believed that it would be "open to objection from every point of view to have the president of one of the [pennant-] winning clubs also serving on the commission during the world's series."[5] Ruppert's recommendation was ignored. Baseball was sailing along to the grandest World Series ever like the unsinkable Titanic. What could possibly happen that would require a chairman without a financial and emotional interest in the event?

Game One, at Cincinnati. White Sox pitcher Eddie Cicotte's second pitch hit the leadoff batter, Reds second baseman Morrie Rath. The Reds pushed him around to take a 1–0 lead, but the Sox came back to tie it in the top of the second. The game remained tied until the fourth inning, when the Reds exploded for five runs, knocking Cicotte out of the game. The key hit was by Reds pitcher Dutch Ruether, who pitched a complete game six-hitter in the 9–1 win. The next day's *New York Times* commented, "Cicotte pitched for the Reds."

Game Two, at Cincinnati. Sox starter Lefty Williams and the Reds' Slim Sallee pitched scoreless ball until Williams walked three Reds in the fourth inning. Larry Kopf's two-run triple capped a three-run surge that held up. Both pitchers tossed complete games, not unusual in the deadball era; and although the Sox out-hit the Reds 10–4, they lost 4–2.

Game Three, at Chicago. Rookie southpaw Dickie Kerr pitched a three-hit shutout for the White Sox. Chick Gandil's two-run double in the second inning off Ray Fisher stood up in the 3–0 White Sox win.

Game Four, at Chicago. Starters Jimmy Ring of Cincinnati and Eddie Cicotte of Chicago both pitched terrific games. But two errors by Cicotte allowed the Reds to score twice in the fifth inning. The Sox managed just three hits in the 2–0 Reds win.

Game Five, at Chicago. After a day of rain and no game, the Sox were shut out in a powerful performance by the Reds' Hod Eller. His six straight strikeouts (including Ray Schalk, Nemo Leibold, and Eddie Collins—none of them later suspected in the fix) were the highlight of the game. Lefty Williams shut out the Reds until the sixth, when the Reds broke through with four runs, en route to a 5–0 win and a 4–1 lead in the best-of-nine Series.

Game Six, at Cincinnati. Dickie Kerr was on the hill again for the White Sox, against Dutch Ruether of the Reds. Cincinnati took a 4–0 lead after four innings, but the Sox battled back, with a run in the fifth and three more off Jimmy Ring in relief in the sixth. In the tenth inning, Chick Gandil singled home Buck Weaver, and Kerr made the run hold up, in the 5–4 Sox victory.

Game Seven, at Cincinnati. Eddie Cicotte hurled the Sox to a 4–1 win, as they stayed alive a second straight day. Jackson singled home Shano Collins with the deciding run as Slim Sallee was handed the loss. Oddly, Redland Field was less than half full, even though the Reds had the chance to earn their first championship.

Game Eight, at Chicago. Lefty Williams, who had already lost twice in the Series, got the start and failed to make it out of the first inning. The Reds scored four times and were up 10–1 before the Sox scored four off Eller in the eighth. But Hod settled down and the final score was 10–5. Joe Jackson hit the only home run of the Series, and the Sox got ten hits for a third straight game, but the Reds racked up sixteen in the clinching win.

In winning five of the eight games, the Reds outhit the White Sox 64–59, outscored them 35–20, and out-pitched them, holding Sox batters to a .224 average and 1.63 earned runs per game—compared to the Reds' .255 and 3.68. Both teams committed a dozen errors, and there were rumors after Games Six and Seven that the Reds were losing on purpose to extend the Series and bring in more revenue—or because they were bribed to lose by gamblers.

There were sparkling defensive plays made by both teams and pitching gems on both sides, too. A fan who was simply following the Series without taking sides was probably rooting at the end for a Game Nine to see if Dickie Kerr could win a third time.

There had been rumors of a fix by gamblers before the Series began, and the odds that had the White Sox as favorites dropped sharply. The rumors persisted during the Series, especially after the Sox dropped four of the first five games.

A mid-series editorial in *The Sporting News* commented on the presence of gamblers. There was concern that they were scouting teams and giving "inside stuff" to the players on the team on which they had their money riding.

There is not a breath of suspicion attached to any player, nor a hint that an effort in any manner was made to influence a player's performance—not a chance for that—but there is a repugnance among sportsmen that such organized methods of getting "dope" for gambling purposes should be practiced.

The Sox comeback in Games Six and Seven did much to silence those rumors. But after the Series, there was more than the usual complaining from those who had bet big on the Sox and lost. *The Sporting News* continued to respond to the accusations as if a fix was simply impossible. W. A. Phelon wrote on October 16, "Talk of gambling and thrown games was rife, both ways. . . . If ever a Series was played upon the level, this was the one." To Phelon, the Reds simply "outclassed" the over-confident White Sox.

In the same issue, Henry P. Edwards went on record: "That the Sox were guilty of intentional bad play is something that cannot be swallowed." James O'Leary of Boston went further: "If anybody was 'fixed,' give us his name and the evidence showing that he was fixed, and who fixed him." The "howl" from the gamblers who lost was drowned out in baseball's bible. There was scant mention when an unspecified Chicago newspaper launched a "bitter attack," mentioning several players by name, and promising a "big expose." A fix was unbelievable, and the idea of one would get no more attention unless and until there was some evidence.[6]

Baseball Magazine, a monthly publication that also covered the series, defended the integrity and reputation of baseball with vigor. Its interview with Eddie Cicotte appeared just after the series; the title, "The Basis of a Pitcher's Success," suggests that much of the interview was conducted before the series. But the magazine gave Eddie a chance to defend himself against the "fix" rumors, and he did just that.

> For my first game I will offer no apologies. It was a very hot day and the heat bothered me considerably. But I thought I could pitch my best ball. I was mistaken as the results showed plainly enough. My second game I did pitch as well as I was expected to do. But I was a little over anxious in the field and things broke badly for me.

Lefty Williams also was interviewed in the off-season, and he lamented his pitching of the previous October. "I want another try at a world's series. I suppose I was the goat of the last one and I don't relish the distinction."[7]

Baseball Magazine carried numerous interviews with the victorious Reds, too, making things seem as ordinary as ever. Meanwhile, the magazine's editorials took to task in harsh terms those who dared to suggest the games were not played on the level.

The Cincinnati Reds, without exception, and their manager Pat Moran thought they had won the Series fair and square, and some of them continued to believe that, even after evidence to the contrary appeared. On September 28, 1920, the statement Eddie Cicotte made to a Chicago grand jury told the world that there was a conspiracy among some of the Sox to lose. Reds pitcher Dutch Ruether told Oregon reporter Emmett Watson years later that he shared his reaction with his wife: "Well, honey, I thought I beat the greatest team in the world—and now I find out they weren't even trying." The umpires were shocked along with the fans.

"I was there. I saw them," said the Reds' pitcher from Cuba, Adolfo Luque, who pitched five scoreless relief innings in Games Three and Seven, both Sox wins. "[Jackson and Weaver] just couldn't be playing that way and not playing."[8]

"We had the jump on the Sox in every game," said Jake Daubert, the Reds' first baseman. "We hit Kerr harder than we did Williams," Daubert continued, commenting on the statement attributed to Joe Jackson that the Sox tried to "kick away" Game Three. "The Sox fielding in the third game looked good to me."[9]

Shortstop Larry Kopf and catcher Ivy Wingo told reporters how Cicotte apparently worked hard to make them easy outs.[10]

Pitcher Hod Eller insisted that the Sox were "playing for keeps" in the two games he pitched and won (five and eight), and perhaps they were. Another Reds' pitcher, Slim Sallee, maintained to the end of his life that none of the players on the Cincinnati club realized that the fix was in during the Series. "I didn't realize it at the time. I couldn't believe it, although it was whispered around the hotels and gambling headquarters that something underhanded was taking place."

Reds outfielder Greasy Neale, later a championship coach in the National Football League who had "a remarkable memory, photographic in its accuracy," admitted that there were some "queer looking plays" in Game One. But Neale "contended stoutly that all of the other games were honestly contested."[11]

"Dick Hoblitzell, manager of the Akron team, told me last year [1919] that he suspected the White Sox players," Neale told another reporter. "I told him the Chicago team had played their best."[12]

Neale, in a later interview, said, "There isn't any question but that there were shenanigans in the first game, but remember that the Sox who fell for the fixers weren't paid what they were promised. You can bet your life they were shooting in the next seven games."[13] Neale went on to recall great plays made by the "crooked" Sox, as well as a great defensive play by Edd Roush to retire Felsch in Game Two.

Hall of Famer Roush, who played the outfield in October 1919 beside Neale, was also convinced that the Sox tried to win after Game One, and his recollections were fairly sharp when he was interviewed in 1974 by Eugene Murdock. Larry Kopf, the Reds' shortstop, told Murdock that same year, "We didn't surmise a damn thing. I couldn't figure it out." Kopf did not even recall rumors of a fix.

Roush: "Why, I didn't get a bingle off Cicotte, and every time I faced him he seemed to have a world of speed. I can't yet see how they could play the way they did and throw the games. It is a mystery to me."[14]

The Cincinnati third baseman Heinie Groh said that he had found Cicotte's pitching "as hard to solve as any I had faced during the year. . . . They seemed to be doing their level best to win. We attributed the stories heard around Cincinnati about the White Sox not trying to 'sour grapes' on the part of American League sympathizers."[15] He recalled Swede Risberg saving three runs by leaping to spear a line drive with the bases full. Years later, Groh admitted, "Well, maybe the White Sox did throw it. I don't know. Maybe they did and maybe they didn't. It's hard to say. I didn't see anything that looked suspicious. But I think we'd have beaten them either way; that's what I thought then and I still think so today."[16]

Reds manager Pat Moran:

If they threw some of the games they must be consummate actors, and their place is on the stage, for nothing in their playing gave us the impression they weren't doing their best. . . . It is an astonishing thing to me that [they] could get away with that sort of thing and us not know it.[17]

Reds owner Garry Herrmann, after it was learned that Cicotte had confirmed that a fix was in, was asked if he would surrender the pennant.

I have never given such a ridiculous question any thought. We won the National League pennant fairly and squarely, and we had to beat a team or two to do it that were stronger than the

White Sox playing at their best and on the level. We could not hand the pennant back to the Sox simply because they did not try to win it, and, what is more, we believe firmly that we would have beaten them had every man on Comiskey's team played the string out and on the level.[18]

National League umpire Richard Nallin said he had "no suspicions whatever of any wrong-doing." American League ump Billy Evans said, "Well, I guess I'm just a big dope. That Series looked all right to me." When the scandal broke, umpire Ernie Quigley was shocked:

He said he never saw a team try harder to win, and that they were beaten on the square by the superior strength of the Reds. He cites the wonderful catch made by Eddie Roush in the second game, which saved that contest, and also a great play by Morris Rath in a later game [Game Four]. But for these two plays the White Sox would have won at least two more games, which would have meant the series for them.[19]

Say it ain't so, indeed.

Almost a year had passed. There were no videotapes to replay and scrutinize, only a handful of grainy film clips. The box scores were silent about player intentions. Even those who had watched the Series with suspicion were not certain about who was playing to win and who was not or about which games were "thrown." Some of the accused players denied that anything was "crooked."

Before looking again at what happened on the diamond in the eight games of October 1919, we will take a closer look at something baseball has tried hard to keep off center stage: the cover-up of the fix, which started right after Game One ended. Or maybe sooner.

3

THE COVER-UP

To understand the Black Sox Scandal, the magic word is cover-up. *And so it was from the day the 1919 World Series fix began.*
—Eliot Asinof, *for ESPN Classic's website*

The largest fiction was that Comiskey was unaware of the fix.
—Jerome Holtzman in *The Commissioner*

On the day that the 1920 World Series opened, Joe Jackson and Lefty Williams were in Greenville, South Carolina, taking time out and visiting a local attorney. Now indicted, they realized that Comiskey's lawyer was not looking out for their best interests after all. According to the Chicago Times *of October 6, 1920—and it is just a squib, not two column inches long—they* "had no further comment to make other than the statement that if the investigators probe thoroughly they may find men higher up in baseball at the bottom of the scandal."

POWER SKIRMISHES

There are really two cover-ups. The first has to do with the Big Fix; for over eleven months, the American public was kept in the dark about the throwing of the 1919 World Series. But there is a larger cover-up that continues until today. "The Black Sox scandal" and "eight men out" are phrases that perpetuate this second cover-up. In this chapter, we will look at the first cover-up.

For the moment, we will set aside the gamblers and the ballplayers who knew of the fix. What set the cover-up in motion?

To answer this question, we need to know who engineered the cover-up. The tempting short answer might be Charles Comiskey, the owner of the White Sox. But just as it would be impossible for one player to throw a

World Series, so it would have been impossible for Comiskey to pull off the cover-up by himself. And indeed, it seems that he had plenty of help:

> To me, baseball is as honorable as any other business. It is the most honest pastime in the world. It has to be or it could not last a season out. Crookedness and baseball do not mix. [Baseball] has become immeasurably more popular as the years have gone by. It will be greater yet. This year, 1919, is the greatest season of them all.

The words above are Charles Comiskey's. He understood well that baseball needed to have a clean image or it would lose its appeal. He continued:

> The reason for the popularity of the sport is that it fits in with the temperament of the American people and because it is on the square. Everything is done in the open. What the magnates do behind the scenes the fans care nothing about.[1]

Comiskey also understood baseball fans pretty well. He knew they wanted a clean sport in a clean ballpark that would not clean out their wallets to get in. They wanted to talk and read all about the players—and they could not care less about the magnates unless they made trades to improve (or wreck) the home team. In fact, the fans knew only as much about what went on "behind the scenes" as the magnates wanted them to know.

Alfred Austrian, Comiskey's lawyer, surely advised him on how to protect his investment—his team:

> Comiskey told Austrian of the suspected fix and that he had withheld the Series paychecks of eight players, implicated by rumor and subpar performances. He then asked whether he should call them in and confront them with accusations. Austrian wisely advised Comiskey that, even if guilty, the conspirators could not be expected to admit it without hard evidence of their betrayals, and that the best course was to hire a private detective to investigate the rumors.[2]

On the witness stand in Milwaukee in 1924, Austrian said that Comiskey first came to him to discuss the fix "between mid–latter October 1919." Baseball was ruled by the National Commission in 1919:

the league presidents were Ban Johnson (American League) and John Heydler (National League), and the swing vote was Garry Herrmann, who was, coincidentally, the owner of the Cincinnati Reds. The National Commission was weak; it is generally agreed that Ban Johnson was baseball's czar before the arrival of Judge Landis in 1921.

Ban Johnson had marketed and battled his Western League, renamed the American in 1900, to major league status in 1901. Johnson curbed rowdyism and supported his umpires, making baseball more fan-friendly than ever, and his league's influence over the game was seen at the box office, as attendance, and the value of each franchise, rose. Johnson had risen from Cincinnati sportswriter to league president to "dictator" of what was in effect a multimillion-dollar corporation, Major League Baseball. And he would have a central role in the events of 1919–1921.

John Heydler had recently succeeded former Pennsylvania governor John K. Tener as head of the National League. Some months after Tener resigned, he complained about Johnson's authoritarian ways:

> It took quite a while before the Commission meetings really got going. . . . First Johnson and Herrmann had to get themselves in a frame of mind for the entertainment of business. That was an extended process. Then Herrmann would say, "Well, we have the case of Jones and Doe to settle." "Don't you think we should do so and so about this, Garry?" Johnson would say, and Herrmann would announce, "Well, then it is decided." All this time I would be an interested spectator, unable to get in a word of advice or opinion. . . . And so it went at the meetings of the national commission.[3]

In 1914, Tener had disagreed with Johnson over whether to fight the upstart Federal League to the finish, as Johnson wanted. When the commission ruled against Tener in 1918 over the rights to a player named Scott Perry, the league president drew the line. For a time, it looked like the National League might secede and the leagues would go to war again; the 1918 World Series, already in jeopardy because of World War I, might not be played at all because Tener would boycott any planning. His resignation saved the peace, but Johnson still ruled.

Many people believe that the scandal that arose in 1920 over the fix was the last straw and toppled the National Commission and that Judge Landis was seen as the perfect man to repair baseball's image. But in fact, the commission's days were numbered even before the 1919 World

Series was played.[4] The need for better government had been plain since 1918, at the latest.

Just weeks before the 1919 World Series, Ban Johnson had been making charges of gambling at the parks and investigating them, and White Sox owner Charles Comiskey, chairing an executive session of a majority of the members of baseball's board, criticized Johnson for failing to come to the meeting and submit his findings.[5] Four fans had been arrested for gambling at Comiskey Park a few days before, and $50 had been collected from them, and the Sox owner probably wanted to know if other teams were losing paying customers, too.

Whether Landis was actually offered the commissionership in September 1919 is unclear. He publicly withdrew his name from consideration for the post when the owners published a list the following February of five men who were being considered. Of course, he later accepted—on terms that he dictated.

SWIRLING RUMORS THAT THE FIX WAS IN

It can be argued that the cover-up began as soon as the first game of the Series ended. Up until then, there was nothing to cover up, just the usual "swirling rumors" that surrounded any major sporting event.

The World Series was a betting event, and that meant gamblers bragged of real or phony "inside tips" to attract more money their way. After betting events, losers of bets routinely complained that "the fix was in"; surely it was not their poor judgment that was responsible for their losses. What *was* unusual about the 1919 Series was that the odds that had favored a White Sox win by 2–1, or by as much as 5–1, swung to the Reds as Game One got closer.[6] To the professional gambler, this meant that the fix *was* in. The cover story was that Eddie Cicotte, the White Sox ace, had arm problems:

> The scene in Cincinnati that week of October 1 was pure carnival. Devotees, dilettantes, and denizens of the netherworld all descended upon the Queen City . . . ready for almost anything. Any "action." There the sports, wearing heavy gold watches called "turnips" on their watchchains along with other paraphernalia which could be safely carried, including gold knives, gold cigar cutters, gold toothpicks and gold ear-cleaners which doubled in brass for reaming out pipes and which all could be converted into cash in any pawnshop on a moment's notice, congregated, offering Cincinnati money.[7]

Because professional gamblers knew early on, it seems likely that the baseball establishment knew, too. If that sounds strange, it is because today baseball has distanced itself from gambling. But in 1919, the relationship was close. Underworld kingpin Arnold Rothstein was once a partner with baseball kingpin John McGraw in a pool hall, and he was no stranger to Giants owner Charles Stoneham's box at the Polo Grounds.

One of Chicago's nationally famous gamblers, Mont Tennes, was a friend of Charles Comiskey. Herbert Asbury cites the Illinois Crime Survey of 1929, which stated that "if the complete life history of Mont Tennes were known in every detail, it would disclose practically everything there is to know about syndicated gambling as a phase of organized crime in Chicago in the last quarter century." Tennes monopolized the racing news by purchasing a telegraph service, and he apparently knew of a plot to fix the World Series as early as August 1919:

> From 1900 to 1930 Mont Tennes was a name linked with gambling, fabulous wealth and the making and breaking of police chiefs. He was denounced as [Chicago's] gambling king, attacked by reform organizations, bombed occasionally and sometimes arrested. But the accusations against him were seldom proved, and no one knew whether the stories of his millions were fact or fiction.[8]

Eliot Asinof in *Eight Men Out* has Tennes informing Comiskey of his doubt about the Series' honesty the evening of Game One. He also has him telling Comiskey that a St. Louis gambler named Joe Pesch had told Tennes that he (Pesch) had three White Sox players—Gandil, Risberg, and Felsch—on his payroll, and for $200 per week, they supposedly would throw two or three games a week. Asinof notes no sources for this conversation, but many sources have Tennes being Comiskey's early source of a reliable tip.

Bill Veeck quotes from the diary kept at the time by White Sox secretary Harry Grabiner, who was, in effect, the general manager: "The first intimation that there might be something wrong in the World Series and that the baseball players might be implicated therein was really brought to our particular notice when [Mont Tennes] called me on the telephone . . . after the first game."[9]

On the witness stand in the 1924 Milwaukee trial, Comiskey said he was phoned by Tennes at 6:00 a.m. He sent an intermediary, Norris L. "Tip" O'Neill, to check out Tennes's story. O'Neill, once a manager in and president of the Western League, was working in 1919 with the White Sox business office. Perhaps nobody was closer to Comiskey than the witty Irishman O'Neill, and he could be trusted with this unique scouting assignment.

O'Neill was also a Woodland Bard. The Bards were basically close friends of Charles Comiskey. It is worth pausing here to take a closer look at them.

THE WOODLAND BARDS

After the turn of the century, Charles Comiskey had instituted an annual camping trip to a club in the northern woods of Wisconsin, usually in the fall, after the baseball season ended. "Prominent men in all walks of life and from different sections of the country" were invited, and so the Jerome Hunting and Fishing Club on Trude Lake, near Springstead and Mercer, Wisconsin, achieved a national distinction. The parties usually included sixty or more campers.[10]

The lodge was "some fourteen miles by rough logging trail, or nine miles by foot trail, from the railroad station at Mercer."[11] It was not possible to drive a car to Commy's "mecca" until many years after he obtained it. The camp was "almost a county"—it covered thousands of acres. Its six buildings were arranged in a quadrangle known as "the Loop" and included a log cabin called "Home Plate" that was built just for Comiskey. Another building, "the Morgue," had no stoves. A large, two-story log house dubbed "The German Village" could bunk forty guests.

In 1907, soon after Comiskey and his friends bought the club, the Woodland Bards were organized. Membership was obtained by making at least one visit to the camp, which was open winters and summers for Commy's friends. A zoo was started up, and in 1919 it grew to include nearly three hundred deer, a herd of elk, moose, and buffalo. Monte the antelope and Minnie the doe, a mother of twelve, became famous for their tricks on unsuspecting guests. Sixteen miles of high wire fence encircled the property to keep the "pets" from straying.

Mentions of the Woodland Bards appeared from time to time in the newspapers and magazines of the day. For example, in 1914:

> Last fall up in the north woods of Wisconsin, to which Comiskey each year takes a party of friends on a special outing, the owner of the White Sox presented [former ace pitcher] Ed Walsh with $3,000, to be divided into two equal parts and applied to the education of the great pitcher's small sons. That is Comiskey.[12]

Comiskey usually took his party north on a special train for a two-week outing.[13] The Woodland Bards, no doubt, included the movers and shakers of their era. And the shape of baseball may well have been influenced by their autumn and winter meetings in the northern woods of Wisconsin, where there was surely a lot of drinking,[14] and perhaps a little gambling. In *Baseball: The Golden Age,* historian Harold Seymour says "On one trip Garry Herrmann predicted he would be a failure at hunting, but a reporter wrote that he did all right, for within twenty-four hours he shot a 'furious demi-john and laid a raging magnum lifeless on the plain.'"[15]

Was this fall ritual event a factor in the movement of Babe Ruth from Harry Frazee's Red Sox to Colonel Ruppert's Yankees? (Could a sober man make such a blunder?) Or in the alliance that made Landis the game's czar? No one knows. But clearly the Bards were like an "inside-trading" network—one that put people looking for baseball tips in touch with those who had tips to give.

Other events in the summer of 1919 surely caught the attention of the Bards. The actors on Broadway went on strike on August 7, closing down some theaters. There was a nationwide wave of strikes that summer, and it included the steel industry and the Boston police. Papers of the day feared the Bolsheviks were at work, stirring up American workers and moving the country toward communism—"the Red Scare."

There was only one Commy involved with the White Sox's near strike in the summer of 1919, though, and he was management, not labor.[16] Ballplayers' salaries going into that summer were not raised, because no one was certain that the fans would return to baseball after the war. They did, and the players noticed and made a plea for raises; but they had no leverage. Their underpayment stung. Kid Gleason agreed with them and took their case to Comiskey . . . but was turned down.

We think of "insider trading" today in connection with tips on the stock market. But in 1919 gamblers fed on tips, too, and if they found out that the starting pitcher was hung over or had an arm that was not 100 percent, they might bet on that information.[17] It boggles the mind to imagine the flurry of telegrams and phone calls that must have flown among the Woodland Bards when rumors of the fix were flying, starting before the first game.

Besides gathering at the Wisconsin camp, the Bards congregated regularly at Comiskey Park, in their Trophy Room. The Bards' room was in the center of the offices and reception rooms that were built over the half-dozen entrances to the ballpark. In 1919, the Bards' membership was several hundred. Besides "trophies of the chase and the rod" brought back from Wisconsin, the Bards' room housed " . . . priceless mementos from the ball field—gifts from the great of the earth, prized souvenirs collected from every part of the world [on the 1913–14 White Sox–Giants World Tour]. Open house, with the good things of life on tap, is kept 365 days a year. There is not a country on earth which has not had its representatives inside its four walls."[18]

The long list of Woodland Bards included Garry Herrmann, Johnny Evers, Joe Kelley, and John McGraw—all Hall of Famers except for Herrmann.[19]

The 1913 and 1924 world tours—Commy's White Sox and McGraw's Giants traveling literally around the world playing exhibition games—were "the supreme extension of the Woodland Bards, a group Comiskey headed that entertained players, managers, even media members, deemed favorites of Comiskey's. They hunted, fished and caroused out of a cabin in Wisconsin."[20]

In one of his several White Sox histories, Richard C. Lindberg has a whole chapter on the Bards, complete with photos and a menu from 1917.[21] The Bards were founded by Robert Emmet Cantwell and Joseph C. Farrell, two rabid fans who championed the Sox and Comiskey, and chartered in 1907. (The 1906 "Hitless Wonder" ChiSox had defeated their crosstown rival, the dynastic Cubs, so baseball rooting was at fever pitch in the Windy City.) The name "Woodland Bards" came along in 1912.

The Woodland Bards appear to have been very similar to Boston's "Royal Rooters." In 1903, Boston's Rooters had tormented Pittsburgh Pirate players and fans during the very first World Series by singing a version of a song called "Tessie." So the Woodland Bards came up with their own chant: "Oh, Sox, bring home the rocks, no hostile knocks, no dreadful shocks shall scare you. Sox! bring home the rocks!"[22]

About 280 Bards traveled to Cincinnati for the first twoSeries games. On October 2, 1919, the *Chicago Times* reported:

> In the present series seemingly unlimited amounts of money to be placed upon the Reds appeared from the same source in Cincinnati after the first game. Much of it was covered by the Woodland Bards to their sorrow. . . . It did not seem to be Cincinnati money.

The *Herald and Examiner* reported that the Texas oilmen in the Bards, alone, had "left behind $50,000 in Cincinnati." The Bards by one account lost $33,000 just on Game One.[23]

Newspaper accounts of the 1919 Series mention the rooting presence of the Bards.[24] George E. Phair, in his regular "Breakfast Food" column in the *Chicago Herald and Examiner*, wrote this poem after the Sox dropped Game Two:

A bard is known as one who loves to write
Or sing a song of innocent delight.
But there is gloom among the Woodland Bards.
They are not singing any songs tonight.

Bards' president Joe Farrell, writing in the *Chicago Tribune* the day after Game Two, noted that the early defeats in the Series "made a crimp in their wallets"; a visit to the racetrack to bet on some "sure things" helped "some of the Bards out of the hole." Farrell noted that the Bards had been visited in their "office" (the Cincinnati headquarters where they partied on the road trip) by Tris Speaker, Ray Chapman, Grover Alexander, Pat Moran, and a number of former ballplayers—including "Big Bill Burns, the old Sox pitcher, now a prosperous oil man." It is doubtful that Burns would have been welcome if the Bards had known that he was a go-between in the fix and carried "guilty knowledge" that might have saved the gambling Bards a small fortune.

George Phair revealed his feelings about the Bards' singing after Game Three, a Sox victory: "There were no song boosters present, all of which greatly added to the joy of the occasion." Charles Dryden, also of the *Herald and Examiner*, commented after the Sox's loss in Game Four: "Small schools of fish strayed into the Bards room, where water is known as a plain and simple fluid employed in rinsing glasses and feet—sometimes. One lady fish invaded this waterless aquarium to partake of Mr. Comiskey's boundless hospitality."

When the train pulled out for Cincinnati before Game Six, just eighty-one Bards (including Comiskey's party of twenty) were on it. A Cincinnati newspaper had "not more than 100" Bards on board. Joe Farrell was one, and he announced that he had already made reservations for the 1920 Series, predicting a rematch between the Sox and Reds.

The Bards hung on a while after the fix was revealed, but it was not the same; chalk up the Bards as another casualty of the Big Fix. Irving Vaughan wrote in the *Chicago Tribune* that the Wisconsin camp broke up when its members disagreed with the plans of Comiskey and Johnson to modernize the plumbing; but much more had gone wrong among the Bards. Comiskey built another wooded retreat near Rhinelander, Wisconsin, and it was there that he spent most of his last years and there that he died. This scene of the Bards' room at the ballpark was not long coming once the Bards learned of the fix:

> The old room, lonely, dark and dusty now, is decorated with prints of sporting scenes, trophies of the chase, old baseball pictures and so on. There are pelts of bears, mounted heads of deer and stuffed animals brought from strange lands some Woodland Bard had visited. There are sturdy old chairs in a row, with no one sitting in them.[25]

COMISKEY AND JOHNSON

It is obvious that Charles Comiskey was well connected. In Axelson's biographical sketch is the suggestion that if he wanted, Commy could have been mayor of Chicago. But he stuck with baseball. "Politics and baseball don't mix. I would rather have a pennant-winning team than be mayor," he stated for the record.[26] His ballpark, which opened in 1910, cost him $750,000 but was turning a profit in 1919. Like many owners since, Comiskey endeared himself to fans by keeping admission prices low.

Comiskey also cultivated friendships with reporters, wining and dining them, so that they checked with him if they had any doubts about whether their stories were suitable for public consumption. The pressmen might as well have been on the White Sox's payroll:

> [Comiskey was] a rich boss who made great show of his open-handed generosity by buying drinks for political barflies and sports writers and contributing to charities. . . . He would roll out a keg of venerable whiskey, as smooth as honey, and set a long board of free lunch at a cost of a hundred dollars or so, and people would get to singing harmony and toasting the Old Roman with never a thought of the salary standards of the greatest ball club ever assembled.
>
> . . .The players got almost no hearing, and some of them thought the writers silenced their grievances in print for free drinks.[27]

Westbrook Pegler was a young reporter in 1919: "Comiskey was a good-time Charley, a handshaking politician and an extravagant host who poured fine Bourbon and took it neat himself, and would admonish younger men to do the same because 'that soda water will rot your guts.'"[28]

Robert C. Cottrell has documented well how Comiskey's "reputation as an icon was well-deserved," and he observes that "no baseball executive ever received more favorable press than Comiskey," both in Chicago and in baseball's national publications.[29] "Best Liked Magnate in the Game" pronounced a 1914 *New York Evening Journal* headline.

Again, the fix, suspected before the Series, seemed to be confirmed to the White Sox management after Game One by Mont Tennes. Testifying in Milwaukee, Comiskey said that when Tip O'Neill reported back from his meeting with the Chicago gambler Tennes, he informed the Sox manager, Kid Gleason, who told the players, before Game Two, that the team knew what was going on. (Chick Gandil recalled the confrontation with Gleason as taking place after Game Two.) "I told Gleason to take out any player who did not appear to be doing his best." Comiskey said that he then sent O'Neill to tell National League president John Heydler.

There is no mention in Harry Grabiner's diary of the Sox management confronting the players during the Series. It seems likely, however, with the rumors of a fix so thick, that Gleason probably spoke of them to his team, and in fact, several players confirmed that he did. When Judge Landis ruled against the reinstatement of Buck Weaver in 1927, he referred to a meeting between Gleason and the team during the Series, at which Gleason stated that something was wrong.

James T. Farrell has made the observation that "drastic action by any one of [those who knew or had suspicions—he mentions Comiskey, Gleason, Schalk, and reporters Hugh Fullerton, Ring Lardner, and Westbrook Pegler] after that first game of the Series could have blown the whole conspiracy into the open."[30] There was much talk, but no action.

Another loss in Game Two provided further reason to worry. According to Grabiner's diary, when the teams returned to Chicago for Game Three, Grabiner phoned John Heydler with the news of the fix. This does not square with Comiskey's memory, over four years later, but in any case, a higher authority was notified. Grabiner did not call Garry Herrmann, because he was president of the Reds and Comiskey "had no confidence in his integrity."

Calling Ban Johnson was out of the question, as he and Comiskey had been feuding for years. This feud, between the still-reigning czar of baseball, Johnson, and one of the sport's most popular and powerful owners, Comiskey, cannot be overlooked or underestimated as a factor in any attempt to understand the cover-up of the fix and its undoing.

Although they had once been very close friends, in 1919, Comiskey and Johnson had indeed become practically mortal foes, each the other's nemesis, like Holmes and Moriarty or Giamatti and Rose. When Ban Johnson was fresh out of law school and working as a reporter in Cincinnati, Comiskey, then manager of the Reds, induced him to get into baseball. Soon after Johnson took over the struggling Western League, Comiskey bought the Sioux City franchise and moved it to St. Paul; and when Johnson was ready to challenge the National League in 1900, Comiskey led the invasion of Chicago. John Kieran: "They worked hand-in-hand and shoulder to shoulder. They rose to success together. They were cronies, brothers in blood, Damon and Pythias."[31]

But less than two decades after conquering the National League, they were scheming against each other, using the thrown Series of 1919 as their weapon in a titanic power struggle. There are several versions of a fishing story that has served to illustrate, and perhaps to explain the origin of, the split that developed between the one-time close collaborators. They were both sportsmen (it was part of the job description of the magnate), and on one occasion, one of them caught a mess of fish and shipped them to the other as a gift. However, the ice melted, and the gift was taken as an insult. In another version, Johnson sent the fish and they arrived in good shape, but what Comiskey needed was outfielders and Johnson had just nixed an acquisition Comiskey made. "Am I supposed to play the bass in left field?" Johnson: "That was a good joke, and I appreciated it as such when it was told to me."[32]

In another tale, Johnson was invited to go along with Commy and the Woodland Bards for a good old boys' day in the woods.[33] Johnson was assigned the task of bringing home the partridges for dinner. He tried his best but couldn't hit a feather. His suspicions aroused, he fired at a nearby tree, and then he fired again at closer range. "Not a scar." Johnson pried open one of his shells to find it was filled with wadding and explosive but nothing solid. Some believed *that* was the end of a beautiful friendship (as Bogie might say). But it was not. Johnson: "That was a good joke and I enjoyed it, and have often told it as a good yarn. It did not offend me at all."[34]

The Sporting News reported that Comiskey and Johnson made their annual visit to the Wisconsin woods together after the 1918 World Series, with just a few of the Woodland Bards along (because of the war). That suggests that the real split between these two giants began during the 1919 season, as the old National Commission was fading and a struggle for power had baseball owners forging alliances. Comiskey wound up siding with the New York and Boston owners when Johnson vetoed the late-season trade of Carl Mays to the Yankees; the trio would line up later with the eight National League owners to crown Judge Landis as the game's new commissioner.

Toward the end of his life, Ban Johnson discredited the fish stories as reasons for the break between himself and Comiskey. The real reason, he said, was that he refused to side with Comiskey in a dispute over pitcher Jack Quinn, who pitched well for the Sox at the end of the shortened season of 1918.[35] Chicago was slow to buy his contract from his minor league team, and the New York Yankees beat them to it. David Fleitz agrees that this decision "completed the rupture between Johnson and Comiskey." It is said that Comiskey screamed at Ban Johnson in a league meeting of that day, "I made you, and by God I'll break you!"[36]

But Charles Comiskey denied that the Quinn dispute had caused the breach with Johnson. He stated that even before Quinn, he had disagreed with the way Johnson was running things.[37] Even close to the end of their long and storied lives, the men were still sparring over how they and their relationship would go down in history.

In 1929, Comiskey reacted strongly to an article in a flattering weekly series on the retired Ban Johnson written by Earl Obenshain for the *Cleveland Plain Dealer*. Besides accepting Johnson's explanation of his rift with Comiskey, Obenshain stated that Johnson "never carried personal feelings into differences over policies" and that "deep in his [Johnson's] heart he had personal regard for his enemy [Comiskey], because of their old associations." As evidence, Obenshain cited how Johnson acted to save Comiskey further embarrassment when the indicted players went to trial.

> There was indication of this when the evidence was being accumulated for indictment of the Black Sox for selling out the 1919 World Series. The state's attorney in charge of the prosecution advised Comiskey should be indicted along with the players, [based] on certain evidence in his hands. He said it would make the case stronger—one of conspiracy, knowledge after the crime on the part of the employer of the players or something along that line. Johnson put his foot down. He would not hear of such a thing.[38]

Comiskey's letter to the Cleveland paper called that paragraph an unmitigated falsehood. On the contrary, it was I who procured the confessions that caused the indictments of the players ... I spent many thousands of dollars uncovering this conspiracy, and did not receive either directly or indirectly the slightest assistance from Johnson or the American League.[39]

Comiskey went on to recall how he informed Heydler "immediately after the first game" of the Series, having no confidence in Johnson. "Johnson discarded my suspicion. . . . To us it appeared that Johnson took not the slightest interest in our efforts to clean up the scandal and to have the guilty parties indicted or punished." In fact, Comiskey wrote, Johnson obstructed the White Sox investigation by getting to the St. Louis gamblers first. Finally, Comiskey charged that Johnson never gave to the American League owners an accounting of just how he spent the $40,000 they gave him to investigate.

Responding to Comiskey a month later in the *St. Louis Post-Dispatch*, Johnson could think of just one disagreement he had with Comiskey before the Quinn problem. That was during the 1918 season, when Johnson urged American League owners to close their ballparks voluntarily, as the country was engaged in war. Comiskey, along with Clark Griffith and Harry Frazee, opposed the plan, and Johnson "was very much incensed at the opposition." Johnson took his case to Washington, calling on labor leader Samuel Gompers, who arranged for a meeting with President Woodrow Wilson. Wilson did not comment, but later the War Department declared baseball was a "non-essential occupation," and players were indeed subject to the "work or fight" order.[40]

There was an exodus of players into shipyards, steel mills, airplane manufacturing, chemical or electrical plants, farming and other exempt occupations, as well as into the military. More than 220 players (of 300-some) vanished from the rosters.[41] Attendance dropped sharply, and finally the owners closed the parks, rather than try to muddle through with replacement players. Johnson:

> That was very humiliating. It would have been much better if we had closed voluntarily. It did baseball no good and it took some time to overcome the harm that was done by the unwise decision. . . . Perhaps that is what Comiskey means when he says he was opposed to my policies prior to the Quinn decision.[42]

Most sources have Comiskey and Johnson as bitter enemies until their end. Certainly, in 1919–21 their feud was at its peak, and much of it was carried on in public. But at least one source has Comiskey sending his son to Ban's St. Louis hospital room to shake his hand before Johnson passed away in 1931. Commy's death followed soon after in the same year.

HUGH FULLERTON'S VERSION

Hugh Fullerton is best known for the articles he wrote in the months just after the Series, in which he repeatedly called for an investigation into the rumors that the Series had been fixed. Fullerton never claimed to know the full story of the fix; he believed only Comiskey, Johnson, Herrmann, and Austrian knew that. But after those four men had died, Fullerton recalled for *The Sporting News* how he had first heard of the fix and what he did about it.[43] His memoir is in some ways as remarkable and startling as his early efforts to combat the cover-up of the fix.

Writing for a syndicate, Fullerton was in Cincinnati the day before the Series, and that morning, he met Detroit sportswriter Joe Jackson, and they went to a speakeasy half a block from the Sinton Hotel. There they met a Chicago gambler at the bar, and when Fullerton introduced him to Joe Jackson, the gambler thought that he had met the ballplayer and asked Fullerton if it was Cincinnati in straight games. (Jackson was believed by the gambling network to be one of eight ballplayers in on the fix.) Fullerton and the reporter Jackson understood the gambler's mistake and strung him along, kidding him and assuring him that Cincinnati would win five straight.

Then "the boys from New York" came into the bar and said that they had a tip "straight from Arnold Rothstein." A.R. said he had been approached but refused to finance the fix, and added that it was safe to bet that someone had agreed. Fullerton then called one of the White Sox (elsewhere he identifies Eddie Cicotte), who denied the rumor and scoffed at it; Fullerton asked him to keep his eyes and ears open. Then Fullerton met the former pitcher Bill Burns, who advised Fullerton to "Get wise and get yourself some money."

That evening, at a party across the river in Kentucky, talk of the fix was "free—too free." Returning to his hotel, where he was rooming with Christy Mathewson, Fullerton told Matty about the rumors. Matty exploded, "Damn them! They have it coming to them. I caught two crooks and they whitewashed them."

(Writing just after the scandal broke, Fullerton had recalled Mathewson's reaction this way: "Damn them, they deserve it," answered Matty. "They whitewashed two players after I caught them with the goods and presented the affidavits to them."[44] Hal Chase had been cleared by National League president John Heydler, February 5, 1919. The second player may have been Heinie Zimmermann.)

Hugh and Matty were still talking at 3:00 a.m. when Cincinnati manager Pat Moran broke angrily into their room, thinking that Fullerton had taken one of his pitchers out to get drunk. Matty calmed Moran down and assured him that he had the wrong reporter.

The next morning—the day of Game One—Fullerton heard from "two big-shot Chicago gamblers" that the fix was in, and Fullerton went to Comiskey. *Comiskey said he had already heard about it.* Commy was furious because Ban Johnson was doing nothing about it. Comiskey said *Johnson knew about it, too—before Game One.* "I urged him [Comiskey] to forget his feud and call on him to act." Comiskey refused angrily. Fullerton then went to Ban Johnson. "I think Johnson had already heard rumors. I put it to him straight that the evidence indicated a crooked series." He scoffed and said it was just Commy squealing.

The previous October, Ban Johnson had arrived for Game Five of the Series a bit late and somewhat tipsy and unable to deal with an ad hoc player committee bent on striking in protest of their Series wages.[45] In 1919, his arrival was delayed by a car wreck. So the National Commission, "for the first time in history, failed to hold a meeting before the [first] game began. The game seemed to go along just the same."[46] But we are left to wonder if, given more time to be convinced by Fullerton and others, Johnson would have at least delayed the Series in order to be sure that the games would be played on the level.

Fullerton next cornered Pittsburgh Pirates owner Barney Dreyfuss and demanded that Dreyfuss "force Ban Johnson to make some move." (Fullerton may have chosen Dreyfuss over John Heylder because Heydler had exonerated Hal Chase, making Heydler, in the view of Fullerton's friend Mathewson, part of the problem, and not the solution.) Dreyfuss, who emerged as the strongman for National League policy after John Tener resigned, had arrived in Cincinnati with two trainloads of Pittsburgh rooters and had declared that the Reds would win the series.[47]

When he heard Fullerton's charges, Dreyfuss became enraged. Fullerton: "I lost my temper and raised Cain with him and with the entire baseball set-up, calling them a bunch of whitewashing bastards who were letting a bunch of crooks get away with it because they were afraid of losing money."[48] Fullerton told them that he heard five White Sox players were in the plot, and he named all five. Dreyfuss went to

Comiskey, but the Series was not halted for an investigation. Damon Runyon thought the reason for this was obvious. "The magnates let the series go through to a conclusion and pocketed the gate money when many persons in baseball were hinting that something was wrong."[49]

If Fullerton's recollections are accurate—and they seem to square with those of sportswriters J.G. Taylor Spink, Fred Lieb, and others—then there can be little doubt that the cover-up began *before* Game One. They also give some credence to the story that Comiskey ordered Kid Gleason to remove any player who seemed to be lying down and that Gleason probably warned at least some players, including Cicotte, before Game One. Whether the warning caused any player to play to win, instead of to lose, cannot be known.

Gleason may have done more than warn his players that they were being watched. He may have threatened them. According to Hugh Fullerton,

> Bill Gleason is as honest a man as breathes, and a fighting man. He believed that crooked work was going on. He told his players [sometime between Games Two and Three] to get out there and play honestly or answer to him. He threatened to choke or kill some of them. He was fighting hard.
>
> . . . In the last game Gleason made his final effort. He first proposed to take out of the game every man under suspicion and send out a team of makeshifts upon whose honestly he could rely. He was told that the act would make a farce of the series. He then declared himself. He stated that if he saw any evidences of crookedness that day he would use an "iron" on the guilty player, meaning a gun. The Kid was desperate.[50]

Writing in 1927, perhaps with October 1, 1919, in mind, Hugh Fullerton reflected on how hard it was to blow a whistle on a fixed game. "It is difficult for a reporter to get evidence. The honest players object to squealing and the dishonest ones cover up." Steve Klein has pointed out the irony that put corrupt ballplayers in league with the owners—both needed to conceal evidence of a fix to protect their investments. Fullerton summed it up succinctly: "The fact that organized baseball's settled policy for years of 'keeping quiet for the sake of the sport' has been the very thing which has made crookedness possible, is overlooked."[51]

THE YELP OF A BEATEN CUR

When and if Harry Grabiner phoned John Heydler with Comiskey's suspicions that the Series was fixed, Heydler gave the expected reply: there are rumors of fixes every year. Testifying before the 1920 grand jury, Heydler said that after the Series he suggested to Johnson that they join in a libel suit against newspapers, which printed suggestions that a fix was in, in order "to have all possible information brought out in court." But he added that he didn't press the point because he did not believe a fix could occur.[52]

In Heydler's account, he recalled Tip O'Neill, who accompanied Comiskey to Cincinnati, telling him the morning after Game One that Comiskey was "all broken up" and suspicious that something was wrong. Comiskey called him on the phone the morning of Game Three, and, accompanied by John Bruce, secretary of the National Commission, Heydler went to Comiskey's ballpark office. Comiskey said Gleason was convinced that "someone had reached the Sox players," and they (Comiskey and Gleason) "had talked the matter over and felt that an investigation should be made." Heydler took the matter to Johnson, who agreed to investigate it. Heydler, trusting that things were in safe hands, backed off.[53]

Coming on the heels of Heydler's tesimony, Comiskey's admission to the grand jury that he had had suspicions as early as just after Game One drew large print in many newspapers. He insisted that he had done his best since then to clear things up but just had not been able to come up with any evidence. He added that he thought Johnson was sincere in his own investigation—"for a time." But then he suggested that Johnson was using it "for his own personal gain"—to knock the Sox out of the 1920 pennant race and tilt things for Cleveland to win.

In his biography of Ban Johnson, Eugene Murdock notes Johnson's "repeated references to the need for 'crackdowns' on gambling" all during his long administration. Like some owners, Johnson was concerned about the growing presence of gamblers at games, and on at least two occasions, Johnson "hired private detectives to go into ball parks where rumors of gambling were rife and collect evidence." Johnson:

> One report [of a game being thrown] was so specific that it even detailed the price—$300 per player for each game tossed. Convicting evidence naturally was hard to obtain and perhaps we indulged a doubt, or at any rate encouraged the hope that such reports were canards.[54]

Conscious that baseball's image was threatened, Johnson "did what he could to suppress" the gambling problem while trying to solve it at the same time. The antigambling crusade was more vigorous in Johnson's American League. Murdock notes that, when Johnson advised Harry Frazee to expel gamblers and end the open betting at Fenway Park, Frazee refused.

After the 1917 season, Johnson and St. Louis Browns owner Phil Ball had gone to the detective agency headed by Allan Pinkerton and explained the problem. Pinkerton replied that he needed the consent of both leagues. "I must have free access to all parks of both leagues and if the National will join you I think I can do you a lot of good."[55] But Johnson received no cooperation from the National League president.[56] It may have been at this time that Allan Pinkerton expressed to Johnson his contention that Arnold Rothstein was the "prime mover" behind the fixers who had infiltrated baseball, an opinion Johnson came to share later.[57]

He may also have had information that a professional gambler from St. Louis, Henry "Kid" Becker, planned to fix the 1918 Series. But Johnson could not raise the funds to investigate. The owners of the American League clubs rebuffed him.[58] The league office was "cash-strapped from the war" (the 1918 season had ended a month early due to the war), otherwise the Black Sox might have been on different feet.[59] But Becker was cash-strapped, too, and was "unable to raise enough money to justify 'framing' the series and he called it off."[60] Becker was shot dead by a "highwayman" on April 15, 1919, but St. Louis gambler Carl Zork and his associates survived. And what better way to honor a fallen comrade than to make his dream come true the next October? But the idea of the fix (to be implemented later by Carl Zork, Abe Attell, and Rothstein) probably did not originate with "Kid" Becker. Rather, it was as old as the Series itself.[61]

John Heydler said that he had asked Harry Grabiner if the club official objected to his taking the news to the American League president. Grabiner: "Heydler never referred to the matter again either during the Series or after and he stated that he would let me hear from him."

Ban Johnson's alleged reaction to John Heydler's news produced the second most famous quote from the story of the scandal: "That is the yelp of a beaten cur." The remark was widely circulated, and if Comiskey was behind the spin, it is easy to see why. It "documents" that Johnson was informed early on but did nothing. He wrote off the message from the White Sox as whining, sour grapes, a lame excuse in the wake of two losses. No doubt Johnson was delighted to see his archrival's team on the ropes early. The remark portrays Ban Johnson as turning a blind eye to the fix and Comiskey as blowing the whistle.

And because the remark contains the word *beaten*, it suggests that Comiskey did not know of the fix until after Game One at the earliest, and probably after Game Two; until then, his team had not been *beaten*.

But it seems more likely that this was Comiskey "covering his rear"[62]— because an owner who failed to report his suspicions would be violating a basic baseball rule, perhaps risking the forfeiture of his franchise.

Like the other famous quote, this one has survived in a variety of versions: (1) the yelp of a beaten cur; (2) the whelp of a beaten cur; (3) the whine of a whipped cur (Comiskey); (4) the bleat of a sore loser; (5) the crying of a whipped cur; (6) the response of a beaten cur; and finally (7), "that's the wail of a sore loser."[63] And like the other famous quote, it may have never been actually uttered at all. Ban Johnson denied ever making the statement.

In fact, Johnson "said many times that he sat through the entire series . . . [without] the slightest notion of a conspiracy. If there was any gossip of a questionable nature [after Game One] . . . I do not recall it. Nor was there any brought to our attention after the second game." He freely admitted that looking back, he could see how the games were thrown.[64] Johnson responded to the rumors of the fix by traveling to St. Louis shortly after the Series, proof that he took them seriously then, if not sooner.

What Ban Johnson did recall was that "The day the series opened in Cincinnati there were rumors of trickery on the part of certain members of the White Sox. The stories were not taken seriously by anybody."[65] But Hugh Fullerton took the rumors very seriously. He just could not get others to do anything about them.

While Harry Grabiner's diary (which was found after Asinof wrote *Eight Men Out*) has the initial communication being a phone call from Grabiner to Heydler after Game Two, other sources have Comiskey himself going to Heydler in the middle of the night, in their hotel, after Game One. A letter penned by Comiskey in 1929 also has the communication after Game One. Baseball historian Harold Seymour believes Grabiner's account. In any event, Comiskey had early knowledge of the fix. If he did not hear it first from his own contacts in the gambling community, and then from Hugh Fullerton, he surely heard it from his manager, Kid Gleason. Taylor Spink believed that Gleason took his suspicions that "something lousy was going on" to Comiskey after Game Two, prompting Comiskey to contact Heydler.

But was the message from Comiskey, whenever it was delivered, news to Ban Johnson? Probably not. Taylor Spink of *The Sporting News* had confided to Ban Johnson that stories of a fix were all over Cincinnati. Johnson allegedly replied, "Do you know, Hugh Fullerton told me the same thing."[66] Ban could read the papers, hear the rumors, smell the fix. He had wanted an investigation the previous October. Did he fear that if he made waves again, the football would again be yanked away, and he'd be Charlie-Brown-flat on his back?

Writer Fred Lieb has Comiskey making his midnight ride to Heydler (and Heydler to Ban Johnson) after Game Two on the train heading back to Chicago. Lieb said he got this information directly from Heydler. And he makes this judgment: *this* is when the investigation should have been started. Instead: "the whelp of a beaten cur!"[67]

DID MANAGER GLEASON CONFRONT HIS TEAM?

In his book *Eight Men Out*, Asinof has Kid Gleason looking for Cicotte after Game One but not finding him until after dinner that evening. Cicotte and Risberg are in the Sinton Hotel lobby when Gleason arrives, and the manager confronts them in front of a hundred people about what they are doing. "Anybody who says he can't see what you're doing out there is either blind, stupid or a goddam liar!" Asinof then has Fullerton lead Gleason away. Gleason then goes to Comiskey, armed with a batch of telegrams that he has received. Commy has had his own telegrams. In the middle of the night, he takes his suspicions to Ban Johnson, via John Heydler.

There is some evidence that Gleason did confront his team, particularly Eddie Cicotte (as we will see later). Reflecting on Harry Grabiner's account of what the White Sox did in response to the fix rumors early in the 1919 Series, the late Bill Veeck noted that no one in the Sox management "called in the players to warn them they were being watched nor did they direct the manager to warn them."[68] But that simply does not appear to be the case.

Just weeks after the 1919 Series was over, reporter Harry Williams was told by an unidentified White Sox player that Gleason was puzzled by the poor showing of the Sox early in the Series. "He called us together and told us he had heard that bettors tried to reach some of the players. The men denied that they had been approached, let alone entering into any agreement." Williams heard rumors that four men played suspiciously, but he named no one.[69]

Swede Risberg recalled from the distance of 1927 that it was after Game Two that Kid Gleason "called up in the clubhouse and accused us of laying down." Asked if anyone denied it, Swede said, "John Collins said it was a lot of bunk."[70]

In 1959, reserve outfielder "Honest Eddie" Murphy—who had batted an astronomical .486 in 1919, with seventeen hits in thirty-five at bats—recalled Kid Gleason holding a team meeting after Dickie Kerr won Game Three. After two disappointing and suspicious losses, Gleason challenged the team. "We can win." And Gleason added, "I hear that $100,000 is to change hands if we lose." By most accounts, that figure was right on the money. Murphy: "I believe [Gleason] told the story to Comiskey and almost anyone who would listen."[71]

Reporter Irving Vaughan recalled that Gleason's clubhouse speech was given after the Sox manager was sure there was "treachery afoot" and that Gleason challenged the guilty players to step forward.[72] Apparently none did.

On the Sunday when Game Five was rained out, nearly all the Sox appeared at the park, but there was no "skull practice or board of strategy meeting." Kid Gleason told a *Chicago Tribune* reporter, "We just talked things over among ourselves."

After the Sox dropped Game Five, the *Tribune*'s James Crusinberry portrayed Gleason as puzzled. "He clearly indicated that something was wrong and that he intended to find out what it was." If Gleason had helped convince his players to play to win after Game One or Game Two, his frustration, confusion, and skepticism after losses in Games Four and Five is easy to understand. Yet the closest Gleason came to blaming the loss of the Series on the meddling of gamblers was when he told the *Tribune* on October 10, 1919, "Something was wrong. I didn't like the betting odds. I wish no one had ever bet a dollar on the team."

When Ban Johnson met with gambler Arnold Rothstein long after the Series, Rothstein claimed that he urged Giants manager John McGraw to inform Kid Gleason before the Series started that there was a conspiracy afoot. (McGraw strongly denied this.) But Gleason had his own contacts in the world of the gamblers and fixers, even if McGraw failed to contact him. So did Comiskey. Therefore it seems highly probable that Gleason knew about the $100,000 bribe, and that—as "Honest Eddie" Murphy recalled later—he spoke freely about it to others. Of course, those others had to include the team that he had led to the pennant in 1919. Gleason said little about the fix for the record later, but his communication to his team, especially his ace pitchers, may have resulted in the fix being called off right after his confrontation.

AFTER THE SERIES

"I blame Ban Johnson for allowing the Series to continue. If ever a League President blundered in a crisis Ban did."[73] The words belong to

Charles Comiskey, and they imply that Comiskey did his job, blowing the whistle by informing Johnson, but that Ban failed to follow through. Once the fix became public knowledge, someone had to take the blame. But of course, Comiskey could have pulled out of the Series after he knew the fix was in. But he was covered—he had told his baseball superiors. It was in their hands now.

The Giants' manager John McGraw, who had as many connections with gamblers as anyone, was asked about the rumors of a fix being in. "Maybe it's all so much hot air, but you can be sure of one thing—it will take a thousand gumshoes to prove anything."[74] Of course, first it would take the will to *hire* a thousand gumshoes. Baseball had shown in the past that its will to investigate was wanting. In 1919, that had not changed much. But the power struggle at the top changed the world of baseball, and this would ultimately ruin the cover-up.

The Series had gone on with no hitches more serious than a problem with the ticket distribution in Cincinnati for Game Seven. The rumors continued, but the season and postseason were over. Comiskey said that he did not call in Jackson or any of the other players regarding his suspicions, based on the rumors.[75] Instead, he immediately—the day after the Series ended—went public in defense of his players, offering a reward of $10,000 for anyone with hard evidence of the fix. "I believe my boys fought the battles of the recent world's series on the level," he proclaimed.[76] At least one newspaper had the reward at $20,000. In all probability that was a typo. But the point was made. If there was evidence, Comiskey wanted it. And as soon as it started coming his way, he buried it.[77]

Some sources have Comiskey calling the players in after the Series, to pick up their final paychecks of the season and their World Series money and to be interrogated on the subject of the fix. Apparently Eddie Cicotte was sent for, but he

> dressed and left the park without going to the office. Comiskey then held the pay checks of seven players, perhaps eight. He sent word to them that their money was there and to come and get it. He held it for weeks and then upon advice of his attorney, he sent it to them.[78]

Donald Gropman has Comiskey hearing the details of the fix from Chick Gandil and Happy Felsch, citing Harry Grabiner's diary; but that detail is not in the excerpts in Veeck's book. However, it is in the transcripts of the 1924 Milwaukee trial.

Comiskey testified that he spoke with Chick Gandil first, then Happy Felsch, the day after the Series. Happy said, "I wasn't in on it." Comiskey was questioned further: "You told Gandil he was the ringleader?" He replied, "I told Gandil he was the ringleader and he denied it, and I says, 'Well, you may have the opportunity to prove it.' He said, 'I will come and prove it any time you call me.'"[79]

Comiskey must have also had been peppered with information from his field manager, Kid Gleason. Gleason had trusted the word of catcher Ray Schalk, who knew better than anyone when Cicotte and Lefty Williams were pitching to win—or not. Gleason also had a collection of telegrams. One of them was sent by his friend, a young reporter named Jack Lait, after Game Five. Lait was one of the first to predict a scandal was on the horizon.[80]

Again, questioned on the Milwaukee witness stand, Comiskey was asked, "Did you speak to the players collectively about it, that is, all together?" He replied negatively, but added that he had spoken to his players individually.

> Some of them were of the impression that the games were not played right, and I think it was at the suggestion of—I think it was Mr. Schalk, that brought this young man that got me connected with this theater man that said he would get Redman [Harry Redmon, owner of the Majestic Theater in St. Louis] to tell who he would play.[81]

Comiskey was then asked, "[Clyde] Elliot?" and he replied, "Elliot, yes. We had talked, and did everything we could, but never succeeded in getting anything." (The Clyde Elliot–Harry Redmon connection will be revisited below.)

A few reporters alluded to the rumors of bribery and tampering and fixing and "framing." On October 19, both Bill Macbeth of the *New York Tribune* and W. A. Farnsworth of the *New York American* wrote of their suspicions. In his columns in the weeks and months that followed Macbeth continued pressing the National Commission to take the lead in an investigation, even though the commission was practically useless, a lame duck that was doomed.[82] But most of the reporting was business as usual. With the exception of one journalist: Hugh S. Fullerton.

Fullerton, who was closer to Comiskey than most pressmen, reported right after the Series that seven players would not return for 1920. Under oath at the 1924 Milwaukee trial, Fullerton insisted that he did not get the seven names (which were not specified) from Comiskey. Rather, he had found "gossip, not legal proof." But Fullerton "revealed much later" that he was quoting Comiskey in his October 10 assertions.[83]

Fullerton had agreed to feed Comiskey anything he could find out from his sources in the press. He was sure that Comiskey would act on the knowledge he had. After the Series, checks were given to the Reds and White Sox, Kid Gleason accepting for the latter. But Comiskey held up sending out checks for the losers' share to the eight players he suspected. And he held his breath.

When asked on the witness stand in Milwaukee why he suspected these eight particular players, Comiskey said that he had read about it in the papers. In Fullerton's story of October 10, there were no names.

But according to historian Lee Allen, "a rather disreputable sporting publication, *Collyer's Eye*, printed an article that not only alleged skullduggery but actually named the eight players who would eventually be indicted."[84] (Lee Allen apparently had not seen the series of articles that ran in *Collyer's Eye*, starting October 18, 1919, and culminating with a triumphant claim of vindication on October 2, 1920, after the scandal broke. The *Eye* had just seven players involved; Buck Weaver did not make their list.)

But *Collyer's Eye* did not go public with the seven players' names until November 15, 1919. That is the earliest Comiskey could have possibly read of any names in the papers, except that of Lefty Williams, which the *Eye* printed on October 25. More likely, Comiskey received the names of the suspected players from Ray Schalk or from other players whom he interviewed before they left Chicago after the Series ended. Or Comiskey may have used his Woodland Bards connections to find out the names. Chicago baseball notable Charles Weeghman testified in 1920 that Mont Tennes told him right after the Series that he had lost $30,000 betting on the White Sox and knew the result had been fixed by gamblers. "He named the seven [White Sox] players to me."[85]

Fullerton and Comiskey did not meet between the end of the Series and late October. By then, the eighth name (McMullin') had been ferreted out (probably from Harry Redmon—see below) and added to the seven that they (and probably Schalk) had on October 10. "They just bunched the whole of them," Comiskey insisted on the stand in Milwaukee.[86] And that was true, as far as the rumors went. And the eight names have remained "bunched" to this day.

It seems likely that Comiskey believed that Chick Gandil was a ringleader and that he told Chick that he would not be welcome back the next season. The club owner would go through the motions, sending the first baseman a contract. Gandil would reject it and stay in California. In an interview that appeared in a California newspaper in March 1921, Gandil stated that the first contract he received was for $4,000—the same as his 1919 salary. He turned it down, and the Sox offered him $5,000—still a thousand below what Chick wanted. Nearly every other player was getting a handsome raise. Then, "Grabiner sent word that negotiations were off."[87]

Meanwhile, Comiskey's reward money produced some results. The St. Louis theater owner and gambler Harry Redmon, who had lost either $5,500 or $14,000—betting on the Sox to win Game Three apparently cost a number of gamblers their shirts—wanted revenge . . . and some of his money back. Redmon at once became a person much in demand by both Comiskey and Ban Johnson.[88]

The day the Series ended, two Sox fans had called Kid Gleason and arranged a meeting at Comiskey Park for the next day. Gleason and Harry Grabiner met with a certain Max Ascher and with film producer Clyde Elliot.[89] Elliot told the White Sox representatives about the fortunes of his great friend, Harry Redmon. Gleason and Elliot were in East St. Louis debriefing Redmon within two days.

Redmon said he could name the ballplayers who met with gamblers, and the gamblers they met—but he would not implicate any gamblers, knowing better. He gave the White Sox the names of Sleepy Bill Burns, Abe Attell, Arnold Rothstein, and four other St. Louis gamblers. He also gave them the names of eight players he believed were in on the fix. It appears that Redmon wanted $5,500 for this information, probably the same amount he lost betting on the Series. Ban Johnson: "All that came of this, I believe, was a threat by Gleason to whip one of the parties."[90]

Hugh Fullerton confirmed that last detail. He believed Kid Gleason had gone to St. Louis right after the Series

with the avowed intention of "getting" the man who was accused of bribing the players. He cornered that man and is said to have choked him and tried to force a confession from him, besides offering $5,000 for the names of those implicated. The man said he was afraid to squeal for fear he would meet the fate that another St. Louis gambler who had been killed [probably Kid Becker], had met. This was told to me by one of Gleason's close friends. I never asked Bill about it.[91]

Comiskey's $10,000 reward for information attracted at least one other interested party.

Joe Gedeon, a second baseman for the St. Louis Browns, and perhaps a link between the players and the St. Louis syndicate, stepped forward. When Gedeon testified before the grand jury after signing a waiver of immunity, he said that he had heard about the fix on a tip from a White Sox player—he wouldn't disclose the name, but the grand jury said they knew it anyway. It was Swede Risberg. Gedeon bet and won $600. He said that the gamblers got a "bad bumping" on Game Three, which frightened them, and they met to raise $25,000 still due the Sox players.[92]

There is no record of Redmon or Gedeon receiving payments of $10,000 or any lesser amounts from the White Sox. Comiskey would pay nothing for Redmon's names; he wanted to see hard evidence.[93] Both Redmon and Gedeon later met with Ban Johnson, and Gedeon agreed to testify when Johnson was looking for witnesses to bring the case to trial. For all his efforts, Gedeon was later banned along with the Sox players, the ninth man out.

But Redmon would apparently rate a second interview by the White Sox. The St. Louis theater operator would later recall (to the grand jury) being in "the [Chicago] office of Comiskey's attorney, Alfred Austrian, with [gambler] Joe Pesch, when the 'sellout' of his players was described to Commy. We refused to accept any part of the $10,000." Redmon also recalled that he and Pesch first heard of the fix from another St. Louis gambler, Carl Zork. Joe Gedeon also implicated Zork and recalled a meeting where he (Gedeon) was asked by Abe Attell and Bill Burns if the "'solid eight' had thrown down their purchasers." Gedeon told the grand jury that this was the first time he realized he was involved in an "unethical" deed.[94]

Comiskey's version of the communication in the fall of 1919 with Redmon was that the club had sent Gleason and Elliot to Redmon prepared to pay the $5,500 he was asking, but his representatives found that Ban Johnson "had already been with him so our plans to secure the full information were blocked."[95] Ban Johnson's version was that he had gone to St. Louis only after the White Sox contacted Redmon and others. "There I found the first convincing evidence that something really was wrong."[96] If Grabiner's diary is close to being accurate about the timing of the first contact with Redmon, then Johnson's trip to St. Louis probably closely followed that of Gleason and Elliot. Redmon's second contact with the Sox, in Chicago, must have been devastating for Comiskey, if Redmon mentioned his having met with Johnson. Now any reward would appear to be "hush money."

Johnson later told a story ("the tip that went astray") about how, while he was in St. Louis, he had learned that "but for the merest slip, based on the overconfidence of a stockholder in the St. Louis American League Club . . .   [I] would have been notified after the first game that the series was being tossed in the interest of gamblers."[97] Johnson claimed that had he received that tip, he

> would have at once called the commission together to discuss action with the probability that the series would have been halted or perhaps called off, until the atmosphere could be cleared. But the information never materialized and left us blundering in the dark.[98]

"The tip that went astray" story clears Johnson, just as "the whelp of a beaten cur" tale clears Comiskey.

Bert Collyer, whose newspaper had named seven of the players who were later indicted, may have "made an offer to show Comiskey the evidence but was not given a chance for the ten grand."[99] Or he may not have wanted a reward—only the chance to help rid baseball of the gambling menace. *Collyer's Eye* announced in a headline November 8, 1919, "Eye Refuses to Accept Any Part of $10,000 Reward."

So it appears that the baseball powers—Comiskey and Johnson—refused to give credence to Bert Collyer and the *Collyer's Eye* stories. The *Eye*, after all, was a gambling publication. But then there were Fullerton's charges. And Redmon's story was more than rumors and hearsay. They really had more than enough information to take stronger measures themselves, or to go to the legal system. And perhaps, if the struggle for power had not been raging, they would have.

Going to the law must have at least occurred to them. Maclay Hoyne, an Illinois state's attorney who left office after losing a bid for reelection in fall 1920, said that he spoke right after the Series with Charles Comiskey.

> [He] came to me and told me that he felt sure that he had been 'jobbed' by some of his players. He asked me as a friend, not an official, to help him get the evidence against the crooked players. He said he would pay all the expenses and so I sent one of my men along with the team on their training trip last Spring, but we were not able to secure enough evidence to do anything.[100]

Hoyne was replaced by Robert Crowe. He was later suspected of taking with him when he left office the grand jury statements made by Cicotte, Jackson, and Williams, as well as their signed waivers of immunity.

And so, no loud whistles were blown. As each day passed, the fix faded away a little more.

COLLYER'S EYE INVESTIGATES

Only *Collyer's Eye* kept up the pressure. Following its October 18 issue mentioning the gambler Attell, the *Eye* on October 25, under the headline "Involve White Sox Pitcher," named Claude "Lefty" Williams. In its November 8 issue, Frank O. Klein declared Eddie Collins and Ray Schalk "clean as a hound's tooth" in the rumors, while noting that Schalk had accused Cicotte of being in on things. A week later, the *Eye* headline read "Discover 'Pay Off' Joint in White Sox Scandal?" and the paper named as suspects seven of the eight players who were finally indicted. That November 15 issue also reported the involvement of gamblers from New York, Pittsburgh. St. Louis, and Chicago.

On December 13, the *Eye's* headline read "Catcher Ray Schalk in Huge White Sox Exposé." Schalk had suggested (as Fullerton had written back on October 10) that seven of his teammates would be missing come spring training—and he named all seven. Buck Weaver was not on his list; the seven others who were later indicted with Buck were.

When *The Sporting News* contacted Schalk for more information, he "denied his statement and said he saw nothing wrong with the Series." He valued his job, and he talked the party line. A sportswriter in Joe Jackson's winter home wrote that "It seems to us that if he [Schalk] made the statement as described, Schalk talked too little, when he talked at all." The reporter complained that Schalk should have been more specific and told *why* seven "important team members" would not be returning for the 1920 season. He spoke for many editors when he wrote "Ray Schalk should either tell what he knows, if he knows anything, or he should say nothing. We have had enough of rumors indefinite and lacking foundations that can be unearthed."[101]

Collyer's Eye's investigation and reporter Frank O. Klein received from the baseball establishment the same treatment dished out to Hugh Fullerton. Abuse crashed down, their reputations were called into doubt, and both reporters were dismissed as mindless muckrakers out to sell their papers with sensational headlines. On October 2, 1920, after the scandal was made public, the *Eye's* business manager Hugo L.

Eberhardt wrote in "The Editor's Horn" that the *Eye* had actually been very cautious, holding off releasing their stories until their inquiry "found actual fire behind the elusive smoke. . . . We were for clean sport and advocates of it at no matter what cost." Crediting Bert Collyer for his "persistency and vigor," Eberhardt added, "Devoid of animosity, with no axe to grind, with nothing but the slogan 'Clean Sport,' in mind, Bert refused to let his paper be swerved from a relentless investigation."

The *Eye* was proud that it had used "caution and good judgment." For his own part, Bert Collyer said,

> I was sorry to have to do it. It has been my policy to stand for fair deal in sports, square racing, honest baseball and boxing and wrestling free from fakery. No sport or game can continue that is contaminated with dishonesty and crookedness. My paper is successful because the public knows it to be absolutely on the square and fearless in exposing fraud and fakes, whenever they are found in any branch of finance or sport.[102]

COMISKEY'S DETECTIVES

Comiskey hired a private investigator, who checked on the suspected players' bank accounts and ran down leads. Comiskey would later say that his probe found nothing substantial, only rumors, hearsay, and innuendo. He would later claim to have spent ten to fifteen thousand dollars on this fruitless investigation. However, the detective he hired, John R. Hunter, was called to testify at the 1924 Milwaukee trial. Alfred Austrian, Comiskey's lawyer, had often used Hunter's Secret Services of Illinois, but not for this kind of sleuthing. Hunter's bill was $3,820.71.

Hunter said that he was employed by the White Sox from November 3, 1919, until his services were discontinued on May 8, 1920. According to Hugh Fullerton, Comiskey "had detectives watching the players" as early as after Game Two.[103]

Hunter had interviewed McMullin, Gandil, and Weaver in California, but got no information from them. Asked "Were you told that Charles Comiskey learned that Jackson received $5,000?" Hunter replied that he was not. He recalled that Comiskey had talked with Felsch after the Series: "There was some reference to that, but I can't recall what was said."

Q: "Were you told to avoid those sources of information that might pick up something that might be embarrassing to Comiskey, or to the White Sox?" A: "No, sir."

That was a great question, because it appeared from the report presented by Hunter to Comiskey—his letter dated May 11, 1920, was an exhibit at the Milwaukee trial—that that was the way this investigation was conducted.

The Sox decided not to send Hunter to Savannah, where Joe Jackson wintered. Much was made in the Milwaukee trial of this point; it seemed to indicate that the Sox knew that Jackson had nothing to offer them but the hard evidence of the $5,000 he was given. We can imagine Comiskey also wanting to save money by *not* having Hunter travel to Savannah.

Charles Comiskey's "primary sin," according to baseball historian Jules Tygiel, was not his tight budget or his slavish management style, but his "subsequent efforts to protect his team and investment by covering up the scandal and undermining the prosecution of the participants."[104] It looks very much like the investigating Comiskey did— through his employees, his reporter friends like Fullerton, and his paid detectives—was carried on to ensure that any hard evidence found would remain hidden from public view.

Some have wondered if Comiskey could have later salvaged the careers of Buck Weaver and Joe Jackson, based on what he knew—that Buck took no money and played to win, and that while Jackson took $5,000, he made an effort to communicate with his team about the fix, and apparently played every game to win as he told the grand jury. But if Comiskey tried to save even one of the players that had become "bunched" together, then it would become evident that he had early knowledge of the fix. And that right after the Series, even as he was offering a reward for proof that was not just "rumors and hearsay," he certainly knew enough to call for an investigation.

Comiskey decided to try to treat all of the suspected players the same way. He suspended them after they were indicted, hoping that somehow they could be cleared. Comiskey had been instrumental in the hiring of Landis as commissioner, so he could hope that the judge might repay that favor, especially if the players were found innocent in a court of law. Perhaps Landis would fine and suspend those more guilty than others, and be lenient with those who had given their best in the Series.

But Landis, acting perhaps on his instincts about what was needed to save baseball's image, decided that no mercy could be shown. There had been too much forgiveness in the past, too much wrist-slapping, and too many blind eyes turned to the problem. His verdict drew a clear line in the sand, and so, from then on, players knew exactly what they were risking when they even spoke with persons with gambling interests.

JOHNSON'S INVESTIGATION

Ban Johnson was investigating, too. In fact, there was a race on: Comiskey collecting all the evidence that he could, to keep the lid firmly on, Johnson scrambling for witnesses, to blow the lid off—but only when the time was right. Some historians believe that when Comiskey re-signed seven of the eight suspected players over the winter of 1919–20—he had to offer them contracts by February 1 or risk losing them to other teams—the healthy raises that each received was partly "hush money." They were to keep what they knew to themselves in case Ban Johnson or one of his agents asked.

Comiskey denied that he so instructed his players. In a deposition for the 1924 Milwaukee trial, Comiskey said that when he signed his players for 1920, he had nothing definite to connect anyone with the scandal rumors. "The salary increases were demanded of him, Comiskey said, and he was forced to pay them."[105] But that was not quite true; no owner was forced to give a raise, no matter how deserving of one the player might be, because the reserve clause meant that players had no leverage in bargaining. Bob Hoie has pointed out that the entire Sox team received raises of about 32 percent, with no significant difference between the suspected and the clean Sox.

So if the raises represented some "hush money," the whole team was being rewarded for their silence. More likely, the raises simply reflected the improved financial condition of baseball, and particularly of the American League champions.

Was Johnson out to wreck the White Sox, so he could buy the team himself, at a bargain price? That theory is supported by the diary entries of Harry Grabiner.[106] But against it must be weighed Johnson's long and consistent interest in ridding baseball of gambling's influence, and a case can be made that this was the stronger motive in his investigative efforts.

The Comiskey–Johnson feud was common knowledge and could well have been at work as a motive stronger than Johnson's vice or virtue. Chicago was a big town, but it had become increasingly clear that it was not big enough for both Comiskey and Johnson.

Since Western League days, Ban Johnson had made his headquarters on the twelfth floor of the Fisher building in Chicago. While this office with its several anterooms was the center of official action, a cozy spot on the first floor might well have been called the "nerve center" of the American League. This ornate barroom was known at first as "Danny's," but later, when it came under the management of John V. Burns, it was called the "J. V. B. Club." A passageway ran from the northeast corner of the main room to another little room with a long table. There were scattered chairs and couches, sufficient to accommodate a dozen people. "It was in this little room," wrote Taylor Spink, "that the American League was created out of the brains of Charles A. Comiskey and Ban Johnson, and it was there the league's great battles were fought and won in the early days of the loop."[107]

Because Johnson's investigation ultimately had more to do with the undoing of the cover-up than the cover-up itself, it will be detailed in chapters 5 and 6. It is mentioned here because Johnson's activities were undertaken out of the public eye, when Johnson had passed up every opportunity to blow his whistle on things, starting, perhaps, before the 1919 Series started.

The National League and the Chicago Cubs carried out their own investigations, too. But whoever found hard evidence of the fix would find themselves in a dilemma. If they chose to blow the whistle but could not prove it, they would risk going down in history as a villain, and not a hero. And they might be sued for libel. There had to be convincing proof, or the charges would not stand. The word of a gambler was not sufficient evidence for a trial, even if a ballplayer corroborated it.

The players who were in on the fix probably had calculated that the chance of being caught was small.

Even if caught, the pattern of disciplinary action by baseball officialdom (up until then]) was a financial slap on the wrist, followed after a "decent interval" by reinstatement, if the players desired it, or at worst an unpublicized, graceful exit from the game.[108]

Standard operating procedure in major league baseball had been "don't look for problems," and if fixes were discovered, they were ignored or dealt with quietly. Who could have guessed that this one would send its participants down in history as traitors to the game, and worse?

Baseball was an American institution, and attacking it was becoming like burning the flag. Fullerton was accused of being an "improbable muckraker" when he went public with his suspicions, and his friend Comiskey did not rush to his defense. In fact, he continued to publicly squash the rumors of the fix and to defend his players. Fullerton's stubborn faith in Comiskey blinded him to the owner's motives.

THE STORM PASSES

Comiskey was relieved when the fix rumors faded away into the winter. He went about receiving signed contracts, and the salaries contained nice raises. Comiskey and other owners were adjusting to brighter economic times. After the shortened 1918 season, baseball bounced back and fans came out in record numbers. The raises also reduced the vulnerability of players to gamblers and fixers who might want to work together in 1920.

Providing a real distraction from the fix rumors in the off-season was that very public struggle for power in the baseball industry. Comiskey declared war on Ban Johnson, and thanks to the Carl Mays case, which wound up in court, he had allies in the owners of the Yankees and Red Sox. Johnson's supporters, the "Loyal Five" (the owners of the American League teams in Detroit, Washington, Cleveland, St. Louis, and Philadelphia) helped him wrest control of the board away from Comiskey. The schism put the decision for Garry Herrmann's successor on the back burner, as Comiskey and his allies threatened to leave the American League to form a new, twelve-team National League (the twelfth team would be the first of the Loyal Five to break ranks). But cooler heads at last prevailed and a truce was declared.

One incident that almost lit the fuse that had been sputtering for Hugh Fullerton was the announcement in February 1920 that the Chicago Cubs would not offer utility infielder Lee Magee a contract for the coming season. Magee claimed that he was being unfairly blacklisted and took his case to the press, which eagerly fanned the flames of a public argument between Magee and his lawyers on one side and National League president John Heydler on the other. In March, Fullerton leaped into print once again, saying that "the action of Magee opens the entire field of investigation of the scandals and whispers of the past fall and winter."

> For the last six months I have been hammering away striving to force the powers of organized baseball to make a full and complete investigation of the stories that have been circulated. They have promised, have declared that they would go to the bottom of the scandals. So far as I can learn only Comiskey, owner of the Cubs [*sic*], has made a serious effort to do so.

SILENCERS PUT ON EVERYBODY

Fullerton continued,

I have been trying to persuade some of the players whose names have been used in connection with the scandals of last year [1919], the year before and the last world's series to force the leagues either to clear their names or prefer formal charges. From most of these I have secured not even an answer.[109]

Magee threatened baseball with "bombs," at one point saying he would name four National League players who were involved with gamblers. But in the end, his headlines "fizzled" as all he could present to Heydler was "the old Hal Chase case." The Lee Magee case remained in the news as the 1920 season opened and went to trial in June. Magee lost. No other players supported his charges, and several denied them. Heydler and Cub president William Veeck recalled Magee "confessing" to them before the case went public, and the evidence against Magee (including a check on which he had stopped payment) outweighed his claim that he had been double-crossed.

The Cub organization was lauded for dealing firmly and decisively with a clear case of game-tossing, even though Magee's team had won the game in question. It was a step forward after Hal Chase's exoneration by league president Heydler and "an everlasting warning to other intending wrong-doers."[110] Perhaps the Magee trial gave Ban Johnson the idea that the courts and the press might be the best places to deal with gambling in his own league—and to clean up that nasty mess left over from the previous October.

Yes, it was spring again, and the 1920 season started up. The cover-up seemed securely in place. Ban Johnson continued to bide his time. The owners of the Major League Baseball teams, "the Lords of the Realm" in John Helyar's famous phrase, were breathing easier. They had dodged an enormous bullet that might have shattered baseball's image and sharply reduced the value of their teams. The outcome of the Magee case had even improved the game's image. But they were not out of trouble. Gamblers would continue to influence players to toss games. For the fixers, it was business as usual, and only a few teams made an effort to bar gambling from the parks.[111]

The 1920s have been called "The Golden Age of Sports." The country found heroes not only in baseball, but also in boxing, college football, and many other sports. Of course, the country was also on the rebound from the First World War, a flu pandemic, strikes, and race riots. The twenties truly roared, the noise having been started by Babe Ruth, who smashed the home run record with fifty-four in 1920. But before the roar, came baseball's darkest hour.

4

SHOELESS JOE JACKSON'S ROLE

I've always maintained that the question "Why isn't Shoeless Joe in the
Hall of Fame?" should be supplemented with "Why isn't Charles
Comiskey out?"
—Marvin Miller in *A Whole Different Ball Game*

I always maintained you couldn't blame Joe [Jackson] for anything.
He was not a very well-educated fellow; they said he couldn't read
or write. I guess somebody talked him into that mess.
—Smoky Joe Wood in *A Donald Honig Reader*

In the previous chapter, we focused on the cover-up that followed the Big Fix. In the next chapter, we will look at how that cover-
up came undone. These are not two, distinct events, although they can
be treated separately. Both the cover-up and its undoing are, in a sense,
still happening.

This chapter is inserted here because of the current keen interest
in one of the players forever associated with the fix, because he was
one of the "eight men out." Joe Jackson is singled out here not because
of his fame, but for his unique role in the events surrounding the 1919
Series. Later, we will look at Jackson's performance in the 1919 World
Series. It was not perfect—it was human. Jackson maintained throughout his life that his performance was the best proof that he was not in
on the fix, but statistics are not conclusive evidence. In this chapter, we
will only explore the evidence that suggests that Jackson was the one
player who wanted to talk about the fix, before and after the Series.

BEFORE THE SERIES

For any pre-series communication between Jackson and his team,
we have only Jackson's word, nothing corroborating, not yet. The ear-

61

liest warning Jackson claimed to have given is reported in a team history. In "The Chicago White Sox," *Sport*, June 1951, John Carmichael quotes Joe Jackson:

> Maybe I ran with the wrong players. Maybe I heard things. But I tried to clear up the mess before it broke and nobody listened. I went to Mr Comiskey three weeks before the Series. I asked him to pull the team out; told him what I heard. He laughed and said, "We got 100 men on guard . . . nothing could be pulled."[1]

Is Carmichael a reputable source? Ted Williams called him "the home run champion of sportswriters"—high praise indeed, considering the source and Williams's relations with the press. But according to another White Sox historian, Richard C. Lindberg, although John Carmichael was commissioned to write the Sox team history,

> Carmichael was a *Daily News* columnist. He ran the "Barbershop" column for many years (1930s–1970s), and was an enthusiastic fan of the Sox. Worked for the P.R. department in the early 1970s after his retirement.
>
> Those sportswriters were topnotch story tellers but poor researchers, who recited anecdotes and yarns they heard in the press box as the gospel truth, and as a result myths and legends became facts in print that future baseball historians had to try to prove but very often could not. This happened to me many times. I would be very skeptical of the Jackson anecdote—other than in this account, I never heard anything to back it up.[2]

Perhaps Carmichael himself was skeptical, because the story from *Sport* does not appear in the book where Carmichael's chapter on the White Sox appears. Instead, he goes with the "legendary anecdote" of "Say it ain't so, Joe," which "italicized Jackson's role in the scandal."[3]

The Sporting News drew some criticism from Major League Baseball for running a feature on Joe Jackson in their September 24, 1942, issue. Baseball officialdom, in the person of Judge Landis, strongly objected to the portrayal of Joe Jackson as a happily retired, successful, contented man, without bitterness and with an apparently clean and peaceful conscience. Fixers aren't supposed to live happily ever after.

When Joe Jackson first left South Carolina to play ball, he found it rough going. He was a southerner, uncomfortable in the big northern cities, unable to read or write. At one point he returned home but was coaxed back. After organized baseball slammed the door shut on Joe Jackson, he still had some spring left in his legs, and he played ball as much as he could wherever he was welcome. Then he was Greenville's again, and in 1942, Jackson summed up his philosophy for *The Sporting News* in these words: "to live in a house by the side of a road and be a friend to man."

The front-page *Sporting News* interview is long, and although it contains no mention of any pre-Series knowledge or communication, it is worth looking up if you want to learn about Jackson's all-time team, how he saw Ted Williams, and much more. It was written by Carter "Scoop" Latimer, the sports editor of the *Greenville News*. Besides photos from Joe's career on the diamond, there are shots of Joe sitting on his doorstep, behind the counter at one of his liquor stores (he was unable to consume sugar or alcohol), smiling as he breaks an egg into a pan in his kitchen, and, finally, chatting with Scoop by his fireplace. Today, it would be called a warm, fuzzy, feel-good interview. But it upset Landis.

Regarding his role in the fix, Jackson pointed to his performance. "The Supreme Being"—and not Landis—"will be my judge." Though not bitter, Jackson still had contempt for the "Say it ain't so" story. "A fabricated scoop," wrote Scoop. "If I had been guilty of 'laying down' in the Series, I wouldn't be so successful today," Joe pleaded. "For I'm a great believer in retribution. I have made a lot more money since being out of baseball than when I was in it—the good Lord knows I am innocent of any wrong-doing."[4]

But there is no mention in this long profile of Jackson making any attempt to communicate about the fix to his team.

In 1949, Furman Bisher interviewed Joe Jackson at his Greenville home. *Sport* magazine ran the article in its October issue, and it is one of the documents that nobody curious about Jackson can pass up.

The interview contains a number of statements that cannot be corroborated, at least not easily, or not yet. For example, Jackson tells of being propositioned by a gambler in front of four witnesses (two couples); he said that he routed the crook and that the folks who saw it "offered their testimony at my trial." Jackson says he went to Comiskey the night before the Series started and asked to be benched. (See below, a version of Jackson's story that appeared in *The Sporting News*, in which his account of "the night before" is repeated.)

Jackson added that Hugh Fullerton was present, and Hugh "offered to testify for me at my trial later, and he came all the way out to Chicago to do it." While it is true that Fullerton did testify at the 1924 trial in Milwaukee, the transcripts do not suggest that he was testifying for Jackson. He was never asked his opinion about Jackson's performance in the Series, or whether he believed that he was in on the fix. Fullerton made no mention of Jackson warning Comiskey about the fix.[5]

If there is any "hard evidence" that can prove that Jackson spoke with Comiskey before the Series, it may be buried somewhere in Hugh Fullerton's unpublished notes or letters—or maybe in a yet-to-be-found cryptic comment that snuck past his newspaper's censors.[6]

With the statements Jackson made in the Bisher interview that we *can* look up, there are some problems. He remembered throwing out "five men at home" (and some writers report that), but he was credited with just one assist in the Series. Jackson recalled Cicotte's deflection in Game Four, which, by most accounts, would have given him a second assist.

Jackson blamed Ban Johnson for "causing the thing to go to into the courts" and for "ruling us ineligible." While Jackson is on the mark about Johnson being responsible for the Black Sox case going to trial, it was Judge Landis who banned the players. In brief, Jackson's memory—never his strong suit—was not entirely accurate by 1949.[7]

When Jackson died in 1951, Bisher himself recalled that interview in his column in the *Atlanta Journal-Constitution*. He remembered Jackson as "a plain and simple man, who thought in plain and simple ways." His weakness, in Bisher's view, had been that he relied too heavily on his friends for guidance; in 1919, he had put his trust in bad hands. Bisher feels that Jackson did not realize he was doing anything wrong.

Bisher recalled that Jackson insisted that he had "played my heart out against Cincinnati" that October and that Joe could recall his play at bat and in the field in detail.

> Joe lived his last years in quiet and comfort, a man who dressed well, drove a Packard, and doted on the respect of his South Carolina neighbors. It is perhaps odd, but when he died, he was chairman of the protest committee of a semipro league around

Greenville. Someone else was always delegated to read the protests and write the committee reports, it should be added.

If Jackson tried to communicate with his team about the fix before the Series, the Bisher article is not conclusive proof.

BEFORE GAME ONE

In *The Sporting News*, on August 17, 1960, Commissioner Ford Frick was applauded for "turning down a request from a television producer [David Susskind] to present a drama involving the 1919 Black Sox scandal." "Banning such a production" was "using common sense." (*The Sporting News* recommended stories about men like Mickey Mantle and following the formula of *The Lou Gehrig Story*.)[8]

But two months later,[9] Frick was criticized by *The Sporting News* for his August ban—he was called a czar and his decision, arbitrary. Yet it seemed that *The Sporting News* really did not want a show on the Black Sox scandal aired. And it said this of Joe Jackson:

> To the best of anyone's knowledge, Jackson took no part in the fix. . . . His problem was that he knew what some of the others were doing and planning and would say nothing about it. Does television know that the night before the Series opened, Jackson begged Owner Charles Comiskey to keep him out of the game and his request was refused? No, we don't think television could do justice to that story.

CBS-TV ultimately used the research it had done for the drama in an episode of *Witness*.[10] It aired Thursday, January 26, 1961, right at the end of the Series' run. Eliot Asinof was listed as "writer"—he had been commissioned to write the teleplay.[11]

In its February 8 issue, *The Sporting News*—with Dan Daniels leading the charge and Jim Anderson following up with the reactions from Greenville, North Carolina—lambasted the program. They picked it apart for its inaccuracies, poor acting, bad casting, and so on. It was the review Max Bialystock dreamed of getting in *The Producers*, but never got.[12]

DID JACKSON "BEG TO BE BENCHED"?

Curiously, inserted in the *Sporting News* blitz on the show was a little box with the headline, "'Begged' to Be Benched in' 19 Series."

The story was from Greenville, so it is likely that Jim Anderson wrote it. The report said Jackson "often told friends" that he had "begged" Comiskey to keep him out of the Series. "'I went to the room of Mr Comiskey the night before the Series started and asked him to keep me out of the lineup,' Joe asserted." Anderson cannot be quoting Jackson—he had died ten years before. "He refused and I said to him, 'Tell the newspapers you suspended me for being drunk, or anything, but leave me out of the Series, and then there can be no question.'" Turned down, Jackson "played his heart out." Then *The Sporting News* criticizes *Witness* for failing to include this appeal to Comiskey.

The bible of baseball, which did not want this show aired,[13] pointed out what it saw as a gross inaccuracy—the omission of the early information Comiskey received.[14]

Assuming for a moment that Jackson *did* ask to be benched—whether he spoke with Comiskey directly or with manager Kid Gleason—why would the request be refused? Because if the fix fell apart, the Sox would need Jackson in the lineup to beat the Reds. And if Jackson had alerted his team to the fix, he was not going to play to lose.

Comiskey and Gleason were also probably knowledgeable about what happens when ordinary people start fiddling with the big-money plans of the underworld. And Jackson, although he was uneducated, was also far from stupid. All of them probably knew that gamblers were involved and that there would be some risk in doing anything to thwart their plans.

Jackson apparently just decided to go out and play the best Series he could play and hope they didn't kill him. If the gamblers had believed that Jackson was in on the fix, and then he had ridden the bench, it might have gotten sticky for him. Of course, this is conjecture.

What did Jackson know, and when did he know it? Here is where the conflicting statements between Jackson's grand jury testimony in 1920, and his trial testimony in 1924, serve to make things confusing. Jackson said that he was approached in Boston by Chick Gandil weeks before the Series and offered $10,000 to be part of the fix. Jackson refused. Gandil persisted, asking him again some time later in Chicago and offering $20,000. Most accounts have Gandil saying that the fix was going down with or without Jackson, so he might as well get in on the action.

Jackson then either refused again or gave his approval, perhaps tacitly, by his silence. In any case, Jackson knew that Gandil was recruiting and something foul was afoot. He may also have known of the plot from Lefty Williams, with whom he spoke often and who admitted being in on the planning.

Here is what Jackson said to the 1920 grand jury about the two offers by Gandil:

> He asked me to consider $10,000 to frame something up and I asked him frame what? And he told me and I said no. [Gandil] just walked away from me, and when I returned to Chicago he told me that he would give me twenty and I said no again, and on the bridge where you go into the club house he told me I could either take it or let it alone, they were going through. They said "You might as well say yes or say no and play ball or anything you want." I told them I would take their word.

In any case, some of the gamblers who testified later believed that Joe Jackson was in on the fix. They had been told he was by Chick Gandil. Gandil also told Eddie Cicotte that Jackson was in. But most sources agree that Jackson did not attend any of the several meetings during which the fix was discussed and then agreed upon. That was Jackson's testimony, too. In the 1924 trial, Lefty Williams testified that he used Jackson's name in the meetings with the gamblers without Jackson's knowledge or permission. (Of course, Lefty was Jackson's friend and trying to help out any way he could, and testimony is not the same as the truth.)

It is possible that the very first time that Joe Jackson discovered *for sure* that the fix was in—that it was not just a rumor, an idea, or a threat—was the morning of Game One. In the Sinton Hotel lobby, Jackson was approached by one of the gamblers, Sleepy Bill Burns. Here is Jackson's account as told to the grand jury:

> [Burns] told me about this stuff and I didn't know so much. He said "Where is Chick?" I said, "I don't know." He walked away from me. I didn't know enough to talk to him about what they were going to plan or what they had planned, I wouldn't know it if I had seen him, I only knew what I had been told, that's all I knew.

Had Burns started talking with Jackson as if he was in on the deal—then backed off and walked away, when he discovered that he was not? That's a possible interpretation. Notice that Jackson says "what *they* were going to plan, or what *they* had planned." According to this account, if he was in the fix, he was not in the know.

So what does Jackson do, now that he knows that the rumors swirling all about are probably more than rumors? Jackson *asks to be benched*. In Harvey Frommer's account, *Shoeless Joe and Ragtime Baseball,* Jackson says:

> I never said anything about it [the fix] until the night before the Series started. I went to Mr Comiskey and begged him to take me out of the lineup . . . if there was something going on I knew the bench would be the safest place, but he wouldn't listen to me. . . .

Frommer's source is unclear. Asinof's account in *Eight Men Out* goes like this:

> Jackson returned the manager's curious stare, and offered that he did not feel good. "I don't wanna play!" he added. Gleason wheeled. "What!" "I said I don't wanna play." Then he added, much too loudly, "You can tell the boss that, too!" He wanted Comiskey to know this.

I asked Eliot Asinof the source for the "begged to be benched" story. He restated his belief that Jackson asked Gleason, just before Game One, saying "I don't want to play!" When I asked if he ever wished he used footnotes in *Eight Men Out*, he answered "No! My sources were an amalgamation of hundreds of conversations, impossible to document." In other words, *sorry—you can't look it up*. To be fair, baseball books written before 1970 rarely had bibliographies, let alone footnotes. Baseball had not yet been discovered by historians, and baseball writers relied on imagination as well as their own style.

There is some speculation that Asinof got the "bench me" story from Happy Felsch, but there is nothing concrete that ties the story to any source that is easy to document. Asinof: "My best recall is that I'd read/heard about it [Jackson's desire not to play in the first game] from a variety of newspaper clips and people. Felsch? Red Faber?" Perhaps Asinof's notes will surface some day and shed some light on this important detail.

Did Jackson ask to be benched? This seems to me to be a crucial question. It has implications for the questions most fans have today about Joe Jackson, and also for the actions of Charles Comiskey during and after the Series.

If Jackson stepped up before the Series, calling attention to the interference of gamblers, and requested that he be benched, then it is hard to believe that he would have given less than his best on the diamond during the Series. He would be a watched man, his every move scrutinized.

If Comiskey was informed of the fix before the Series, then he was covering up all along, not just after the Series. And because Jackson told him, Jackson had to be prevented from giving that information to anybody else; silencing Jackson would be a crucial part of the cover-up. When he learned that Eddie Cicotte had gone to the grand jury to testify, Jackson decided to follow. Comiskey and his advisors did not attempt to stop him, but Comiskey's lawyer took him aside first. We do not know what advice or coaching Alfred Austrian provided. We do know that he made sure that Jackson waived his immunity, something that a lawyer acting on behalf of Jackson probably would not have advised.

In his grand jury testimony, Jackson made no mention of trying to inform or warn his manager or Charles Comiskey about the fix. He said nothing about asking to be benched. The closest he came was his account of a conversation he had with Chick Gandil during the Series:

> "I am not going to be in it. I will just get out of that altogether."
> . . . Gandil said I was into it already and I might as well stay in.
> I said, "I can go to the boss and have every damn one of you pulled out of the limelight." He [Gandil] said "It wouldn't be well for me if I did that." I told him any time they wanted to have me knocked off, to have me knocked off. [Gandil] just laughed. That was the fourth game, the fifth night going back to Cincinnati.

THE MORNING AFTER THE SERIES

Jackson testified in 1924 that he went to see Charles Comiskey the morning after the Series ended. He had received $5,000 from Lefty Williams the night before.[15] When asked, "You got the $5000 right after the fourth game in Chicago, didn't you?" Jackson replied, "The day after the World Series, to the best of my recollection."[16] That contradicted the story he (and Lefty Williams) had told the 1920 grand jury.

[Williams] said the gamblers had crossed him. I don't remember [what I said] but he explained to me that he had used my name in order to wring money out of certain fellows supposed to be gamblers, and I said "you fellows had a lot of nerve."[17]

Jackson may well have received the tainted money earlier in the Series. In their 1920 grand jury statements, both Jackson and Williams had had the delivery taking place after Game Four or Five (they said Four, but they also said it was just before leaving for Cincinnati, where Game Six was played). Jackson also had said in 1920 that he knew of the fix before Williams gave him the money. "I told Williams after the first day it was a crooked deal all the way through, Gandil was not on the square with us."

In any case, at the 1924 Milwaukee trial, Jackson consistently said that on the morning after the Series he had wanted to tell the club owner what he knew of the fix from Williams. Asinof has this in his book, and the story is found in other sources, too. Some accounts have Grabiner saying, "Go home, we know what you want," and slamming shut the window on the office door. Some accounts have Jackson hanging around a while. None of the accounts have him meeting with Comiskey.[18]

Here is how Jackson described it on the stand in Milwaukee: Q: "Did you tell Grabiner why you wanted to see the old man [after the Series]?" A: "Why should I tell him? I told him it was important that I see Mr. Comiskey."[19] Grabiner was apparently so rude that Jackson was still upset with him months later, when they met in Savannah to talk contract.

According to Jackson, Grabiner said in Savannah: "'We have the goods on three fellows, Cicotte, Williams, and Gandil,' and he [Grabiner] said, 'We know Williams gave you $5000, but your record speaks for itself. We know you play baseball to win.'"[20] Grabiner denied that this conversation, or any conversation right after the Series, took place.

When Joe Jackson, Charles Comiskey, and Harry Grabiner gave their stories before a jury in Milwaukee in 1924, twelve jurors listened to their words and their tone of voice and watched their facial expressions—and eleven of them believed Jackson. Juries are not infallible. Their verdict was overturned by the judge, but for the record, they had believed Jackson's 1924 version of things, presumably a version coached by a lawyer looking out for his interests, not those of the Chicago White Sox.

CONSPIRACY THEORY

"What made the situation dangerous was the simple fact that the circumstances and facts that exonerated Jackson condemned Comiskey," writes William R. Herzog II. Herzog's long essay in *The Faith of Fifty Million* (John Knox Press, 2002) details better than most books the case for a connection between the cover-up of the fix and Jackson's banishment.

Chicago lawyer David Carlson:

> It's my theory that [the White Sox's lawyer] Austrian and Comiskey wanted Jackson to confess so they could compromise him. Jackson was in the unique position of substantially embarrassing Comiskey by telling of his attempts to inform him of the fix. If Jackson were indicted, however, he would be discredited. I think the evidence supports this theory.[21]

In Savannah, Georgia, for the winter of 1919–20, Jackson wrote (with the help of his wife) a series of letters to Charles Comiskey.[22] On November 11, 1919, Comiskey offered to "gladly pay your expenses to Chicago" if Jackson wanted to go there and tell what he knew about the Series. On November 15, Jackson wrote that he had been surprised to hear his name linked to the rumors of the fix, and he offered to go to Chicago any time. Twice in this letter, Jackson insisted that he had done all he could to win the Series. There was no reply. Conspiracy theorists might conclude that this is evidence that Comiskey did not want Jackson's story on the record. His investigator was not directed to visit Savannah.

FOLLOW THE MONEY

Before looking at how the lid was finally lifted off the Big Fix, it is worth looking at the "hard evidence" that Joe Jackson might have delivered to Charles Comiskey—that is, the $5,000 that he admitted receiving from Lefty Williams. This "dirty envelope" had the potential to prove the fix to anyone who wanted to believe that it happened and to reveal it to the world. Ironically, the cash that might have made Joe Jackson a hero for blowing the whistle on the fix instead condemned him when he could not prove that he had showed it to his employer.

Follow the money. These words from the Watergate scandal would have taken you, in 1919, to places where a bodyguard would have come in handy, to places from which you might not escape, if you learned anything useful. Indeed, the gamblers were the big winners in the fix, and they made the most money. And although Al Capone was not yet making headlines, prohibition was starting to make underworld figures wealthy—and well armed.

Following the money that the gamblers distributed is not that easy. Eddie Cicotte apparently bought a farm for the "missus and the kiddies, as he said to the grand jury." Chick Gandil, who likely kept a good portion of whatever came his way, went to California, kept on playing ball wherever he could, and apparently kept his money well hidden. Comiskey's investigation extended into the bank accounts of the suspected players, but revealed little.

What about Joe Jackson? That Lefty Williams gave him $5,000 seems certain. That he took it was, in retrospect, a huge mistake. That he took the money to Comiskey (as hard evidence of the fix) is controversial because it is not well documented. That he tried showing it or giving it to Harry Grabiner in Savannah is more believable (a Milwaukee jury seemed to believe it in 1924), but still not certain.

Accounts vary about what Joe and Kate Jackson did with the money "from a dirty envelope." Some are convinced that they either donated it to a hospital or used it to pay for the medical bills for Joe's sister Gertrude. Some are sure that the $5,000 went to a charity. Some assume the Jacksons just spent it on their businesses. They may have done all of these things.[23]

Relying heavily on biographer Donald Gropman, William R. Herzog has Jackson hanging onto the money. He tries to give it to Grabiner after the season but is instructed to keep it. Herzog then, in a footnote, says this about the tainted $5,000:

> Neither Joe nor Katie believed the money was theirs. So they put it in savings and let it earn interest. After Katie's death, the money, which had grown through the years with interest, was donated to the American Heart Fund and the American Cancer Society.

The Jacksons apparently never regarded the money as *theirs*, to spend on themselves.

In fact, Katie Jackson's deposition for the 1924 Milwaukee trial addresses the question about where the tainted money went. Kate testified that she was in the room when Lefty Williams gave her husband the "dirty envelope" that contained $5,000, in large bills.

"Lefty said 'Here is $5,000.'"

Q: "What did he say it was for?"

A: "That he had gotten."

Q: "From whom?"

A: "He didn't say."

Q: "What did your husband say?"

A: "I don't remember."

Q: "Did your husband take the money?"

A: "Yes, sir."[24]

Kate did not recall what Joe told her about it. And she did not recall crying about it, as Joe said she did in his statement for the grand jury in 1920. Nothing was said about what the money was for.

"I've always taken care of Mr. Jackson's money and banked it for him."[25]

Q: "He gave you this $5,000?"

A: "Yes."

Q: "What did you do with it?"

A: "Most of it I spent trying to save his sister." [Joe's sister Gertrude had been hospitalized.]

Kate did not know the total of the hospital bills. She recalled that the Savannah hospital cost $35 per week; Gertrude was a patient there for four weeks. Private nurses cost $35 per week.

Q: "Was the total expense over $1,000?"

A: "Heavens, yes!"

So the money was simply deposited in Chatham Bank, Savannah. A representative from the bank testified in Milwaukee that Kate deposited $5,400 on December 1, 1919, in large bills.

Those who believe Jackson threw the Series argue that he felt guilty about the money—and that although he was upset at getting just $5,000 of a promised $20,000, he continued to see the cash as tainted. And some believe it is more likely that he regarded money the old-fashioned way, as something you *earned;* so because in his mind he had done nothing to earn this money, he was reluctant to spend it except to help others.

But why did he keep it at all? Williams gave it to him—or threw it at him. "He didn't want the damn stuff [the $5,000], and I thought just this way, since that lousy so-called gambling outfit had used my name, I might as well have their money as for him [Williams]," Joe testified in Milwaukee.

Q: "How did you know they had used your name?"

A: "I had Williams' word for it."[26]

Again Jackson described being very upset with his friend Lefty Williams when Lefty told him that he had used his name in the meetings with gamblers, meetings that Joe had not attended. Donald Gropman believes Williams felt sorry about that and offered Joe half of the money he (Williams) had received, to make up for it. "I told [Williams] I didn't want any part of it [the $5,000], it didn't belong to me at all, I didn't want it, knew nothing about it, and I went up to tell the boss."[27]

In the special verdict it considered, the Milwaukee jury at the 1924 trial was given two questions related to the $5,000. First, based on all the testimony (which included a considerable amount from Lefty Williams), did Williams give Jackson the money before all the games in the Series were played set? The jury responded, eleven-to-one, no.

Then they were asked to answer this question: At the time Williams gave Jackson the money, did he tell Jackson that there "had been an agreement between certain ballplayers to lose or 'throw' the games of the World Series, and that the $5000 was his [Jackson's] share of the money received by the players for their part in the agreement?" Again, they responded, eleven-to-one, no.

It may well be that Jackson took the money to Comiskey the next morning, not to turn it over to him, but to show him that he had hard evidence that the Series had been tainted. Only if Comiskey insisted that he needed the cash to show the authorities, would Joe have given it up. Maybe. As it turned out, Jackson apparently could not even get past Harry Grabiner, let alone see Comiskey in private.

How important was money to Joe Jackson in October 1919? As one of the top hitters in baseball, he should have been making at least twice the $6,000 he had been paid since 1917. The next winter he would sign a new multi-year contract for $8,000 a year. The reward of $20,000 for participating in the fix, or just for not doing anything to stop it, must have been very tempting. The chance of being caught must have seemed very slim. The chance of losing a career in baseball because of association with the fix, even slimmer.

While he was still with Cleveland, Joe Jackson was supposedly offered a lucrative sum ($20,000) to jump to the outlaw circuit, the Federal League. On a speaking tour of southern cities, Jackson was asked how important that much money was to him.

One thing Joe tells them is how he turned down $60,000 to play with the Feds for three years. It looked like a lot of money, he said, but there are things in this world to be regarded above money—keeping faith with your friends, for instance. All of which goes to show that you don't have to know how to read and write to be a man of principle and conscience.[28]

Following the money is taking one more trail that branches off in several directions. Jackson took the money, and he kept it; but if he kept it, maybe his team knew that and even instructed him to keep it. He apparently did not spend it on himself. What this all says about the cover-up, and Jackson's character, is a matter of interpretation—and fuel for the hot stove.

5

IT COMES UNDONE

"We will show," [defense lawyer] Mr Ahern said, "that it would have been impossible for Eddie Cicotte, Joe Jackson, Claude Williams, or 'Chick' Gandil to have fixed the games. Before we finish, the jury will be convinced that none of the games was thrown."
—Chicago Tribune, July 28, 1921

Partly because of the movie *All the President's Men*, Bob Woodward and Carl Bernstein became household names for their role in helping to bring the Watergate scandal to light. But even in baseball circles, the names of the men who uncovered the fixing of the 1919 World Series remain tough trivia. If they did it today, they might rate as *Time*'s "Men of the Year."

HUGH FULLERTON

I was disappointed to learn from one of Hugh Fullerton's grandsons that his grandfather left behind no papers or diaries. After all, in the stories he submitted just after the Series, he had names and dates and places—although most were apparently edited out by his supervisors, either for fear of libel, or perhaps at the request of Charles Comiskey. In one of his last interviews, Joe Jackson claimed to have told Comiskey about the Big Fix, in the presence of Hugh Fullerton, before the Series. How great it would be if a journal entry would confirm that tiny detail. Fullerton wrote a series of articles after the 1922 season that were vetoed by Comiskey. They may yet turn up and shed new light on events that were then still fresh in memories.

That said, much of Hugh Fullerton's writing has survived. Some articles are familiar and widely quoted, while others have been overlooked. Perhaps because no one was more convinced about the fix, no one crusaded harder than Fullerton to undo its cover-up. While he is credited today more than anyone else with bringing the fix to light, other events—and not Fullerton's writings—were more responsible for that. But the story of the uncovering of the fix has to begin with Hugh S. Fullerton.

Hugh was born in 1873, and according to Norman L. Macht in *The Ballplayers*, he was "the best-known baseball writer in the country" for the first quarter of the twentieth century. "A titan of the Chicago press box," Fullerton graduated from Ohio State College and started writing in Cincinnati in 1889. He moved to Chicago seven years later, and in 1919 was on the staff of the *Herald and Examiner*. His columns and features were often syndicated. Fullerton also wrote several books, including some fiction. From Fullerton scholar Steve Klein's master's thesis:

> In the decade preceding the fix, Fullerton, a prolific writer, had published more than 100 freelance magazine articles. The majority were for the popular *American Magazine*, the favorite soapbox for the Muckrakers, progressive journalists who pioneered American investigative journalism.

Fullerton was one of the founders of the Baseball Writers Association of America, and he was awarded the J. G. Taylor Spink Award in 1964.

By a somewhat bizarre coincidence, the storyline of one of Fullerton's juvenile fiction books, *Jimmy Kirkland and the Plot for a Pennant* (John C. Winston Company, 1915), involved a conspiracy between ballplayers and gamblers. Even more bizarre, the player most deeply involved was a left-handed pitcher named Williams. The book was published in 1915—a year before Lefty Williams joined the White Sox. While Fullerton's fiction has the team ownership, politicians, and even the police aiding and abetting the fixers, in 1919 Fullerton set Charles Comiskey above suspicion of any wrongdoing, no doubt out of loyalty. In *Plot for a Pennant*, a character named Technicalities Feehan helps uncover the fix—Feehan being, in the words of Steve Klein,

> a baseball writer and thinly disguised stand-in for the author, who notices irregularities in the team's statistics that point to wrongdoing. "I deserve no thanks," Technicalities tells Kirkland, "It's merely in the line of square dealing and justice."

Baseball historian David Q. Voigt quotes Fullerton often in his *American Baseball*, describing how the early game evolved—with Fullerton lobbying for "more dash, less mechanical work, more brains by individuals and fewer orders from the bench." He argued in print for more discipline to curb rowdyism, but also gave a voice to the players who felt stifled by the system. Voigt ranks Fullerton with Ring Lardner, Grantland Rice, and Franklin P. Adams—all-star company—as individual stylists. He says, "In 1919 it was Fullerton's detective work that unraveled the web of fact and rumor and exposed the crooked work of the 'Black Sox.'" But that's not quite what happened.

Rumors of the fix were "widespread and detailed," and were not confined to the playing field and locker room. A hundred reporters must have heard them, but Hugh Fullerton was "inquisitive," and "tracking down rumors was a joy of [his] life" (Voigt). *Thou shalt not quit* was the first of Fullerton's "The Ten Commandments of Sport, and of Everything Else," the title of a 1921 *American Magazine* article. "He was like a bird dog on the scent and never let go of the story," Fred Lieb wrote. "From gamblers, politicians and players, he pieced together a story."[1]

His "tireless digging" was assisted during the Series by Hall of Fame pitcher Christy Mathewson, who had covered the October games for a New York paper. Matty became Fullerton's "expert witness," diagramming each questionable play. "Comparing notes, [they] marked seven plays by the White Sox as highly suspect. In several articles over the winter, Fullerton not only questioned the honesty of the Series but discussed specific plays by specific players that had convinced him that something was amiss."[2]

While several sources mention the series of articles written by Fullerton and including Matty's diagrams, most of the books on the 1919 Series and on Mathewson refer only to the single article in the *New York Evening World* (see below), December 15, 1919. No diagrams accompany the text. But the *Evening World* itself, on February 24, 1920, suggested with some pride that baseball's taking off-season action against players ("three unnamed stars") for gambling "was no doubt inspired by special articles written by Hugh Fullerton . . . several months ago, which pointed out that baseball was headed toward the rocks because of gamblers' activities and suspicion that the last World Series . . . had been tampered with."

Fullerton smelled something fishy before the first Series pitches were tossed. The rumors were flooding the streets, because the money being bet was shifting rapidly away from the Sox to the Reds.[3] Testifying in Milwaukee in 1924, Fullerton said that he heard of the fix before Game One directly from Sleepy Bill Burns—but did not tell Comiskey. As noted in chapter 3, writing in *The Sporting News* in 1935, Fullerton said that he *had* told Comiskey, as well as Ban Johnson (both had already heard about it) and Barney Dreyfuss, but they all chose to do nothing, giving the reason that despite all the rumors, it was impossible to fix a World Series.

Even though he was under oath in 1924, he was not about to embarrass Comiskey, and he could honestly state that he did not tell Comiskey of the fix *first*. Comiskey had been dead for several years when Fullerton wrote his 1935 memoir.

Christy Mathewson may have heard of the fix from Burns before the Series, too. They apparently were on the same train from New York to Cincinnati, and as Dewey and Acocella note, Burns had a "lack of discretion with everybody . . . about fix possibilities"[4] *(The Black Prince of Baseball: Hal Chase and the Mythology of the Game* (Sport Classic Books, 2004)).

The night before the Series started, Fullerton wired all the papers with which he was syndicated: ADVISE ALL NOT TO BET ON THIS SERIES. UGLY RUMORS AFLOAT. In 1935, Fullerton said this message had been sent as a "black face precede to [his] story" and that he had been hoping to "warn the fans that something queer was coming off" and they should refuse to wager. As cautiously as he worded it, only two of forty papers printed the precede. But that was enough to put Fullerton on the record as the first whistle-blower.

During Game One, Fullerton and Mathewson took turns leaving the press box to go downstairs to watch the pitching. Fullerton recalled later that, "after two innings I was morally certain that something was coming off." Matty watched Cicotte pitching and returned to the press box shaking his head. After Game One Fullerton "was forced to admit, 'I don't like what I saw out there today. There is something smelly. Cicotte usually does not pitch like that.'"[5]

Mathewson, in his *New York Times* account of Game One, wrote, "In the third inning of today's game Hugh Fullerton said to me, 'Do you think Cicotte was right?' I replied: 'No, because if he had his usual stuff the Reds would be making more foul tips.'" Matty proceeded to predict again that the Reds would take the Series in seven games, and added, "I never bet on a ball game, but if we get another warm day tomorrow and Sallee starts for Cincinnati, I think I will get down a little wager on the Reds." The closest Mathewson came to suggesting something crooked was going on, was his parting line, ". . . No team to my knowledge was ever defeated by so large a score in an opening [Series] game when each contender was trying its best." (The "Miracle Braves" beat the A's of Connie Mack 7–1 in the 1914 opener, but most other first games had been close.)

That evening, catcher Ray Schalk came into Fullerton's room as he was writing.

> He declared loudly that the pitcher had crossed him in signals at least eight times that game. "Little man," I said, "Keep your mouth shut or go to Comiskey and Gleason. If you make charges against anyone you'll be the goat—you can't prove them, and it would ruin you."[6]

Fullerton, of course, did not follow his own advice. He knew what was happening but could only investigate so far by himself. He pleaded with those who had the resources to carry out a more thorough investigation to get involved. Until their efforts finally bore fruit, Fullerton was "the goat."

> A Chicago newspaperman quoted Schalk as saying in the autumn of 1919 that Cicotte had repeatedly crossed him in the first game of the world's series of that year and had refused to follow his signals. Ray further told of having accused Cicotte of trying to throw down his club, and the two had a battle in the club house. It was Schalk who told Gleason that something was wrong with the series as early as the first game.[7]

Writing just after the scandal broke, Hugh Fullerton said that after Game Two, Ray Schalk,

> the greatest and gamest little catcher in the business, fighting with every ounce of nerve in his body and desperate over defeat, informed Manager Gleason in detail as to what had happened. He told Gleason that repeatedly, in the opening game of the series, Cicotte had pitched straight balls with "nothing on them" when he had signaled for shiners or curves. He said

that in the decisive inning of the second game—the fourth—
Williams had "crossed him" four times, pitching straight balls
when he ordered curves.

"How many times has he crossed you this season?" Gleason
demanded.

"Not once during the year."

Schalk, that evening, in our rooms, told several of us that
things looked bad. He told us about what he had told Gleason.
He had already accused two ball players of crooked work to
their faces, and yet refused to charge them publicly with trying
to lose the series.[8]

Fullerton did more than inform baseball's highest authority, before
or right after Game One, as noted earlier. He wrote about his suspicions as strongly as he could, during and right after the Series. His
newspaper's fear of libel prevented him from naming the players he
suspected.[9]

At the Milwaukee trial, Fullerton said that the only player he spoke
to about the fix rumors was Eddie Cicotte, the morning before Game
Two. Apparently thinking Cicotte had lost the Series opener legitimately,
Fullerton asked Eddie to help him "dig up the rumors." In his 1935
recollection, he spoke to Cicotte before Game One.

To write about the fix after the Series was not an easy choice for
Fullerton. "I feared that my branding of the games as fixed might have
wrecked a life friendship with Charles Comiskey." Fullerton sought out
Commy and found him a broken and bitter man. "Keep after them,
Hughie, they were crooked. Some day you and I will prove it." In his
1935 memoir, Fullerton seems to suggest that he checked with Comiskey
around the time that his first article appeared (October 10), but it may
not have been until about three weeks later.

When Fullerton's post-Series syndicated articles appeared, revealing his discoveries about the fix, the fixers, and the money, they were
widely read, and promptly and largely dismissed as "improbable muckraking."[10]

Fullerton's editorial crusade was all uphill, because there was a
strongly and widely held belief that baseball was just too hard to fix.
Historian Charles Alexander cites several "experts" who espoused this
view, including nineteenth-century star Montgomery Ward. But Fullerton insisted that all it took was "honest players not squealing on their

corrupt teammates." He had no difficulty believing in the possibility, because he knew it had happened.

OCTOBER 1919

Fullerton's campaign started with hints in his column following Game Four, a 2–0 Cicotte loss. Cicotte had pitched a terrific game but made a wild fielding throw and botched a cut-off attempt to open the doors for the Reds. Convinced that Cicotte let up in Game One, Fullerton was skeptical that the pitcher's errors in Game Four were accidental. Then, after the Series ended, Fullerton wrote,

> There is more ugly talk and more suspicion among the fans than there has ever been in any World Series. The rumors of crookedness, of fixed games and plots, are thick. It is not necessary to dignify them by telling what they are, but the sad part is that such suspicion of baseball is so widespread.
> . . . The only reason I dignify such stories by mentioning them is to show how generally suspicion has been cast upon the sport by the actions of the magnates in the last two years.

Fullerton is referring here to the failure of club owners to curb the influence of gambling.

What happened during the Series made Fullerton's case harder to make. The gamblers did not deliver the promised payoffs. Some cash was delivered, but it was a fraction of what was promised. Somewhere between the end of Game One and the start of Game Six, the White Sox realized that they were being had and decided to strike back by winning the Series and claiming the bigger prize money. Down four games to one, they took Game Six, 5–4, with Gandil knocking in the winning run. Then they took Game Seven, behind Cicotte's pitching and Jackson's hitting, 4–1. But Game Eight slipped away early—it was Lefty Williams's third loss—as the Reds pounded out sixteen hits in a 10–5 rout.

"One gambler told writer Hugh Fullerton before the [eighth] game, 'All the betting's on Cincinnati. It's going to be the biggest first inning you ever saw.'"[11] Fullerton added this right-on prediction after the Series: "There will be a lot of inside stuff that is never printed." And he called on the club owners to call off the World Series, to make 1919 the last—because he felt the game was now in the control of gamblers.

Ban Johnson's recollection, years later, was that Fullerton's initial article about the Series being crooked "woke up the National Commission. A copy of the story was sent to Comiskey and we awaited his report. None came. Comiskey never replied." Johnson added this, about Fullerton's sources:

> It appeared that Fullerton, traveling between Chicago and Cincinnati during the series, had overheard conversations between one Billy Maharg, an auto salesman, Bill Burns, an old White Sox player, and others. Fullerton, it developed, had heard remarks made by Burns to Mayor John Galvin of Cincinnati about the games being thrown and he had written his story around that.[12]

(Bill Burns testified at the 1921 trial that he had spoken with the mayor of Cincinnati in the smoking compartment of the train he took back from Chicago after Game Five.)

Perhaps the most startling thing Fullerton wrote in his post-Series wrap-up on October 10 was that seven White Sox players would not be returning to play in 1920. He gave no names and did not say why they would be gone. Testifying in the 1924 trial in which Joe Jackson sued the White Sox for breach of contract and back pay, Fullerton was asked about those statements and what was behind them. He replied, "I wasn't convinced of it, no . . . I considered it good enough to shoot at, yes . . . good enough to make a good story for the newspapers. . . . I was convinced that they [the seven players] would not be there, guilty or not—the talk was so strong that they would be out."

According to Harold Seymour, "In fact, Fullerton revealed much later that when he predicted immediately after the Series that seven Chicago players would not be back on the team in 1920, he had really been quoting Comiskey" (*Baseball: The Golden Age*). Of course Comiskey had the players' names; he had their World Series checks withheld.

It wasn't that much later. Right after the scandal broke, Fullerton wrote in his syndicated column that his source for "seven will not return" was the owner of the White Sox. "My authority was Charles A. Comiskey, who then believed that his team had been corrupted." After the final game of the Series,

> Comiskey, in his bitterness, said: "There are seven who will never play on this team again." I did not want to quote him, but, believing him, I printed this prediction. Later Comiskey and I discussed the matter and he said he had been unable to get legal proof, but was still trying.[13]

Fullerton seemed disheartened when Comiskey offered his $10,000 reward after the Series, because Comiskey also called for a return to the seven-game format and a new system for selling tickets. Why did this disappoint Fullerton? Because calling for these reforms was a sign that "in spite of the harm done the game by the world's series, the owners intend to continue that event and ignore the scandals." Fullerton could not see how the owners could "ignore the talk that was rife during the recent series."[14]

And yet at this point, Fullerton himself seems to have joined in the cover-up. He wrote that most fans thought "something was wrong" in the series, but his own opinion was that "this talk is gambler conversation and the loser's alibi." Fullerton recalled being told by someone before the series started that "there was something doing" but Fullerton "scoffed and told him it was impossible." Fullerton and Mathewson scrutinized the games "closer than I ever have watched ball games before." After the fifth game, they compared notes. "Matty remarked to me, 'Have you seen anything wrong?' 'No, I haven't seen a crooked move or an unusual play in the series,' I said. 'Neither have I,' said Matty, 'and I don't believe any ball player is a good enough actor to get away with it and not betray himself.'"[15]

This version of things, appearing in his syndicated column on October 21, is quite different from every other account that Fullerton wrote, which suggests that it may have been written at the direction of an editor or heavily edited after he wrote it. Fullerton also told the story of his being informed that Game Eight would feature "the biggest first inning that ever happened in a world's series"—but Fullerton added that he hunted up his source after the game and "he denied knowing anything—he had just been talking. That is the way these rumors start. No one can ever run them down or get any proof." It is almost as if Fullerton wrote this column with a gun to his head.

ASSASSINATION ATTEMPT?

Writing in *Liberty* magazine in 1927, Fullerton said, "I was assailed from all directions and an attempt was made to assassinate me. This only strengthened my conviction that the series was crooked."

"The chief attacks came from publications connected with organized baseball. I was informed that I would be driven out of the game."[16]

The gambling syndicates may indeed have considered knocking Fullerton off, as his was the loudest whistle-blowing. Here is a detailed account, from an article Fullerton wrote:

The attempt to shoot me was made under the viaduct of the Illinois Central at Fifty-third Street in Chicago. My wife and I were to start for New York early the following morning. [That places the event as most likely in November 1919.] I went downtown to bid some friends good-by, and was followed by a man whose face I knew. A new subway was being built under the tracks and I started under it, then remembered an errand and went back to a drug store. Returning through the dimly lighted subway I was accosted by a man who demanded to know if I was Fullerton. "No, Crane," I exclaimed, using the first name I could think of, and brushed past. As I stepped into the light another voice cried: "That's the ——" and two shots were fired. I started to run, fell, and the men fled. I got up unhurt and fled in the other direction, into a garage. Fearing I would be held as a witness and our trip East spoiled, I made no complaint, not even telling the family until we left the city. But I was satisfied that, if the crooks thought it important enough to get me out of the way, there must be much truth in the charges against the players.

Fullerton had first left Chicago at 7:00 a.m. the day after the Series ended, the day his first "exposé" appeared, for a two-week vacation in Frankfort, Michigan. When he returned, he did not meet with Comiskey for another week or so; then they met for several hours over lunch at a restaurant across from the ballpark. Fullerton agreed to investigate and report back to Comiskey. After a few more weeks he moved to New York.

Fullerton continued to write the syndicated column that had carried his account of the Series. Several times each week, all through October, November, and December of 1919, "On the Screen of Sport" appeared in newspapers such as the *Atlanta Constitution*. He referred a number of times to the World Series just concluded, and he called for reforms. On November 6, he reported that after the Series, a number of newspaper owners and editors, disgusted with the "continual scandal and persistent refusal of the magnates to reform," came to the conclusion in informal discussion "that they would not permit their papers to be used to advertise and boost the baseball business until the owners decided to clean up."

Baseball's players and owners were hurting the game, and that was hurting the newspapers—so the pressmen agreed to cut down the space given to baseball, and only print the bare details of the games unless the whitewashing stopped and the clean-up started. Fullerton wrote that this pressure from the press had worked once before, in Chicago.[17] But there is no evidence that this plan went anywhere in 1920—not with Babe Ruth's homers exciting fans.

In that same column of November 6, Fullerton noted that "a lot of the players who participated in the series have not yet received their checks. . . . Oddly enough, they do not seem to care much. . . . Queer, isn't it?" Several players *had* contacted the team and the American League office about those missing checks, but Fullerton was trying to fan anything that looked like a flame that might spark an investigation.

When the National Commission met that fall and discussed changing the rules for the shine ball, spit ball, and other trick pitches, Fullerton compared the commissioners to Nero fiddling while Rome was burning. "There are reforms needed in baseball that may save the game and I fancy we can struggle along with a bit of paraffin on the ball or a rough spot on the curve until those things are settled." Fullerton called for "the expulsion from the game of every player connected in any way with gamblers or gambling . . . the immediate and searching investigation of the world's series scandal . . . and the barring from all connections with the game of every gambler."[18]

DECEMBER 1919

Fullerton had written on October 10 that seven White Sox players would not be back the next spring. He was confident that Comiskey would do something. Ray Schalk made a similar statement to a Chicago reporter, but when he was contacted by *The Sporting News* and asked to be more specific, he refused to comment. "Now what does Ray Schalk know?" *The Sporting News* asked.

The *New York Times* also followed up on Schalk's leak:

> "It was all wrong to say that I said that seven members of the White Sox would be missing when the 1920 season started. It is not true that I said such a thing. If I had made that charge I would willingly come out and give the names."
>
> Schalk is a player whose word is respected, and those who know him at all scoff at the charge that he involved seven members of the Sox in the scandal rumors.[19]

Of course, Schalk *had* named seven of his teammates in the December 13 issue of *Collyer's Eye*. Himself pronounced "clean" by the *Eye*, Schalk had been nevertheless caught up in the rumors. To Oscar

Reichow of *The Sporting News*, Schalk said that he presumed that it was because he was the only White Sox player wintering in Chicago that he was pressured to answer reporters' questions. "If I were elsewhere, I probably would never have been mentioned in any way."[20] Schalk denied being Fullerton's source and insisted that the charges that he "fathered the idea" were all wrong. He also denied fighting with any of the Sox pitchers during or after the Series.

Life went on, but the Big Fix refused to be swept neatly under the carpet. The *Chicago Herald and Examiner* had printed what turned out to be Fullerton's parting shots from that city on October 10 but did not follow up. Nelson Algren: "[Fullerton's] own paper, roaring daily . . . about corruption in public life, fled like a hare when confronted by the need for simple honesty."[21] But they were not alone. The press had no interest in damaging baseball's image. Besides, like stock market reports and the comics, boxscores sold papers.

Fullerton apparently had made his decision to move to New York before the 1919 Series. One of the top sportswriters in the country, he probably could have landed a job anywhere. But his move had nothing to do with the assassination attempt in Chicago and probably had nothing to do with the fixed World Series.

Once settled into his new job at the *New York Evening World*, Fullerton was discouraged and disillusioned by the failure of baseball to respond to the fix rumors. He felt like he wanted to quit writing baseball. He went to the managing editor, John H. Tennant, saying, "I'm sick and tired of writing about a game that has gone crooked. That Series was fixed." Tennant then directed him to write a special series on it. Fullerton said that a Mr. Daly of the *Morning World* also instructed him to investigate, as the paper had a report from St. Louis about gamblers influencing the Series. Tennant reportedly said, "It's hot, but this story has to be told." Even toned down and with names removed, the story was a blockbuster. So Fullerton's courageous series broke not in Chicago, but in New York. And Fullerton never really did stop writing about baseball.[22]

MONDAY, DECEMBER 15

Fullerton's byline appeared with the article, "Is Big League Baseball Being Run for Gamblers, With Players in the Deal?" on December 15, 1919. The World Series was only two months down in history. The two leagues had met and adjourned and had not dealt with the issue of gambling and the fix rumors at all; to Fullerton, their silence was inexcusable.

Fullerton wrote not so much about the fixed Series, as about the fact that so many people in so many different cities were talking about the apparent success of gamblers in fixing the Series—and baseball officialdom was not doing much about it. He was clearly bothered that baseball's reputation as a clean sport had been sullied more than ever before. And it pained him.

As forcefully as he could, he called on baseball to settle things. If the fix was in, the guilty needed to be punished. If they were found innocent, wonderful—baseball's reputation would be restored. He put baseball on trial. He focused on the American League, which, "smirched with scandal, held [their annual fall] meeting, wrangled, fought and blackguarded each other, and separated without an effort to clear the good name of the sport." He was dismayed that the American League had closed its eyes and ears, hoping the whole thing would just go away.

Some of the owners wanted, like Fullerton, a full investigation. And "some are for keeping silent and 'allowing it to blow over.' The time has come for straight talk. How can club owners expect writers, editors and fans to have any faith in them or their game if they make no effort to clean up the scandal?" He then fired these strong words at a specific target: "If one-quarter of the charges that Ruppert, Comiskey, Frazee and Huston made against President Ban Johnson of the American League are true, Johnson should be driven forever out of baseball. If they are not true, the men making the charges should be driven out." Fullerton was allied with Comiskey, an enemy of Ban Johnson. This contingent of dissatisfied American League owners would unite a year later with the National League owners to remove Ban Johnson from power and replace the three-man National Commission with a commissioner.

Fullerton seemed to be as upset about Cincinnati manager Pat Moran's charges that certain persons tried to get his players drunk before the first Series game, as he was about the gamblers' nasty business. And he took Moran to task for keeping *that* quiet, because it meant the crime went unpunished.

Fullerton saw the charges against the seven White Sox players as "more directly injurious" to baseball than those against the owners. Why? "The public has for years had little faith and much disgust in the officials and club owners." Accusations of cheating leveled against players were not new, either. What had Fullerton so incensed was that "never before have players been so freely charged." And that the crime was going unpunished.

Fullerton was not grandstanding. He was a reluctant crusader.

I have steadfastly refused to believe this [the conspiracy to fix the Series] possible. Some of the men whose names are used are my friends and men I would trust anywhere, yet the story is told quite openly, with so much circumstantial evidence and with so many names, places and dates, that one is bewildered.

Later, in his detailed account in the *Atlanta Constitution,* Fullerton would recall, "It was my misfortune to be compelled to reveal the truth concerning the play of the series. . . . The way of cleaning the sport seems to have been to banish reporters who dared to write the truth."[23]

Fullerton considered Comiskey an honest man, but he was sure that Commy knew the whole story, "knows perhaps more than anyone else." He applauded Comiskey's offer of a $10,000 reward and his hiring detectives. Just as he fought against the belief that baseball *could* be rigged, then that the Series *was* rigged, so Fullerton seemed to cling to the hope that Comiskey would act by banning the guilty players. He pointed to the feud raging in the American League as the only thing that had prevented Comiskey from investigating all charges.

Then Fullerton explained why he seemed to be the only writer out on this particular limb. "For nearly two years I have been working to discover some evidence of what has been going on." He was not referring here to the 1919 Series, but to the gambling rumors that had been plaguing the game. (Earlier, he had referred to activities Hal Chase had engaged in when with the Reds and which his manager Christy Mathewson would not tolerate.) A Boston gambler had told him that the syndicates "had men" on every team. Fullerton scoffed, but sure enough, some of the players named wound up in trouble. In July 1919, a Chicago gambler took Fullerton aside and questioned him seriously about the honesty of baseball. "I told him it was straight." He knew the gambler was also a fan, and his suspicions were aroused.

Hugh Fullerton had also had suspicions about several World Series before 1919. Writing for the *Chicago Times* on October 16, 1912, right after Boston won a series from New York, Fullerton wrote: "There is a bitter taste remaining in the greatest series of games ever played, for today Boston boycotted its ball club and the rumor that the series was fixed and all prearranged ran through the town. Half the people believed it." Perhaps for Fullerton, October 1919 was just the last straw.

Finally, Fullerton gave his eyewitness report on the gambling scene he observed on the eve of the 1919 Series. He was told as soon as he arrived in Cincinnati that the first two games were a sure bet. Yet the heavy betting was not convincing—Fullerton knew gamblers "considered themselves wise" but were also "the biggest suckers in the world" when they heard tasty rumors.[24] Nevertheless, Fullerton went to Mathewson with what he had heard, and Matty ridiculed the rumors. But they were both so suspicious by now that they sat together and took notes of every play in the Series that seemed like it *might* be crooked. They found seven.

His last exhibit for this trial on paper was this:

> Twenty minutes before the final game in Chicago started, I was taken aside by a gambler, who told me to plunge. I was mad by that time, and demanded that he come through with some proof or shut his mouth, that he was a crook and accusing others. He laughed and remarked:
>
> "You ought to have cleaned up on it—tipping one team and playing the other."
>
> I was mad all the way through, but wanted to learn something, so I asked:
>
> "What do you know about to-day?"
>
> "It'll be the biggest first inning you ever saw," he said.
>
> These things, and worse, are printed in the Western cities. The club owners know all about them.

And he had this concluding line: "The baseball authorities must go to the bottom of the entire matter of gambling."

TUESDAY, DECEMBER 16

The *New York Evening World* followed up the next day with an article, "Col. Huston of Yankees Favors Gambling Crusade." The part owner of the New York American League team, Tillinghast L'Hommedieu Huston, was in sympathy with the *New York Evening World* stand regarding gambling in baseball. He declared that "no stone should be left unturned to rid the game of evil" and noted that the Yankees spent "large sums of money" annually to keep down betting at the Polo Grounds.

This article had no byline; it referred to Fullerton's article of the day before, repeating some of his charges. Huston also added that the gambling rumors were nothing new. He and Col. Ruppert employed detectives and private investigators to "smash any public betting that may show its head at the Polo Grounds."

WEDNESDAY, DECEMBER 17

"Scandal of World's Series in Baseball Will Not Down; Here Is a Way to Settle It." Fullerton's Monday article has acquired the label "blockbuster" over the years, but it was his Wednesday article that perhaps deserves that adjective even more. In it, Fullerton gave baseball a plan for uncovering the conspiracy that he was certain had ruined the Series.[25]

Fullerton began by stating that after two months of work by his detectives, Comiskey had been "unable to find evidence of dishonesty" among the White Sox in the recent World Series. He had had detectives at work "since the night of the second game of the series in Cincinnati when one of the best-known gamblers in the country [Mont Tennes] went to him and told him the stories that were being circulated through the underworld of sport."

Comiskey and Gleason had both worked hard but had been unable to prove or disprove anything. This was not good enough for Fullerton. He demanded a verdict: guilty or not guilty. "Mr. Comiskey, unaided, probably cannot discover the truth. It is not the seven players who are indicted by common gossip that are on trial. It is the good name of baseball and the honesty of hundreds of players who are not mentioned."

Fullerton felt that the recent meetings of owners had started "a concerted movement . . . to put the silencer on the story of the series. To drop the matter and follow the policy of 'allowing the public to forget' is probably the worst possible thing that could happen to the sport in the United States."

He then suggested that Judge Landis—who would not become commissioner for another year—be asked to get involved. Fullerton praised Landis for saving "the organized part" of baseball by not ruling on the Federal League case until the owners came to their senses and settled out of court. Landis loved baseball. "I happen to know that Judge Landis has been keenly interested in the current stories of the World's Series. He has heard the entire story and was shocked and grieved."

Landis, Fullerton believed, could hear testimony from the players and the gamblers. "In fact, I think the gamblers concerned will tell him more in confidence than could be drawn from them on the stand under oath. They trust him. He need not mention the source of his information without their consent."

Who should Landis interrogate? Gamblers named "Karl Zork, Ben and Lou Levi of Des Moines, Eddie of Boston, Tim of Des Moines, Abe Attell, Bill Burns, Joe Pesch, and Redmond" [Harry Redmon]. Then, question Mont Tennes, "chief of the gambling fraternity of Chicago," and Arnold Rothstein. Then, Comiskey's detectives, manager Kid Gleason, writers James Crusinberry (of Chicago) and Ed Wray (of St. Louis), as well as Fullerton himself ("I will volunteer to appear and tell all the facts I know"), and finally, ballplayers Ray Schalk and Eddie Collins. (Years later, Fullerton said that even if Landis had met just with Bill Burns, "all of the facts" would have come out, months before the 1920 season started instead of in its final days.)

THURSDAY, DECEMBER 18

"Comiskey Has Been on Point of Dropping Several Men." Fullerton thought the fans were aroused, and "demands for an entire cleaning up of baseball and a thorough investigation of the scandalous charges made in connection with the recent World Series are pouring in."

Fullerton was having two big laughs: first, from the perception that he was making charges of "crookedness." "I never said or insinuated that the seven ball players accused by common report are guilty" (although saying that they probably would not be back for Opening Day was close). Again, baseball "MUST investigate and either throw out the men or exonerate them completely." What nagged at Fullerton was silence, "whitewashing."

The other laugh Fullerton had was from the accusation that he was an enemy of Comiskey and an ally of Ban Johnson. "That will get a laugh even from Johnson. Comiskey broke me into baseball. He was my first friend in the game. We have stuck together in everything—and always will."

Fullerton went on to list what Comiskey had done so far. He had offered a reward "for proof of crooked work." He had been at the point of dropping "a number of players—not because he found them guilty, but because of the talk about them." But he had held off, waiting for positive evidence. "He is going to secure it. The row over the Carl Mays case has delayed his operations." (Boston Red Sox pitcher Mays had quit his club, and the New York Yankees had signed him, but Ban Johnson protested the deal; eventually the case went to court.)

Comiskey, according to Fullerton, "is badly broken in health and growing old." The trip around the world had almost ruined his health, and now the Mays case and his feud with Johnson were impairing it further.

Fullerton devoted the rest of the article to the Mays case and the jockeying among owners in the American League. Some owners were trying to sell their teams "on a rising market," but Comiskey would not sell; his team and ballpark were his monument.

The same day, the *New York Evening World* ran another article under this banner: "Frazee and Grant, Hub Club Owners, Favor Any Reform to Curb Gambling." The owners of the Red Sox and Nationals believed that baseball was honest, but that there should be no limit to any action to keep it clean. Frazee was responding directly to Fullerton's charges.

The national commissioners were polled for their views. Heydler (of the National League) was not ready to comment and "intends to be out of town on a holiday vacation" the rest of the month. Garry Herrmann was expected to quit his post "within a few days." Ban Johnson "is so engrossed with affairs of his own organization" that he had no time for National Commission business, "no matter how pressing it may be."

Immediately following the above article was one titled "American League Has Not Begun an Investigation of Reported Gambling"—at least that's what league secretary Will Harridge reported. The issue "probably would be taken up" at the next meeting. "Disclosures made by Hugh Fullerton have evidently caused every one to draw into their shells." Comiskey repeated that his investigation "had proved the reports to be groundless." The rumor that Ban Johnson had started an investigation right after the Series "was denied at his office."

FRIDAY, DECEMBER 19

"National Commission Chairman to Stamp Out Baseball Gambling." Garry Herrmann—"if I remain at the head of the National Commission"—pledged to "wage a hot fight against betting in ball parks." He could not believe that his Reds had not won the last Series fairly. Pat Moran had wired Herrmann denying that gamblers had gotten two Reds pitchers drunk.

SATURDAY, DECEMBER 20

"Judge Landis Asked to Take Charge of Investigation." In the *New York Evening World,* Fullerton called on Landis and Comiskey to take action. He was encouraged that "practically every owner and manager" was eager to clean up baseball. "Some object to any further exposé of the recent world's series and the attendant scandal which has become an annual part of the show."

Fullerton said that the most direct charge was not connected with the Series. It was the claim made the previous July by a professional gambler to another that he had three of the Chicago White Sox on his payroll and that they would, for a consideration of $200 a week each, throw one game a week as selected by him.

But Fullerton hastened to add, "This may not have been true." The gambler who had heard it did not believe it and "refused to enter into it." Fullerton's digging had suggested that this story was "the starting point from which all the scandalous stories have spread."

Again he declared that "a complete investigation" was necessary and nothing less would suffice. Fullerton asked Judge Landis if he would accept "the responsibility of conducting an investigation if the powers of baseball are willing to submit the entire matter to him and assist him in bringing witnesses before him."[26]

Fullerton asked Comiskey "to use all his influence" to bring the investigation about. "There is small use to ask Ban Johnson" because Johnson felt anything that he did

> would instantly be construed as an attack by him on Comiskey. Johnson has been the strongest opponent of gambling ever since he has been in office. One of the big things in which I have always stood by him has been his fight against the gamblers, and some of Johnson's troubles with club owners have grown out of his activity.

Fullerton had been assured that Johnson "would have taken steps in this scandal immediately after the series" but for his troubles with three club owners, "which would have resulted in a misunderstanding of his motives."

Letters had been pouring in for Fullerton, most "scoring" him and a few offering evidence, which he was trying to investigate. Much was hearsay. One mentioned the name of a player new to the scandal.

Fullerton had no proof, "but one thing is certain: Gamblers stated that they had 'put over' the thing and they solicited capital from others on the ground that they could control the players." This "solicitation" was not just before and during the Series, but during the season as well, and "the Chicago White Sox were not the only team mentioned."

Two days before, Fullerton had thought the owners and managers were behind him. Now he wrote, "The powers of baseball appear to have overlooked the peril."

Fullerton then reviewed rumors of fixes in previous World Series. After the 1910 Series (Cubs–Athletics), Fullerton "investigated the thing for a week." He found that the rumors were started by men "who were betting the other way." In 1912 (Red Sox–Giants) rumors had Tammany politicians fixing things; again, an investigation showed the rumors were started by men "backing Boston heavier than ever."

When Fullerton heard the rumors before the 1919 Series, he thought gamblers were "working the old gag." But this time, the money was being wagered in the direction that the rumors ran. In fact the first really suspicious thing that became public was that a gambler went to a club owner and told him the men who were betting the big money were crooked and advised him to take a look around. He was suspicious, not of the players, but of the men who were gambling, and he stated frankly that anything they bet on heavily was crooked or they believed it to be so.

Fullerton ended with a kind of peace offering. He was encouraged that the owners were changing their attitudes. "If they can drive out the gamblers there is no further danger of attempts to tamper with the players."

HAPPY NEW YEAR

In the January 2 *World*, Fullerton "Wishes Magnates a Scandalless New Year." Ironically, in September 1920, the greatest scandal in baseball history would make headlines. But in January, Hugh Fullerton could sit back and write "An Interesting Open Letter to the Club Owners," as the subheadline put it. He also addressed it to the national commissioners.

Fullerton stated his belief that Charles Comiskey "is taking serious and honest steps toward cleaning up all the scandal concerned with the World's Series." Meanwhile, the warring factions in the American League seemed to be moving toward a peace settlement. Urging the owners to follow through on their pledges to clean up baseball, Fullerton characterized 1919 as a year "of financial prosperity and prostitution of the sport to finance." He repeated some of the main points that he made in the series of articles that appeared in December. "Whether any player or team has acted dishonestly it is not for me to say. If I had proof of any crooked dealing I would shout it."

Fullerton responded to those who were blaming him and other writers for starting the stories about the fixed Series. "These stories were not started, nor were they circulated, by baseball writers. They started before the series was played, were circulated during the series, and were so widespread in the West that detectives were employed to watch players." Fullerton argued that it was Comiskey's offer of a reward for evidence of a fix that had "placed the scandal before the public. Up to that time I never had mentioned it." (Apparently his October 10 article stating that seven White Sox players would not be back next season did not count.)

The National Commission had done nothing, and its credibility was gone; if it pronounced all players innocent, no one would believe it anyway. "Comiskey is conducting a deep investigation. One thing the fans may rely on is that Comiskey will go as far as he can to dig up the truth." And that was true; but Fullerton thought that Comiskey would then reveal that truth, instead of burying it even deeper.

Perhaps aiming at Ban Johnson, Fullerton wrote, "One member of the commission at least knew about the stories that were going around the morning of the second game of the series." (Later, Fullerton would write that he confronted Ban Johnson before Game One, after talking with Comiskey, and both had already heard the stories. Neither acted. Not with a record take on deck—each game would bring in well over $100,000 in ticket sales and concessions.) "Had he done his duty he would have started the investigation then and there. He did not." Fullerton saw the policy of silence "for the good of the game" at the bottom of it all.

Fullerton recalled taking a two-week vacation after the Series to go hunting and fishing, then returning to a Chicago where everyone knew the stories of the fix. He was "questioned by some one every few feet on the streets. When I protested ignorance they smiled. Twice I was accused of 'being in on it.'"

Responding to a club owner who had demanded that he prove his charges, Fullerton wrote that he had never made any. He was upset that this owner wanted things "kept quiet for the good of the game."

It would not hurt baseball even if the men accused should be found guilty. If they were kicked out the fans would believe the owners honest in their efforts to keep the sport clean. Remember that only seven out of more than 200 are even accused by gossip. Are not the others entitled to protection?

Fullerton insisted that his motive was not to hurt baseball. Nor was he reacting with animus because his dope for the Series went wrong. No, he wanted to prevent the Reds from being robbed of the honors they had won. For twenty-seven years, Fullerton had argued that "it is impossible to make baseball crooked." Players may lose games on purpose, but they cannot get away with it for any length of time. He even had argued this during the recent World Series. "How can a writer who wants to be fair and honest continue writing baseball unless it is proved to be fair and on the level?"

Finally, Fullerton took this parting shot at the magnates: "You have made a good start to the new year. Keep it up. The one big thing to do is to make the sport the thing. So long as the gate receipts are more important than winning games there can be no real reform."

Ironically, the same day that Fullerton's bombshell was exploding in New York, December 15, the *Chicago Tribune* ran the headline "Comiskey Refutes Series Charges Against White Sox." Possibly given a courtesy tip by Fullerton, Comiskey announced that his investigation, begun right after the Series, showed that the rumors of a fix were entirely unfounded. "I am now very happy to state that we have discovered nothing to indicate any member of my team double crossed me or the public last fall."

Chicago Tribune writer I. E. Sanborn noted that the investigation was continuing and Commy's $10,000 reward for evidence was still good. Sanborn added:

> Although the details of the "scandal" are probably known to every one who speaks baseball, it may be necessary to inform a few. In brief, it was to the effect that six, seven or eight White Sox [the number varied according to the source of the rumor] met in a hotel room . . . and split anywhere from $20,000 to $100,000—depending on the narrator—of a gambling clique's bankroll under an agreement to let Cincinnati win the world's pennant.

Sanborn also gave a colorful description of how frustrating it must have been for those "running down" the rumors.

> Every "lead" that promised anything at all was chased to a finish and always ended in a circle—Jones heard it from Smith, who got the indisputable facts from Brown, who was told it was absolutely true by Levitsky, who knew the parties who framed and pulled off the deal, and when Levitsky was rounded up he invariably got his information from either Jones or Smith. That has been the net result of the investigation.

Sanborn, like Fullerton, had warned his readers "not to wager better than even money on the White Sox" before the Series. But he was quick to explain that was based on his belief that the Sox were "overconfident and not in good physical condition for a hard fight," having clinched their pennant too recently. Sanborn's views were typical and unwittingly contributed to the cover-up. Fullerton's nagging pleas, pointing to precisely the right people to interrogate, were almost unique.

JANUARY 1920

In 1924, Fullerton gave Comiskey credit for keeping him active in pursuit of hard evidence. They corresponded in January 1920, when Fullerton had become discouraged; Comiskey motivated him to keep at it for six or seven more months. Comiskey testified that Fullerton had told him that he was "detailed by the *New York World* to go out and run down the rumors of crookedness." Comiskey said that he told Fullerton, "I have nothing substantial." When Fullerton was disheartened, Comiskey said, he told Hugh to "keep on it." The scandal bothered Fullerton, but baseball continued to appear in his columns in the summer of 1920.

THE RESPONSE TO FULLERTON'S CHARGES

If a reporter today wrote a similar story, charging, for example, that a superstar and six or seven of his teammates on a pennant-winning team received money from gamblers for giving the World Series to their opponents, and it ran in *Sports Illustrated*, he and the magazine would be instantly in the glare of the media. The reporter would be forced to produce evidence, and if he had it, he would be famous.

Hugh Fullerton, unfortunately, had only, as Fred Lieb later observed, the word of "gamblers, politicians and players." And he had a scorebook marked with seven suspicious plays—which, *Baseball Magazine* noted, using Fullerton's own words, "might equally have been caused by the accidents of the game." He did not have the power to bring the truth to light; all he could do was rail against the American League owners and Ban Johnson, who *did* have the power, for failing to do more.

Fullerton was crushed for his attack on baseball. The establishment assailed him and his reputation was ruined. *Baseball Magazine* called him an "erratic writer" who knew so little about baseball that he thought games could be fixed! As late as August 1920—right before the fix was brought to light—*Baseball Magazine* editorialized about the "malignant ingenuity" of Fullerton, "for whose action there was not the slightest excuse."[27] *The Sporting News* also defended baseball's integrity against the charges Fullerton had made. Fullerton's career seemed headed for a gloomy finish.

ABANDONED BY MATHEWSON

Christy Mathewson, who had sat beside Fullerton and charted the suspicious plays, took off in the opposite direction, blaming the White Sox loss on overconfidence and arguing that the Reds' superior pitching had turned the tide. The closest Matty came to hinting at a fix was in his *New York Times* column after Game One: "No team to my knowledge was ever defeated by so large a score in an opening game of the world series when each contender was trying his best."

Mathewson expert Eddie Frierson believes Matty took his diagrams of suspicious plays to the National Commission and asked that he not be associated with them or be called to testify, should it come to that. Frieson's guess is that the diagrams were destroyed. He thinks Mathewson just did not want to be involved or be a part in any official way of "bringing down the game" he loved.[28]

Writing in his *New York Times* column a few weeks after Fullerton's bombshell, Mathewson credited Comiskey for not ignoring the rumors of a fix, applauding his posting of a reward for evidence.

> Many professional detectives have been working on the case and many amateurs have presented themselves with hearsay evidence, but as no real facts have been brought to light it is only fair to conclude after this length of time that the rumors were false. My personal opinion, as an eye witness, is that every game of the series was decided on the merits of the two teams.[29]

It is interesting to compare Fullerton's crusade with the writings of the man who sat beside him in the Series looking for those questionable plays. Christy Mathewson believed, like many others, that baseball games were very *hard* to fix, and to fix a nine-game Series was impossible—too many players would need to be involved, and there would surely be leaks. Mathewson once wrote five arguments demonstrating how ridiculous he thought it was to question the honesty of the Series.[30] "It's just unthinkable." When the post-Series rumors of fixed games were still swirling, *Baseball Magazine*'s F. C. Lane expressed the view of many when he wrote that the idea of a player who would toss a game for a few thousand dollars, at the risk of his career, made no sense.

Matty also had predicted—against the early odds—that the Reds, the team he had managed in 1916–18, would win the Series. Here is what he wrote in the *New York Times* on September 28, 1919, just before the Series: "There is no question that Cicotte will be a powerful figure in the series." The headline on the day of Game One: "Pitchers Are the Important Factors," and the subheading: "Cicotte May Not Be Fit." Eddie's ailment was the cover story for those odds sinking so quickly as Game One drew close.

Of course, the fix *was* in—everybody would find this out the following September. But as Hugh Fullerton wrote mightily about the suspicious play by the Sox in the Series just ended, Matty took off in the opposite direction. "Baseball Not Crooked in Spite of Big Bets on Games, Declares Christy Mathewson" was the headline of his October 16 *Times* column. "I honestly think that if ball players on a world series team found their fellows trying to toss one off, they would kill the guilty ones. . . . Assuming some ball players could be fixed, not enough could be reached."

He wrote what everyone wanted to hear, to believe. His October 19 column defended the Reds' "riding" of White Sox players. The bench jockeys had been especially harsh on Collins and Jackson. Matty said it was all part of the game.

On October 23, Matty gave another reason why the Sox lost: "Overconfidence is the bane of champions." And he gave all kinds of examples from history. The Sox were just the latest one. Overconfidence "did in the Sox, and almost did in the Reds when they were up four games to one."

In December, Hugh Fullerton's strongest charges to date had appeared in the *New York World*. Matty responded: "Baseball Gambling Opposed by Matty" was the headline. But he did not get to gambling until deep into the article. Then he quoted the Reds' manager Pat Moran: "I was looking close, saw nothing." Matty called for a 60–40 split of proceeds between winning and losing teams, so the incentive to stretch the Series out longer (for more revenue) would be gone.

Because ghostwriting is always a possible factor in the columns that appear under the names of athletes, we should not be too quick to judge Christy Mathewson.

Other writers who probably knew of the fix, like Ring Lardner and Damon Runyon, left baseball writing and moved on, although there is good reason to believe that Lardner was more soured by the advent of the lively ball and the worship of home runs. Hugh Fullerton would return to sportswriting after the fix was uncovered, but he spent much of the rest of his life working for *Liberty* magazine and then in the movement to return the McGuffey textbooks to America's classrooms.

FULLERTON A DON QUIXOTE?

Was Fullerton a Don Quixote? He took a huge risk, and lost. He underestimated baseball's ability to keep the lid screwed tightly on the scandal. Fullerton had a blind spot when it came to the Sox's owner (in a 1923 letter he referred to Comiskey as "my dearest and perhaps oldest friend, who would protect me, even at his own expense, if he thought I needed it, and would never do anything to hurt me"), and this ultimately cost him. He imagined that the baseball owners and Ban Johnson had consciences to which he could appeal with passion and logic. He may have hoped that his voice would be joined by writers in every major city, and his articles would be the snowball that started an avalanche. But instead, by itself, his case had more like a snowball's chance in hell.

Did Fullerton accomplish anything? I think so. His singular attempt to clean up baseball, even though it failed, at least brought to national attention the very real problem of baseball being strangled by gambling. Fullerton had had enough; he just could not take it any more. But baseball's owners were not about to air their dirty linen (or sox, in this case), not if they did not have to, and no one was making them.[30]

DUELING INVESTIGATIONS

Because the story of how the cover-up of the fix of 1919 was uncovered is long and complicated, it is tempting to sum it up in a few words: Toward the end of the 1920 season, a grand jury was convened in Cook County, and after three White Sox players confessed, indictments and a trial followed. That hardly does justice to the "chain of events" or "chain reaction" that blew off the lid. (John Lardner (one of Ring's sons): it "went off in scattered pops, like a string of firecrackers" [see note 29].) In fact, there was no neat chain of events, all linked together and easy to trace. The unraveling of the fix happened more like a Rube Goldberg cartoon—a series of complicated contrivances, fascinating to watch, that produced a simple result.

From the day Comiskey was convinced that some of his players were lying down in the Series—and this was very early, because the first two games confirmed all the rumors he had heard—he seemed to be doing his best to simultaneously collect all the evidence he could and suppress that evidence. He knew at once that if the fix became public knowledge, he could lose the service of some of his most talented players. The White Sox team was a dynasty that drew well, and it was capable of bringing the World Series to Comiskey Park again.

Comiskey must have felt relieved when the Sox started playing to win in October 1919, and certainly the fix was easier to hide because the Sox did win three games. But it seems clear that Comiskey had enough evidence right after the Series to act. And he did: he withheld the series checks of the eight players whom he had heard—from gamblers and reporters, and probably Gleason and Schalk—were involved.

Ban Johnson was probably convinced early on, too. He started his investigating right after the Series. The previous October, the owners had rejected his request for funds for an investigation of a series fix. This time, he would not ask, he would just do it. And he did it walking a tightrope because the National Commission was falling apart, and if he stepped on too many toes, and blew a whistle on a fix that he could not prove, he would lose his chance to name the new czar. But if he could prove Comiskey's team was guilty of crooked play, a strong opponent would be sidelined in the struggle for power.

There were other investigations, too, but the two that mattered were Comiskey's and Johnson's. A race was on: if Commy and his men could reach potential witnesses first, they could pay them off and keep them silent. If Johnson could find them first, then he had more ammunition. For a 1929 memoir, Johnson told Irving Vaughan that his first move was to go to St. Louis after the Series "on a tip that a bookmaker named Carney [betting commissioner Thomas M. Kearney] could and would tell the story. From him I learned how Abe Attell had induced Western [Des Moines, Iowa, and St. Louis] gamblers to get in on the sure thing."[32]

So the 1920 season began—as if nothing happened. And it almost ended the same way. No one can say if Ban Johnson would have let it end peacefully; he might have, if it meant his being the czar or controlling the new power structure. As it turned out, he did not have to blow the whistle himself. Here is how the lid came off.

To recap, Hugh Fullerton and other reporters had known about the fix from the start of the Series. But their editors would not let them blow the whistle—name names, that is—because of a lack of hard evidence and a fear of libel suits. Fullerton pushed hardest and was rewarded with the scorn of the baseball establishment. Major League Baseball owners, by 1919, had a way of handling rumors of fixed games: they buried them as deeply as possible. Even when the evidence seemed to be unambiguous (the Hal Chase case) Major League Baseball preferred to close its eyes. And this worked. No need to alarm the paying fans. Players who were untrustworthy could be let go quietly. Yes, isn't that better than a public hanging?

Ed Bang, sports editor at the *Cleveland News*, covered the Series and was suspicious after the second game. He could not get his managing editor's permission to write the story of the fix. "Practically every sports writer in the press box had valid suspicions that there was something markedly wrong . . . but it was one of those things that was impossible to prove on the basis of performance."[33]

Bang called Cicotte and Lefty Williams to his office when the White Sox came to Cleveland in the 1920 season.

> "You know," said Bang, "this story's going to break any time. I happen to know you two fellows are going to be mentioned. Personally I don't think you had a thing to do with it. (The old oil, we always thought.) And now tell me what you know about it and I'll write a story that will be favorable to you and help clear your names."
>
> [Cicotte] laughed. "Hell, Ed, every place we go that story comes up. There wasn't anything wrong with the series, and if there was I'd tell you honestly."
>
> . . . Every place the Black Sox went that season, which was 1920, the sports writers tried to break the story. They knew definitely by now that the series was a fake. The gamblers had been double-crossed and they had started to talk—but not for publication.[34]

Abe Attell told Joe Williams in 1944,

> What I never could understand is why the blow off took as long coming as it did. People knew it in Peoria and knew it six weeks before the series. But I guess the answer is that baseball is such a great and decent game that they wouldn't believe their own ears and eyes.[35]

On July 17, 1920, a chance meeting took place in New York.

> According to Eliot Asinof in *Eight Men Out*, Ring [Lardner] and [reporter] Jimmy Crusinberry were talking in a New York hotel when [Sox manager] Kid Gleason called to tell them that Abe Attell, one of the fixers, was spilling the beans at Dinty Moore's restaurant and speakeasy. After they heard Attell out, Crusinberry filed a story that [*Tribune* sports editor] Harvey Woodruff declined to print for reasons of potential libel. But the scandal was bound to emerge in full....[36]

In *Hustler's Handbook*, Bill Veeck notes that Woodruff was a "confidant" of Ban Johnson. You can just see Kid Gleason *aching* for the press to blow the whistle. He had probably invested in a lot of whiskey to get Attell talking about it, and he summoned Lardner and Crusinberry —not Hugh Fullerton, who was a Comiskey loyalist.

In Crusinberry's account many years later, he recalled that he and Lardner "walked into the bar, stood close to Gleason and Attell, ordered something to drink, and then just listened." As Gleason predicted, Attell recognized neither writer.[37]

Crusinberry was silenced but got around his editor later. Lardner? He had been a close friend of Eddie Cicotte, and when he learned that he (and the world) had been betrayed, he was profoundly disillusioned. According to biographer Jonathan Yardley, Lardner was disgusted by the fix, and when the public refused to share his reaction, he became even sourer.

However, Crusinberry was now convinced of the fix. And that was significant. Why? Because the next month, lightning struck.

THE AUGUST 31 CUBS–PHILS GAME

"The day before [the August 31] game between the Cubs and Phillies, Kansas City gambler Frog [actually H. A. Frock] Thompson received the following telegram from a Chicago pitcher: BET $5,000 ON OPPOSITION."[38] The identity of the pitcher was kept secret, but the fact that the Cubs' would-be starting pitcher on August 31 was Kansan Claude Hendrix raised suspicions about the sender of the telegram.

There were reports that other gamblers were super-active, with huge amounts going down on an otherwise insignificant Tuesday game between the Cubs and Phils. Nothing was at stake here; they were both second-division clubs. Cubs' president William Veeck received several phone calls and half a dozen telegrams, and he yanked the Cubs' starter Hendrix and sent out Pete Alexander to win one. Pete won twenty-seven times for the Cubs that summer, but not on August 31.[39] Veeck's announcement, on the day of the game, that he had hired detectives was reported in newspapers across the country.

Detroit owner Frank Navin wrote Ban Johnson on September 1 with reports of gambling activity in his city on the Cubs–Phils game. He stated that $10,000 was bet and also said that he was told that big bets went down on clubs to beat Pittsburgh when a certain Pirate pitcher starts. Navin suggested that Johnson forward his letter to National League president John Heydler, so Heydler could investigate.[40] Johnson did pass on the information to Heydler.[41] Meanwhile, other telegrams found their way to Chicago newspapers.

In Grabiner's diary is the suggestion that Ban Johnson had been "waiting patiently" for Charles A. McDonald (some sources have it MacDonald) to be made chief justice in Chicago, and now the time was right to convene the Cook County grand jury. The real purpose had little to do with the Cubs–Phils game—Johnson and "the conspiracy" (as Grabiner called them) were out to wreck Comiskey and the White Sox so they could purchase the franchise.

Johnson had completed his investigation in June. The Sox had the successful coal company operator Edward Fleming acting as a mole, traveling with Ban Johnson and reporting back to Grabiner.[42] There was a month left in the season, and the American League race was tight—Cleveland, New York (Ruth was swatting like no one had ever swatted before), and—those damn White Sox! Johnson was determined to keep the Sox out of another Series.

In baseball, timing is everything. Time now to go to court, to knock the Sox out of the race—the hard way. And if things went his way, Johnson could knock Comiskey out of baseball and put his man, Judge McDonald, in charge.

Crusinberry published a letter on the front page of the *Tribune*'s sport section calling for an investigation, and public pressure started building. The *Herald and Examiner* headline on September 2: "Bare Baseball Scandal. $50,000 Bet on Cubs and Phillies. Sure Thing Game." Gamblers from "Cincinnati, Detroit, Boston and Chicago alleged to have asserted they 'fixed it' [the August 31 game] so the Phils would win."

In a letter dated September 4, Frank Navin told Johnson. "I've been advised that there are five or six other games on which the gamblers are trying to make big bets." One game was between the Cubs and Phils, and "who pitches won't matter" (implying that there were many players in on it).[43]

On Saturday, September 4, a front page headline in the *Kansas City Times* announced, "K. C. Bookmakers Drop $101,000 in 'Philly Run.'"[44] The same day, Veeck went to the Chicago papers with the charge that the Cubs–Phils game of August 31 was fixed. He called on the Chicago chapter of the Baseball Writers Association to assist in the investigation. The *Herald and Examiner*, first to break the story, quoted Veeck:

I want the baseball reporters of the Chicago dailies to meet and select from their members a committee of three to investigate the charges in connection with the most thorough investigation, including the engaging of detectives and such attorneys as the sporting writers' committee determined.

On Sunday, September 5, the Chicago chapter of the Baseball Writers' Association announced that they would examine whether the Cubs–Phils game had been fixed.[45] The same day, the *Chicago Tribune* carried the news that William Veeck had put the Burns Detective Agency on the case. On September 6, Veeck told the *Tribune* that he would let the baseball writers question his players.[46]

JOHNSON AND MCDONALD

On the Sunday when the story of the alleged fix appeared in Chicago's papers, Ban Johnson received a telegram from Judge Charles McDonald to meet him at once at the Edgewater Beach golf course.[47] When Johnson arrived, the judge inquired if the charge that the August 31 game was crooked was sufficiently serious for the grand jury. "Most decidedly it is," Johnson replied. "Then," McDonald announced, "I will lay the matter before the Cook County Grand Jury Tuesday" (the next day was Labor Day).[48]

Was Ban Johnson waiting until "his man," Judge McDonald, was in position to direct the twenty-three members of the grand jury toward the rumors of the fix of the 1919 Series? McDonald had been elected chief justice of the Cook County criminal court July 6, 1920. He succeeded Judge Robert E. Crowe on September 7 and that same day directed the September grand jury to turn its attention to baseball—not the 1919 Big Fix, but the August 31 Cubs–Phils game—and to baseball pools. "Jurors Cheer as Judge Orders Baseball Quiz" ran the *Chicago Tribune* headline on page 9 the next day.

James Crusinberry, writing in *Sports Illustrated* in 1956, recalled, "Maybe there was no truth in the report [of the fixed game of August 31], but Ban Johnson seized upon the chance to fluster the National League by asking a grand jury to investigate the matter, which it did." Was Johnson merely trying to "fluster" a rival league? Or did he know that any real investigation of gambling in baseball would lead to a look at October 1919?

The Sporting News would later give full credit to Judge McDonald for taking "'direct action' against baseball crookedness" by starting the grand jury investigation, forcing it "against very strong 'influences,' political and otherwise." The paper suggested that McDonald was later slandered for his pioneer efforts, and "accused of seeking certain favors [the post of chair of baseball's National Commission] as a reward."[49]

Ban Johnson now asked the American League owners for permission to employ a detective agency to help investigate the problems of baseball gambling that the Chicago grand jury were taking up. The Chicago Pinkertons wanted no part of the investigation. Washington's Clark Griffith wired his okay to employ any agency, while Detroit's Frank Navin gave his consent to secure the McGuire Detective Agency. James Tate, general manager of Tate's Industrial Protective Association, General Detective Services, wrote to Ban Johnson to ask for the job. "We know all the gamblers and their tricks and the manner in which they embarrass people."[50]

Early on there was a hint that the August 31 fix might not have been the main target of the grand jury. On September 9, the *Chicago Tribune* reported that only $3,000 had been wagered on that game in Detroit—the usual amount—not the $10,000 that Frank Navin claimed earlier.

In his column September 11 in the *Kansas City Post*, sports editor Otto Floto expressed his faith in the "man of the hour" in the crisis, Ban Johnson.[50] "However, Johnson cannot act on the strength of mere idle gossip.[51] He must be shown tangible evidence."[52]

Joe Vila wrote an article that appeared in the *New York Evening Sun* on September 13, in which he claimed that the first two games of the 1919 Series were "framed up." He said that half a million dollars was bet on the Reds to win Game One. J. Louis Comiskey, the White Sox treasurer and son of the owner, immediately sent a telegram to Vila, asking him to come to the grand jury if he had hard evidence of his charges. Apparently, he did not.[53]

Around September 21, the list of those who were going to be subpoenaed to come before the grand jury appeared in certain newspapers (the *Los Angeles Times* was one). It included celebrities, like George M. Cohan (who was reported to have lost $30,000 on the Series, although there is some hint that he found out about the fix and hedged his bets); Ban Johnson, Comiskey, and the baseball establishment; players, including the "clean" or "square" Sox; gamblers like Mont Tennes (who supposedly lost $80,000 on the Series, even though he may have had word in August 1919 that a fix was in the works); and reporters like Ring Lardner and sports editors. In the middle of that list were the names of publisher Bert E. Collyer and reporter "Frank O. Cline" (Klein), of *Collyer's Eye*. But apparently neither Collyer nor Klein was ever given the chance to testify. The *Eye* had tried to blow the whistle on the fix and cover-up in the months right after the Series, but whatever evidence their investigation had turned up was kept off the record.

The grand jury hearings did not begin until September 22. In the meantime, James Crusinberry of the *Chicago Tribune* had been chomping at the bit to go public with what he and Ring Lardner had learned about the fix from Abe Attell, two months earlier. The *Herald and Examiner* had broken the story about the gamblers' big take on August 31. "Not to be outdone, the *Tribune* gauged that the public was fed up with baseball's foot-dragging." Crusinberry "arranged for a prominent Chicagoan named Fred M. Loomis to write a letter to the editor demanding a thorough investigation."[54]

Crusinberry kept the authorship of the Loomis letter secret for thirty-six years. Here is an excerpt:

> There is a perfectly good grand jury located in this county. The citizens and taxpayers of Illinois are maintaining such an institution for the purpose of investigating any alleged infraction of the law. Those who possess evidence of any gambling last fall in the World Series should come forward and present it in a manner that may give assurance to the whole country, so that justice may be done in this case where the confidence of the people seems to have been so flagrantly violated.[55]

Woodruff had finally given Crusinberry a green light to do something. The Loomis Letter appeared on the front page of the *Tribune* on September 19. The *Trib* supported the letter with more columns, one mentioning that the "bonus checks of eight players on the White Sox team were held back" after the Series. This pressure spurred the grand jury decision to widen its scope and take a look at baseball's gambling problems—especially that big one left over from last October.

So now, according to historian Lee Allen, there were "three phases" to the grand jury hearings: the August 31 Cubs–Phils game, the 1919 World Series, and the business of baseball pools. The *Chicago Times* estimated conservatively that 100,000 fans just in Chicago regularly played the pools. The *Chicago Tribune* had the number at 400,000 tickets a week, costing $150,000. Some editors regarded the pools as the root problem for baseball, involving more people and money than any "fixed" games, even those in a World Series. The *St. Louis Post-Dispatch* reported that a single baseball pool made profits of over $100,000 in a single season. But once the information about the Big Fix started flowing, the other phases were soon forgotten.

In his September 20 *Kansas City Post* column, Otto Floto noted that Ban Johnson was now working hard to make wagering on ballgames a felony. Johnson was looking at New York's law, which penalized those found guilty of bribing ballplayers with one to five years in prison and fines of up to $10,000.

According to the September 23 *Kansas City Times*, Veeck gave the grand jury an "armfull [*sic*] of reports" from his private investigations, but it included no proof against any Cub player.

The telegram received on August 30 by the Kansas City gambler Thompson had been seen by newsman Otto Floto, a staunch Johnson backer. Floto was not sure that Claude Hendrix had signed the telegram, the *Kansas City Times* reported.[56] But on September 24, Floto wrote to Ban Johnson about the evidence he had. Later Johnson would write to Floto about how the publicity that the disclosure of betting on the August 31 game received had handicapped the exposure of more gamblers.[57] Floto's letter about the Thompson telegram was finally entered as evidence to the grand jury on October 29.

Also on September 24, Floto wrote in the *Kansas City Post*, whose motto was "So the People May Know," that he knew people in Kansas City who made large wagers on the August 31 game. Trying to help Johnson implicate Abe Attell, Floto wrote that he recalled Attell "betting thousands" in the Sinton Hotel lobby in October 1919. According to Floto, Attell was told of the fix by a Chicago gambler named Levy and was betting big for Rothstein. Floto added that Levy was now "awful sore on Abe Attell"—perhaps for driving down the betting odds. Floto sent the same information to Ban Johnson in a letter.

Hendrix and Thompson denied having any connection to the now infamous August 30 telegram, and later, Veeck denied to the grand jury that any of the messages he had received implicated Hendrix or any other player.

Veeck suggested that possibly gamblers had started the rumors about the August 31 game so Alexander would not be available to pitch his next scheduled start—or to get the Cubs to switch from Hendrix, "a comparatively weak pitcher," to "Alexander, one of the best in the league" (*Kansas City Times*, October 2, 1920). The gamblers then bet on Chicago to win on August 31.[58]

One of the telephone calls Veeck had received came from some-one who gave an address that did not exist. All of the messages came within a space of forty-five minutes, and detectives could not locate any of the six telegram senders.[59] "The club itself had been made the 'sucker' in the case."

The *Chicago Tribune* opined that "the report from Detroit that perhaps the bookmakers there had sent the wires of warning to the Chicago club seems plausible to those familiar with the methods of gamblers who make book on baseball."

Harry Grabiner's diary has the White Sox's "spy" in Ban Johnson's camp, Edward Fleming, suggesting that the wires were arranged to be sent not by gamblers at all, but by Ban Johnson, so that McDonald's grand jury would convene, but then shift its attention to the 1919 Series. In any case, the grand jury ignored the allegation about Hendrix, and never bothered to call him to testify. They were after bigger game now.

When Hendrix was released the following February by the Cubs, Veeck noted that this had nothing to do with the August 31 fix and there was no evidence implicating Hendrix. Unfortunately for Hendrix, sloppy reporting by the press gave many fans a mistaken impression that has hurt his reputation.

THE GRAND JURY ZEROES IN

James Crusinberry testified before the grand jury, and in his view, it became a whole new ballgame. Crusinberry later took full credit for turning the hearings around. Assistant State's Attorney Hartley Replogle had told him, "If I hadn't been a witness, the whole case would have been whitewashed."[60] Oddly, the newspaper accounts barely mention the testimony of any reporters. They may have been reluctant at the time to trumpet themselves or their rivals.

The information Crusinberry heard from Attell could have impli-cated Rothstein and others. Kid Gleason had told Crusinberry after Game Two about telegrams he received during the Series from friends in New York, Philadelphia, New Orleans, San Francisco, Havana, and other places, about the fix. Gleason said that he had given that evidence to Comiskey. Crusinberry:

> I testified for more than an hour. I told the jury of the incident
> with Attell and Gleason, and named Arnold Rothstein as the big
> gambler behind it. I told them that I had heard that Hal Chase,
> the ex-ballplayer who had been dropped from several clubs for

his nefarious activities, conceived the plot to throw the Series and had conferred with Gandil as to which players they would dare approach.

Comiskey and Johnson testified. Comiskey accused Johnson of trying to wreck the White Sox and pointed to Johnson's stock in the Cleveland team.[61] The 1920 American League race between the Chicago and Cleveland teams was still neck and neck. Johnson fired back, and by all accounts, it got ugly. Johnson reported everything he had turned up. Comiskey cited his own investigation, but he apparently contributed little to the hearings.

Garry Herrmann wrote to Ban Johnson in reaction to the Comiskey testimony that had been leaked to the press. Herrmann said that he had written Comiskey right after the 1919 Series, had sent him the Fullerton article, and had given him leads to St. Louis gamblers.[62]

RUBE BENTON'S TESTIMONY

Sometime during the summer of 1920, New York Giants pitcher Rube Benton bragged that he won $3,800 betting on the crooked World Series of 1919. He later said that he was only kidding, that he had really won just $20. But someone overheard his earlier remark and "got that to Johnson." Johnson stated publicly that he heard Benton had won $1,500, to which Benton replied later, that if Johnson really believed that he had won big, "he is wandering in vague realms of superheated imagination."[63] In any case, Benton wound up on the grand jury witness stand.

Rube Benton testified about tainted games at the end of the 1919 season, and he named names. The one that made a difference turned out to be that of a Chicago third baseman nicknamed Buck—Buck Herzog, of the Cubs.

Ban Johnson, having been told about Rube Benton, probably was responsible for having him called to testify. Taking credit for the grand jury breakthrough, Johnson recalled later that

the impenetrable wall was first pierced by a pair of affidavits produced on September 23 by Buck Herzog of the Cubs. His name had been linked by Pitcher Rube Benton with the throwing of the Cubs–Phillies game. [This was not the August 31, 1920, game that had been under scrutiny, but a Cubs–Phillies game in September 1919.] In the affidavits, made in May 1920, [two Boston Braves ballplayers] Tony [Norman] Boeckel and Art Wilson, charged that Benton had told them of winning $3,800 on the *fixed 1919 series* after receiving information in a telegram sent by Hal Chase. [Emphasis mine.][64]

Benton testified that he saw a telegram sent by a Bill Burns to Jean DuBuc, another Giants' pitcher, and DuBuc confirmed this. But the information in the wire was likely from Chase. DuBuc produced the telegram before the grand jury.

The September 30 *Sporting News*, having gone to press after Benton's testimony but before all of its repercussions, praised Benton as "the first player to lend a hand in cleaning up baseball" and noted that

if other players who perhaps know even more would come as clean, the bottom of the rotten mess might be reached and the guilty gang put in the penitentiary, which is too good for a player who would throw down the game and the public which has trusted in its honesty.

Before that edition of *The Sporting News* hit the stands, other players—players who knew much more than Benton—would step forward.

The *Chicago Tribune* reported on the Boeckel and Wilson affidavits and printed them in their entirety on September 23, mentioning not only the tip Benton had received about the Series, but the detail that Cincinnati would win the first two games and the Series. The same day, *Tribune* reporter James Crusinberry quoted Assistant State's Attorney Replogle "baring the fixed World Series" by declaring that among the "very good stuff" brought out by the grand jury its first day was that "five to seven players on the White Sox team" had been involved.

Buck Herzog, manager of the Cincinnati team in 1914–15, when Benton was with the Reds, claimed that Benton had mentioned his name to the grand jury to get even for several disciplinary actions Herzog had taken, once after Benton had broken into Herzog's desk to learn the players' salaries, and once after Benton attacked Doc Miller with a knife in a poker game argument.

The National League had investigated the 1919 Cubs–Phils fix charges, and in June 1920, President Heydler had cleared Herzog of any wrongdoing. Benton may not have known this when he testified to the grand jury, because the incident, which also involved Heinie

Zimmermann, had been neatly covered up along with its references to the fix of October 1919. Heydler had told everybody to keep quiet about it.[65]

On September 24, Rube Benton testified for a second time, and he admitted that Hal Chase, who played for McGraw's Giants in 1919, had tipped him off about the crooked 1919 Series, but he denied that he won $3,800 on the tip. Chase said, as Benton recalled, that the White Sox were going to lose the first two games and the Series. Benton claimed that Chase won $40,000 betting on the information he had received from Burns, although Chase later denied profiting very much.

Chase himself did not testify at the grand jury hearings. In a 1941 interview, Chase said he had been willing but was denied the $500 in expenses he requested to cover his traveling from California. Although Chase was indicted, he avoided the trial when California refused to permit his extradition.

Bill Burns was implicated when Benton testified that he had seen a telegram from Burns to Giants pitcher Jean DuBuc. (Several years later, Benton noted that the Giants were in Canada when the telegram arrived on the morning of Game One, Burns advising DuBuc to bet all he could on the Reds to win. Benton said he put down $20 on Game One—the only bet he ever made. He added that all of the players in the room had seen the telegram.)

Jean DuBuc, who finally testified on October 4, corroborated Benton's story, adding that he had told Burns that he had heard rumors of a Series fix at the end of the 1919 season. Burns had told DuBuc that he was heading for Cincinnati and that if he heard anything there, he would send a wire to DuBuc. Finally, DuBuc recalled seeing Burns talking with Hal Chase in late September.[66]

Detroit owner Frank Navin, in a letter dated September 24, asked Johnson in a postscript, "Why don't the grand jury have Gleason and Schalk? If Gleason tells all he has told to different people, it will be very interesting."[67]

Newspapers reported on September 25 that Benton claimed that a $100,000 pool had been delivered to the White Sox players by a Pittsburgh gambling syndicate.[67] Benton said he had been introduced to an agent of this syndicate, which operated in both leagues.

> We discussed various players on the team. Buck Weaver's name was not mentioned, nor were the names of Jackson, Eddie Collins, John Collins or Ray Schalk. Five players were men-

tioned by [Cincinnatian] Hahn in the course of conversation.
Four are: Eddie Cicotte . . . Claude Williams . . . Chick Gandil
. . . and Hap Felsch. . . . I do not recall the name of the fifth
man.

Gamblers had approached these players, Benton said. That's all he
knew for sure. Cincinnati newspapers were quick to note that the Hahn
Benton described was not the old Reds pitcher Frank "Noodles" Hahn,
long since retired. Benton's Hahn was never identified further in the
hearings. (In a September 25 letter to Ban Johnson, Reds owner Garry
Herrmann said that he knew betting commissioner Philip Hahn very
well and added that Benton had his facts wrong "in many instances."[69])
Philip Hahn, a racetrack man, traveled to Chicago himself and denied
all of Benton's charges.

Benton then suggested to the grand jury that they would do better
to call in Eddie Cicotte to tell them all about this. Cicotte, of course,
started and lost Game One, the game on which Benton bet, the day he
saw Bill Burns's telegram.

From Detroit, Heydler attacked Benton, saying his testimony to the
grand jury contradicted what he had earlier told Heydler. Fighting hard
to keep on the lid that was now rapidly unscrewing, Heydler insisted
that all National League games during the 1919 and 1920 seasons had
been won or lost strictly on their merits.

Regardless of the alleged attempted "fixing" *of the first two
games of the last world's series* [emphasis added; note that at
this point, no one was saying that the Series had been fixed,
only that the first two games had been tampered with], I always have contended, and do now contend, that the best team
won the pennant on the level.[70]

Movieman Clyde Elliot testified, and afterward confirmed for reporters, not only that he had early knowledge of the fix, but that he
would give the grand jury evidence that White Sox officials had known
about it, "yet took no steps to dismiss the guilty players."[71]

The names of the eight players whose 1919 World Series checks
had been held up appeared on September 25 in newspapers across
America. Ban Johnson is a probable source of those eight names; as
league president, Johnson had fielded the complaints of several of the
players (Gandil, Cicotte, and McMullin) when the checks were tardy.

The *New York Times* also carried an "inside story" of the plot to fix the Series, furnished to the grand jury by an unnamed source (the *Chicago Tribune* ran a similar piece, crediting Abe Attell,). The boxer's understanding was that only five players were in on things and only $15,000 was delivered to them. Curiously, the boxer agreed in the main with the account delivered a few days later by Billy Maharg: that the ballplayers initiated the proposition, that Rothstein was contacted but refused to get in, and that other backers were found, so that the players were offered $100,000.

The mystery man added that "four members of the team were known to be honest beyond question—two pitchers, two outfielders, and an infielder." Of course, that is five players, and the absence of a catcher (Ray Schalk) is conspicuous. If the reporter misunderstood, and Attell was in fact giving hints about the five players he believed were in the fix, the quotation makes more sense, although it is hard to believe Attell would think either Risberg or Gandil were not involved. (We know Attell later maintained that Weaver was "guiltless" and claimed to have tried to clear Weaver with Landis.) Perhaps because the *Times* source was undisclosed, this story did not shake the baseball world.

But things were warming up.

Indicating that his grand jury testimony would be illuminating, Ray Schalk declared [*New York Tribune*, September 26], "It is up to the baseball players themselves to protect the sport. If they are going to drag me into this I am going before the grand jury and tell all I know. I will mention the names of men on my own team.[72]

Schalk later said that he never showed eagerness to go to the grand jury, even though the September 26 papers reported that he "wishes to tell all." He also denied that he fought in September of 1920 with several of the crooked Sox during the Series, but he did express his doubts about "the honesty of two pitchers in the World Series—especially during the last two months."[73]

With the names of eight Sox players now in the news, and Ray Schalk, Eddie Collins, and Kid Gleason all stepping into the on-deck circle, the grand jury had to choose whether to call in the players. The American League race was red hot, and on September 27, the White Sox beat the Tigers at Comiskey Park, their tenth win in eleven games. The grand jury decided not to call any White Sox players to testify until either the 1920 season had run its course or the Sox were out of the race. This was noted in the *Chicago Tribune*, along with the detail that Assistant State's Attorney Hartley Replogle had conferred with Comiskey and Gleason while at the White Sox game the day before.

Subpoenas had been issued earlier (on September 25) for Eddie Collins, John Collins, Ray Schalk, and reserve Eddie Murphy to appear. None were among the eight whose checks had been withheld after the Series. Pressure was building. "There is still no intention of calling any of the eight men whose world series checks were held up last year," Replogle announced.[74]

Former Chicago Federal League owner Charles Weeghman testified that he had bet and lost big on the White Sox, even though he had been told by gambler Mont Tennes in August 1919, in Saratoga, that the Series would be fixed, something Weeghman said Tennes confirmed to him after the Series, when he named seven Sox players.

Tennes denied Weeghman's story.

> I'm willing to tell [the grand jury] all I know about baseball and betting on baseball—but I can tell them nothing about fixed games. I know nothing about fixed games. I never told Charley Weeghman about fixed games. Weeghman's intentions are good, I'm sure, but I believe he was misunderstood. Whether Weeghman and I met at Saratoga I can't say. I remember meeting him at the racetrack last summer. Of course we talked baseball—one would have to talk baseball with Charley. . . . I bet on the White Sox. I lost my bet and made no cry of fraud.[75]

THE MAHARG INTERVIEW

Then another bolt of lightning. Former boxer Billy Maharg, now an auto worker in Philadelphia, made a phone call to Izzy Meyer, the sports editor of the *Philadelphia North American*. Maharg had read in the papers about a $10,000 reward that was being offered for evidence. He thought he had some. Ban Johnson, in his *Chicago Tribune* memoirs, stated that Maharg was motivated by the prospect of claiming Comiskey's $10,000 reward for information.

Soon Maharg was talking at his place, the Haymarket Hotel, with his former fight manager, H. Walter Schlichter, who now worked for the *North American*. Maharg had played some baseball, and once was both roommate and chauffeur for his lifelong friend, pitching great Grover Cleveland Alexander. Soon Maharg and Schlichter were talking about the grand jury hearings, and it became plain to Schlichter that Maharg knew something more than the average fan about what happened in October 1919.

Schlichter[76] told *North American* reporter James Isaminger to do some sleuthing, then interview Maharg. "Maharg at first denied any knowledge of 'fixed' games, but finally admitted that he and Burns were the first men approached by White Sox players," Isaminger wrote in his blockbuster article, which appeared on September 27 and quickly made headlines across the country.

Isaminger's exposé was a chance to repay an old favor. In 1905, Ban Johnson had recommended him to the *North American*.[77] The headline, "Gamblers Promised Sox $100,000 to Lose," corroborating the leaks from the Chicago grand jury, rocked baseball. Ban Johnson later said that the interview "caused a panic in the ranks of the players."[78]

Maharg's narrative must have at least panicked Eddie Cicotte. While Rube Benton had only suggested that Cicotte be asked what he knew, Maharg named the Sox ace as the instigator of the fix, who sold the idea to Bill Burns and Maharg. In fact, Cicotte was the only player Maharg named besides Lefty Williams. He also pegged Abe Attell as the point man for the gamblers. Abe had sent a fake telegram using Rothstein's initials, but Maharg said "A.R." was never involved.

Maharg told Isaminger that he thought eight White Sox players were in on the fix. He also said Games One, Two, and Eight had been tossed. He mentioned that he had bet on Game Three, along with Bill Burns, and both had lost everything on it.

Maharg: "The players told Burns that if they lost behind Cicotte and Williams, they wouldn't win for Dick Kerr, the busher." Burns later testified that he had indeed been told that but did not recognize it as a double cross until after the Sox won Game Three. Maharg's knowledge was partial, but still electrifying.

Maharg could have read much of the story he told in the September 25 *New York Times* or the *Chicago Tribune*. Exactly when he met with Isaminger is unknown.

EDDIE CICOTTE STEPS FORWARD

Reporters from the *Chicago Herald and Examiner* moved on the story out of Philadelphia as soon as it arrived in their town. "Long after midnight" they called on Eddie Cicotte, "waking him from sleep to tell him of Maharg's statement."[79] Initially, Cicotte denied meeting or knowing Maharg. He had not responded when Rube Benton had mentioned his name to the grand jury, and he was not about to talk to the press now.

There are varying accounts of what happened next. We can only wonder what might have been the next event, if the schedule had had the White Sox on the road—in Boston or New York, for example. But they were in Chicago and had an off day.

On the morning of September 28, so one version goes, Kid Gleason went to Comiskey and asked if Commy wanted him to call in Eddie Cicotte. As the pressure from the grand jury mounted, Gleason had seen Cicotte look increasingly agitated, ready to crack. Comiskey, in this account, agreed to let Gleason fetch Cicotte.

Another account has Cicotte volunteering himself. "Eddie is said to have talked first to his priest, who had suggested that he go to the owner."[80]

In a third version, William Sullivan, an investigator for the state's attorney's office in Chicago, had a role. Sullivan had gone south to spring training with the Sox prior to the 1920 season, at Comiskey's invitation. He was unsuccessful at that time in confirming the team's suspicions about the fix but said that on the night of Monday, September 27, Eddie Cicotte came to him saying, "I've got a load on my chest." Sullivan sent him to Comiskey.[81]

Sox lawyer Alfred Austrian gave yet another account. He said that the Maharg article prompted a meeting of the White Sox management. Austrian recalled asking Comiskey and Gleason, "Who would be most likely to tell the truth?"[82] Eddie Cicotte was then "sent for,"[83] and he went to Austrian's office with Harry Grabiner. "Eddie's attention was drawn to the morning paper" [the Maharg accusations], and he was asked if he had been a party to a crooked deal. "He denied it." Asked if he received any money, Cicotte (according to Austrian) denied it at first, then admitted to all present that he did. He then named seven other players.[84]

In 1921, Cicotte testified that he had been brought to Alfred Austrian's office by Harry Grabiner, Comiskey's secretary.

> He introduced me to Mr. Replogle, and said, "He is the Assistant District Attorney and is going to take care of you if you come through." Replogle said: "We have got the goods on you and we want you to come clean." He and Austrian then told me: "If you will tell us everything we will save you from going to prison or even from paying a fine."
>
> Mr. Replogle and Mr. Austrian took me to the Criminal

Court Building and I was introduced to Judge McDonald. The Judge said I had [to tell] all I knew and asked me what I knew about the gamblers. I said that I made a full and complete statement, and McDonald said to Replogle, "Go ahead and indict him." I then said to Judge McDonald, "Judge, Mr. Austrian and Mr. Replogle promised me that they would take care of me and that I would not be indicted." McDonald said, "Are you trying to bull me?" I said, "I'm telling you the truth." Replogle then took me before the Grand Jury after his talk with McDonald. On the way over I asked him whether his promise and Austrian's still held, and he said "Yes. You can depend on us. We will take care of you. Everything goes as we say."[85]

In *Eight Men Out*, Eliot Asinof has Eddie reporting to the office of lawyer Alfred Austrian. After sweating for an hour in an anteroom, Eddie breaks down when he finally talks with Austrian. Austrian takes him to Comiskey, who tells Eddie to tell it to the grand jury. After Austrian has Eddie sign away his immunity, he accompanies the pitcher to the hearings.

The accounts in which Comiskey, Gleason, Grabiner, or Austrian initiate things all suggest that the White Sox officials deserved credit for the Cicotte confession. Incredibly, Austrian later claimed credit for turning the attention of the grand jury toward the 1919 Series.[86] We may never know the exact role of the White Sox management, but it seems clear that Cicotte voluntarily went to his team, then to the grand jury.

There were just three games left in the 1920 baseball season. The White Sox were only a half game out of first place. No Sox players were going to be called before the grand jury until the pennant race was decided. Despite everything that had appeared in the papers to date, members of the grand jury were still telling reporters that indictments were unlikely. No one had expected Cicotte to step forward.

BEFORE THE GRAND JURY

Alfred Austrian was working hard that day on behalf of his client—Charles Comiskey. He told Cicotte, and later Jackson, not to worry, that they would be taken care of, that the grand jury was out to put away the gamblers. The three players whom he advised—Lefty Williams would come in the next morning—all signed away their immunity. (The gamblers who were later indicted knew enough—or were advised by their counsel—not to.) The players did not have their own lawyers to look out for their interests, they only had Austrian.

The 1921 trial would begin with Cicotte, Jackson, and Williams taking the witness stand in turn and denying that they had signed away their immunity knowingly; they all added that they had been told by Judge McDonald that if they "came through" they would be taken care of. Jackson stated that he was drunk. Judge McDonald followed the players on the stand and denied promising them immunity, although he did sympathize for Williams, whose salary was so pitifully low.

> It was as rare in 1920 as it is today for a suspected felon to appear voluntarily before a grand jury and confess his crimes. Even more peculiarly, both Cicotte and Jackson waived immunity and paved the way for their confessions to be used against them. . . . The ultimate in incredibility: Both players were acting on the advice of counsel.[87]

A case could be made that the person who finally uncovered the fix of the 1919 Series was the same person who many think initiated it in the first place—Eddie Cicotte. The latter is hard to determine; Chick Gandil was probably a ringleader, too. But Gandil himself credited Cicotte for being the key person in the undoing of the cover-up of the fix. Gandil admitted that for a long time, he held a grudge against Cicotte for confessing. Without that, he thinks, no one would have ever found out about the fix.[88]

Interviewed in March 1921, just six months after Cicotte's confession and four months before the trial, Gandil was only slightly more sympathetic. He recalled that Comiskey had promised Cicotte a bonus in 1917 and refused to pay when Cicotte came up a game short. (He did not mention the size of the bonus, nor did he accuse Comiskey of tampering with Cicotte's starts.) Gandil said that when Cicotte confessed, he "probably had a crying jag on. . . . He boozed a lot during 1919 and maybe he agreed to do something crooked while full of redeye."[89]

Two months later, advised by his own lawyer, D. P. Cassaday of Detroit, Eddie Cicotte tried to bargain with the courts to avoid any punishment except banishment. An unidentified state official had "let it become known that but for Cicotte's testimony the [grand] jury never would have had sufficient evidence to indict more than one or two persons," and chances for any convictions would have been slim.

"Before Cicotte confessed we had reams of hearsay evidence," said this official to-night, "but none of it would have held in court. . . . In order to get the evidence necessary we had to have a confession. We were certain that Cicotte knew more than many others whose names had been given us, so we went after him. Of course, we have to concede something to such a witness and we'd rather see Cicotte free and convict the rest than to let them all get away."[90]

The state official refused to say whether immunity had been granted Cicotte before he testified. Of course, it had not; it had been waived.

Back to September 28. That afternoon, Jackson either heard about Cicotte or was called in by the Sox. Or he called Judge McDonald to proclaim his innocence (Asinof) but was told by the judge that he knew Jackson *was* in on the fix.

In Austrian's account from the 1924 witness stand, Jackson came to his office alone. He told Austrian that he heard that he had been implicated. "He denied it." Then, Austrian said, he told Jackson to tell the truth, and Austrian would help him out with Judge McDonald. Jackson stated that he had received $5,000 after the fourth game. Austrian noted that the next day, Lefty Williams told him that Jackson got the money and was in on the fix. Jackson and Williams both told the grand jury that the money was exchanged after the fourth or fifth game, but in 1924, they both swore that it was not until the Series was over.

Austrian had taken notes when he spoke with Cicotte and Williams but, curiously, had not made a single memorandum in his meeting with Jackson. He spent between one and two hours with Jackson before leading him to the grand jury.[91] "I didn't ask him [if he'd done anything on the ballfield to throw the game to Cincinnati] and he didn't tell me."[92] It was enough for Austrian to know that Jackson accepted money that probably originated with the gamblers—an opinion shared by many today. "I didn't think a man couldn't have money in his pocket under the scheme that he had, in my judgment, and play honest baseball, or do anything else honest."

The Judge [McDonald] said Jackson called him up after Cicotte talked to the jury and said he was not implicated. Fifteen minutes later he called up and said he wished to tell all. . . . He told me that he had heard that "Swede" Risberg had threatened to "bump him off." He asked protection. I gave him two bailiffs.[93]

Jackson was confused when he went to Alfred Austrian. On the witness stand in the 1921 trial, Jackson recalled Austrian telling him that he would be indicted in a few minutes, and that he needed a lawyer "damn bad." Apparently Jackson was reluctant to go to the grand jury at first, but Austrian "promised if I'd tell what I knew I would not be prosecuted. Austrian told me they weren't after the ball players but wanted to trample the gamblers under their feet."[94]

Ben Short, Jackson's lawyer in the 1921 trial, asked Jackson if Austrian told him that "Cicotte had been taken care of, and you would be, too?" Jackson replied,

> Yes, and he said that after confessing nothing would be done with me and I could go anywhere—to the Portuguese Islands if I wanted. Then they sent two bailiffs with me when I left to protect me, and the bailiffs and I went out and got good and drunk.[95]

Jackson's later recollections of his time with Austrian, Replogle, and Judge McDonald were "plentifully sprinkled with accounts of 'hooch' parties and stories of how he had been promised everything if he would only talk."[96]

Something Austrian said to Jackson in the time between his initial phone call to Judge McDonald, insisting that he was not implicated, and his second call, promising to tell what he knew, changed Jackson's mind, and his life. Afraid of being indicted, Jackson found reassurance and safety in Austrian's advice. It appears that Jackson was told to give the grand jury what they wanted, something that could be used to punish the gamblers.

> Austrian finally persuaded me to talk. On the way to the jury room, Replogle told me they promised to take care of Cicotte and would do the same for me, but that I'd never be able to play ball again.[97]

Before meeting with the grand jury, Jackson had a short private conference with Judge McDonald in his chambers. Replogle then "came a-running in, het up, and it was then they told me Cicotte had done gone down town and I could leave after I testified."

Replogle, McDonald and Austrian told me I'd never be prosecuted and the only way I'd be used would be as a witness. All I wanted to do was tell my story and get out—drunk or sober.[98]

Asked in the 1921 trial if Jackson said that he played the 1919 Series to win, Judge McDonald said, "He told me that he played hard, but that he could have played harder."[99] That was something Jackson had said privately to McDonald. To the grand jury, he stated that he played every game to win, at bat and in the field, and that is the way the grand jury foreman later recalled Jackson's testimony—not as a confession that he played to lose.

The trip to the jury room that followed Jackson's talk with McDonald was like "running the gantlet of newspaper cameramen."

Jackson hung his head and covered his face with his hands. Replogle tried to keep the cameramen away. They refused and there was a volley of flashes. Jackson cursed newspapermen gamblers and baseball and fled to the security of the jury room.[100]

In the 1921 trial, Judge McDonald recalled it somewhat differently. He said Jackson "asked if he could go before the jurors without his teammates knowing. I took him the rear way. We met a George Wright, a reporter, on the way, and he flashed the story to the newspapers."[101]

The afternoon grand jury session had opened with National League president John Heydler and the New York Giants' John McGraw testifying. Then Joe Jackson appeared. Like Cicotte before him, and as Lefty Williams would do the next day, Jackson signed a paper in the grand jury room, because he was instructed to do so. He had no idea that it was a waiver of immunity so his testimony could be used against him. The newspapers reported that when the indictments were announced in the grand jury room after his testimony, Eddie Cicotte broke down and cried. Jackson, now half drunk and dizzy from his meetings with Austrian, McDonald, and Replogle, probably was not aware that he was indicted as he addressed the grand jury.[102]

Jackson, who could not read the waiver of immunity, said he was half drunk when he signed and believed the paper contained only his address. "Judge McDonald told me that if I talked I would not be indicted, I wouldn't have to go to jail, put up bonds or anything. All they wanted, they said, was my address."[103] In several other accounts, Jackson said he would have signed his own death warrant. In one he said Replogle "read a lot of stuff from a paper to me. I don't know what it was. He said it was a waiver or something."[104]

Jackson was supposed to meet the following day with Judge McDonald. "But I got on a big party and got drunk. I had the judge's two bailiffs with me." Asked if he left town when he was done at Replogle's office, Jackson said, "No I got teed up again."[104] Would a cold sober Joe Jackson have told a different story to Judge McDonald the day after his blurry, contradictory testimony to the grand jury? We will never know, just as we will never know if the bailiffs who kept Jackson under the influence of alcohol were following somebody's instructions, or just enjoying a very pleasurable assignment.

DID THE PLAYERS CONFESS OR NOT?

James Kirby, looking at the grand jury statements of Cicotte, Jackson, and Williams—not as they were published, but as they were read into the transcript of the 1924 civil action by Jackson against the White Sox—said that he found the texts disappointing. "They admitted agreeing to a fix with gamblers to accept cash . . . but all three players also told the grand jury that they played to win."[106]

Jackson wanted to tell what he knew. Austrian may have advised him, in the words of Eliot Asinof, "To deny your involvement will prejudice the grand jury. Do you understand that?" Jackson wanted to stay out of trouble. So he testified. He said he let up some. And then he said he played every game to win. In the newspapers the next day, no one reported the latter. Whatever Jackson actually said, it went down as a "confession."

It was the exceptional newspaper that reported, either right after the grand jury statements, or later, that "neither Jackson nor Williams had made any admission of 'game-throwing' to the grand jury, and that the fixers of the Series were unknown to them."[107]

Joe Jackson: "There never was any confession by me. That was trumped up by the court lawyers. They couldn't produce it in court. They said it was stolen from the vaults. Does that sound right?" Jackson said that the "confession" was one of the shoddy tricks played against him.[108]

On September 29, the *Los Angeles Times* printed an Associated Press night-wire story, which included this "leaked" information: "Officials of the court, desirous of giving the national game the benefit of publicity in its purging, lifted the curtain on the grand jury proceedings sufficiently to show that great hitter, Joe Jackson, declaring that he deliberately just tapped the ball."

But that is nowhere in Jackson's grand jury testimony that we can read today. No one has argued that the surviving testimony is incomplete, although it is puzzling to understand how the session—if it lasted about two hours—could be filled by the pages we have. (Some accounts have Jackson on the stand closer to a half hour, which matches the testimony better.) In any case, the statements Jackson may have made on the evening of September 28, hours after his afternoon appearance before the grand jury, could have been made for the consumption of those he feared—his teammates and the gamblers they had double-crossed.

A number of papers also reported that Cicotte and Jackson had been arrested or jailed after their testimonies. They had not been. The *New York Times* has Jackson leaving the grand jury room "walking erect and smiling." He was reported to say, "I got a big load off my chest. I'm feeling better. I'm willing to tell the world now, if they'll let me." Hartley Replogle commented, "He's gone through beautifully and we don't want him bothered," as he ushered him through the crowd and into a car, still with his new bailiff friends.[109]

The next day's *Times* carried a different version. Instead of being escorted away and protected by Hartley Replogle from reporters, Jackson is instead surrounded by a group of small boys. One asks, "It isn't true, is it, Joe?" to which Jackson replies, "Yes, boys, I'm afraid it is." Whether it happened or not, this wire-service story was simply too poignant not to pass along.[110]

6

SCANDAL, TRIAL, AFTERMATH

"This 'blowoff' [of the lid off the fix] is due to Mr. Comiskey's action," Mr. Austrian said. "As soon as he knew what the state of affairs was, he ordered me to go ahead. We rushed the evidence to the grand jury and are now [as he was speaking] having Mr. Jackson tell what he knows of the affair. This is due to Mr. Comiskey's desire to get at the bottom of the scandal and to have the matter cleared up at once."
—Lawyer Alfred Austrian, September 29, 1920, Utica Daily Press

THE DAY AFTER

The morning of September 29, Lefty Williams met with Alfred Austrian, who told him that the team would take care of him if he cooperated. Williams answered a series of questions, then signed the statement, then signed a waiver of immunity. He was then taken to the grand jury, where his statement was admitted as evidence. It appears that he did not testify further or answer any other questions in front of the grand jury. Judge McDonald denied making promises of immunity to any of the players, but later said that he had the most sympathy for Williams. Lefty told the Judge that his salary in 1919 was only $2,800. McDonald told him that "if he came clean, that I believed the trial court would make a record of it."

Also in the news the day after the Cicotte–Jackson twin bombshells, was the "confession" of Sox outfielder Oscar "Happy" Felsch in an interview by Harry Reutlinger in the *Chicago Evening American*. "Reutlinger was looking to secure his scandal facts first-hand from one of the players. He was advised to visit Felsch, who was uneducated but considered affable enough to talk."[1] Eliot Asinof, who interviewed Felsch, said that Reutlinger went to Happy "armed with a bottle of Scotch, and quickly got him to open up." Felsch said he was in on the Big Fix, but never really had the opportunities to do much to throw the series.

> I didn't want to get in on the deal at first. I had always received square treatment from "Commy" and it didn't look quite right to throw him down. But when they let me in on the idea, too many men were involved. I didn't like to be a squealer and I knew that if I stayed out of the deal and said nothing they would go ahead without me and I'd be that much money out .... I suppose that if I had refused to enter the plot and had stood my ground I might have stopped the whole deal. We all share the blame equally.... I'm not saying that I double-crossed the gamblers, but I had nothing to do with the loss of the World Series.[2]

In *Baseball: The Golden Age,* Historian Harold Seymour wondered if Joe Jackson and Happy Felsch were "protesting too much" in their testimony —if they were making "worried attempts to convince the gamblers that they conscientiously tried to lose." From this safe distance, it is easy to forget how real the risk was, of not keeping one's word with the underworld. (Rothstein came to an unpleasant end for not paying a gambling debt, when he dropped a small fortune in a card game he decided was rigged and was shot to death.) Remember, Jackson feared bodily harm from Risberg, and that was why he was given a heavy escort out of court.[3] "The Swede is a hard guy." If he thought *Swede* was hard, how about the thug that had threatened his friend Lefty Williams and Lefty's wife, and possibly Cicotte? This is just something else to keep in mind in looking at the statements that became public record—gamblers read the papers, too.

Mostly eclipsed by the stories about Williams and Felsch was the testimony that Giants' manager John McGraw gave to the grand jury on September 29. He said he released Hal Chase and Lee Magee on the advice of John Heydler, who had told McGraw that Magee had confessed (behind closed doors) to accepting bribes from Chase. McGraw "patted Benny Kauff on the back" for reporting to McGraw that Heinie Zimmermann tried to bribe him, but McGraw made no charges against Jean DuBuc.

Also in the press that day, New York detective and Rothstein crony Val O'Farrell linked Kauff with Bill Burns and a gambler named Orbie, and said that these three had been the first to approach Rothstein.

O'Farrell suggested that McGraw dispatched Kauff to Toronto mid-way through the 1920 season because Rothstein had informed the Giants' manager about Kauff's problems with the law.[4] McGraw also linked Kauff with gambler Abe Attell.[5]

In Joliet, near Chicago, a fan accused Cub third baseman Buck Herzog of being "one of those crooked Chicago ball players," and stabbed Herzog in the fight that followed.

SAY IT AIN'T SO

Fred Lindstrom in *A Donald Honig Reader* (Simon and Schuster, 1988):

> There is that marvelous story of the young boy who accosts Joe Jackson outside of the courthouse and tugs on Joe's sleeve and says, "Say it ain't so, Joe." Well, that story might be apocryphal, but it nevertheless symbolizes what we felt, because we were so close to those fellows. By close I mean of course from a fan's perspective, and even though that is not at all intimacy it can lead to greater disillusionment because those fellows were part of our fantasies.

The day after Jackson's statement to the grand jury, the *Chicago Herald and Examiner* carried a story about a "little urchin" who grabbed Jackson's coat sleeve as he left the building, and asked "It ain't true, is it Joe?" The reply is, "Yes, kid, I'm afraid it is." To which the urchin exclaims, "Well, I'd never have thought it."

Hugh Fullerton's more famous and vivid account appeared the day after the *Herald and Examiner* version, in a New York paper. It is not clear whether Fullerton was writing from Chicago, covering the grand jury, or embellishing from his New York office, reading wire reports.[6]

As a kid growing up in Chicago, writer Nelson Algren had idolized Swede Risberg. One of his essays captures the disillusionment of the day much more powerfully than the "Say it ain't so" story, which may well be fiction.

> Out of the welter of accusations, half denials and sudden silences a single fact drifted down: that Shoeless Joe Jackson couldn't play bad baseball even if he were trying to. He hit .375

that series and played errorless ball, doing everything a major-leaguer could to win. Nearing sixty today, he could probably still outhit anything wearing a National League uniform.

Only, I hadn't picked Shoeless Joe. I'd picked the man who, with Eddie Cicotte, bore the heaviest burden of all our dirty Southside guilt. The Black Sox had played scapegoat for Rothstein and I'd played the goat for The Swede.[7]

Writing about "Say it ain't so, Joe," Algren has Jackson, "Getting bewildered a little: 'I wish to God it warn't.' It wasn't too hard to bewilder Shoeless Joe."[8]

John Lardner (one of Ring's sons) believes Shoeless Joe's exit line: "'Yes, boys, I'm afraid it is,' said Shoeless Joseph."[9] But Lardner believes the story because it appeared in four different papers the next day. (Ruth's called shot appeared in countless places, but it can still be traced back, I believe, to sportswriter Joe Williams.) Reporters often stole and borrowed from each other, and they were not above embellishing their stories with made-up quotes.

A quote from the *Los Angeles Times* of September 30 comes closest to the saying that is now so familiar: "Tell us, Joe, that it ain't so." Their story had no by-line.

White Sox historian and reporter Warren Brown: "I don't think it ever happened. It's like most good stories. It was made up."[10] A later Sox historian, Richard C. Lindberg, agrees that "There is no truth to the famous 'Say it ain't so, Joe' quote associated with Shoeless Joe Jackson."[11] But there seem to be equal numbers of skeptics and true believers; some of the latter even claimed to be eyewitnesses to the event.[12]

Donald M. Ewing's obituary had the former Associated Press night city editor and reporter helping to break the scandal and "the famous 'Say it ain't so, Joe,' episode," along with a Charles Dunkley.[13] "Ewing left [the courthouse] with Jackson and as they made their way through the hushed crowd one tiny youngster stepped up to the outfielder and tugged at his sleeve," wrote Oliver Grambling in "AP, The Story of the News."

Dick Schaap also gives Ewing credit for the initial story. Schaap himself did not believe the precise words "Say it ain't so, Joe" had ever been spoken, but he interviewed both Ewing and James Crusinberry, who said they "covered the grand jury hearing and followed Joe Jackson out of the building after his testimony."

Ewing told Schaap that a group of youngsters "confronted" Jackson, and one asked, "It isn't true, is it Joe?" Jackson then faced the group and replied, "Yes, boys, I'm afraid it is." "We didn't even put it on the wire until five or six hours later," Ewing added. "I certainly never expected what happened afterward."

Crusinberry recalled for Schaap the youngster "grasping Jackson's hand and begging, 'Say it isn't so, Joe. Say it isn't so.'" Crusinberry's account has Jackson moving silently away and stepping into a waiting car. So the eyewitness accounts of Ewing and Crusinberry vary somewhat. But they do counter the claim of the one person we know for certain was present, Jackson himself. Jackson gave credit to a writer named Charley Owens for making the story up. However, Bob Stanton of the *Chicago Daily News*, a contemporary of Owens, maintained to Schaap that Owens was not responsible. He thought Ring Lardner or Crusinberry wrote it first, but wasn't sure.[14]

Is it possible somebody yelled to Jackson, "Are you drunk, Joe?" (because he looked hung over), and a kid called out, "Say it ain't true, Joe!"—and Jackson gave him the reply that the reporters wanted to hear? It really doesn't matter, it's a handy red herring—it was in 1920, and it still is today. It keeps our attention focused on the ballplayers and on October 1919, missing the bigger picture of gambling in baseball and baseball's determination to insist that the game was clean and honest. People who have never heard of the Black Sox know "Say it ain't so, Joe." It's stuck in America's consciousness like a commercial jingle.[15]

The late baseball researcher Jack Kavanagh believed that the most likely "Say it ain't so" story was James T. Farrell's,[16] and not the famous one reported by Hugh Fullerton. Farrell recalls a fan calling out to Jackson and Felsch, as they walked under the Comiskey stands one last time on September 27, "It ain't true, Joe." Other fans, men and boys, picked up the cry. "Farrell's account has the ring of historical truth."[17]

Walter Camp recounted yet another story making the rounds in the wake of the revelation of the fix:

A small boy, an embryo "sand lot's player," was, shortly after the scandal, found out in the yard breaking his bat into kindling wood and crying silently. This, perhaps better than anything else, describes the attitude of the "fans" of the country when this disclosure burst upon them.[18]

OUT IN THE OPEN

With Cicotte's confession, the dam that held back the truth about the fix burst open. In the days that followed, there would be more players in the headlines. The press reported that Joe Jackson had confessed on the heels of Cicotte, but the statements he allegedly made to reporters after, about how he "struck out in the clutch" and "just poked at the ball with men in scoring position" and "let up in the field" appear nowhere in his grand jury testimony. *The statements that do appear, about playing every game to win, at bat and in the field, were reprinted nowhere.*

The press explained the apparent breach of confidentiality that the grand jury hearings required by saying that the officials of Judge McDonald's court were only "desirous of giving the national game the benefit of publicity in its purging" and that this justified their "lifting of the curtain on the grand jury proceedings."[19] There is enough mis-information in the stories that appeared following Cicotte's and Jackson's testimony to make one wonder if the reporters were offering rewards so tempting that the court officials either embellished what they remembered or simply told the pressmen what they wanted to hear.

The *New York Times* reported that the eight indictments had been made possible not just by the two "open confessions" of Cicotte and Jackson, but by "evidence obtained by the Cook County Grand Jury by Charles A. Comiskey"—giving the White Sox owner credit for delivering the players, perhaps, because Comiskey had apparently not turned over any other evidence. The *Times* also suggested that the $20,000 that Jackson was promised was his "asking price" instead of a figure that he apparently rejected.

The *Washington Post* dug up and quoted a story that Eddie Collins had written during the 1919 Series for the *Boston Post*.[20] In this article Collins commented on how unusual it was that Cicotte committed two errors in an inning and on how they had cost the Sox the game. "Overanxiousness on his part" was likely the cause of the wild throw to first. "Why he interfered with Jackson's throw home following Kopf's single to left still remains a mystery." The *Post* gave this bit of history the headline, "How Eddie Collins Saw Ed Cicotte Throw Game." Of course, Collins himself never made that accusation.

Buck Weaver and other players protested their innocence. But eight names had been linked together, and their joint removal from the White Sox roster made it appear that they had all done something wrong.

Eight checks had been held up after the Series, eight names had sur-faced in the coverage of the grand jury.

Catcher Ray Schalk loved to talk baseball, but about all most people could get him to say about the dark days of 1919–21 was "It was a bad thing—let it die." Even when offered large sums of money for the exposé he could have provided, Schalk refused to talk. But he did share one memory, and it appeared a few months after Schalk's death.[21] He recalled the day when Comiskey came into the clubhouse to tell the accused players that they were through with baseball. Schalk admitted he viewed the scene "with mixed emotions. Some of the guys broke down and cried." Paul Gardner:

> Baseball, which the owners liked to present to the public as a lady of undefiled virtue wrapped in the American flag, was suddenly naked, and she looked like a cheap whore. That was bad enough, but the tergiversations of the owners, as they tried to decide whether to expose the full extent of the scandal or to hush it up, made matters quite a bit worse than they need have been.
>
> The *New York Times* said flatly that "the men financially interested in the game are incompetent to run their own busi-ness" and it was a view that was widely shared. The owners faced a dilemma: either to continue business as usual, hoping that all would blow over, but facing probable catastrophe if it did not, or to appoint an independent "strong man" to clean up the sport, hoping that public approval of such a move would, in the long run, outweigh any scandals he might uncover. While they argued, the pressure mounted to the point where there was no alternative: it would have to be a strong man.[22]

On September 30, John Heydler called for a new governing struc-ture for baseball. "The disclosures at Chicago show the futility of an organization like the National Commission ruling an activity of such country-wide interest as baseball." Heydler pointed to the Comiskey-Johnson feud and the team ownership of Commissioner Garry Herrmann (who had resigned from the commission in February 1920) as factors that had prevented an immediate, unbiased investigation into the 1919 Series fix.[23]

Heydler added that, for the record, he wanted to answer the printed rumors about the fix right after the Series with a libel suit against a Chicago paper—probably *Collyer's Eye*. He suggested that to Ban

Johnson but "did not press the point" because he didn't think fixing a series was possible. Heydler said a libel action would "have all possible information brought out in court." And that is probably why the lawsuit idea was dropped.

Cleveland would finish two games ahead of Chicago to win the American League pennant. The grand jury hearings continued as the World Series was played out. The hearings concluded on October 22, and the indictments of eight White Sox players and a number of gamblers were handed up to Judge McDonald—Ban Johnson's choice to be baseball's savior and new commissioner. But on November 12, 1920, the owners selected Judge Kenesaw Mountain Landis.[24]

Comiskey had been in damage control mode. He sent checks for $1,500 to each of the players on the White Sox who were not indicted— the difference, he stated in his letter, between winning and losing Series shares. (In fact, the winning share for the Series in 1919 was $5,207.11, and the losing share was $3,254.36; Comiskey should have paid his clean Sox $1,952.75, instead of $1,500.) Comiskey's letter, and the grateful response of the loyal players, were both released to the press.

The owners of the Yankees, Ruppert and Huston, urged Comiskey to issue a full statement of what his team had done to investigate the rumors that had now been proven true. Comiskey's statement was carried in full by *New York Times*. It amounted to a denial of any covering-up.[25]

Comiskey recalled hearing Redmon's story some time in November, instead of right after the Series, on October 12. He insisted that Redmon's evidence was not at all convincing but was "vague and uncertain," and he contradicted Redmon's testimony to the grand jury, as Harry Grabiner had done right after Redmon testified ("His story seemed to be merely the hard-luck yarn of a loser"[26]). Comiskey claimed to have spent around $10,000 on hired detectives, when in fact he had spent much less, and the investigation had been a sham. He repeated that he had informed Ban Johnson via Heydler during the Series. He noted that Johnson had also interviewed Redmon and "must have reached the same conclusion, because he took no action as the President of the league."

Comiskey added that when the grand jury was convened, he had turned over all the evidence he had (what that was has never been made clear). He declined postponing the hearings until the World Series was over, and it was his team's lawyer that procured the players' confessions; he suspended the players as soon as they were indicted, destroying his team and costing him "many hundreds of thousands of dollars. I took my loss without a pang or bit of sadness," even though he had been betrayed. The press continued to focus on the players, not those who owned and ran baseball.

The grand jury submitted its final report on November 6, and the *New York Times* headline ran "Finds Baseball Generally Honest." The report called for a new federal law that would make offering or accepting bribes to throw games a criminal offense. The leaders of baseball were said to be guardians who could be relied on to keep baseball above suspicion and honest. The jury emphasized that the few players who confessed to taking bribes had expressed "remorse and self-contempt" and that their voluntary testimony showed how "cheap and petty" they felt and how "their loss of self-respect was in no wise compensated by the sums that were accepted."

"Grand Jury Adjourns, but Ban Johnson Has Just Started" ran a *Sporting News* headline on November 11. Johnson was disappointed that the grand jury had not indicted a St. Louis gambler who could have given them twenty more names of ballplayers in both leagues who were "mixed up in dishonest work."[27]

But Johnson's investigation was sidetracked in the struggle for power that took place that winter. Johnson would find himself and five loyal owners faced with a possible schism of the American League. The movement to crown Landis as commissioner was gaining momentum.

THE RESPONSE OF AMERICA'S EDITORS

Collyer's Eye, the gambling publication that had printed an "exposé" in a series of articles starting soon after the 1919 Series, championed its editor. In its October 2 issue, Bert E. Collyer's picture appeared with this caption:

> The man whose ceaseless effort in the face of the most strenuous opposition, even threats, resulted in the exposé of the World's Series scandal. In discussing the sources of his information, Mr. Collyer quizzically remarks, "Oh, yes, there were plenty of people willing to hand me the dope. All of them were willing to call the other fellow an -?-?-?-? but always they added, when they did so, 'But don't say I said so.'"

With Cicotte confirming that the fix indeed was in, *Collyer's Eye* recalled its efforts to achieve what finally had been accomplished by

Chicago's grand jury, nearly a year after the Series ended. The indict-ments handed up were "the vindication of a remarkable series of sto-ries printed in this paper. . . which were the first in time and value of news to inform our readers of the possibility of the baseball scandal."[28]

On October 9, an article appeared in *Literary Digest*, with the title "The Flaw in the Diamond." It begins by quoting the *Wall Street Journal*: "The Joliet [Prison] baseball team should have a pennant chance next year." Clearly, even before any players were tried, some editors had the crooked players behind bars.

Hugh Fullerton took the occasion, writing in the *New York Evening World*, to call for a housecleaning of baseball "from cellar to garret. Nothing but a change of heads of organized baseball and a wholesale expulsion of players can save the national game."

Writing in the *New Republic* magazine that same month, Hugh Fullerton might well have used the title "I Told You So" instead of "Base-ball on Trial." Fullerton had been right about the fix, but instead of complaining about the way he had been treated, he calmly and thought-fully noted that baseball "has received a blow from which it will be a long time recovering." He recounted what was found out when the players confessed before the grand jury and recalled his suspicions and his charting plays with Mathewson during the 1919 Series. He called on ballplayers who suspected that their teammates were controlled by gam-blers to speak out.

Fullerton pointed out how gamblers had corrupted the image of horse racing in many parts of the country. Gambling had been a serious problem in baseball for more than twelve years. Fullerton mentioned at least three other World Series that had been tainted, without saying which ones or going into any detail. He described the clearing of Hal Chase after Mathewson charged him with fixing games as a green light for players to play dishonestly without fear of being discovered or punished.[29]

Fullerton repeated that the climate of baseball had been such in the 1919 season that gamblers could openly boast of owning players on various clubs, and no one blinked an eye. "Through it all the officials in charge of baseball adhered to their policy of curing an evil by declaring it did not exist and by using their influence over consciously or uncon-sciously subsidized sporting writers to suppress the accusations and punish those who demanded an investigation."

This is as close as Fullerton got to "I told you so." The scandal was now public and the players banished, but Fullerton was not satisfied. He cleared Comiskey but took this parting shot: "Baseball hardly can be purged of crookedness while among those who own clubs are men who are themselves gamblers and interested in gambling businesses."[30]

With the scandal now out in plain sight, Fullerton wrote to *Baseball Magazine* requesting a retraction and an apology for its caustic attack the year before. "I desire most of all to know who inspired the attack, in plain English, what person in organized baseball ordered you to write it?"

It printed his letter in the December 1920 issue, but replied "with neither apology nor retraction."

> We have no comments to make upon this letter. Nor would we waste our time and space upon this particular individual were it not for the recent turn of events which makes it advisable to define our attitude toward the gambling rumors of last fall, which formed the basis of Mr. Fullerton's attacks.

Instead, they piled on Fullerton again for "picking up an ugly story" and "blowing it up into a muckraking tirade against organized baseball." The *Baseball Magazine* editors had attended the 1919 Series just as Fullerton had, and they heard the same rumors. They interviewed a number of players and some of the owners and "could find nothing more substantial than a hazy mass of unfounded suspicion." They were aware that an investigation "was being conducted, quietly, normally, sanely." Fullerton's "attack was vicious, premature, unfounded," and the magazine was simply defending baseball. It was building up while Fullerton was tearing down.

Baseball Magazine gave Fullerton no credit at all; his crusade had in no way hastened or helped the investigations. It compared him to a weatherman predicting rain—he had nothing to do with causing the rain. "Events have played favorably into Mr. Fullerton's hands in a manner which is probably gratifying to him," *Baseball Magazine* said. "We begrudge him none of his personal triumph."

With the fix in the spotlight, few writers called attention to the cover-up that had nearly succeeded. One who did, James P. Sinnott of the *New York Evening Mail*, predicted that the hearings in Chicago were "only the beginning," and observed that papers that tried to "'run down' the [to them] well-known scandal of last year 'were handicapped by an apparent dislike of publicity on the part of organized baseball.'"

Literary Digest recalled Fullerton's declaration right after the 1919 Series that "there are seven men who never will play on this [White Sox] team again." Of course, they did play. Then this curious line: "Afraid of the consequences of their acts, Fullerton says, 'they failed (last year) to come to Comiskey's offices for their season and World Series paychecks, even after the owner of the team asked them to come.'" Fullerton may not have been aware of Comiskey's refusal to see Jackson after the Series and Jackson's repeated offers that fall, in letters, to come tell what he knew—or, more likely, Fullerton is passing on here a cover story from Comiskey.

Dan Daniel of the *New York Herald* wondered about the wagers that were paid off on the Series. "As the series was thrown by the White Sox it was legally 'no contest,' and should be treated as such in the official records of the major leagues." Daniel called on the National Commission to strike the Series from the records, "and take from the Reds the official title of world's champions of 1919."

The *New York Globe* thought the grand jury hearing marked the end of reputable baseball, but the *Brooklyn Eagle* predicted baseball would survive, as it had survived the scandals of the 1870s. The *Indianapolis Star* felt that baseball as a whole should not be condemned because of "a handful of players." The *St. Louis Globe* took a philosophical stand: there are crooks "in every employment and profession," and why should baseball be any different?

The *New York Telegraph* made this point: the fix was engineered not by *gamblers*—that implies taking risk—but by "sure-thing grafters." The players were traitors, to be classed with those "soldiers or sailors who would sell out their country and its flag in time of war," added the *Philadelphia Bulletin*.

The *Digest* said that an editorial from the *Kansas City Times* was representative of opinions from editors all over the country. "The owners, managers and players have got to convince the public that the game is square. Unless they can do that, baseball must ultimately go the way of horse-racing. The public will not stand for a crooked sport."

The editors across America also believed, in this moment of crisis, that baseball was worth saving. The *New Orleans Times-Picayune* hoped that "the exposures have come in time to permit its rescue."

The *Digest* reported that Comiskey had suspended the indicted players, and beneath a photo captioned "The Old Roman of Baseball," they quote Commy as saying he will "run out of organized baseball" the guilty players, "even tho seven of the players have a cash value of $230,000." (Not that they were being paid anywhere near that much by Comiskey.)

Finally, the *Digest* quotes Cicotte at length. It mentions Jackson's darker statements but does not report his insistence that he played every game to win, at bat and in the field. Lefty Williams and Happy Felsch get brief mention. Happy "adds that he was told the games were already 'fixt,' and that he might as well have his share of the spoils." The *Digest* also contained several cartoons from Chicago papers; one from St. Louis has a gambler digging a grave for baseball, beside those of boxing and horseracing.

BUT WOULD THERE BE A TRIAL?

Even as the first evidence of a World Series fix trickled into the grand jury hearings, indictments of ballplayers did not seem probable. "The authorities" who were leaking information to the press said that they would be content to "purge the game of any taint of scandal . . . for the good of the sport,"[31] but a trial to bring individuals to justice was not likely. Gambling was a widespread practice that was unregulated, and baseball was a sport, and cases involving bribery to influence the outcome of games had not been routinely brought into the court system. However, with the player "confessions" on record and the names of at least several gamblers in hand, the grand jury indictments meant that there would be an attempt to put those accused on trial.

But this was baseball, where "it ain't over till it's over." Just months after the hearings ended, the grand jury papers and the signed confessions vanished. In 1929, Ban Johnson recalled for the *Chicago Tribune* that the disappearance was discovered in December, when Judge Robert E. Crowe took over as the new state's attorney.[32] Most sources agree that Rothstein and Comiskey probably had teamed up to make this happen, through their lawyers and other intermediaries. Rothstein must not be implicated. Comiskey was still hopeful that some, if not all of his players could be cleared and play for him again, perhaps after serving suspensions or paying fines.

Landis's term as the game's first all-powerful commissioner began in January 1921. Soon after he took office, Landis let it be known that even if the players were not found guilty in the courts, they would not necessarily ever play ball again. Pressed by *The Sporting News*, he did not mention names or numbers, leaving others to speculate if he would punish the players according to the level of their participation in the fix or possibly forgive players against whom there was little or no evidence. But Landis was, without doubt, now in charge.

For a time, it appeared that there would be no trial. The players who had confessed repudiated their statements and asked to be reinstated so they could go to spring training. But Judge Landis squashed their hopes, placing them on an ineligible list until they were cleared.

Imagine Johnson's reaction when the evidence that the grand jury had collected—from gamblers and ballplayers—vanished into the Chicago winter. After all this—no trial? *Say it ain't so!* Sure enough, the original indictments were dismissed and the case dropped.[33] But with the strong support of Browns owner Phil Ball, Johnson was determined to revive the case. At its next meeting, "the American League teams had resolved that all guilty parties in the fix should be punished and [the owners] allocated $50,000, if necessary, for the purpose."[34]

There was talk that the new baseball czar, Landis, would make his own investigation. Johnson at first waited, then went to Landis. Landis said he planned to pursue the matter no further, but regardless of what the jury found, he would bar all crooked players from the game.

Johnson recalled his conversation with Landis going like this:

At [State's Attorney Crowe's] suggestion, therefore, I went to see Commissioner Landis. It was up to him to prosecute the players and I wanted to give all the assistance I could. . . . At Judge Landis' office I asked him what progress he had made and he said: "None."

"Are you hopeful of making any?" I asked.

"No."

"How long have you been of that mind?" I asked him.

"For two weeks," he answered.

"And you have not notified me? You know the American League has given its pledge to prosecute and it must be done. Are you through?"

"I am," he replied.

"Then we will take it up," I told him. Then the commissioner asked me if I did not think that people would think that it was due to my enmity for Comiskey that I was following this thing up.

"I can't help what people think," I replied. "As I see my duty, I intend to perform it."[35]

Johnson added that Landis did not regard it as his duty, because "the affair had taken place prior to his election as commissioner." Johnson later said that this is when he first "lost faith in" Landis and started to break from him. "I had decided he didn't want to cooperate."[36]

The trial was indeed in jeopardy. *The Sporting News* reported that it "looked like the combination of lawyers for and against a baseball cleanup . . . had pretty well destroyed the hope of ever getting the indicted ball players to trial. There was so much evidence to be digested, and the criminal courts were so congested with other cases, and all that."[37]

But Ban Johnson was now free to go ahead. He flew into motion, traveling great distances, "a two-month odyssey," to "reassemble the evidence and rebuild the case."[38] "Johnson worked like a beaver; he traveled 10,000 miles in following leads and digging up evidence, pursued Bill Burns, one of the fixers, into Mexico, even induced Bill to bring a trunkful of evidence back to Chicago."[39]

Fred Lieb may be exaggerating about how much evidence Bill Burns possessed, but there may have been a trunk involved with Ban Johnson's pursuit of this witness, as we will see shortly. In Johnson's memoirs, he gives this project the title "Going It Alone." A decade later, perhaps to challenge Johnson's story of a one-man crusade, Comiskey noted that the directors of the American League had approved his request for $40,000 to investigate, and another $10,000 to employ a lawyer to work with the prosecution. The American League also picked up the tab for the trial itself.[40]

Hugh Fullerton wrote in his column that "Judge Landis has a big job on his hands," namely, deciding exactly whom to expel from baseball for their knowledge of the fix and for wagering on that knowledge. Fullerton wrote that he knew Rube Benton had talked with his friends about the fix before the Series and had bet and won some money, although he "three times changed his story about the amount he won." But Benton was not the only one; he "had plenty of company on his own team [the Giants]."[41]

A few weeks later, Fullerton again reminded Landis publicly that Benton should not be expelled by himself, because that "would be unfair to him unless all the others who bet receive the same treatment." In Fullerton's view, if all the guilty Giants were duly punished, "not much will be left of the team." Fullerton was hopeful that Heinie Zimmermann's recent public attack on Giants manager John McGraw would "open up the entire manner of crooked practice in baseball and give us a real housecleaning."[42]

When the prosecution moved to delay the hearing of the Black Sox case until after the 1921 season was over, Landis repeated the official suspension of the accused players. Many White Sox fans had hoped that an off-season trial would clear at least some of the players before opening day. Now they grew impatient with the slow process of bringing the case to trial. Hugh Fullerton wrote,

> The fans believe something is being covered up . . . that organized baseball is afraid to have the entire truth known and that the stalling is not for the purpose of collecting further evidence, but because the baseball club owners do not want all the truth known. This is not my opinion . . . but the view of a score or more who have written me, and who certainly reflect the general opinion among fans.[43]

But Fullerton applauded Landis's action of barring the indicted players, which removed Comiskey from "an unpleasant and ticklish situation." The Comiskey–Johnson feud was center stage again— Johnson, "the guiding genius of the prosecution," and Comiskey, "the one legally responsible to lose if the players choose to try to bring suit." Fullerton pointed out the conflict club owners felt, when faced with the desire to keep their teams intact, but also to help the sport clean house. That, said Fullerton, is where baseball could rely on Judge Landis.

JOHNSON ENSURES A TRIAL

Historian Lee Allen: "The fight to convict the Black Sox was largely the work of Ban Johnson, who labored tirelessly to track down witnesses and make the accusations stick." Johnson had the financial support of the American League owners. The Browns' Phil Ball told Johnson "that if the crooked White Sox players weren't prosecuted he wouldn't remain in baseball."[44] Johnson's work resulted in new indictments against the original thirteen and five more gamblers, handed up March 26, 1921.

Johnson's task of trying to collect enough evidence for a trial was not undertaken entirely alone. J. G. Taylor Spink of *The Sporting News*, a Johnson supporter, put Johnson in touch with St. Louis gamblers.

But the first thing Johnson did was to go after Billy Maharg. *Philadelphia North American* reporter James Isaminger, whose interview with Maharg had appeared the day before Cicotte's grand jury appearance, arranged for a meeting at a Philadelphia hotel. Here is Johnson's recollection of that encounter.

> Maharg told his story naively, as if there was no thought in his mind of any wrong doing. But he was willing to make amends or he wanted revenge—so he became our star witness. I at once took him back to Chicago with me . . . and he made his deposition.[45]

With Maharg's story, Johnson now needed corroboration, and that meant he needed Sleepy Bill Burns. But Burns was in hiding. According to Spink, Johnson bought a trunk and gave it to Mrs. Burns, so she could make a trip to Mexico, and that's how Johnson found Burns's hideout. But there are other accounts.

Isaminger and Johnson exchanged telegrams on April 5, the reporter giving Johnson two Texas addresses for "the man you want to know. . . . All must be confidential." Isaminger suggested that Johnson send Burns a Western Union telegram. Johnson replied that Burns should have no knowledge that he was being sought. But on April 19, Maharg wired Burns with the word that "Ban and I will be in Ranger [Texas] Friday evening at latest . . . going to do something for you relative to our trouble."[46] Maharg asked Burns to reply to the American League office in Chicago. Instead, Burns took off across the Mexican border.

On April 25, Johnson wrote to Harry L. Davis, governor of Ohio. He told Davis that Bill Burns had been reindicted and had fled from Texas to Mexico. Then Johnson asked Davis to lobby the governor of Texas for his help.[47]

According to the *Chicago Times*, the story of how Burns was found was "a wild west thriller, filled with moonshiner's gun play, rattlesnakes, wolves and the discomforts of the chaparral cactus trail." Bill Maharg, in Chicago, was asked by Ban Johnson and the district attorney to accept the assignment of tracking down Burns. Maharg, who had spent a year with Burns at his Texas ranch, had been fishing and hunting with the quarry south of the border and knew the terrain. But it was not an easy trek.

Maharg learned Burns was fishing on Devil's River, and Maharg's rented car took two weeks to make it to the reunion. In the American League records of the scandal are numerous handwritten letters from

Bill Maharg to Ban Johnson describing his trip to retrieve Bill Burns, "fording through Texas looking for Bill."

Once Burns was found, it took a few hours for Maharg to persuade him to be another star witness in the Black Sox trial. Johnson later said,

> "Together with . . . a State's Attorney assistant [John F. Tyrrell], I went there [to Del Rio, Texas] and got [Burns's] story. We also induced Burns to come back to Chicago with us. With this evidence we had the keystone of the arch and thereafter the building was easier but slow."[48]

Burns testified in 1921 that Maharg had promised him immunity from prosecution, "at the instigation of Ban Johnson." Burns also received $300 in expenses from Johnson, and more money had been promised.[49] These admissions helped support the defense's case that Burns and Maharg were pawns of Johnson, whose feuding with the Sox's owner Comiskey was widely known, and that the gamblers had told Johnson what he wanted to hear.

The story of the "capture" of Sleepy Bill Burns—like Sir Henry Morton Stanley's search for Dr. David Livingstone in Africa nearly fifty years earlier—would have sold a lot of newspapers. Johnson was contacted by James Isaminger and John C. Eckel, both of the *Philadelphia North American*. Johnson replied,

> In order to keep Burns beyond the reach of the lawyers for the defense, we were obliged to "put him away." If the Texas story became public property our most important witness might be uncovered by the enemy. Just as soon as he is in our possession, I will have no objection to a full write-up of the chase through Texas to the Mexican border.[50]

Protecting Bill Burns from those who would intimidate or buy him off became a priority for Johnson. However, there was at least one "sighting" of Burns while he was "put away." A *Chicago Tribune* reporter recognized Burns as the indicted man for whom "detectives have combed the continent," as he was "calmly walking in Dearborn street" (in Chicago) with "a short, stout man of middle age." The reporter trailed Burns and his companion from Dearborn and Madison north to the Cunard building, where he and Burns took the elevator to the tenth floor. Burns then entered the office of John Tyrrell's law firm—also the firm of Charles V. Barrett, Ban Johnson's lawyer.[51]

That evening, the reporter phoned Ban Johnson and told him that he had seen Bill Burns and implied that Johnson had been in the law office to meet with Burns. Johnson denied seeing Burns and asked the reporter to "publish nothing concerning his presence. It might hurt our case."

> "Whom do you mean by we?" he [Johnson] was asked.
>
> "Why, the state's attorney's office. Anything that is said should come from Judge Crowe's office."
>
> "Is it likely," Johnson was asked, "that evidence is being gathered to be presented at the trial in July that may incriminate Owner Comiskey of the White Sox?"
>
> "O, I really couldn't say anything about the case," was his quick reply. "I don't think anything should be said at this time."

Two weeks before the trial began, Johnson wrote to New York lawyer James R. Price that he was pleased to learn in a letter from Burns that "he has not been approached by the enemy." He also instructed Price to "discontinue the [New York City] Pinkerton men tomorrow."[52] Chicago Pinkertons guarded Johnson's star witnesses, Burns and Joe Gedeon, and brought them safely to the courthouse to testify.

With Burns and Maharg in hand, the prosecution was ready to go to trial. But the criminal court system was clogged with cases, and the Black Sox trial could not even get into the legal system's on-deck circle. Wrangling among the lawyers also made it difficult to proceed faster than a snail's pace. Another opening day came and another season started its long journey toward another October, and the public was losing interest in the fate of the indicted men.

Commissioner Landis and Ban Johnson helped break one deadlock between the lawyers, but it took Judge "Direct Action McDonald"[53]—the one who had called the original grand jury—to step in with the solution. He took the case out of the overcrowded criminal courts, out of the hands of Judge John Sullivan, and put it into another court qualified to act as a relief tribunal. There, a judge set a date for the entering of pleas, and the trial followed soon after.

THE PLAN TO KIDNAP ABE ATTELL

Ban Johnson was determined to bring to justice not only the lower-level gamblers who had been indicted, but also those who had hatched the plot and bankrolled it. In a telegram Johnson sent on May 24, 1921, to reporter Frank G. Menke, he said that he needed witnesses to place Attell in Chicago before and during the 1919 Series. On June 2, Johnson wrote to Menke again, this time to enlist his help in publicizing the coming trial. He wanted national exposure that would result in indictments for Arnold Rothstein and Abe Attell. A few weeks later, Menke asked Johnson for a statement on the menace of gambling. "I would insure publicity of same under your signature in every city of size in America." The next day, Menke wired to ask for "skeletonized facts" and offered to write the piece for Johnson.[54]

So determined was Johnson to bring Attell to justice that, days before the trial began, he and Chicago lawmen hatched a plan to abduct him. They were certain that Attell would be ringside at the "fight of the century"—Jack Dempsey vs. Georges Carpentier, on July 2, in Jersey City, New Jersey. Johnson:

> One of the State's Attorneys went to New York with a detective. The plan was to seize [Attell] at the train and railroad him to Chicago. All the necessary papers were drawn to bring this about, but some one got to an official and he sold out for $5,000 and the plan failed. Corruption and the lure of easy gain runs all through this sordid story.[55]

Ban Johnson had a conference in New York with Arnold Rothstein during the grand jury hearings, and the *Chicago Tribune* reported that Johnson returned to Chicago convinced that although Rothstein admitted that he knew about the "frameup," he had not been in on it himself.[56] Johnson changed that view about Rothstein's involvement over the next months, as he learned more and gathered evidence for the coming trial. He was also convinced that Rothstein was behind the missing grand jury papers.[57]

The surviving letters and telegrams sent and received by Ban Johnson in the spring of 1921 suggest that he and his friends were networking all over the country for evidence that could help convict the indicted players and gamblers.[58]

THE TRIAL

The Black Sox trial began on June 27, 1921, and ended August 2. It was "vigorously contested"[59] all the way, from the eight days of jury selection to the wrangling at the end over how the jury was to be instructed before their deliberations. A Cubs' fan named William Kiefer was excused from jury duty because he never visited the Sox's park and Cubs' fans were assumed to be prejudiced against their cross-town rivals.[60]

When robbers blew the safe at Comiskey Park on July 11 and made off with $3,000 (the Yankees and drawing card Babe Ruth were in town, which always meant big takes at the box office), the press showed that it had doubts about the facts ever making it to the public. "Owner Charles Comiskey denied reports that the safe contained papers pertaining to the former White Sox players now on trial."[61]

The players were defended by a "dream team" that included Michael Ahern, later "Al Capone's favorite lawyer";[62] Thomas Nash; Ben Short; and James "Ropes" O'Brien, who earned his nickname as a prosecutor noted for winning convictions—and hangings. Initially, O'Brien was retained by Ban Johnson as a special prosecutor, but he switched sides before the trial.

Whether Charles Comiskey contributed to pay for this group of "Chicago's finest" has never been certain, but it seems very likely. Again, everything suggests that Comiskey held out hope that some or all of the players would be reinstated after they were acquitted, perhaps after paying fines or serving suspensions. The appearance for the defense (!) of Kid Gleason, Eddie Collins, and Ray Schalk just could not have happened without Comiskey's permission. Bill Veeck Jr. believed that Comiskey never dreamed Landis would throw his players out of baseball if they were acquitted.[63]

Comiskey's nemesis, Ban Johnson, had not pressed for the trial to clear the names of individual players, but to clean up baseball's damaged image. The sport had begun to expel players who had gambling ties. But there had never before been a public trial of this magnitude.

Ban Johnson was confident that the story he had pieced together "from the testimony of the witnesses, from the stenographic records of the confessions of the players and from the testimony of betting commissioners and others connected with the affair [would] stand up before a jury."[64]

Johnson refused to give Comiskey and the Sox organization any credit at all for the clean-up of baseball.

> We did think that we had not been rendered assistance from one interested party—the Chicago White Sox. Before the trial opened, Judge Barrett of our counsel talked to an official of the White Sox

and said, "We have been working on this case for three solid months and we have not had an iota of cooperation from the Chicago club. I want you to understand that we feel you have not rendered us the slightest assistance in the preparatory work."[65]

The press coverage of the trial noted that the defense team contended continuously that Ban Johnson had instigated the prosecution because of the feud between himself and Comiskey. The star witnesses for the prosecution, Bill Burns and Billy Maharg, knew of the feud and the defense claimed that they were hoping to collect Comiskey's $10,000 reward money by assisting Johnson.

The defense lawyers took turns hammering at Johnson in the hours they spent summing up before the jury. Johnson, they said, controlled who testified and who did not, steering things to wreck Comiskey's team, while the real villains, Rothstein and Attell and Sullivan, went unpunished. They chided him for telling what he knew to the grand jury "in the dark," but not in the bright light of the courtroom. They urged the jury to not let Johnson run them.[66]

None of the players testified, except to repudiate the statements that they had made to the 1920 grand jury. Their silence may have been a good defense strategy, but in the long run, it worked against them. What were they hiding? White Sox historian Richard C. Lindberg suggested that "a deal had been reached. The players agreed to remain silent about the Comiskey 'plantation' in return for unspecified protection."[67]

The prosecution asked for five years in jail and fines of $2,000 as punishment for the accused players. The lawyers argued with Judge Hugo Friend for nearly five hours over how the jury would be instructed. On August 2, after less than three hours of deliberation, about 10:40 P.M., the jury reached their verdict, and at 11:22 P.M., the judge and defendants were back in the courtroom for the reading of that decision. Before the jury delivered their verdict, Judge Friend stated that "there was so little evidence against Felsch and Weaver, that he doubted whether he could let a guilty verdict stand" against those two players. (Friend had disallowed Felsch's interview with Reutlinger as evidence.)

All players and gamblers were acquitted of the conspiracy charges. Without any clear confessions, and with scant evidence, the fraud charges were difficult to prove—a longshot. (There was no law in Illinois that prohibited "fixing" or throwing games.) Historian Harold Seymour described the trial as superficial at best, farcical at worst. No serious effort was made to uncover the full truth about the scandal or to really grapple with the gamblers. By containing the mess within limited perimeters and focusing primarily on the ball players, the trial served the interests of both the gamblers and the baseball industry.[68]

Indeed, the focus of the trial was kept squarely on the players and the handful of low-level gamblers. Hugh Fullerton was among those who were disturbed by this seeming whitewashing.

The names of a dozen persons, not hitherto connected with or even suspected of complicity in or [of having] guilty knowledge of the fixing of the 1919 world series have been openly flaunted during this trial. There is no doubt that many more persons were actively implicated in the plot to debauch the national game than those indicted and prosecuted. The startling evidence is that dozens KNEW of the plot—had guilty knowledge and were willing to participate in the profits or advantages accruing from such knowledge—who perhaps were not guilty of actual wrongdoing.[69]

The "not guilty" verdict was greeted with wild enthusiasm by the players, who were quick to congratulate each other and the jury, while shouting to the reporters over the cheering crowd. Eddie Cicotte leaped to his feet and pounded Joe Jackson on the back, then was the first player to the jury box. There, he thanked foreman William Barry, as the party continued for several minutes, with Judge Friend smiling his approval.

LANDIS'S EDICT

After the trial, the players celebrated at a local restaurant into the wee hours, but when they awoke, Judge Landis's verdict—the one that counted more—had come down. All players charged—and McMullin—were banished. They could apply for reinstatement, but it was unlikely that Landis would change his mind. Here is the well-known Landis edict:

Regardless of the verdicts of juries, no player who throws a ball game, no player that undertakes or promises to throw a ball game, no player that sits in conference with a bunch of crooked players and gamblers where the ways and means of throwing games are discussed and does not promptly tell his club about it, will ever play professional baseball.

Landis's ruling would be criticized as harsh and unfair to the players who may have done little or nothing to actually throw the Series of 1919 and who had never confessed to anything. But no one could doubt the ruling's effectiveness. Baseball had been sliding down the path that had destroyed boxing and horse racing, but Landis's verdict, along with the amazing slugging of Babe Ruth, had turned things around and restored the faith of fans. There would be more reports of thrown games, thrown before and after the 1919 Series, but Landis was careful to keep them from becoming anything like the Black Sox scandal.

Landis's priorities seemed to have been: (1) save the image of baseball, so the franchises would retain their financial value to the owners; (2) cover the owners and previous baseball leadership, who had known about the gamblers for years and done nothing (they may have even gambled themselves—some certainly had ties, as Fullerton and others pointed out a few times); (3) deal with only the public scandal (the 1919 World Series fix), in a decisive, firm way. Although Joe Jackson and/or Buck Weaver could have been sorted out from the others who conspired to fix games and then followed through on their plans, Landis wanted to keep it short, sweet, and simple, and it was a bonus having a star like Jackson in the accused group, because "no player is above the new law." Landis may also have been remembering Jackson's "slacker" image from 1918, but that seems incidental.

While the public and the sporting press generally applauded the expulsion of the Black Sox at the time, historians aware of the bigger picture of gambling in baseball look back on the action with doubts about its fairness.

To protest this arbitrary judgment on any grounds is to run a twofold risk: that of undermining one of baseball's most sanctimonious myths, and that of awakening the ghost of Landis. Yet the fact is that the players were denied their civil rights by the application of baseball law. Today such a ruling could never happen lest it evoke a heavy lawsuit; and even in 1921 its imposition was a legal error, resting on the moral consensus of baseball owners who were supported by the general public—all apparently unaware of the implication for civil liberties but overaware of their own pious definitions of sin and evil.[70]

In Chicago, where the rumors of a fix had been thickest after the 1919 Series, receipts were up by about a half million dollars in 1920. In 1921, the summer of the trial, attendance was down only slightly. Babe Ruth hit fifty-nine home runs. Baseball had survived.

THE LARGER COVER-UP

Comiskey's motives for wanting to keep the fix hidden are easy to understand. He and his lawyers had these priorities: (1) cover Comiskey, so he would not lose the franchise; (2) cover up the fix, so he would not lose a huge investment; (3) cover the players, so if they were reinstated, they would still be White Sox property. But his cover-up was part of a larger one. Baseball was in the grips of gamblers. If the public found out, the sport would be endangered, if not doomed. Living with "guilty knowledge" and the threat of being exposed with that knowledge for almost a year must have been very painful for Comiskey.

On the heels of the grand jury indictments, *The Sporting News* took Comiskey to task for suppressing what he knew, "to the shame of baseball." He had been "posing as a reformer" and was now a wreck of the beloved figure baseball once knew.

But there was more to keep out of the public eye. Baseball was seen as a sport, an entertainment, a *pastime*. And it was in baseball's interest to keep it that way. In fact, baseball was also a business, and a big one. Franchises in 1919 were at or approaching the million dollar mark in worth. Baseball was also a monopoly. Its "reserve clause," in every player contract, bound players to their teams, prohibiting them from playing anywhere else. This meant that players had no bargaining power at all. They could accept the contract offered or find a different line of work. Players disgruntled about contract negotiation might hold out, but they found no sympathy from reporters and they almost always gave in and signed.

Charles Comiskey has been painted as an evil monster, and as a "typical purveyor of the business ethics of the era"[71]—either way, in the words of Pogo, "it's a mighty soberin' thought." Comiskey maximized his own profits and spent little on his players. Yet he could be generous with them, too, rewarding good results with bonuses or helping veterans in financial trouble. What is hard to keep in mind when observing how attendance soared and revenues rose after the war is that as poorly as Comiskey's players were paid, they were still making wages well above what they would receive back in the mines and mills. The Civil War didn't end all kinds of slavery, the slave owners had learned to disguise and legalize it.

The Federal League was another factor in the baseball economics that led to the 1919 World Series fix.[72] When the Federal League collapsed in 1915, American and National League owners tried to recoup the losses they had suffered—and World War I was not making it easy. Many salaries in 1916 were cut or frozen. It really was not until the war ended that baseball started getting back on its financial feet, during the 1919 season. That is why the Sox protested their "wartime" wages and appealed for a better deal that summer, almost causing a strike.

Before the Federal League folded, it had taken Major League Baseball (MLB) to federal court, complaining about restraint of free trade and antitrust violations. Chicago federal judge Kenesaw Mountain Landis (a high school dropout who got interested in the law while working as a court reporter) sat on the case until the Feds were out of business. At one point he interrupted the trial to declare, "Both sides must understand that any blows at the thing called baseball would be regarded by this court as a blow to a national institution." Landis's "strategic inaction"[73] scored big points for the judge with MLB, which named Landis as its first commissioner.

But another lawsuit was filed, this one brought by the Federal League Baltimore club and accusing the National League and the American League of acting as an illegal monopoly. The Baltimore complaint was that MLB destroyed the Federal League by buying up some of the Federal League clubs, thus inducing all of the Federal League clubs except Baltimore to quit the league. The Sherman Act forbade monopolies by big businesses, so what was at stake in this case was the very definition of baseball—was it a sport or was it a business?

So, for baseball the business, the timing of the disclosure of the Big Fix could not have been worse.

> Revelations about baseball being sold out were appearing in the newspapers daily *while the appeal was being heard.* And when you think about it, what does a crooked player believe? *He believes that baseball is a business, not a sport. . . .* So the appeals court which ruled in favor of Organized Baseball heard the case with a monster looking over their shoulders: the

monster of professionalism run amok. . . . This unusual circumstance is reflected in an odd decision.[74]

The case lingered on and was appealed until it was finally argued at the Supreme Court on April 19, 1922; the case was decided on May 29, 1922, with Justice Oliver Wendell Holmes delivering the opinion. The Federal League was dead and its corpse cold, and one of the defendants, the old National Commission, was long gone, too, having been replaced by the commissioner, Landis. Yet the decision of 1922 has stood up until the present. Baseball was granted an exemption from the antitrust laws.

"The business is giving exhibitions of base ball, which are purely state affairs." Baseball was not interstate commerce, because the travel required in the leagues was "a mere incident, not the essential thing."

Economic reporter John Helyar has called the decision "a piece of fiction that would grow sillier with each passing year. But it undergirded everything about the way baseball operated."[75] The reserve clause was safe, as the draft would be later; baseball answered only to its own authority, its absolutely omnipotent commissioner.

In pondering the lessons of the fix and cover-up, I have come up with a maxim. It is a twist on the one we associate with Lord Acton, about power corrupting. Here it is: Power covers up, and absolute power covers up absolutely—but not permanently.

The scandal of 1919–20 was not "eight men out" for throwing the Series. That is only how it went down in history. The scandal was that baseball was being preyed upon by gamblers. That the owners, thanks to the reserve clause, ruled over the players as masters over slaves. Players could accept the contracts offered, or they could go into farming or back to digging in mines. As baseball boomed into the national pastime, money poured in. But it only trickled in for the players. The owners knew about the gamblers, as did the league presidents. By labeling the event the "Black Sox scandal," they conveniently swept a lot under the rug, safely out of the public's sight.

Fans across the country wanted to believe baseball was not rigged. They were eager to believe that the fix of the 1919 World Series was an isolated incident. (Actually, a lot of fans disbelieved that the fix really happened, even after Sox players confessed.) Is it any different today? Americans want to believe that corporate America is not run by greedy CEOs and boards of directors—that the Enron case (for example) is an isolated exception to the rule. However, it does not look that way.[76]

Baseball itself never investigated what happened in the 1919 World Series. No one asked what baseball personnel, besides the infamous eight players, were involved with the fix, profited from it, or knew about it before, during, or immediately after the Series ended. No one asked what Charles Comiskey knew and when he knew it. No one asked what Ban Johnson and the National Commission knew, and when.

The trial of the Sox brought to public attention the shabby treatment of ballplayers by owners. Revolts by players, such as that in the Federal League, had exposed the owners as tightwads. What was really shocking was that the system that seemed so slavish was perfectly legal. Club owners were making fortunes, and there was nothing to force them to give the players a penny more than they cared to. Baseball was a mirror of the country, but it was best that the fans did not realize that, not when the reflection suggested the immoral, greedy, but legal exploitation of labor.

The term "Black Sox" predates the scandal. If the root of the fix was Comiskey's tightness with his money and his deceitful ways with his employees, the term "Black Sox" illustrates theses qualities. In 1917, Comiskey had decided to take the cost of laundering the uniforms, fifty cents per wash, out of his players' paychecks. In response, the Sox refused to wash their unis—which got quite dirty. (The rest of the story? One version is that Comiskey gave in, paid for the laundering, then deducted the cost from the Sox's World Series shares. Another has him removing the uniforms from the lockers and fining the players.)

But was Comiskey such a Scrooge? Some researchers think not, and argue that the 1919 White Sox—while underpaid—may have had the highest payroll in baseball. Several of the banned players expressed remorse for having wronged an owner who had treated them if not well, then at least better than they had been treated elsewhere in baseball. Modern skirmishes between players and owners may make us sympathetic to the plight of one side or the other, according to which we see as the greediest. But in the case of Big Fix, as in contemporary conflicts, it is not at all clear that the owner was any more or any less greedy than the players.[77]

LABOR RELATIONS

An incident in the 1921 trial illustrates how sensitive baseball was about its labor relations. On the witness stand, Charles Comiskey was asked if he ever "jumped" teams (broke a contract) as a player, and he became highly agitated in defense of his image.[78]

What had gotten Commy so upset? After all, Comiskey had been a member of the Brotherhood of Professional Baseball Players. The brotherhood was formed in 1889 "to protect and promote the rights of players." Eventually, the brotherhood produced its own league, in 1890, and when the story broke, *The Sporting News* ran it under a succession of three headlines: (1) THE BROTHERHOOD; (2) Every Man But [Cap] Anson Pledged to Jump the League; and (3) The Greatest Move in the History of the National Game.[79] But, lacking money and organization, the brotherhood was gone by the start of the 1891 season. Bill Veeck summed it up as "a one-year disaster"that was motivated by a revolt against the reserve clause.

And Veeck adds this: "Charles Comiskey, as manager of the St. Louis Browns . . . quit his job and threw in his lot with the players." Veeck calls this Comiskey's "one foolish descent into altruism" (which is not quite accurate). Noting that Commy might even have written the bylaws of the brotherhood himself, Veeck speculates that Commy might have held onto the bylaws to prove that he "had always been sympathetic to the just aspirations of the working man."[80]

When Ban Johnson, as president of the Western League at the time, looked back on the brotherhood experiment, he noted that while Comiskey had gone to the new league, the man who would later battle him over salaries and work under him during the crisis in October 1919—Kid Gleason—had not.[81]

In 1889, with Charles Comiskey as their player-manager (the innovative first sacker hit .286 with 102 RBIs), the St. Louis Browns finished second, three games back of Brooklyn, in the American Association—then a major league. But in 1890, who's on first but Comiskey, with the Chicago Pirates in the Players League (also considered a major league); he also managed them to a 75–62 forth-place finish. Because he was a playing *manager*, Comiskey was probably not subject to the reserve clause—that is Veeck's observation. So *technically*, while he certainly did "jump" to the Players League, he may not have broken any contract. In any case, there were no hard feelings; in 1891, he was back in St. Louis, as player-manager, finishing second again. Then Comiskey was off to the Cincinnati National League team, where he played and managed three more years before hanging up his cleats and his—whatever managers hang up.

The "playing manager" was an economic move, and sometimes a necessity—times were very tight for baseball back in the days of rising and folding franchises and leagues. By having the manager play, a salary was saved. But the position must have strained even those who, like Comiskey, were deemed to be good at it. As players, they shared the same plight as the rest of the roster—they traveled with them and ate with them and played cards with them. But as managers, accountable to the owners (or designated middlemen), they had to maintain some distance, too. After all, they were "management."

The dual role can create awkward situations. At best, the player-manager becomes an ombudsman, someone who can take real grassroots problems higher and get them resolved or who can communicate the reasons behind policies that are hard to understand from the grassroots. Comiskey was apparently a well-respected player-manager.

A former player might be expected to be a more understanding and generous owner. And perhaps Comiskey does not deserve the title of "the cheapest skate in town" (Veeck). Every owner wielded the reserve clause. It may well be that his secretary, the man who often negotiated player contracts, Harry Grabiner, deserved the title more than Comiskey.

But Comiskey's tirade in the 1921 trial, reacting to charges that he had been a renegade player, shows how far he had come since 1890.

Some may wonder why Comiskey, after the lid was blown off the fix, did not try to save at least Buck Weaver, whom he knew was not in on the scheme and who received no money; or Jackson, whom he knew played to win and who tried to show his team the money that Williams had given him. I believe that Comiskey and his advisors could not risk sorting out individual roles in the fix, because that would show that they knew who *had* played at least some games to lose, who *had been* in the conspiracy, and who *else* had received money. Defending Weaver or Jackson was simply too risky. It was difficult enough to control the spin, with the story kept in its oversimplified version. *Eight players conspired with gamblers to lose the Series.* Eight names were linked in newspapers across the country. Each received identical letters from Comiskey, notifying them of their suspension, soon to be banishment.

The press was kinder to Comiskey than it might have been when the cover-up came undone. For example, John Sheridan of *The Sporting News* surely realized that Comiskey must have known of the fix right after, if not during (or before) the Series. But he chose to underline Comiskey's doubt and his reluctance to falsely accuse anyone without harder evidence.

I was inclined to censure Comiskey for not cleaning house last fall. Commy had moral, if not legal, proof of the iniquities since confessed by his players. The grand jury investigation told Commy little that he did not know a year ago. He probably did not know how many of his players were involved in the faking. But he is too keen a baseball man not to know trying from not trying when he sees it. I asked Si Sanborn last week why Commy did not run the rats last fall. Si said that Commy did not know absolutely who was guilty, how many, how deeply, and that he feared greatly that if he made a wholesale cleaning he would hurt some innocent man.[82]

REFLECTIONS ON THE COVER-UP

Most interesting about Bert Collyer's efforts to bring the fix to the light of day, as Comiskey (and the baseball establishment) fought to keep it buried, are the motives that were in play. A scandal—and who knew how far it might extend, if a really thorough probe was made by independent investigators?—could reduce baseball to the level of the discredited sports of horse racing and boxing. Baseball's clean image had not only made it attractive for fans and betting America, but it made the team owners millionaires. Baseball was a legal monopoly, a business in which players were in fact slaves. Yes, their "plantation" was a wonderful diamond inside a cozy park, where they were cheered and idolized by thousands of fans—but their status was fragile and totally dependent on their owners. They were property. They could accept the contracts they were offered or go back to jobs where they would *work*, not play, for a living. The owners had a good thing going, and they knew it.

Bert Collyer made his living by selling advice to gambling Americans. His paper offered tips on stocks, horse races, and fights. (In the twenties, the *Eye* named college football all star teams, so odds on that sport were also likely to appear in the *Eye*.) If baseball games could be *fixed*, that removed the element of *chance*, which is so necessary to gamblers. The fix of the 1919 World Series hardly damaged baseball at all—fans continued to believe, despite all the rumors, that baseball games were unfixable, as surely as the Titanic (before it sank) was thought to be unsinkable. But the rumors of the fix shook those who were bettors or who depended on bettors—like Bert Collyer's publication's readers.

So the folks who blew the whistles first and loudest were not the baseball owners or the National Commission. No, they were Bert

Collyer; Harry Redmon of St. Louis, who had gambled and lost big; Billy Maharg and Sleepy Bill Burns, who both claimed to have bet on the Reds to win Game Three—and lost big. (In the Lee Magee case, it was Boston gambler Jim Costello who provided the key testimony and evidence.) And so, ironically, it was "the dark side" of the marriage between gambling and baseball that was most anxious to clean things up. Baseball would, of course, take full credit.

UNSUNG HEROES?

Does this event have its equivalent of Frank Wills, the security guard whose alertness while making his rounds at the Watergate, led to the arrest of five burglars and the eventual undoing of a president? A case can be made for the first whistle-blower, Hugh Fullerton; for those who convinced Bill Veeck Sr. to call for an investigation of the suspicious August 31 Cubs–Phils game; for Judge McDonald, who convened the grand jury; for James Crusinberry, whose letter (under Fred Loomis's name) nudged the grand jury to look at the 1919 Series; or for reporter James Isaminger, whose interview with Billy Maharg may have been the catalyst that caused Eddie Cicotte to confess.

But perhaps the most obscure contribution to the unraveling of the cover-up came from someone that the books written on the subject to date do not mention at all. And that would be St. Louis lawman Elias W. Hoagland.

Just as with Frank Wills at Watergate, Hoagland's story begins with the detective-sergeant making a routine check. He and his partner Jim Vasey

> noticed a couple of flashy characters in the Hotel Jefferson [in St. Louis], a hotel which normally didn't attract that type of clientele. "They were sport-jacket fellows and they were moving around a lot on the elevators and in the dining room," Hoagland said. "we thought we'd keep an eye on them. After about a week, we spotted them coming out of a smoke shop that had often been raided as a bookmaking joint.[83]

Hoagland and Vasey found out that the two strangers were meeting with "characters the police had been arresting regularly as 'big name' gamblers. The trail got pretty hot and we decided to move in." The officers followed their suspects to their hotel room, flashed their ID, and were let in. "It turned out they were pretty well-known gamblers.

One of them owned a place in Long Island City, N.Y., and the other was a racetrack man."

The suspects balked when Hoagland decided to take them in, and they demanded to see a warrant. "We told them we didn't need any on a charge like this." What the charge was is not clear. While the suspects were detained at the station, Hoagland returned to the Jefferson to search their room.

"There were a lot of telegrams from big gamblers, and one I'll never forget. It read, 'Beware of Dickie Kerr. POISON.' The telegrams named names," said Hoagland. He turned them over to J. G. Taylor Spink, and Spink summoned American League president Ban Johnson, "who, up to that time, had been running into a stone wall with his investigations."

Johnson sifted through the telegrams and letters, which were filled with the names of White Sox players. Since the records from the 1920 grand jury hearings and the material used in the 1921 trial are not available, it is uncertain that Hoagland's find was ever used—or deemed admissible. Nor is it clear that Johnson ever "ran into a stone wall" in his investigations of the fix.

"Beware of Dickie Kerr. POISON" sounds like a message that would have been sent during the Series to warn gamblers that Games Three and Six, the two that Kerr won, were *not* fixed, and to bet on the Reds in those contests would indeed be "POISON." A number of gamblers, including Burns and Maharg, claimed later that they lost small fortunes betting on Game Three; these men apparently were not the recipients of that telegram, or else they misunderstood its warning.

Elias Hoagland and his partner Jim Vasey were proud but obscure heroes who deserve recognition for their small, but perhaps illegal role in "the start of the whole thing." If it is hard to ascertain just who deserves what blame in the fix—it appears that assigning credit for its uncovering can be tricky, too.

WHAT IF LANDIS HAD BEEN COMMISSIONER SOONER?

Judge Kenesaw Mountain Landis dealt firmly with players suspected of tossing games, and his edict put the fear of hell into players who even *thought* about asking a gambler for the time of day. But he also overpunished some players, and overlooked much—thus keeping more dirty laundry out of sight. A look at an incident that took place just two years after the Black Sox trial provides some insight into how Landis might have reacted if he had been commissioner when the cover-up of the Big Fix of 1919 started to come undone.[84] It also sheds some light on the plight of the only newspaper that made a serious attempt to investigate the rumors of the fix after the 1919 Series—*Collyer's Eye*.

On August 18, 1923, *Collyer's Eye* printed a story by Frank O. Klein about two or three Cincinnati ballplayers who, according to Klein, had been approached by gamblers and offered $15,000 each to toss a game with the Giants. Its eye-catching headline: "Scandal Rocks Baseball—New Plot to Bribe Stars: Full Exposé." The *Eye* claimed that Ban Johnson was on the case and that the newspaper had traced the trail to a certain New York real estate office. Ban Johnson may have been the only baseball authority who was open to receive help from Collyer in the war against gamblers, because Johnson knew Collyer's "knowledge of big gamblers who tried to corrupt and fix racing" was a valuable weapon.[85]

National League president John Heydler called the players, heard them deny the story under oath, and listened to the testimony of several writers who covered the Reds. Then he was urged by Landis to encourage the Cincinnati team to sue *Collyer's Eye*. He did, and the Reds announced that they would sue.[86]

Heydler said that he had investigated at once, even though *Collyer's Eye* "has no great influence in sport circles and none to speak of in baseball." Their singular attempt to expose the crookedness in the 1919 Series was not mentioned. Heydler further threatened to sue any publication, large or small, if they made unfounded charges. "We are not satisfied to favor clean baseball: we will fight for clean baseball."

Publisher Bert Collyer sent Landis a long telegram "asserting that the gambling fellowship was still active in baseball and offering to provide details. Landis never answered the telegram." Here are some excerpts, as they appeared in the *New York Times*, August 25, 1923:

It is the policy of my newspaper to print nothing without the fullest investigation and verification. . . . I am confident that my editorial staff has adhered to this policy in this instance.

President Heydler's frantic effort to raise a smoke screen behind which to hide is characteristic of him. Heydler was one of the first to yell 'fake' when my newspaper months before anyone else printed the details of the 1919 world's series. We were then [in 1919] threatened with violence, as well as legal prosecution, just as we seem to be now. Nevertheless we produced the unvarnished truth, which proved self-explanatory.

You will recall that it was *Collyer's Eye* which printed the details of the White Sox scandal months before anyone else and that we were then attacked in the same depraved manner by those who wished to cover up instead of remove the ulcer.

I now respectfully direct your attention to the statement of belief of Ban Johnson that a gambling syndicate has been conducting operations on a large scale. Investigations made by my staff and others would seem to verify these apprehensions.

Collyer informed Landis that he had appointed Major Barrett O'Hara, a former lieutenant governor of Illinois, to represent his newspaper in a conference with Landis. Collyer himself was ill and recovering in his native Canada at the time. That Landis had a dim view of Bert Collyer and his publication was made clear in a telegram he sent to the Cincinnati team: "The character of the paper rather refutes any assertion made in its columns. However, any suggestion, even from such a source, will receive a thorough investigation."[87] The press reported that O'Hara phoned Landis, but there is no record of a meeting.

Collyer accused Heydler of covering up the lingering connections between baseball and gambling by his quick dismissal of the case. He called on Heydler to resign if he really believed those connections did not exist, and he offered to work with the baseball authorities to root out and break the ties. He also challenged Heydler to make public the names and salaries paid to any and all daily newspaper reporters or sports editors, either by the league or any of its teams. This charge was in response to a number of newspapers rallying to support Heydler. And it drew at least one spirited editorial response in the mainstream press:

> If the National League or any of its members are carrying baseball writers or sports editors on their payrolls for services not legitimately rendered, it would be just as important that this fact be made public as it would to ascertain whether an effort was made to approach members of the Cincinnati club for the purpose of throwing games. Cleaning one room in the house of baseball is not enough.[88]

Frank O. Klein, the "staff investigator" for *Collyer's Eye*, was introduced by the editor of the article that caused this stir as the person who "scooped the world with details of the 1919 world's series scandal."[89] Klein had been sent from Chicago to Cincinnati to look into the rumors that implicated infielder Sammy Bohne (Cohen) and outfielder Pat Duncan, a star for the Reds in the 1919 Series. Klein heard Rothstein's name "freely bandied about" and wrote that Ban Johnson had his own investigators on the case. His story said only that Bohne and Duncan had been approached "by the agent of the gamblers" and that there was "no direct evidence" that either had accepted bribes. Klein added that the fact that the Giants won the Series only "gave color to the charges."

Heydler had cleared the players, and so did Landis.[90] The official spin given to the story had *Collyer's Eye* printing "tirades against players" and making unfounded charges out of, according to Landis, a spirit of malice. "Baseball is O.K.," Landis proclaimed, "It is being run straight."

The libel lawsuit was filed by the Reds against *Collyer's Eye* on September 7, 1923. Collyer's counsel O'Hara, trying to head it off, stated that Bohne and Duncan were "fine young fellows, gentlemen in every sense of the word, and highly rated both as ball players and as honorable individuals."[91] But he pressed for a full investigation, because he was certain that there had been "enormous" betting in Chicago and because "a sudden flood of money was poured in, one day before the series opened," which money was traced to New York. O'Hara called on baseball to find out if bettors on the Giants were unusually active in Cincinnati, too.

The case dragged on, with both sides sparring occasionally in the press. *Collyer's* said that "despite the discussion and common knowledge of the same, for reasons unknown, Heydler, Landis and Herrmann were unable or unwilling to take action to eradicate or remedy the corrupt practices" [of open gambling on the Giants–Reds games].[92] Collyer continued to insist that the case was not about the reputations of two ballplayers, but about the lingering tampering by gamblers. Baseball stood firm, insisting that gambling was no longer an issue.

Judge Landis's persistence finally got the case tried, before Judge Walter C. Lindley in Chicago federal court. Both players were cleared of charges on February 21, 1928, although the court awarded the players just $50 each, instead of the $50,000 for which they were asking. The players' reputations were saved, and baseball was spared another scandal. "Both the game, and players Bohne and Duncan, have been vindicated before the American public," Landis proclaimed.[93]

Bert Collyer's call for baseball to examine the gambling influence had been silenced—again.

A NEVER-ENDING STORY

Steve Klein has noted how Fullerton "experienced the frustration of trying to serve two masters: organized baseball and his conscience." Klein's research has turned up a letter Fullerton wrote to Joseph Medill Patterson, the owner of the *Chicago Tribune* in 1923, which illustrates this.[94]

In the letter Fullerton recalled that after the 1922 season, he tried to write a series of articles, "64 separate pieces by his count," on Comiskey for the *Tribune*. But the newspaper insisted that Fullerton clear the articles with Comiskey. Four of the articles dealt with the World Series of 1919, and Harry Grabiner, Comiskey's secretary, "laid [them] aside entirely." Fullerton and Grabiner worked on the rest of the articles for five hours, with Comiskey present and being "extremely entertaining. . . . We had another morning and revised the stuff. When we reached the crooked worlds series both Commy and Grabiner warned me that we must be careful in dealing with it. We took the four articles I had written and literally revised them to pieces—and they still were not satisfactory."

On the same day Fullerton was writing to Patterson, the sports editor of the *Tribune* sent a note to the newspaper's attorney, informing him that the articles would not be printed. "Mr. Comiskey has informed me today that he would not under any circumstances permit the series of articles written by Mr. Fullerton to go out, even with the corrections he has tried to make in them so that they would be truthful and readable." The next day, the *Trib*'s lawyer wrote Patterson: "I saw Grabiner today and there is no doubt that the series as written by Fullerton could never be approved by Comiskey. Fullerton was not accurate in anything from all reports."[95]

Patterson killed the series. The next time Fullerton wrote about the 1919 Series was for *Liberty* magazine in 1927, four years later. Steve Klein believes, and I hope, that the Fullerton series vetoed by Comiskey in January 1923 may yet be found.[96]

Fullerton hoped to have his series on Comiskey in the *Tribune* before Opening Day 1923. But there were lawsuits in progress that complicated things: Jackson, Felsch, and Risberg were suing the White Sox for back pay and damages to their reputations. Comiskey and Grabiner were concerned about what Fullerton wrote—it might show up in a courtroom. But it must have stung Fullerton when his "dearest and perhaps oldest friend"—the man he wanted to honor—snuffed it out, even after he invested hours editing it with Fullerton and Grabiner.

Because extinct newspapers like *Collyer's Eye*; yellowed trial transcripts; obscure letters like those unearthed by Steve Klein and other chance correspondence involving the baseball authorities, the White Sox management, the players and the reporters who covered the events but were unable, or unwilling, to go public with what they knew—because all of these exist—the full story of the fix, its cover-up, and its undoing may take many more decades to be told.

Even as this book was being readied for publication, exciting new information came to light. The fourth article in Frank Menke's 1924 series (see chapter 1), missing from *The Sporting News*, was printed in Menke's regular *Mansfield News* (Ohio) column. And it seems that Menke was writing about Joe Jackson and the cover-up in 1923, and probably earlier, too.

Also found (it was buried in his files for more than fifteen years, Mike Nola said) was the elusive eighth article in the 1929 series that Earl Obenshain wrote on Ban Johnson (see chapter 3). The *Cleveland Plain Dealer* had halted that series at six; the *Marietta Times* printed all ten installments, but the eighth had vanished from their records. However, the *Oakland Tribune* carried "The Eighth Obenshain," and it was a blockbuster.

Obenshain—editor of *The Sporting News* in 1919 and later employed in Ban Johnson's office—accused the owners in both leagues of "following a 'hush' policy, dropping the players without a noise and preventing an airing of dirty linen." They feared the loss of the fans who were already suspicious about the ties between players and gamblers. Then he stated something that can only be appreciated by those who understand how baseball worked so hard to discredit Bert Collyer and his publication, *Collyer's Eye,* by burying the *Eye* so deep that it has taken more than eight decades to bring it to light:

> The story of the exposé of the 1919 sell-out and the efforts to punish the guilty parties would not be complete without telling the part that *Collyer's Eye* had in the case. The fearless action by that publication in publishing evidence of crookedness, which it had obtained, gave much heart to Ban Johnson in his own investigation.

Not only does Obenshain write positively about Bert Collyer's role, he credits *Collyer's Eye* with keeping Ban Johnson on the case. Probably it was a bit more complicated.

"But the Collyer story convinced Ban Johnson, up to that time loath to believe the rumors buzzing about his ears, that something was rotten about the 1919 World Series, and with the evidence put into his hands [did Collyer turn something over to Johnson?] he began an inquiry that led to such an accumulation of testimony and confessions that baseball was amazed at the revelations." This is very flattering for Johnson, but it is a terrific oversimplification.

Such articles are like pieces of a giant puzzle, waiting to be found and assembled. I do not expect to see the puzzle completed in my lifetime or perhaps ever. But it is now clear that those pieces are scattered all over the continent, there for the finding, by anyone willing to track them down.

7

SHOELESS, KNUCKLES, AND LEFTY

JOE JACKSON

Joseph Jefferson "Shoeless Joe" Jackson was born around 1888 in Pickens County, South Carolina. He batted .408 in his first full season, for Cleveland in 1911 and was dealt to Chicago in 1915. His lifetime batting average of .356 is the third best all-time, behind Ty Cobb and Rogers Hornsby. His .375 average led both teams in the 1919 World Series. His story is surely the most complicated to tell.

Joe Jackson, by all accounts, seems to have been a simple man. But his tale is anything but simple. Earlier, we looked at his role in the Big Fix and the cover-up of the fix. Here, I will discuss Jackson's performance in the 1919 World Series. I will furnish as much evidence and testimony as I can to help readers make up their own minds about Shoeless Joe Jackson.

Joe Jackson once played a game in his socks because his feet were so badly blistered. After a hit landed him on third base, a nearby fan praised him as a "shoeless son of a gun." Besides that great nickname, he had a sweet swing that Babe Ruth said he copied. He batted his way out of the mills of South Carolina into the country's imagination, with a .408 average in 1911, his first full season. He never hit below .300 after that, and his .356 lifetime average is a well-known baseball statistic.

Less-known facts: he played more games for Cleveland than Chicago, after he broke into the majors with the Philadelphia A's; he was traded to Cleveland in a 1910 even-up for Bris "The Human Eyeball" Lord, who went on to hit .310 in 1911 and .256 lifetime—exactly 100 points under Joe; he was traded to the Sox midseason 1915 for

Braggo Roth, two other players, and the curious sum of $31,500; because of World War I, he played in just seventeen games in 1918. He hit .382 with twenty triples in 1920, the season *after* the 1919 World Series.[1]

Did Joe Jackson Play the 1919 Series to Win?

This question has remained controversial since it was first posed to the American public in 1920. In his statement to the grand jury, when details of the fix were starting to leak out through the wire services and newspapers, Jackson admitted taking $5,000 from his friend, Lefty Williams. He also denied doing anything to earn it:

> Q. Did you make any intentional errors yourself that day? [Game Four]
> A. No, sir, not during the whole Series.
> Q. Did you bat to win?
> A. Yes.
> Q. And run the bases to win?
> A. Yes, sir.
> Q. And fielded the balls at the outfield to win?
> A. I did.

This testimony went unreported. Instead, the newspapers quoted Jackson (or fabricated quotes) saying that he struck out in the clutch, just poked at the ball, and threw the ball short a number of times, giving Cincinnati runs. Eddie Cicotte had confessed earlier that day. Jackson's statement went reported as a confession, too, in most accounts. "Say it ain't so, Joe" has become a familiar phrase. Jackson always denied that there ever was a confrontation between a small boy and his fallen hero, even as he always pointed to his performance in the Series as evidence that he played every game to win. Let us now examine that evidence as best we can.

We cannot go back to October 1919. If we could, I am not sure it would make any difference. Thousands of fans watched the World Series games that fall and saw nothing out of the ordinary. The White Sox's opponents, the Cincinnati Reds, were sure that they had won the Series fair and square. The umpires noted nothing strange.

Reds manager Pat Moran went on record in the grand jury hearings.

> We defeated the White Sox fairly and squarely and I challenge anybody to prove otherwise. To my mind all these reports about fixing White Sox players are bunk. I kept pretty good watch on

things as you may imagine, and I didn't see the least thing that appeared out of the way. As far as I know there was very little betting on the Series.[2]

The reporters covering the games for Chicago and New York as well as the wire services did not write about plays that looked suspicious as if deliberate errors were being committed. Even reporters who were pretty sure that the fix was in could not be certain.

Why? Because that is the nature of baseball. Players trying their best still make errors. The best hitters can strike out in the clutch, the best pitchers can lose their effectiveness and look awful for an inning or two. If you are convinced that "the fix is in," you will find suspicious plays in *any* ballgame. If you are not on the lookout, you will not see anything except baseball.

In the 1917 World Series, which the Sox won, Joe Jackson managed only seven hits—all singles—in six games. His average was .304, with only two RBIs. Nobody accused him of anything. Lots of players, Hall of Famers, climb onto October's stage and fizzle. Another Jackson—Reggie—went 2-for-16 in the 1977 playoffs and 2-for-18 in 1982, and in fact has a lifetime .227 for forty-five playoff games. That's *Mr. October*. Of course, he did better in the World Series.

My point? The World Series has always been a pressure cooker, in which stars have struggled while obscure players have become national heroes. In a sense, it's a perfect target for fixers: the pressure can explain away errors, temporary wildness, the strikeout in the clutch.

JACKSON AT THE BAT

Those who believe Jackson was in on the fix often make statements like this, regarding Jackson's performance in 1919: "In the first five games, Joe Jackson came to bat with eleven men on base and never drove in a run. In the last three games, when the fix was off, he drove in six runs and hit the only Series home run . . . . He didn't hit in the clutch in the first five games." (Whether the fix was in for Games Three, Four, and Five is not certain.)

One of baseball's top researchers, Bill Deane, has a great reply for those who would judge players strictly by how they did in certain games:

Look at two other players in the 1919 Series. Player "A" went 2-for-18 (.111) in the first five games of the Series, failing to score or drive in a single run. But, in the last three games, after the fix was off, he went 5-for-13 (.385), with two runs and an RBI. Player "B" went 2-for-15 (.133) in the first five games, but 4-for-13 (.308) with three runs, two doubles, and four RBI in the last three, after the fix was off. In light of this new evidence, perhaps it is not too late to get Eddie Collins and Edd Roush expelled from the Hall of Fame. (From an e-mail exchange.)

Of course, Deane is being facetious here, illustrating the folly of drawing conclusions from such small sample sizes.

"Out of Position" in the Field?

Another argument sometimes made goes like this: "Jackson was not charged with any errors in the Series, but he played out of position, he let balls fall in for hits, and three of the Reds' triples went to left field, where triples are rare."

There is a difficulty in using play-by-play accounts to prove anything. In Appendix A, the seven Cincinnati triples are described using six different "eyewitness accounts" for each. There is rarely a consensus about exactly where these hits landed. For example, the last Reds' triple was either along the right-field line or to the fence in right-center. Probably it hugged the line—Gandil, who played first base, had a shot at it, according to the *Cincinnati Enquirer*—but if you consult only the Neft and Cohen account, Gandil never had a chance at the ball.

In any case, Jackson's name is nowhere mentioned in any of the accounts of any of the triples. Was he playing out of position? Or was he playing where he should have been, if the pitchers were trying for outs, and not tossing up hittable pitches? Or was he playing where the scouting reports said that he should play—reports gathered by Fred McMullin, who was in on the fix?[3] There is no way to know for sure. In 1927, Buck Weaver went on record saying that he had no recollection of anyone playing out of position in the Series. At the same time, Kid Gleason, Sox manager in 1919, said of a 1917 incident what surely held for 1919: "If there had been anything wrong . . . I would have known it. I knew everything that went on around the club." It seems likely that Gleason would have spotted anyone playing out of position, called time, and moved them.

Here is another account suggesting that the Series may have featured some "playing out of position":

In Game Five, the excitement is caused by Hod Eller fanning six Sox batters in a row, a new Series record. The Old Timer does note in the sixth inning, "Slow fielding on the part of Felsch and Jackson and a wild throw by the former put Eller on third on a poke to left center that was [ruled a double.]" Later, in the same inning "Duncan hit a fly to Jackson and Roush scored after the catch when Jackson threw wide of the plate." Roush was on third with a triple "which again caught the Sox outfield out of position." The Old Timer is sure that the Sox "lacked their old fight."[4]

Whether this account was written before the fix was uncovered or after is not clear. In any case, it is likely that no player on either team played perfectly in the eight games that fall.

Here is another example—Greasy Neale's run-scoring double in Game Four:

For some reason or other, Jackson, unnoticed, played in close back of shortstop when Neale, who is a heavy swatter, came to the bat. Neale's slant, which would ordinarily have been easy picking if Jackson had been playing back in his regular place, went over Joe's head and along he went through a lot of spiral evolutions to get to the ball. It dropped to the turf just as he got his hands on it.[5]

Because there was a runner on second at the time, perhaps Jackson had moved in to get an edge if there was a hit in front of him. A few moments earlier, his perfect throw to the plate had been deflected by Cicotte, so Jackson may have wanted to eliminate the cut-off in the future, if and when he could.

William R. Herzog II believes Jackson was recalling this play in a 1949 interview in *Sport* magazine, when he was asked if he saw any suspicious plays: "[N]ow that I think back over it, Cicotte seemed to let up on a pitch to Pat Duncan, and Duncan put it over my head. Duncan didn't have enough power to hit the ball that far, particularly if Cicotte had been bearing down."

Herzog believes Jackson confused Duncan with Neale, and that is probably the case, as Duncan had no extra-base hits in the Series. Another possibility is that Jackson played shallow because he thought Duncan, and not Neale, was at bat, and it stuck in his memory that way.

In any case, Jackson recalled that Cicotte was "not bearing down." Most play-by-play accounts simply describe Neale hitting the ball over Jackson's head, without reading anything more into it.

Reporter Hugh Fullerton thought that Neale's hit was carried over Jackson by the wind. Finally, Greasy Neale himself said in a 1961 interview, "When I hit the ball over Jackson's head to score Kopf, it was written that Jackson played in too close for Neale, a long ball hitter. I was strictly a singles hitter."[6]

JACKSON'S FIELDING AND RUNNING ABILITY

But was Joe Jackson a top-notch outfielder who usually ran down everything hit his way? Because his glove has been called "the place where triples go to die,"[7] one might think so. But Allen Barra argues that Jackson's lifetime statistics suggest that he was slightly below average in the field (and as a baserunner).[8] His "range factor" (2.02 putouts per nine innings) is below the league average of 2.12 for his thirteen seasons. For a comparison, Barra notes that Ty Cobb's range factor was 2.35, and Cobb was not regarded as a great fielder. And Jackson's numbers would likely have dropped some as he slowed down with age, if his major league career had continued beyond 1920.

In the 1919 Series, Jackson handled the sixteen balls hit his way flawlessly and was charged with no errors. He also threw out a runner at home and might have had a second assist if substitute catcher Byrd Lynn had not fumbled his throw in the sixth inning of Game Five. Most accounts agree that Jackson's peg home in Game Four, deflected by Cicotte, could have given him another assist, if the runner had not held up at third. Near the end of his life, Jackson's failing memory had him throwing out five runners. But the record shows one.[9]

Barra further doubts those who insist Jackson had great speed, by pointing out that while his stolen bases numbers are impressive (202 lifetime, most of them in his Cleveland days), in the seasons for which we have "caught stealing" figures (1914–16, his peak seasons for steals, and 1920), his success rate was just over 53 percent—not very good.[10]

THE TESTIMONY OF OTHERS

In looking at how others recalled Joe Jackson's performance in the Series, other players will come up, too. Because baseball is a team sport, pulling aside the performance of a single player can be difficult and sometimes misleading.

Ray Schalk

The White Sox catcher Ray Schalk was one of the first players to suspect that the Series was being thrown. His impatience in Game Two with Lefty Williams was visible. *Collier's* reported shortly after the 1920 grand jury indictments that Schalk knew something was wrong before the middle of Game One and that Cicotte and Williams "crossed him" in Games One and Two. The magazine also said that "the conspirators were known because, in the clubhouse after the games, the honest [players] drew aside and refused to mingle with them. Then they knew that sooner or later their crime would be exposed."[11]

Collier's underlines this by quoting Eddie Cicotte saying, "We felt all the time that we would be exposed." But *Collier's* does not mention that the White Sox team was not known for its "mingling" in the best of times or that it had been divided into cliques since well before October 1919. In the words of Eddie Collins, the Sox "seethed with discord and bitterness. Time after time they were close to open fighting with fists among themselves. And still they won going away [in 1917]."[12] Cicotte's statement may have been true for him, as he seemed to have the strongest misgivings, once the plan was under way.

Schalk likely convinced his manager Gleason about the fix early on; Gleason had received telegrams, and then Comiskey talked with him. Schalk said little about the fix later but did tell others that he believed Joe Jackson and Eddie Cicotte both played the Series (if not, at least in the case of Cicotte, every game) to win. (More on this in the section on Cicotte below.)

Christy Mathewson

Hugh Fullerton had heard the rumors of the fix before the first game. So he asked the retired star pitcher Christy Mathewson, who was covering the Series for a New York paper, to sit between himself and Ring Lardner and to let him know if he saw anything suspicious. Mathewson knew what to look for—he had been instrumental in having Hal Chase put off the Reds for tossing games, when Mathewson managed them. Mathewson was one of many who believed that a Series could not be fixed, but he agreed to sit with Fullerton and look for anything suspicious. The result was seven circles in their scorebook.

It is commonly believed that after the Series, Fullerton wrote about the suspicious plays in his columns and included the "diagrams" from Mathewson. But these columns have yet to be found.

In his research for *The Celebrant*, Eric Rolfe Greenberg identified seven suspicious plays, in three different games, all Chicago losses.[13] One play was made by Shano Collins, who was never associated with the fix. And none of the plays suggest Jackson was playing crooked; in fact, the last play (Cicotte's muff on Jackson's strong throw home) suggests just the opposite.

Cincinnati won Game Four, 2–0, scoring both runs in the fifth inning. Almost every account of that inning has Joe Jackson's peg home being on line and destined to beat the runner. In a 1956 interview, Chick Gandil said that he called to Cicotte to cut off the throw.

An official scorer of the Series, James C. Hamilton, testified under oath that he saw just one suspicious play in all the games—on Jackson's throw home in Game Four.

> He threw a ball from center field to the plate; the ball was apparently going to Schalk to catch the runner at home plate. Cicotte intercepted it by jumping in the air, knocked it down and booted it and the runner scored . . . . The throw, to my eye, would have gone to home plate . . . . It was a good throw.[14]

Because it was the most memorable misplay by the White Sox in the tainted Series, Jackson's throw and Cicotte's deflection have been written about more than any other event on the diamond that October. Author James T. Farrell, who was a teenager in the stands at Comiskey Park for the game:

> I remember this play vividly, even now [in 1957]. There was Joe Jackson. He fielded the ball on one bounce and got off a quick, accurate throw. As the ball sailed in, I knew that the Cincinnati runner would be out if he tried to score. He didn't. He merely made a stab at going on . . . . [Cicotte's] play didn't seem right.[15]

Charles Dryden of the *Chicago Herald and American* apparently never saw Cicotte deflect the peg from Jackson, and in his account the next day, "Kopf singled to left and Duncan halted at third until Jackson threw the ball high to Schalk. The pill rolled to the stands and Duncan scored." But other stories in the same issue, including Hugh Fullerton's, noted it was Cicotte's error that let in the run.[16]

Baseball biographer Ray Robinson has detailed Christy Mathewson's presence at the 1919 World Series as a columnist for the

New York Evening World.[17] Through August 1918, Mathewson had been the manager of the Cincinnati Reds; they were a third-place team when he left to join the Army's Chemical Warfare Service in France. Therefore, the White Sox's opponents in the 1919 Series were largely "his team," though Matty spent the 1919 season as a coach with John McGraw's Giants. Throughout that season Mathewson looked askance at Hal Chase, suspecting he was crooked. It took a while for McGraw to be similarly convinced, but eventually he pulled Chase out of the lineup.

> "Nobody can kill the game of baseball, except the public," Matty said not long after the Chase incident. "However, a baseball player who does not do his best every day—the best he can possibly do that day—should be disciplined and if he persists should be released." Mathewson's keen eye for the game and for slacking made him an ideal partner for Hugh Fullerton as they sat in the press box together and logged the questionable plays. But of course Matty himself did not raise any of his own suspicions in his newspaper columns. The risk of being sued for libel may have intimidated him.[18]

Robinson has Matty's scorecard "cluttered with red circles" (the suspicious plays). Robinson's account largely agrees with that of Greenberg, with these exceptions: he has Matty faulting Lefty Williams for throwing a steady diet of fastballs (Greenberg has Matty faulting Williams for his wildness); he has Felsch misplaying a fly ball; and "an errant throw home by Shoeless Joe drew another red circle." I was unable to find another source to agree with Robinson about this last play, so Robinson may have confused Jackson, one of the eight men accused, with Shano Collins, a clean Sox. Robinson adds this note:

> No man had been more concerned than Matty about the purity of baseball. . . . Yet, he continued to show broad tolerance for the alleged sins of those eight Black Sox. "There is such a thing as condemning the acts of these men and still forgiving the individuals," he said. "I don't think Kid Gleason and the rest of the White Sox wanted to see their former comrades sent to the penitentiary for violating the trust placed in them by the fans. They would not have been human if they did. Even a judge must dislike sentencing a man to jail, unless he is a most hardened criminal."

Charles A. Comiskey

Hugh Fullerton called Sox owner Charles Comiskey the man who may have known more about the fix than almost anyone. In the 1924 Milwaukee trial, Comiskey took the witness stand and was interrogated about whether Jackson played the Series to win or not.

We might expect Comiskey to be a witness hostile to Jackson. In 1918, Joe Jackson, originally deferred from service as a married man, was reclassified 1-A. He passed a physical and was set to be inducted into the Army, when he got an offer from a shipbuilding company in Delaware. Jackson took their offer and went to work building ships— an important wartime occupation.

To no one's surprise, there were those who regarded players who took jobs in the "paint and putty league" as draft-evaders and slackers. What is harder to understand is why Comiskey suspended and publicly criticized his star player. (Hugh Fullerton went after Jackson, too.) Jackson was "the first prominent player to decline service" and took the brunt of the heat from sportswriters.[19] (Babe Ruth joined a reserve unit and kept playing in the majors.) Jackson's teammates supported him.[20]

When the war was over, and Comiskey "saw that Joe Jackson still drew large crowds [in 1919] through the turnstiles everywhere the White Sox played, [he] smugly announced that he was glad he had not listened to the critics who'd wanted him to get rid of slacker Joe."[21] This was before recording technology arrived, and the press was too indebted to Comiskey to rerun his earlier condemnations of Jackson.[22]

On the witness stand in Milwaukee, and standing to lose over $16,000 if the jury found for Jackson, Comiskey testified that Jackson had played the Series to win. And not just the Series, but every game Jackson had ever played in a White Sox uniform.

But it took him a while to get there: "Did you observe anything dishonest about Jackson's playing in the eight games of the World Series?" he was asked. "No." Q: "Did Jackson play dishonest baseball in the World Series?" Commy: "He said he did." Q: "I am asking you." Commy: "Why sure he played—you are asking me now—why, yes." Comiskey then recalled one play when Jackson was in too close, and the ball went over his head. He could not recall which game; "8th inning, I think." Later, Jackson's lawyer Ray Cannon noted that it was Edd Roush, a left-handed batter, who drove it over Jackson's head for a double, in the second inning of the eighth game.

Comiskey said Jackson had played "his usual game" in Game One. Comiskey had been sick and missed Games Three and Four. Pressed later on by Cannon:

During the time that Jackson played as a member of your base-ball club, from the year 1915, I think it was, down till the time he was suspended, on the 28th of Sept, 1920, do you know of one dishonest move or act committed by Joe Jackson while on the base-ball field?

[Comiskey's lawyer Hudnall objected saying that Jackson was discharged for something he did off the baseball field.]

Comiskey then answered: "No." Court (clarifying): "On the ball field?" Comiskey: "On the ball field."[23]

And apparently Comiskey was consistent in this evaluation of Jackson. His grandson has sworn for the record that the Comiskey family's belief was that Jackson neither conspired to throw nor attempted to throw any or all games in the 1919 World Series.[24]

The 1924 Milwaukee Jury

The Milwaukee jury did not hear only Comiskey's recollections of Jackson's play. They also heard Lefty Williams's deposition, in which he said Jackson and Buck Weaver had played perfect baseball. It seems that the defense lawyers conceded that Jackson played excellent base-ball on the field in October 1919 and chose to try to prove he was released by the club for having some role in the conspiracy to throw the Series. In any case, after hearing all the evidence, the jury was asked to decide whether Jackson "did unlawfully conspire with Gandil, Williams, and other members of the White Sox Club, or any of them, to lose or 'throw' any of the base ball games of the 1919 World Series to the Cincinnati Baseball Club?" Eleven of twelve answered, "No."

Juries are not infallible, but their verdicts are significant because jurists have an advantage over those who can only read trial tran-scripts. In the Watergate trial, the *tapes*—not the transcripts—were admitted as evidence. Jury members were given transcripts to use as guides, but they were repeatedly reminded to pay attention to what they were *hearing*.[25]

If only we had *tapes* from 1920 and 1924! What in Jackson's testimony was said after a long pause, or with emphasis, or with sar-casm? If we could *hear* the testimony, would we be better able to determine if he was more convincing, more sincere, more sure of him-self, when he said he played to win? When he said he was promised $20,000 but received only $5,000, did that sound like something rehearsed, or something spontaneous and candid?

Henry H. Brigham was listening to every word Joe Jackson said before the Cook County grand jury in 1920. Henry Brigham had been the grand jury foreman. Brigham stated on the witness stand in Milwaukee in 1924 that Jackson, in his 1920 statement, had denied being in the conspiracy. Jackson said that he had given his best effort, Brigham recalled, and "he didn't admit that he threw the games . . . or any game."[26]

Q: "Did he [Jackson] testify in substance that he was making his best effort all through the play?"
Brigham: "Yes."[27]

Brigham affirmed that Jackson had said in 1920 that he had tried to see Comiskey after the Series to tell what he knew. (Brigham also admitted that "the Grand Jury had made no investigation of Comiskey's conduct pertaining to the running down of rumors after the 1919 Series." He denied that the grand jury ever considered indicting Comiskey; "No, he was liberal and cooperative.")

The jury in Milwaukee, by eleven to one, believed the version of events that Jackson had given to them on the stand. Judge John J. Gregory, however, dismissed their verdict, stating that the discrepancies between Jackson's 1924 testimony and his 1920 testimony amounted to perjury. The case was settled out of court.

If it was plain to the grand jury foreman that Jackson said he had played the 1919 Series to win—as the surviving statements made by Jackson confirm—then why did *no newspaper* report Jackson's insistence that he played to win? Why did his grand jury testimony go down as a simple confession, instead of the self-contradictory account of a confused witness? The grand jury hearings were supposed to be "secret," but they were full of leaks that got lots of newspaper column space. Why is it that no one leaked Jackson's, "I tried to win all the time?" It may be that the papers took the spin that baseball officialdom wanted them to take.

Jackson at the Bat

Joe Jackson himself always pointed to his performance as the proof that he had played the 1919 Series to win. His twelve hits stood as the World Series record for decades.[28]

Almost everyone at least suspected that the first two games had been tossed. In Game One, Jackson went hitless—apparently after

Charles A. Comiskey, owner of the White Sox in 1919. According to would-be whistle-blower Hugh Fullerton, Comiskey knew before the first game of the World Series started that "the fix was in." *National Baseball Hall of Fame Library, Cooperstown, New York*

Judge Kenesaw Mountain Landis, baseball's first commissioner, was hired by baseball's owners to repair the game's image in the wake of the scandal. *National Baseball Hall of Fame Library, Cooperstown, New York*

Landis's tight-fisted banishment of eight players was effective, but probably unfair. *National Baseball Hall of Fame Library, Cooperstown, New York*

William J. "Kid" Gleason, manager of the Sox, was left holding the bag when some of his key players conspired with gamblers before the 1919 Series. "He stated that if he saw any evidences of crookedness that day [Game 8] he would use an 'iron' on the guilty player, meaning a gun. The Kid was desperate," wrote Hugh Fullerton. *National Baseball Hall of Fame Library, Cooperstown, New York*

Eddie Cicotte's testimony to the Cook County grand jury on September 28, 1920, confirmed the fix. Whether Cicotte did anything "crooked" after he hit the first batter he faced is not at all certain. *National Baseball Hall of Fame Library, Cooperstown, New York*

Not only was Joe Jackson famous in 1919, so was his trademark bat, forty-some-ounce, thirty-four-inch-long Black Betsy. He apparently named his other bats, too. *National Baseball Hall of Fame Library, Cooperstown, New York*

Rube Benton's grand jury testimony in September 1920 was a crucial step in bringing to light the shadowy events of the previous fall. The *Sporting News* praised Benton as "the first player to lend a hand in cleaning up baseball." *National Baseball Hall of Fame Library, Cooperstown, New York*

In 1927, Buck Weaver took the occasion of hearings called by Judge Landis to look into a 1917 scandal to ask for reinstatement. Weaver continued to try to clear his name until his death in 1956. *National Baseball Hall of Fame Library, Cooperstown, New York*

Only one publication—one published for gamblers—seriously investigated the rumors of a fix after the Series was over. When the scandal broke nearly a year later, *Collyer's Eye* declared that it had been vindicated.

Most baseball histories give reporter Hugh Fullerton credit for blowing the lid off the cover-up. But his pleas for Major League Baseball to investigate fell on deaf ears, and the baseball establishment discredited him, despite his long history of concern for and contributions to the sport. Pencil sketch by *Ray Evans*, courtesy of Hugh Burns."

I Recall

By HUGH FULLERTON

Charles Comiskey

TWO years always stand out in memory whenever "Don't you remember?" sessions which last all night if old-timers get together. One is 1906, the most dramatic and sensational in baseball history, and the other 1919, the year of the Black Sox scandal.

There has been so much discussion of that scandal, and so much criticism of baseball officials and club owners for not investigating and exploding the plot, and so many wrong tales told, that I recall vividly almost every incident.

Many persons have asked me, "Why didn't someone do something when so many persons knew something crooked was coming off?" The plain answer is that they did not believe a fixed series was a possibility.

I was working for a syndicate then and was to meet the boss and some of the others—including Christy Mathewson—in Cincinnati the day before the series was to start. I knew all the White Sox and the majority of the Reds and most of them were my friends, and the idea that anything crooked was being planned never entered my head. Early in the morning before the series started, I met Joe Jackson, the Detroit sporting writer, and we went to a speak-easy to get an eye-opener. The place was half a block from the Sinton, where we were stopping. In the bar, we encountered a Chicago gambler. I knew him by sight, and he knew me. After a time, I introduced him to Joe Jackson. He looked surprised, thinking the grizzled old reporter was the ball player. He drew me aside and asked if I had talked with Joe about the "fix"—and asked me to learn from Joe whether it was to be Cincinnati in straight victories. Thinking him a crank, Joe and I started kidding him and told him Cincinnati was to win five straight games.

Many Rumors Floating Around.

We laughed over the idea, neither thinking of it seriously. An hour or so later the boys from New York came in, and with them odd rumors. They had the tip that the series was fixed. The tip came straight from Arnold Rothstein, who had told friends that he had been approached, but refused to finance the crooks, but that it was safe to bet someone had.

All day, the rumors increased in strength. I called one of the White Sox who was my friend, and went over the rumors with him. He denied that anything was doing and scoffed at the whole story. I asked him to keep his ears open and see what was going on, if anything, and he promised to do so. And all the time he was one of the principals in the plot. About noon, I was going across to the telegraph office and met Bill Burns. I had known and liked that odd, interesting character when he was pitching for Chicago. I did not mention the stories but we talked for a few minutes about the series and he said: "Get wise and get yourself some money." It was not what Bill said, but the way he said it that startled me.

That evening, a crowd of us went to a road house in Kentucky and had a party, at which talk of the series being fixed was free—too free. I came away and reached the hotel, where I was rooming with Matty. We were sitting up in bed talking over the situation. I was telling Matty all about the rumors I had heard, and of the odd actions of some of the boys, when he suddenly exploded out of his usual calm and said:

"Damn them," (meaning the club owners) "they have it coming to them. I caught two crooks and they whitewashed them."

We were still talking at 3 in the morning when Pat Moran, wild with anger, broke into the room, charging me with taking one of his pitchers out and trying to get him drunk. I had not seen the pitcher, and was mad, Pat was madder, until Matty cut in and assured him that I had not been with any of the Cincinnati players. As a matter of fact, Pat was right about the player—but he had the wrong reporter.

The following morning, early, I talked with two big-shot Chicago gamblers, who told me flat-footedly that the series was fixed for Cincinnati to win.

* * *

Comiskey and Johnson in Feud

I WAS much upset and went to Comiskey to urge him to take some action. He already had heard about it. He was furious, because, he charged, Johnson would do nothing. I urged him to forget his feud with the league president, and to call on him to act. He refused angrily.

I then went to Johnson. I think Johnson already had heard rumors. I put it to him straight that the evidence indicated a crooked series. He scoffed and said it was just Comiskey squealing. Unable to make any progress, I cornered Barney Dreyfuss, and demanded of him that he, in the interests of the sport, act so as to force Johnson to make some move. Barney was enraged that anyone should accuse players of framing a series. I lost my temper and raised Cain with him and with the entire baseball set-up, calling them a bunch of whitewashing bastards who were letting a bunch of crooks get away with it because they were afraid of losing money.

I told him that five of the White Sox were in the plot—and named the five—I told him a lot of things as facts which I couldn't prove, and he only got madder and more indignant. I think, however, that our angry interview scared Barney, for he went to Comiskey—or Comiskey sent for him.

In the first game, Matty and I took turns in slipping from the press box and going downstairs to watch the pitching. After two innings, I was morally certain that something was coming off. Matty watched Cicotte pitch and returned shaking his head.

Before the game was over I was morally certain that the rumors were based on truth. That evening, while I was writing, Ray Schalk came into the room. The grand little man was in a high state of excitement and he declared loudly that the pitcher had crossed him in signals, at least eight times in that game, and that Cincinnati's victory came from hits made off pitched balls thrown exactly opposite to his signals. "Little man," I said, "keep your mouth shut, or go to Comiskey and Gleason. If you make charges against anyone you'll be the goat—you can't prove them, and it would ruin you."

The night before the series started I sent out a short message marked "black face precede to story" warning the fans that something queer was coming off, and to refuse to wager on the games or series. To show the faith of people in the honesty of baseball, only two newspapers out of 40 would print that precede, cautiously as it was worded.

When the series finally ended, I feared that my branding of the games as fixed might have wrecked a life friendship with Charles Comiskey. I sought Commy and found him, a broken and bitter man, in a small place near his park. We talked and suddenly he struck the table with clenched fist and said: "Keep after them, Hughie; they were crooked. Some day you and I will prove it."

It took almost a year to do it, but little by little, the evidence piled in, and proof accumulated. Then came the confessions and the clearing up of baseball's worst blight.

But today, more than 15 years later, the full story never has been told and never will be, because Johnson, Comiskey, Herrmann and Alf Austrian, the only ones who knew it all, are dead.

Ever loyal to Charles Comiskey, whistle-blowing reporter Hugh Fullerton waited until after Comiskey passed away to reveal in a memoir that he had informed the baseball authorities—before Game One started—that the fix was in. *The Sporting News Archive* asking, or by some accounts "begging" to be benched. Does it seem likely that a player planning to give less than his best effort would call attention to himself by asking to be benched? Jackson told the grand jury in 1920 that he knew for sure that something fishy was going on when he was approached by a gambler the morning of Game One. The gambler (Bill Burns) thought Jackson knew all about the fix, and left him quickly when he realized that he did not. The encounter may have shaken Jackson and made him feel like he could not take the field that day.

> He was afraid of Gandil and even more afraid of Risberg. He was also afraid of Gleason, Comiskey, Grabiner, Collins and Schalk. He couldn't swing at a bad pitch and he couldn't throw badly. One fly ball dropped between him and Felsch: that was as close as he came to making a Series error; while outhitting everyone on both clubs. Yet he felt he wasn't playing to win.[29]

Sickened because he knew that some of his teammates were playing to lose, Jackson gave his all in the Series. But he knew the gamblers thought he was in on the fix—the meeting with Burns confirmed that. What would happen to him, to his wife, if they found out he was not?

Keeping in mind especially the argument that Jackson played hard in the games the Sox won, but let up in the games that were tossed, here is how Jackson did in Game Two: He went 3-for-4. And for those who say Jackson was just poking the ball to the opposite field, Game Two has him hitting a Texas leaguer behind second that he hustled into a double; a single to left (behind a single by Weaver, both hit off the first pitch, and a rally was afoot); and a hard smash to right that the first baseman knocked down, then threw late to pitcher Sallee.

The Spalding Guide's description of the 1919 Series has a number of interesting sidebars. One lists "Failures to Advance Runners" for both teams. Felsch led with 12; then comes Groh with 11; Gandil, Kopf, and Risberg with 9; Collins, Daubert, Neale, and Jackson with 8; and Roush with 7. But if you read the play-by-play, both teams made some super plays on defense. So these numbers by themselves do not tell the whole story.[30]

The *Guide* also tracked "Runners Advanced," game-by-game (so readers have to do the addition). Jackson went 0-for-4 in Game One, but he advanced more runners (2) than any of his teammates. In the Series, Jackson led his team with 15, and only Edd Roush, with 16, had more. (Edd had a big Game Eight with 4 RBIs and 8 runners advanced.) Second on the Sox? Felsch 13, then Gandil 10 and Weaver 8. The clean Soxers, Schalk and Eddie Collins, advanced 5 each. Rookie Pat Duncan of the Reds, someone who *never* comes up in the story of the 1919 Series, had 13 advances, and the *Guide* credits his unexpected timely hitting (8 RBIs) as no small factor in the Reds' victory. It may seem less important today, but in the deadball era, advancing runners and sacrificing was everybody's job and often meant the difference between victory and defeat. Jackson hit to the right side to advance runners in Games One, Four, and Seven.[31]

Yet it is easy to see why some people have concluded that Jackson "failed in the clutch, but hit when it did not mean much." Some of his outs were made with men on, sometimes in scoring position, while some of his hits were "wasted." That is common in baseball—but if it happens when the beholder thinks that a fix is in, it raises suspicion.

Supporters of Jackson note that when his team was leading or was trailing by three runs or less—two examples of "clutch" (in position to extend a lead or put his team closer)—Jackson batted .435 (10-for-23). The statistics can probably be sliced and diced a dozen more ways, but they remain silent witnesses to Jackson's intention in each at bat.[32]

Baseball history suggests that Ty Cobb's intensity in each game, and each at bat, was by far the exception to the rule. It is more "normal" for players to streak and slump, to conserve their energy at times and go all out at others, and even in a World Series, few "rise to the occasion" at every opportunity.

To sum up: Joe Jackson's performance in the 1919 World Series was, on the surface, exceptional. He hit well against a staff rated better than that of the White Sox by Christy Mathewson, who had managed the Reds. He hit safely in six of the eight games, with five multihit games. He fanned just twice in thirty-two trips to the plate. To suggest that he intentionally hit better in certain games than in others is to suggest that he could rack up hits at will, whenever he wanted, which is ridiculous. Batters can look awful in "Home Run Derby," when the pitchers are serving up whatever the batter wants. But even accomplished hitters make outs more often than they get hits, and often the outs come in the clutch.

On the other hand, Jackson's .375 average, his team-leading six RBIs, his hitting the only Series home run, and his errorless play on sixteen chances are not proof of his playing "straight," any more than his hitless Game One is proof that he was playing that game "crooked." Teammate Dickie Kerr, whose two wins were also multihit games for Jackson, had his doubts about Jackson's intentions, but this comment, made later to reporter Joe Williams, underscores the difficulty of knowing for sure even for eyewitnesses:

> You know he was such a remarkable hitter it was almost impossible for him to swing without meeting the ball solidly. I recall one game in the Series—the second, I believe—when he got a hit trying to ground out. He chopped down on the ball and it took such a high hop that the Reds' second baseman couldn't reach it and Jackson looking pretty apologetic about it, too, had to go to first on the single.[33]

Joe Williams's interest in the White Sox of 1919 may have stemmed from a conversation he had with Joe Jackson in the spring of 1920. Williams, a southerner, approached Jackson and asked him about the rumors that the Series was had been fixed and that Jackson had been in on it. Jackson swore "on his mama's grave" that he had played it honest, and he argued that if he had been in on the fix, the way he hit, the gamblers "would have had him killed long since."[34]

What was going on inside Jackson during the Series? Dickie Kerr did not know, nor does anyone else. Was he playing *every* inning of *every* game to win? Or did he let up some, just poke at the ball, fail to hustle in the field a few times? Testifying before the Cook County grand jury, Jackson told two stories, and they contradicted each other, and no one asked him to choose one or the other. So both are on the record, giving fuel to those who believe he was in on the fix and to those who believe he was not. Jackson was in court again in 1924, and that time he was crystal clear about his performance. And he went to his grave without ever changing his story again.

A "Jury" of Writers and Historians

What do baseball historians and authors believe on this question? Most think Jackson played to win. Here is a quick survey of twelve views from the last forty-some years:

Eliot Asinof wrote in 1963's *Eight Men Out* that Jackson "mumbled his innocence."[35] He has stated that he felt Jackson was more a victim than anything else.[36]

Victor Luhrs, in 1966, was sure Jackson was not in on the fix. On the question of how many players fixed how many games, Luhrs is more conservative than most writers. But in the light of the Milwaukee trial testimony and depositions, Luhrs's conclusions may not be so far-fetched. He believed just two games were tossed (Games Two and Eight) and just three players were playing to lose (Williams, Gandil, and Risberg). "Shoeless Joe could no more play dishonest baseball than a mouse sitting on top of a cheddar wheel could go on a non-cheese diet." For Luhrs, Jackson's innocence is proved by his performance in the Series.[37]

Historians David Q. Voigt and Harold Seymour, both writing before Jackson's testimony was accessible, have differing views. Voigt does not focus on Jackson but he gives the impression that he thinks Jackson *was* in on the fix.[38] Seymour gives the impression that he does not think Jackson threw any games and that he thinks the statements attributed to Jackson that suggest he was not trying hard to win may have been published to shield him from the underworld, who had paid the players to lose.[39]

Writer Nelson Algren, who knew Chicago pretty well, felt Jackson had played to win. He was "never so sophisticated that he could play baseball badly for a price."[40] Jackson biographer Donald Gropman: "His performance . . . seemed to give the lie to his confession."[41] The only author to make extensive use of the 1924 transcripts, Gropman is perhaps the strongest advocate for Jackson among writers and historians.

Baseball historian Charles Alexander in 1991: "Obviously Jackson played to win."[42] Biographer Harvey Frommer in 1992: Jackson's performance was "that of a player beyond reproach."[43] Baseball researcher Jack Kavanagh in 1995: "No one can be sure."[44]

David Fleitz, whose 2001 Jackson biography is perhaps the best-documented, believes Jackson must have done something to earn the money he accepted from the gamblers.[45] William R. Herzog II, writing in 2002, was convinced to the contrary: "He played to win. The record exonerates him."[46] Daniel A. Nathan, in 2003, is not interested in the question in his cultural history of the scandal, and he believes the evidence to be inconclusive.[47]

Once upon a time I imagined that a "jury" made up of the twelve historians and writers in my survey above might settle the question. But even though their "verdict" here finds Jackson innocent by roughly two to one, it is not that simple. The twelve men did not have equal access to all of the information that is now available—not that they would unanimously come to the same conclusions if they did. But that fact makes the theoretical "trial" unfair at its roots.

Baseball fans, almost by definition, disagree with each other. They love to argue, especially over All Star selections and the membership of the Hall of Fame. While the question of Joe Jackson's role in the 1919 fix is great fuel for the Hot Stove, it is not a typical baseball question. And while everyone is free to have their opinions, not all opinions are equal. Even those of historians are not equal, if they do not have the same evidence to assess. Are the views of contemporaries more believable than those writers who live decades later? For example, pitcher George Uhle's view:

> Joe Jackson was on the Cleveland team before I got there. Shoeless Joe. Somehow or other he got over to Chicago. He was a terrific hitter. My first year in the league, 1919, was when the Black Sox threw the World Series. But Joe was too dumb to get involved in that. He didn't get into it, he really didn't. He wasn't that smart. I mean, they may have talked to him about it and all, but it didn't sink in. He didn't try to do anything to lose. He had a hell of a Series. In fact, he didn't have anything to do with the planning of it. I know that from conversations with other players at the time, some of who[m] knew some of the stuff."[48]

On the question of Jackson's eligibility for Cooperstown, only one opinion counts, that of the commissioner. Happy Chandler, who succeeded Judge Landis, was interviewed after he left office, and said, "I don't think [Jackson] ever did anything in connection with that scandal. It's an injustice that ought to be corrected by the baseball people."[49] Unfortunately for Jackson, Chandler himself never acted on that belief, if indeed he had held it when he held baseball's highest office.

After the Ban

According to today's Greenville, South Carolina, guide for tourists, Joe Jackson played his first games of baseball at age thirteen on "the trampled dirt field beside Brandon Mill" (on Greenville's west side). Playing on the mill team meant $25 or more in tips in a single game. Eleven hours in the mill paid $1.10. And the guide has this understatement: "This financial incentive goaded him to improve."

The story of Joe Jackson is that of the American Dream turned nightmare. He rose from dirt fields to national fame, and his name could be recalled today in the same way we recall Ty Cobb and other deadball era celebrities—except that something happened to prevent that, and we are not even sure just what it was. His story in baseball has no happy ending. Joe Jackson's pro ball career effectively ceased with the decree of Judge Landis in 1921, although Jackson kept playing wherever he was allowed. In the late 1920s, Jackson returned to Greenville for good, and there he was regarded as a local hero.

In every interview Jackson gave before his death in 1951, he seemed a bit disappointed with the way his time in baseball ended, but he was far from bitter about it. He and his wife had lived a comfortable life among friends, and he had been successful in several businesses.

Greenville County, where Greenville is located, honored Joe by restoring and landscaping the old Brandon Field—now Shoeless Joe Jackson Memorial Park—and by designating a stretch of U.S. Interstate 123 as "Joe Jackson Memorial Highway." On July 13, 2002, a statue of Joe Jackson was dedicated on the plaza at the West End Market. You can look it up.

EDDIE CICOTTE

Eddie Cicotte started Game One for the White Sox and gave up six runs before leaving the game in the forth inning; the Reds won, 9–1. Cicotte started Game Four, pitched a brilliant complete game, but lost 2–0 due to his own errors in the fifth inning. He started and won Game Seven, 4–1. His grand jury confession on September 28, 1920, was crucial to the confirmation of the fix.

Edward Victor Cicotte was born in 1884 in Detroit and broke into the major leagues with his hometown Tigers in 1905. After a stint with Boston, Eddie arrived in Chicago during the 1912 season, and he emerged as one of the league's aces in 1917 when he won twenty-eight games, leading the White Sox to a pennant and a world championship. In 1919, Eddie won twenty-nine.

THE SIGNAL

The gamblers and players involved in the fixing of the 1919 Series disagreed on a lot of things, but they all seemed to agree on one detail: the way Eddie Cicotte dealt with the first batter of the Series would be the signal that the fix was in.

Why did they need a signal? Because by the time Game One rolled around, news of the fix was rippling out across the country. Players were telling family and friends, and gamblers were giving out (or selling) tips in their networks. It must have seemed too good to be true, like finding out the score of the next Super Bowl before the opening kickoff. But no one was sure. There had been much wrangling in the negotiations. Cicotte's participation was vital to the fix, because the White Sox ace would likely get three starts.

Cicotte insisted that he needed to win one game, to throw off suspicions. By some accounts, the players were indifferent about which five games they should lose. The gamblers wanted the first two or three. Betting and winning early meant having more money to bet as the Series went along.

Cicotte insisted on getting $10,000 up front, before he threw a pitch—exhibiting a very healthy distrust of gamblers. The other players in on the fix, whoever they were, surely regretted not insisting on their money in advance. Some felt downright cheated when they wound up with only $5,000—not much more than a winning Series share.

And so the signal was set up: the first Cincinnati Reds batter would either be walked or hit with a pitch by Cicotte. Anything else, and the fix was *off*.[50]

Second baseman Morrie Rath, a .264 hitter who drew sixty-four walks in about 600 plate appearances during the season, stood in. The first pitch—*called strike one!* Freeze frame, please.

Who threw that pitch? Was it the Eddie Cicotte who did not really want to go through with the fix? Was he flipping a coin, leaving it to fate? If Rath swings and connects, the fix is off? And Eddie goes on to win three games—carefully returning the cash, lest his fingers be broken—or worse?

There is some evidence that suggests that Cicotte really thought that returning the $10,000 he received before the Series was an option. In his deposition for the 1924 Milwaukee trial, Eddie was asked about Game Four, the one in which he pitched very well but lost by a 2–0 score because of two errors, which he himself made. Q: "If Chicago had scored more runs would you have given up more?" A: "No, I would have given back the $10,000 with interest if the Sox won the Series."[51]

Is there any basis for the theory that Cicotte was leaving things up to fate with that first-pitch strike? First there is the fact that he indeed threw a first strike. Then there is this statement of his from 1920, "The first ball I pitched, I wondered what the wife and kiddies would say if they ever found out I was a crook—yet I had the $10,000."[52]

Cicotte was absolutely filled with regret and remorse when he was escorted by Comiskey's lawyer into the 1920 grand jury hearings, in progress. His repeated "I was only thinking of the wife and kiddies" as his noble motive became a saying almost as famous as "Say it ain't so, Joe." Cicotte's testimony was made sobbingly by a man who had been through "hours of mental torture, days and nights of living with an unclean mind, the weeks and months of going along with six of the seven other crooked players, and holding a guilty secret, and of going along with the boys who had stayed straight and clean and honest—boys who had nothing to trouble them—say, it was hell."[53]

Then there are the statements of Cicotte's 1920 grand jury testimony, which were used when he was deposed for the 1924 Milwaukee trial. Cicotte to grand jury: "Well, I went into the first game and tried to walk Roth [Rath], and I hit him." Q: "You wanted him to get on base?" A: "Yes. But after he passed, after he was on there, I don't know, I guess I tried too hard. I didn't care, they could have had my heart and soul; that is the way I felt about it after I had taken that money. I guess everybody is not perfect."[54]

These statements echo what Judge McDonald recalled of his conversation with Cicotte, before Eddie appeared in front of the grand jury.

> He started the first game, he told me, with the intention of walking the first man. Instead he hit him with a pitched ball. After that he said his conscience hurt him and he realized that he was doing wrong. He regretted his action, but he did not return the money.[55]

Hugh Fullerton had confronted Eddie Cicotte with the fix rumors the day before his first start.[56] So Cicotte knew that *lots* of people knew what was going on, before he threw that first pitch. Soon after the Series ended, Cicotte recalled that first game. "It was a very hot day and the heat bothered me considerably. But I thought I could pitch my best ball. I was mistaken, as the results showed plainly enough."[57] He added that the pressure of being in the spotlight had caused him to wake up with a start, every night of the Series. "You are so deep in the thing that you eat and sleep baseball. And the result is that you can't eat as you ought to and your sleep is pretty well broken." Later Cicotte would recall, with regret that he had taken the bribe, "I lay awake all one night thinking and wishing that there was some way I could go out there and win that Series myself."[58]

When Cicotte's grand jury testimony was read at the 1921 trial, it confirmed some of gambler Bill Burns's story.

> The former pitcher told of hitting Rath, the first man up in the first game, while trying to walk him, but said he played his best after that. "I pitched my best afterwards. I didn't care what happened. They could have had my heart and soul if I could have gotten out of the deal—I guess that was the trouble; I tried too hard and played poorly as a result." Speaking of another game, Cicotte said that while playing he "wished some one would come out and shoot him."[59]

Cicotte had hinted to reporters right after he spoke to the grand jury that he had changed his mind after hitting Rath. "I pitched the best ball I knew how after that first ball. But I lost because I was hit, not because I was throwing the game" (the *Cleveland News*, September 29, 1920). But the headlines confirming that the game had been fixed eclipsed Cicotte's claims that he had been pitching to win after all.

Eddie Cicotte seems to have been the player with the keenest conscience—if he had not confessed, the grand jury might have stalled where it was stuck and handed up no indictments. With Eddie's statements confirming the fix, the members of the grand jury had the evidence they needed. (This was also Chick Gandil's opinion.)

There is yet another possible explanation for that first strike Eddie Cicotte threw. Take another look at the list of betting odds in chapter 2. Yes, fans bet on whether the first pitch of the Series would be a ball or strike—just as they bet today on the coin flip for the Super Bowl. Maybe that is why Cicotte was not worried about Rath swinging at the first pitch in October 1919. It may well have been a "tradition" to take that first one—because there was money riding on it. Eliot Asinof imagined it this way:

> Schalk called for a fast ball, aware that the batter, Rath, would probably take the first pitch. Cicotte nodded, then as if to let the whole world know, cut loose a fast ball that Rath could not hit on the best day he ever had. . . . It would be the last good pitch he would throw all day. . . .
>
> [Rothstein] tried to put himself inside Cicotte's head, wondering at the defiance of the man. What really was going on? He could sense the possibility that this entire venture might

prove to be a bad mistake. . . . He had bet $325,000 on the Cincinnati Reds already. . . . "Rath hit by pitched ball" . . . He immediately left for his midtown office, determined to get as much money down on the Cincinnati Reds as possible.[60]

There was one other factor operating when Eddie Cicotte took the mound to pitch Game One of the 1919 Series. Cicotte had developed a superstition about pitching openers.[61] In 1917, Eddie Cicotte watched Lefty Williams start and win on the season's Opening Day; Eddie then won his first start, and twenty-seven more games as the Sox took the pennant. In 1918, Cicotte started the opener and lost, lost his next three starts, went 12–19, and the Sox finished in sixth place. In 1919, Cicotte again watched Williams pitch and win the season opener; Eddie won his first twelve starts, finished 29–7, and the Sox were back in the World Series.

There is no evidence, however, that Cicotte asked for a bye for the opener of the 1919 Series. Perhaps he and his manager recalled that he had started and won Game One in the 1917 Series, pitching a 2–1 complete game. Besides, Cicotte was the team ace, and not starting him would have seemed suspicious. But in baseball, superstitions can play a hidden role in events, and if Cicotte was pitching to win in Game One, he might well have felt jinxed when his defense let him down in the fourth inning.

Some writers and historians think that Joe Jackson and Lefty Williams were coached by Comiskey's lawyer, Austrian, to help the grand jury out by giving them something they could use against the gamblers. Could Austrian have coached Cicotte as well to say that he had not played to win? All three players later repudiated their grand jury statements. There is no reason to assume that Cicotte was alone in giving a version that was strictly his.

Did Cicotte Pitch to Win?

Cicotte's 1924 depositions reopen this question. At first it may seem far-fetched—most of us are used to thinking that Cicotte confessed to "throwing" his first two starts in the Series. Since he lost decisively, 9–1, in Game One, and literally threw away Game Four himself, his confession seems believable. Of course Cicotte was guilty of conspiring to throw the Series; it may have been his idea in the first place, and most sources have him as a ringleader, with Gandil. He had a motive; he was making half of what he should have been making. Yet there have been alternative points of view, held even by those who never read his statements in 1924.

Victor Luhrs wrote *The Great Baseball Mystery* in 1966, three years after Asinof's *Eight Men Out*. Luhrs believed that Cicotte played to win but that "he was in such bad mental shape as a result of his involvement that he was hardly fit to pitch the opener."

Luhrs goes on to make two arguments. It is true that Cicotte got shelled in Game One. But in the fatal fourth inning, when he was knocked out, he made a dazzling defensive play on Kopf (but Risberg cost him a double play); and then he *again* seemed to get the third out, but Greasy Neale's pop fly to short was not held by Risberg. No error, but Eddie really had gotten his man. Given the extra outs, the Reds took advantage and went on to rout the White Sox, scoring five runs with two outs. In Sanborn's *Tribune* account, the Reds' rally "hung on the toenail" of Kopf beating Risberg's throw to first.

Regarding Cicotte's Game Four goofs, Luhrs thinks Cicotte made a good play to stop Duncan's hot grounder, when he could easily have let it pass, and his wild throw was an honest mistake. "His deflection of Jackson's throw to Schalk [a few plays later] was *simply too glaring to have been crooked*." (Emphasis mine.) It truly stood out as the worst play of the Series. Luhrs may have been right; in his 1924 deposition, Eddie Cicotte said that he tried to win Game Four.[62] After the Series, Cicotte explained his mistakes in Game Four like this:

> My second game I did pitch as well as I expected to do. But I was a little over anxious in the field and things broke badly for me. But the worst break from my angle, was the fact that Ring, my opponent, was pitching air tight ball. When you are shut out you are shut out, that is all there is about it.[63]

Ban Johnson recalled that Eddie Collins and Ray Schalk told him that Cicotte had "disobeyed orders" in deflecting the ball, "thereby indicating to them that something was wrong."[64] But by Game Four, that something was wrong was not a secret, and every miscue must have been seen as suspicious at best. And a memoir by Eddie Collins does not support Johnson's recollection:

> Joe [Jackson], coming in fast, scooped up the ball and rifled a good throw towards home to head off Duncan. But the Reds' outfielder had stopped at third and Cicotte attempted to cut off

the throw. At times during my career I saw a ballplayer, attempting to make a catch, or attempting to cut off a throw, inadvertently swipe the ball toward the stands. That was my reaction when Cicotte's glove tipped Jackson's throw and sent it rolling off the field of play.[65]

Cicotte's glaring muff was criticized by his manager Kid Gleason after the game. The cut-off had been unnecessary because "Kopf had no more intention of going to second than I have of jumping into a lake." The play confirmed for Reds pitcher Jimmy Ring "that there was some horseshit going on," especially when Schalk stared at Cicotte and Cicotte stared at center field, rather than face his catcher.[66] But Cicotte's intention remains uncertain.

Some sources claim Cicotte was a veteran pitcher who played his position well, so his errors *must* have been made on purpose. But in fact, Cicotte was a poor fielder—seventy errors in his fourteen-year career for a .942 lifetime fielding average. Compare that to his fellow Sox starters Williams's .955 and Kerr's .953; and to the Reds' starters Ring's, Ruether's, Sallee's, and Eller's respective .967, .972, .973, and .980.[67] The stats—70 Es, .942, thirty-sixth worst all-time—by themselves do not mean that he was a terrible fielder, but they suggest that Cicotte under normal conditions was no stranger to muffs. And his situation in October 1919 was hardly normal.

Batting in the second inning of Game Four, with two outs and the bases loaded, Cicotte worked the count to 3–2, then hit a sharp grounder into the hole between first and second. It took a web gem play by the Reds' Morrie Rath to retire the side.

This amounts to hearsay evidence, but in Harry Grabiner's diary, he recounts the story of the fix that the Sox obtained from gambler Harry Redmon, in which he said that Cicotte and Weaver were "crooked in the first game" and then "turned." In other words, Harry Redmon thought Cicotte had played Games Four and Seven to win.

Hugh Fullerton wrote later that he had heard a story after Game Three about a meeting of the players and gamblers that morning. "Williams and Cicotte refused to go any further with it and . . . there was a stormy time."[68]

What about his confession? Luhrs believes Cicotte lied to the grand jury. He was caught in a real bind: having taken $10,000, by 1920 he knew that it was impossible to "give it back with interest"—the thugs with whom he had bargained were not nice guys. As Jackson may have done, he may have told the grand jury, and reporters later, a version of things that was prepared for the eyes and ears of gamblers.

On the witness stand in the 1921 trial, Bill Burns testified that in the plotting of the fix Cicotte said that he wanted to win his second game "so as to help him out in making his next year's contract." Burns added that the other players agreed that they wanted to win that game for Eddie. In Burns's story, the fix was *off* after Game Two, and the Sox really were trying to win from Game Three on. And Cicotte was "supposed" to win his second start, Game Four, *even if the fix was still on*.

Cubs secretary John Seys testified at the same trial that Abe Attell had told him not to bet on the Reds for Game Three, because the Sox were going to win. If that was true, Attell may have been expecting Cicotte to pitch and to win. Dickie Kerr said Gleason had Cicotte and himself both warm up for Game Three, then gave the start to Kerr, which upset Cicotte. Kerr: "I think [the reason the gamblers never approached me] was that if Cicotte and Williams got beat in the first two games, Gleason would not dare to take a chance and pitch anyone else but them until we evened up the Series with the Reds."[69] Reporter Hugh Fullerton wrote a year later that Gleason, having found out about the fix, threatened his players, and "spoiled the plans of the gamblers by sending little Dick Kerr in to pitch."[70]

In his grand jury statement, Lefty Williams said that he spoke with Cicotte on the second trip to Cincinnati, after the Reds had won four of the first five games. "I told him we were double-crossed and that I was going to win if there was any possible chance. Cicotte said he was the same way." Burns's testimony suggests that Cicotte probably was pitching Game Four to win but that Williams may have been lured back into the fix for Game Five, even though the "solidarity" of the conspiracy, never clear or very strong, had dissipated.

Would Comiskey have doubled Eddie's salary for the 1920 season if he thought he had lost two games on purpose? Or would he more likely have told Eddie to retire a little early, he would not be welcome back, as Comiskey may well have told Gandil?

Edd Roush's Recollection

Edd Roush, the Cincinnati Hall of Famer who played center field for the Reds in 1919, was always skeptical that the Series was fixed, and like many Reds (and Reds fans, no doubt), he believed that the best team won, without any help from their opponents.

After he retired, Roush told a number of stories, some of which appeared in Lawrence Ritter's oral history classic, *The Glory of Their Times*, and some of which appeared in other books and articles. However, in the transcripts of the Ritter tapes, there are some comments by Roush that did not make it into *Glory*.[71]

After Game Two, a newsman/gambler named Jimmy Widmeyer,[72] Roush's "deep throat" source for one story that concerns Cicotte, asked Roush if he heard the "squabble" that the White Sox got into after Game One. Widmeyer said that the Sox tossed the game, but the $20,000 they were promised was not delivered. Roush quoted Widmeyer: "They had a meeting in Cicotte's room. . . . Gleason found out about it and he went up there. They had a heck of a go-around. I heard it because my [Widmeyer's] room is right next to Cicotte's."

Roush told Ritter that the Sox players beat up one of the fixers until manager Kid Gleason was finally sent for. "'They didn't get their money and they decided to go out and win if they could.' Well, I didn't pay too much attention to that," Roush said. His anecdote seems to be corroborated by a *Sporting News* article:

> Williams and Cicotte said [to the 1920 grand jury] that after the awful howl was raised they decided they had better pitch real ball in the closing games of the Series, but by that time things were so upset on the team because of accusations, threats, etc., that it didn't make much difference whether the conspirators tried to play ball or not.[73]

Jimmy Widmeyer took Roush aside sometime between Games Seven and Eight and told him, "they got to some of the players on your own ball club." Roush spoke up in the dressing room and asked if anyone had been contacted by gamblers. Starting pitcher Hod Eller said, "Yup" (to Ritter, Roush said Eller had been offered a bribe of "five $1,000 bills")—then told how he had threatened to punch out the fellow who made the offer. "I don't like those kind of guys." Manager Moran then called an impromptu meeting in the shower room —Moran, Roush, Eller, and Jake Daubert. Moran made it clear that he would yank anyone he suspected of doing anything fishy. Roush said that he thought no more about it, until the next season.[74]

> It began to come out when Cicotte spilled the beans, see. He finally just up and spilled the beans. He told the same damn story that was told to me, see. That after the first ball game

they didn't get their money and they went out and tried to win. Well, the writers have done everything but print what he said, see. Because the writers said that Cincinnati never had a chance. . . . I could never figure that out myself, see, why those newspapermen was with the White Sox so. How the hell does a newspaperman know about a ballplayer? How the hell do they vote on a man for the Hall of Fame, anyhow? I can't figure it.[75]

In *Glory*, Ritter includes the Hod Eller anecdote, but nothing about Cicotte and what was *not* printed from his grand jury testimony. Roush seemed to suggest that the media of the day, the newspapermen, latched onto the Big Fix story at least partly because it would explain why the team they picked to win the 1919 Series, the Sox, had fared so poorly against the Reds. And the "smaller" the fix was—for example, if it was in for only the first game or two—the worse their predictions looked. And the smaller the story, too. One or two fixed games, not such a big deal, but a *fixed World Series!* Again, Roush and his teammates thought had they won fair and square and saw themselves confirmed as the better team.

Roush's stubborn insistence that the Reds beat the Sox fair and square may be rooted in the information he received from his source, Widmeyer.[76] Roush evidently believed that the fix was off after Game One, as Widmeyer said. Roush said he was "convinced and satisfied" that the Sox were trying to win after the opening game. Roush also insisted that the Reds had the superior pitching, and while the White Sox had the better hitting, "pitching is 70 percent of the game."[77]

Roush elaborated on the story he got from Widmeyer, whom he characterized this time as a gambler, in an interview with Joseph Reichler:

He told me an amazing story. He told me that certain well-known gamblers had told him eight White Sox players had been fixed to throw the Series to the Reds. He told me how a lot of gamblers, including himself, had lost a lot of money in the first games betting on the White Sox, before getting wise to what was going on. He then said that some smart crooks, angry at the double-cross by the New York gamblers, began figuring out a way to get even and at the same time recoup their losses. After the first two games, they figured out a deal whereby, if they could get the Reds to throw the Series, they would clean up because by now everyone figured the Reds were set to win.[78]

Widmeyer did not know if the gamblers had succeeded in getting to any of the Reds, but "hinted there was a strong possibility that they had." Roush got angrier, the more he heard. He then described to Reichler the team meeting before Game Eight.

> I was still burning so I stood up and said out loud so that everybody could hear, 'I hear someone in this club doesn't want to win today.' You could hear a pin drop. 'Well, I'll be out there in center field watching every move, and nobody better do anything funny. No damn crook is going to rob me of my winning share of this Series.'[79]

Manager Pat Moran took Roush aside, and Roush told him everything he had heard. "I was still mad, and I told him, 'I'm not going to go out and run my legs off if we have someone on the team who doesn't want to win.'" Moran then called in Hod Eller and the rest of the story unfolded as Roush had told others. One wonders if there was not a similar confrontation in the White Sox locker room after Game One or Two.

Only His Catcher Knew for Sure?

Did Cicotte play to win? Again, for most of the time since 1919, that seemed like a ridiculous question. It still seems unlikely that Cicotte gave his best in the entire Series, but now there is more evidence to consider. The Cincinnati Reds thought he had pitched to win, as did the umpires. What about his catcher, Ray Schalk? A number of sources have Schalk physically fighting with Lefty Williams for not pitching to win, and some of them have Schalk showing similar displeasure with the staff ace, Cicotte. But then how to explain anecdotes like this one from Bill Werber:

> In 1932, the Yankees sent me to play for the Buffalo Bisons under Ray Schalk, the old White Sox catcher. He was a feisty little Dutchman and regaled us with stories of his eighteen years in the big leagues. He caught every game of the 1919 World Series for the so-called Black Sox against the Cincinnati Reds and was emphatic that Shoeless Joe Jackson and Ed Cicotte gave their best all the way. I always believed that as the catcher for the team, he was in a position to know.[80]

Did Schalk physically assault Cicotte, as well as Lefty Williams? Nelson Algren, in a poem in which he sometimes confuses players, may be recalling this fight in his account of a story he imagined or heard about Lefty Williams "handing Cicotte a dirty envelope with no one but Ray Schalk watching."

Schalk got the left-hander into a pier-brawl under the stands:
Went up to the showers with his knuckles already skinned
And beat Cicotte in front of them all."[81]

What about the part of Cicotte's *Tribune* statement that suggests that one of the eight men suspended was innocent of being in on the fix? He probably did not mean Joe Jackson—Cicotte thought Jackson was a co-conspirator. And he thought that because the team's first baseman, Chick Gandil, his partner in the fix, and/or Jackson's friend, Lefty Williams, told him so. It seems likely that Cicotte meant Buck Weaver. Weaver was the third baseman who was banned, not for doing anything crooked during the Series, but for having "guilty knowledge" of the fix and not reporting it to his team. Buck had sat in on some of the meetings between the conspiring players and the gamblers, but had decided that the fix was not for him. More on Weaver later.

MOTIVATED BY OPPORTUNITY DENIED?

What most people today know and think about the 1919 World Series and its aftermath can be traced to Eliot Asinof's *Eight Men Out*, the 1963 book and the 1988 movie directed by John Sayles. In the book, Asinof suggests that Eddie Cicotte's motive for being in on or initiating the fix had much to do with a bonus of $10,000 that he had been promised in 1917, if he won thirty games. White Sox owner Charles Comiskey, in order to avoid having to pay the hefty bonus, had Eddie benched. In the film, Sayles moves the bonus denied to 1919, and the scene is very sympathetic to Cicotte.

But Asinof's best guess about what made Eddie do it, has not stood up to scrutiny. In both 1917 and 1919, Cicotte had chances to win thirty (he won twenty-eight and twenty-nine those two seasons); there is no evidence that Comiskey prevented it from happening. As Casey Stengel often said, "You can look it up." Box scores are public record.[82]

What follows may seem to some like a tangent. But keep in mind that we are correcting something that, in what many people consider the "definitive" book on the subject, involves the primary motivation of the person who may well have been the initiator of the Big Fix. So it is worth the longer look.

Baseball researcher and writer Rob Neyer was among the first to notice the problem with the Cicotte bonus.[83] Neyer addresses this passage from *Eight Men Out*:

> There were betrayals, too. Like Comiskey's promise to give Cicotte a $10,000 bonus in 1917 if he won thirty games. When the great pitcher threatened to reach that figure, it was said that Comiskey had him benched. The excuse, of course, was to rest him for the World Series.

Neyer wonders where Asinof got this information—there are no footnotes in *Eight Men Out*. "Asinof's source for this is unclear, and one begins by wondering how a story of this nature surfaces forty years after the fact."

The record shows that Cicotte started thirteen times in August and September 1917, with never more than five days between starts. A few times "he pitched on two days rest, and also made four lengthy relief appearances." He had his chances to win thirty, all right, and he led the American League in innings pitched with 347, nineteen more than Walter Johnson.

Neyer found no mention of a bonus in the *Chicago Tribune* accounts. Cicotte had been making $5,000 per season since 1915. So a $10,000 bonus seems absurd in 1917, and even more unlikely in 1919, when salaries were depressed across the board.[84] Before 1917, Cicotte's highest win total had been eighteen, so perhaps a bonus for winning twenty was offered.

There is no doubt that Eddie Cicotte, as one of the aces of the league, *should* have been paid $10,000 a year or more.[85] That is what he received in 1920. The money was there; White Sox secondbaseman and superstar Eddie Collins was making $15,000. There are many who blame Comiskey's wages for the fix; they believe that if the players had been paid fair and decent salaries, they would not have been so willing to risk their careers for $10,000 or $20,000.

But baseball researcher Bob Hoie argues that the White Sox might have had the top payroll in their league and perhaps in both leagues, around $90,000. In 1920, it was around $113,000. Hoie has been unable to find a team with a higher 1919 payroll. Comiskey's "Scrooge" image has spread thanks to *Eight Men Out,* and perhaps to the tendency to read into history modern assumptions about "greedy players" or "tight-fisted owners." Comiskey was probably not exceptionally tight. Every owner wielded the reserve clause as the ultimate closer in contract negotiations. To think of Comiskey as the rule, and not the exception, is hard; but the facts seem to point in that direction.[86]

Comiskey's treatment of his team may have been a factor in the scheme to toss the Series. But it may well be that neither their salaries nor their working conditions were as strong a motive as the chance to make some "easy money" from the gamblers surrounding the sport. And even if the White Sox were the worst paid team, or the worst treated, neither fact would have justified the conspiracy.

So is there nothing at all to Cicotte's claim that he was done wrong—that he was interrupted in his pursuit of thirty wins, with Comiskey pulling the strings to keep him away from a big bonus? Well, there is still 1919—maybe Asinof just made a typo in *Eight Men Out*. Because in September 1919, Kid Gleason displayed what Neyer terms "an extremely strange way to run a pitching staff during the pennant race."

Neyer found that Cicotte had a strong August, winning four of six starts, and he picked up two more wins in relief. He won his first two starts in September—then had a two-week layoff. When he returned (on September 19) with a win over Boston, the *Tribune* announced he was "back in form"—he had walked six in his previous win on September 5, and none on September 19.

The *Cleveland Plain Dealer* reported on September 17, 1919, that Cicotte was suffering from a sore arm. "He told friends it was not lame, but very tired."[87] On October 2, *The Sporting News* carried George Robbins's report on Cicotte; Eddie said that his "arm has responded to rest and treatment the last two weeks." After his September 19 win, he was "allowed to go to his home in Detroit for five days." Starting against the Browns on September 24, Cicotte was hit hard; he was not in the game when the Sox rallied for a 6–5 win.

Responding to questions about Cicotte's arm on the eve of the 1919 World Series, manager Kid Gleason said, "Say, it always was allright and it's just the same now as it was. Those stories about Cicotte having a sore arm were all wrong. He's ready [for the Series]."[88] The same day, the *New York Times* quoted Cicotte saying that his arm *had* been lame a few weeks earlier. Bob Hoie has pointed out that this disagreement between Gleason and Cicotte "is *exactly the opposite* of what one would expect if Cicotte had been artificially held back from winning thirty games in order to cheat him out of a bonus."[89]

But there is some evidence that the conspiracy had been hatched as early as August and probably not later than mid-September. Eddie Cicotte may have seen his chance at thirty wins slipping away as September wound down, but not before the fix was already in motion. So the loss of a bonus was not likely a factor in Cicotte's motivation. While plotting the fix, Cicotte had no idea if he would win thirty or not, or how Comiskey would respond if he did or came close. He did get two starts (one was just a tune-up) after winning number twenty-nine, but the two-week layoff really hurt his chances.[90]

The wire stories and box scores that made it to print in 1917 and 1919 usually did not include pitchers' won-lost records. A pre-Series piece notes that Cicotte won "around thirty" games in 1919. The winning pitchers were not credited in the box scores back then, either. Here is a reason at least for the American League: "In 1913, Ban Johnson not only proclaimed the ERA (earned run average) official, he became so enamored with it that he also instructed American League scorers to compile no official won-lost records. This state of affairs lasted seven years, 1913–1919."[91]

We have come a long way; today we are flooded with statistics immediately and constantly. Imagine a pitcher with a shot at thirty wins today, trying to sneak in number thirty! *Pedro Martinez on the hill tonight, seems like he has around twenty-eight, twenty-nine wins. . . .Well, he's won a bunch of games.*

Some writers, including Sox historian Richard C. Lindberg, speculate that Asinof got the bonus story from Eddie Cicotte himself but never checked it out. Lindberg also believes, as do Bill James and Bob Hoie, that if there was a bonus, it was a small one. The press reported on July 8, 1921, that Cicotte was paid $952.50 a month in 1919 and received a $3,000 bonus.

Lowell Blaisdell wrote one of the most comprehensive and convincing articles about the "legend" of the Cicotte bonus in 1992. Blaisdell argues that Gleason was resting Cicotte in anticipation of needing to use him at least three times in the World Series, with just two days' rest for each start. Gleason said as much to a *New York Times* reporter on September 21. Blaisdell points out that while the legend of the bonus denied was easy to believe due to Comiskey's penny-pinching ways, it "darkens excessively" Comiskey's reputation.

At a deeper level, there probably was another factor, symptomatic of the times. By the early twentieth century the ruthless anti-social actions of many business tycoons was common knowledge. This had spawned the legend that all rich entrepreneurs were by definition bent on exploiting the common man. Who better served from the sports world as the archetype of the "Robber Baron" than the White Sox owner? Was not his assumed refusal to allow his star pitcher to win 30 games a perfect illustration of a rich mogul's heartlessness? And thus has the legend enjoyed a hearty life.[92]

Legends are sometimes impossible to kill, but recently, a piece of hard evidence about Cicotte's bonus has been found. In 2002, Major League Baseball donated approximately 15,000 "transaction cards" to the National Baseball Library in Cooperstown. These were cards kept by the league offices to track movement of players from one team to another and to note the salary and other special features of each contract signed. Among them was the card of Eddie Cicotte. Here is how it reads:

Top line: CICOTTE, E.V. "CHICAGO" Detroit, Michigan

The information on the rest of the card is just typed in a continuous flow, with new information following old.

C.A. with Boston 3/18/12 $3600.00; W R by Chgo & Wash 6/3/12: Rel to Chicago 7/9/12: C.A. 2/17/13 $3600.00: W 3/12/13: C. 3/10/14 A. with Chgo 5/2/14 $4250 ($3500-$1250) for season 1914. Clause 7 eliminated. C. 6/22/14 A. with Chicago 1/9/15 $5000 ($3500-$1500) each for seasons 1915, 1916, and 1917. Clause seven eliminated: C. 1/9/18 A. with Chicago 3/28/18 $5000 ($3000-$1500) for season 1918 (OFC) $2000 advance at time of signing: C. 1/29/19 A. with Chicago 5/2/19 $952.50 ($750-$202.50) per month for season 1919: C.A. with Chicago 5/3/20 $10,000 ($8,000-$2,000) for season 1920, starting on Apr 14 and ending on October 14, 1920: Last two lines first page contract eliminated: Ineligible list Chicago club.

According to historian Bob Hoie, "C" stands for contract and "A" for accepted. Clause seven at that time was the ten days clause. Some contracts note that "Clause 7" is eliminated, and some specify the "10 Days Clause" that allowed a team to cut players loose any time they wanted, giving them just ten days' notice. The removal of that clause (as in Eddie's 1914 and 1917 contracts) gave a player some security; they would be guaranteed their salary for the duration of the contract, unless they did something awful. Like take a bribe.

The fact that Cicotte's card had no mention of a bonus for winning thirty (in 1917 or 1919), does not mean there was none. The cards did include bonuses; but in fact, not all bonuses were contractual, and promises made verbally would not be reflected in the agreements that were copied for the league office, the team and the player.[93]

DEATH THREATS?

George Cicotte, a great grandnephew of Eddie Cicotte, has claimed that Eddie Cicotte's wife was threatened during the 1919 World Series.[94] He also claimed that the scene in the movie *Eight Men Out* depicting Comiskey denying Cicotte a bonus was "highly accurate."[95]

Was there a threat to Eddie Cicotte and/or his wife? That could help to explain why Eddie and almost all of the players associated with the fix were extremely reluctant to discuss their roles, even decades after the fix was uncovered. Some writers and historians believe the threat of violence from the underworld was responsible for their grand and lasting silence.

Cicotte gave just a hint that he might have been threatened when he was deposed before the 1924 Milwaukee trial. After saying that he really did try to win Game Four, he was asked why. He replied,

> Well, because I didn't care whether or not I got shot out there the next minute. I was going to win the ball game and the Series. I didn't care for the money after that. [It is not clear what he is referring to here, probably to his Game One loss.] I lost too many friends there at base-ball, friends that look up to me, and everything depended on it and I couldn't stand it.

Taken together, his 1924 statements suggest that Eddie Cicotte's conscience bothered him, starting at the moment that he accepted the $10,000 to help throw the Series. Whether he had a change of heart right after hitting the first batter in Game One, or after losing Game One, or after losing Game Four, can be argued. What is certain is that he pitched and won Game Seven, that he used the $10,000 to pay off the mortgage on his farm, and that he broke open the scandal with his September 1920 trip to the grand jury.

Below we will look at the evidence for the more famous threat that may have caused Lefty Williams to tilt Game Eight to the Reds. While there are references to death threats in October 1919, revealed later by the players, most are subtle. Joe Jackson was perhaps the most explicit when he said he feared retaliation from his teammate Swede Risberg after he went to the grand jury. But the only evidence of actual violence—and it is thin evidence—has catcher Ray Schalk punishing his batterymates with his fists, for giving what Schalk apparently judged to be less than their best performances on the mound.

NEVER DENIED MAKING A MISTAKE

"Organized baseball is a closed book for me," said Eddie Cicotte in 1927, when fresh scandals were breaking. "I don't care to take part in any of its squabbles."[96] Cicotte stayed away from the Risberg hearing that year and did a good job of staying off the baseball record for a number of decades after. (More on the Risberg hearing later.)

In 1965, Eddie Cicotte finally gave an interview. It was to Detroit reporter Joe Falls.[97] He admitted making a mistake, but was proud that had he made up for it with forty-five years of clean living. His family and friends seemed proud, too. Confession was indeed good for this soul.

> I don't know of anyone who ever went through life without making a mistake. Everybody who ever lived has committed sins of his own. I've tried to make up for it by living as clean a life as I could. I'm proud of the way I've lived and I think my family is, too.

Falls concluded the interview, "As I went down the steps, I waved good-bye to the man in the plaid shirt, the blue denim pants and the tan shoes, but what I noticed for the first time were his socks. They were white."

LEFTY WILLIAMS

Claude Preston "Lefty" Williams was born in 1893 in Aurora, Missouri. Like Eddie Cicotte, Lefty started his career in Detroit. He joined the White Sox prior to the 1916 season. Williams's testimony was delivered to the 1920 grand jury the day after Cicotte and Jackson appeared. Known as a control artist, Williams walked eight in sixteen innings, losing a record three games in the 1919

Series. It is widely believed that Williams and his wife had been threatened with death if Lefty failed to lose the final game of the Series by serving up a big first inning. He did.

There is no doubt that Claude "Lefty" Williams was in on the fix. Losing the final game must have been extremely painful for Lefty—first he had to convince his manager, Gleason, that the fix was *off* (and he could point to Cicotte's win in Game Seven as proof), but then—some believe—he had to hand the Reds a big first inning, or risk losing his wife and his own life. But he got there on his own.

Summing up Williams' pitching in October 1919 is easy. Lefty's wildness cost him dearly in Game Two, a complete game, 4–2 loss in which he gave up just four hits. He yielded just four hits in eight innings in Game Five, a 5–0 loss; the four runs off Williams came in the Reds' sixth inning. Finally, he gave up four runs in Game Eight before he was removed from the mound in the first inning. Three games, one bad inning in each, three losses.

FRIENDS

That Williams gave his fellow-southerner friend Joe Jackson $5,000 is also certain. Lefty later testified under oath that Jackson had not been in on the fix but that his name had been mentioned and that Lefty had represented Jackson to the gamblers—without Joe's knowledge or permission. That's *not* what friends are for. And at least up until then, Williams and Jackson had been very close friends.

> They are neighbors at home in Chicago and roomies on the road and their wives are such chums that what one knows the other knows. Jackson jumped to the shipyards [in 1918], Williams followed. Comiskey forgave Jackson and Joe signed a contract to return. Presto Williams also asks forgiveness, gets it and signs. . . . Williams did not leave the White Sox for a shipyard job because he wanted to escape Army service, for he was safe under exemption—he just went because Jackson did. . . . [He] was going like a house afire last spring [1918] when Joe quit—and he just had to quit along with him.[98]

When the grand jury was meeting in late September 1920, Lefty Williams appeared the day after Cicotte and Jackson at the law firm of Comiskey's lawyer, Alfred Austrian. With his manager Kid Gleason and a court reporter present, Williams responded to Austrian's questions.[99]

Williams's signed statement was admitted into the grand jury hearings. Austrian also had him sign a waiver of immunity, so what he said could be used against him.

Austrian appeared to be taking no more chances. Joe Jackson, the day before, after careful coaching by Austrian, had not been able to swear that he had done anything to toss the games. *At least he kept quiet about Comiskey*, Austrian might have thought. With Lefty, Austrian did all the questioning himself, then delivered the statement with the Qs and As to the grand jury.

Asked about "everyone you talked to" at the meetings, Williams named Cicotte, Gandil, Weaver, and Felsch, and several gamblers. Williams said that he had been promised $10,000 to lose Game Two, but got only $5,000, from Gandil, after Game Four. Later, Williams said he was paid after the Series was over. Williams did not know how much any of the other players received, or even whether Game Three was supposed to be tossed. All he seemed to know for sure was that a lot of money had been promised, and a lot of double-crossing had gone on.

At least in the excerpts of Williams' statement that we have today, Austrian never asked Lefty about Joe Jackson, never gave him the opportunity to clear his friend, or to implicate him. Nor did he follow up on Lefty's naming of other players: they met with gamblers, but did they all agree to participate in the fix? Why not run down the seven names he had and ask Lefty to comment on each?

Lefty's original statement disappeared with the rest of the grand jury material before the 1921 trial. Cicotte, Jackson, and Williams repudiated those 1920 statements, and no player took the stand in 1921 to defend himself or to be questioned. Buck Weaver wanted to, but the defense lawyers made it a package deal, and this turned out to be a winning strategy, at least in court. The "conspiracy to defraud" charges were tough to prove, and the case probably should not have gone to trial. Nor did it need to—rookie commissioner Kenesaw Mountain Landis had made up his mind about the futures of the eight players.

OTHER VERSIONS

Deposed for the Milwaukee trial on May 5, 1923, Lefty Williams said, "The first I heard [of the fix] was in 1920 when I was suspended." He could not recall talking with Gandil about it before the Series. Stonewalling, Lefty insisted that he had spoken with no one and suspected nothing. He had testified once, and that was enough. Promised by Austrian that he would be taken care of, Lefty soon found himself out of his baseball career. He was not eager to be cooperative with the legal system. About all he would admit was that he had made $3,300 in 1917, was cut to $3,000 for 1918, and was cut again to $2,600 for 1919. The $5,000 he had received for his role in the fix was nearly double his salary.

On January 12, 1924, just weeks before the Milwaukee trial began, Lefty Williams was deposed again. This time, he opened up. He was confronted with his 1920 grand jury statements. His general response was that he did not recall what he said in 1920 but that whatever he said then, he had believed to be true then. The fix "has been a thing of the past for me."[100]

Lefty said that he turned down Gandil's first offer to join the fix. Asked about Joe Jackson's role, Williams said that Jackson had "played his regular game all the way through" the Series. He could recall no suspicious play by Jackson. Williams explained that he had used Jackson's name in the meetings with the gamblers, without Jackson's knowledge or permission.[101]

Lefty testified that he had received $10,000 from Chick Gandil. "Gandil told me, 'There is five for yourself, and five for Jackson, and the rest has been called for'"[102]—meaning that the gamblers needed it to make more bets and more money. If that recollection was correct, Williams received the money during the Series, while betting was still going on.

Lefty had expected to receive some money after Game Two, but did not. Later, Williams said that he took the money, counted it, and went to Cincinnati—that would have been after Game Five. Another time, Williams said that Gandil had given him the payoff after Game Three, saying, "There is your dough, the gamblers have called it off." In 1920, he had said he gave Jackson $5,000 after Game Four. He also said he "never got a nickel until after the last two games."[103]

Like Jackson, Williams testified that he "would have kept the money if Chicago won." Whenever it was that Lefty was paid, he said that his wife's reaction was not positive. She was mad—"until I showed her the money. She said 'You have done it. What can I say how I just got it? Let it go and get the best of it.'"

If Lefty Williams was annoyingly vague about just when he had received the money, he was also inconsistent about when he had passed on the $5,000 to his friend Joe Jackson. Did he throw the money on the bed and say, "We have been crossed in some way"—suggesting that a bigger payoff ($20,000 per player) was expected? Williams said that when he delivered the cash, he told Jackson that the fix had just been called off. Again, if that was accurate, the delivery took place *during* the Series.

Despite all the vagueness and contradictions in Lefty Williams's statements, the Milwaukee jury at the 1924 civil suit trial—having heard Williams, Jackson, and Jackson's wife Kate all tell about when, where, and how the $5,000 was given to Jackson—voted in their special verdict by eleven to one, that the money had been given *after*, not during the Series, and that Williams did *not* tell Jackson at that time that the cash was his share of the money received for the players' part in an agreement with gamblers to toss the Series.

DID WILLIAMS TRY TO WIN ANY GAMES?

Jackson consistently said that he had played the whole Series to win. Cicotte admitted to being in the conspiracy, and to at least putting the first batter in Game One on base, on purpose, as the signal that the fix was in; whether he also threw Game One is not certain, but it seems likely; his statements for the 1924 trial make his "crooked" role in Game Four seem less likely. What about Lefty Williams?

Asked in his second deposition, "Did you do anything intentional to throw the games?" Lefty replied, "I did not; I was a little nervous, naturally, and there was three bases made by the shortstop." But later he admitted, "Well, I might have pitched harder if I wanted to." Weighing against this claim are the facts that Ray Schalk confronted Williams, by some reports with a physical assault, after Game Two, and did not insist later to young Bill Werber (as he did about Jackson and Cicotte) that Lefty played to win.

Williams also denied intentionally losing Game Five: "I pitched as hard as I ever pitched a ball game in my life."[104]

Q: "Were you nervous because this [the fix] was on your mind?"

A: "Naturally it did. I was sorry, I wanted to be out of it and not mixed up in it at all."

Lefty also insisted that he had pitched Game Eight to win.[105] Possibly, a death threat was still vivid to him. In his grand jury statement, Williams said that on the way to the park for Game Eight, he told Jackson, "If we have been double-crossed I am going to win this game if I possibly can." Williams also said that he told Cicotte after Game Five that he was out to win because he had been double-crossed. The double-crossing started early in the Series, when the $20,000 payoffs after Games One and Two were not delivered.

If Lefty had made the statement above to anyone before Game Eight, it would likely have been to Gleason, to make sure that he got the start. If he made it up, or was advised by Austrian to say it for the grand jury, it likely was to emphasize the double-crossing that had taken place. Williams never was clear about whether the Sox were "supposed" to lose Game Three or not (neither was Jackson). Communication with Gandil had broken down, and Williams may have been out of the loop for Game Five, or he may have made a personal deal with agents of Abe Attell or Sport Sullivan. Burns and Maharg testified that there were still men who were trying hard to see that the Series went to the Reds, no matter how.

THE FAMOUS DEATH THREAT

In *Eight Men Out*, Eliot Asinof says that a death threat was delivered to Lefty Williams before he pitched his third start, in Game Eight. What is the evidence for this?

"Requiem for a Southpaw" appeared in the December 5, 1959, issue of *The New Yorker*—just after Lefty died. The author, J. M. Flagler, as a young boy (he was born in 1922), knew Lefty Williams as a friend who taught him some pitches in their games of catch. Lefty and his wife, Lyria,[106] lived in a basement apartment below Flagler's family's home. J. M.'s dad recognized Lefty's name and mentioned it to his son, who found himself talking one day with Lefty's wife. She told him it was so—and she wanted him to hear it from her first.

> "He was wrong, I guess, but he was only a youngster when it happened," [Lefty was twenty-six and in his sixth year in the major leagues] she said in a rush. "All those others were doing it, and he didn't understand what it really meant, and besides, he was threatened."

She said that the threat was that, if Lefty did not toss Game Eight, a hired gun would shoot her. Gambler Billy Maharg had hinted at this in his 1920 interview with a Philadelphia reporter.[107]

Arnold Rothstein "is said to have arranged for a Chicago thug . . . to pay a call on Lefty Williams, who was to pitch the eighth game."[108] "The thug" is commonly identified as "Harry F." because he has that name in *Eight Men Out*. He has also been called "the Man in the Bowler Hat"[109] and the "man in a black derby."[110] But did someone really make Lefty an offer he could not refuse—threaten his life and that of his wife—if Lefty was still on the mound after the first inning?

(In Brendan Boyd's fiction, the hit man is in Lefty's apartment when he arrives there the night before Game Eight. The thug drives home his point just before he leaves by ordering Lefty to turn up the heat in his stove after they talk. Lefty does as he is told, and soon realizes that his cat is in the oven.)[111]

In an interview for this book, Eliot Asinof confessed that he named the hired gun "Harry F." when someone suggested that he add a dash of fiction to his account, so that if others "borrowed" it without giving him credit, it would be obvious on what source they had relied. "Harry F." now appears in many books and articles.[112]

Reds star Edd Roush batted against Lefty Williams in that first inning of Game Eight. Was Lefty pitching with one eye on Rothstein's "designated hitter"? Roush recalled pulling a curve ball just fair over first base. "I could just as easily have popped up, or the ball gone foul." In other words, even someone close to the action could not say for sure if Williams was serving up a big inning or if he was the victim of bad breaks.

8

THE OTHER GHOSTS OF SUMMER

DICKIE KERR

Richard Henry Kerr was born in 1893 in St. Louis, Missouri. A rookie in 1919, Kerr won thirteen games for the White Sox. He drew the starts in Games Three and Six, coming through each time with wins. He was not part of the conspiracy, but his story needs to be told, along with those of his "crooked" teammates. When it was later revealed that the support of his teammates, particularly in Game Three, was doubtful, Dickie Kerr became a hero to Sox fans. (While Kerr apparently preferred "Dickey," his name was "Dickie" in most newspapers and remains that way in most books.)

In pursuit of the whole story about the 1919 scandal, there are many sad tales. Shoeless Joe Jackson's is the most famous. Buck Weaver's is probably next.

And then there is the case of Dickie Kerr. He is the White Sox pitcher who won two games in the Series, in spite of everything going on. In Game Three, he tossed a complete game, three-hit shutout; in Game Six, he won 5–4 in ten innings. The 5'7" lefty was a rookie in 1919 and had a 13–7 season. Dickie was not the third-best Sox hurler (behind Cicotte and Williams). Red Faber—who won three games in the 1917 Series—was, but Red was not available for pitching duty that October, so Kerr got the World Series starts.

For his efforts, Comiskey rewarded Kerr with a $4,500 salary for 1920, with the option to sign him in 1921 at the same figure. In 1920 Kerr went 21–9 and was (with Faber) one of the aces left when the season ended. In 1921, with a gutted Sox team in the field, he still managed to win nineteen games.

With three fine seasons under his belt, not to mention the 1919 Series heroics, Kerr was offered either $4,500 or $6,500 for 1922 (accounts vary, but it was probably $6,500, which is what he earned in 1921). In any case, the offer did not include a raise or the multiyear contract that Kerr thought he deserved. And remember, in 1922, baseball income was booming, thanks to the sport's cleaned-up image and to Babe Ruth.

Kerr had had enough. He signed a $5,000 contract to play with a Texas semi-pro team. There he played against some of the banned Black Sox—and for that he was swiftly suspended in 1923 from baseball by Landis. The commissioner lifted the ban in August 1925, and Dickie Kerr pitched in twelve games for the White Sox; he was 0–1, 5.15, and he never pitched again in the majors.

The *Sporting News* obituary of Dickie Kerr quotes him as having said that he had been tipped off by newspapermen that the fix was in after Game Two. When Gleason went to Kerr after Game Two and asked him if he knew anything, Kerr replied, "Yes, but I'm not telling you who told me." We usually think of reporters protecting their sources, but things were reversed in 1919. This anecdote illustrates again how widespread the knowledge of the fix was. The reporters were thick with the gamblers and the players.

TWO SIMPLE TWISTS OF FATE

"Pitching is 75 percent of baseball," according to Connie Mack, who spent sixty years in baseball, most of them as a manager. The percentage he is supposed to have quoted varies to as high as 90 percent, depending on the source, but in any case, it is plain that Mr. Mack gave a lot of the credit for the success of his teams to his pitchers.

To win a seven-game Series, a manager needs either one hot pitcher who can win three and a little help from the rest, or two pitchers who can win two of three starts. In 1919, the Series was best of nine, so the third starter would be important, too. In the eight games played in 1919, the starting pitchers went eight or more innings twelve of a possible sixteen times; the bullpen was a real factor in only one game, Game Six, won by the Sox in extra innings when the Reds' Jimmy Ring, pitching in relief after a complete game win three days earlier, wilted in his fifth inning.

What made the 1919 Series very vulnerable to a fix was that the White Sox had just three healthy starters available. Cicotte was an ace, having finished the season at 29–7, 1.82, in over 300 innings pitched. Lefty Williams finished 23–11, 2.64. Rookie Dickie Kerr was 13–7, 2.88.

Assuming that manager Kid Gleason had knowledge or *very* strong suspicions of the fix after Game Two, what were his options? If he benched Cicotte and Williams the rest of the way, that could draw attention to the fix, even if he came up with excuses. It appears that Gleason consulted with team owner Comiskey after each game of the Series; the choice to go with the team's best pitchers was probably influenced by Comiskey.

But things might have turned out differently if Gleason had had the services of Hall of Famer Urban "Red" Faber, a winner of 254 games lifetime for the ChiSox, including twenty four in 1915 and twenty three in 1920. (It is easy to imagine Red winning 300+ games if the Sox had not been shattered by the fix.) But when October rolled around in 1919, Faber, who had returned from the Navy and chipped in eleven wins in the pennant race, was sidelined with a sore arm and the flu. Catcher Ray Schalk always insisted that if Faber had been healthy in October 1919, there would have been no fix.

And then there was the case of Jack Quinn. Quinn showed early promise by winning eighteen for New York in the American League in 1910, but then didn't do much until he jumped to the Federal League, where he went 26–14 for Baltimore in 1914. When the Federal League folded, Quinn wound up in the Pacific Coast League. In July 1918 this league shut down for the duration of the war (the majors carried on until Labor Day), and the White Sox signed the thirty-five-year-old spitballer for the stretch run. Quinn went 5–1.

The Yankees saw some potential in their former moundsman and did what the White Sox failed to do—they bought his contract from his Pacific Coast League team, Vernon, in late 1918, when Quinn was in a White Sox uniform. The dispute went to the National Commission, where Ban Johnson reigned. Johnson ruled against Comiskey. This explains why Quinn won fifteen in 1919 for the Yankees, not the White Sox, and why Gleason lacked that starter he needed when Faber went down and Cicotte and Williams lay down.

Gleason's Options

Before leaving this topic, let's take a quick look at the other pitchers the Sox might have used. There was Grover "Slim" Lowdermilk.[1] In nine seasons, Slim was a lackluster 23–39 for five different teams— he ended his career with the Sox in 1920. In the Series, Gleason trusted him to pitch just one inning, where he gave up a run, two hits, and a walk. Slim was the only other starter Gleason had. His other relievers were not too effective, although the defense they had behind them was doubtful.

After Lowdermilk, Gleason had only Bill James, who wound up the season pitching his last five major league games for Chicago, having pitched in fifteen others in 1919 with Detroit and Boston; Erskine Mayer, also at the end of his major league career, pitching in just six games for Chicago after coming to them from Pittsburgh; and Roy Wilkinson, who pitched just four games for the White Sox in the regular season.

Gleason probably was more than a little suspicious about the fix when his two aces lost Games One and Two. He was heartened when Dickie Kerr rose to the occasion and won Game Three, which, according to some sources, the Sox conspirators had figured the rookie would lose. Gleason sent Cicotte and Williams out for that second round of losses either because Comiskey said to send them or because he was hoping that they would straighten out after he had confronted them. As for their third starts, they must have convinced Gleason that the fix was off, and now they *really* wanted to win. Can anyone imagine a manager having a worse time in a Series than Kid Gleason had in 1919?

BUCK WEAVER

George Daniel "Buck" Weaver was born in 1890 in Pottstown, Pennsylvania. He broke into the majors with the White Sox in 1912 as a shortsto but changed positions and gradually became one of the league's top third basemen. Buck admitted to sitting in on meetings with gamblers but denied that he ever agreed to be part of the plot to throw the 1919 Series. Most people believe that he gave no less than his best effort in every game. He was banned nevertheless for having "guilty knowledge" of the fix and failing to inform his club.

> The spiked sand at third belonged to an army haircut
> And a bulldog trick of wearing a pitcher down
> Called Buck Weaver—
> A back-of-the-yards plug-ugly spitting blue seal scrap
> Halfway to the pitcher's box after every foul . . .
> A sandlot animal, all heart and hard living,
> Who wound up coaching a girl's softball team
> And no heart left in him at all.[2]

On the eve of the 1919 World Series, Sox manager Kid Gleason presumably wrote a column for King Features Syndicate, in which he called Buck Weaver "among the great [third basemen] of all time."

"Weaver simply loves to play ball," Gleason went on. "Why, he's got a smile on his face all the time, no matter what is happening. Buck is just as much of a kid today as he was when he first came to the White Sox in 1912. Weaver never gives up."

Buck Weaver was a fan favorite whose hard play earned him the respect of his peers as well. He was on a path to stardom, but instead became "immortalized" as the one player who was banned, even though no one doubted that he had given his best effort on the field. His fate was decided by someone who was not even inside baseball in October 1919, and his story has become forever entwined with the ruling made by baseball's first commissioner, Kenesaw Mountain Landis.

America's attitudes toward its favorite sport were dramatically affected by the rumors and then revelations of the influence of gamblers.[3] When the scandal broke, editorial opinions crashed down on the baseball authorities who had done too little to insulate baseball from professional "crooks," and on the gamblers themselves, who were likened to a cancer in the game.

Even before Judge Landis's now-famous cleansing verdict, editors had called for player dismissals to preserve baseball's integrity—and not quiet, no-publicity dismissals, either. America was ready for whatever it took, and the shift in 1920 was to presume accused players guilty until proven innocent. Why take chances? And baseball could act, "because of the public's faith in the judgment and intentions of those who have the game in their keeping," to dismiss players without having "evidence of the same character . . . that might be required in a court of law."[4]

Who was this man who was chosen by the baseball owners to be the "czar" that replaced the weak National Commission, which had been unable to police gambling in baseball?

> Kenesaw Mountain Landis, with his shock of white hair over craggy features and his mail-slot mouth, looked like a statue of Integrity Alerted, just as Harding, elected in 1920, looked like a president. Landis was a tobacco-chewing bourbon drinker who would hand out stiff sentences to people who violated Prohibition. He had a knack for self-dramatizing publicity. He fined Standard Oil of Indiana $29,240,000 in a rebate case (the Supreme Court overturned him) and tried to extradite Kaiser

Wilhelm on a murder charge because a Chicagoan died when a German submarine sank the *Lusitania*.[5]

The colorful sportswriter Red Smith described Landis as "a gimlet-eyed tyrant off the federal bench with a white fright wig and the face of a sanctified billy goat."[6] Landis was a spectator during the 1919 Series, just an ordinary fan. But he would soon emerge as the most influential and powerful force in baseball at precisely the time that the game needed decisive leadership and an image of integrity. The door was wide open for justice, Kenesaw Mountain Landis–style, and it did not really matter if the case of the eight accused White Sox players went to court or not. The courts could not be trusted to make the right calls. Landis could.

One of the saddest of baseball documents on display at the National Baseball Museum in Cooperstown is a letter from Buck Weaver to Commissioner Ford Frick. In 1953, at age sisty-three (he would die three years later), Buck was still trying to clear his name with Major League Baseball. He insisted that he "knew nothing" and "played a perfect Series." When he sued his team, after he was banned from baseball, contending that he deserved the pay for the last year of his contract (for 1921), he won, which (in Buck's view) proved that he was right and Comiskey wrong.

Of course, Landis never really dealt with Buck as a separate case, even though he responded directly to his appeals several times. At least one writer, Hugh Fullerton, wondered what might happen if Weaver tried to sue baseball and proved that he had been expelled by the club owners—would that demonstrate that baseball was indeed a trust, acting to deprive men of their right to earn a living? Would that then affect the lawsuit filed by the Federal League's Baltimore team against baseball, the suit that would eventually result in baseball's antitrust exemption?[7] Landis was very familiar with that suit, and it may have been a factor, however small, in his rulings on Weaver.

Looking back, it is easy to say that Buck might have argued that he was standing up for a high principle: loyalty to his teammates, right or wrong. He would not "squeal" on them any more than he would talk about clubhouse secrets to the press. He might have insisted that such trust was as important as the ability to bunt, and if players were expected to "spy" on each other, they would be policing the game—and that was management's job, not labor's. A player's union would likely argue the same way.[8]

During the 1921 trial, Hugh Fullerton wrote that the indicted men seemed to have the support of the majority of ballplayers, who were "if not in sympathy with crookedness, were at least inclined not to feel unkindly toward the players who disgraced the sport." They took the attitude, "They ain't no worse than some of them owners." And they knew the real scope of the ties between gambling and baseball. Fullerton estimated that "not fewer than a hundred ballplayers had information that something was doing when that Series [the World Series of 1919] started."[9]

If Fullerton's estimate was off by even fifty, it is easy to see that more than a few players took a keen interest in how the law, and Landis, would deal with the "guilty knowledge" that Buck Weaver had. Fullerton himself believed that the players who had kept silent were acting out of "a false sense of loyalty to fellow players, fear of being called a 'squealer'. . . one reason why so few criminals can be convicted is that we teach our kids that a tattletale is something worse than a criminal."[10]

"I am up a tree about Buck Weaver," Charles Comiskey told a reporter before the 1921 trial.[11] "He was one of the stars of the 1919 baseball championship Series. . . . I wonder if it is possible that Weaver is innocent of the charges that have been lodged against him?" He was, and Comiskey knew that he was. The rules Buck broke had yet to be promulgated by the new commissioner.

When you put the Black Sox scandal under a microscope, it is obvious that while the eight men out were all somehow involved, and some were paid for their "services," there were certainly different degrees of guilt. Cicotte and Williams perhaps teaming up to lose five games is clearly on a different scale than the "contribution" of utility man Fred McMullin.[12] Weaver may not have been the only player to give his best, but he may well have been the only one who played to win *and* did not accept any of the payoff money.[13]

Hugh Fullerton was informed the evening after Game Three that a meeting had been held that morning at the LaSalle Hotel. He had not been able to verify the report of the meeting when he wrote about it exactly one year later. Fullerton was told that seven ballplayers had met with Abe Attell and someone else. Buck Weaver "raved and swore and declared he had nothing to do with the losing of the games and that he would not touch the dirty money."[14]

When Swede Risberg dragged an accusation of bribery into the news at the end of 1926—more on this below—he stated that all of the White Sox regulars chipped in about $45 each to pay off the Tigers in September 1917—all except Buck Weaver.[15]

Weaver was banished because he knew what was going on but said nothing. Those sympathetic to his situation and his "thou shalt not inform on friends" ethic like to point out that other Sox knew what was happening. The catcher, Ray Schalk, whose signs were repeatedly shaken off or ignored by Cicotte and Williams, apparently was seen physically fighting with Williams under the grandstand after Game Two and then complained to Gleason. Gleason himself was probably tipped off by numerous telegrams, and he took them, with his suspicions, to Comiskey early on in the Series, perhaps right after the startling loss in the first game. If Gleason had spoken early to his team about the bribe, what would be the point of Weaver going to Gleason, if Buck really was not sure which players were playing to win?

In a sense, the fact that Gleason shared his knowledge of the fix early on[16] made Buck Weaver's case more complicated for Landis and for history. Informed of the planning of the fix, Buck had opted out. He may have tried to talk others out of it, and maybe he succeeded. In any case, probably no one—not the players, and not the gamblers—were sure that the fix was in until after Game One. If Buck had thought about telling someone, once Gleason called his meeting, Weaver had no one to tell; his team knew. Landis' insisting that Buck should have informed his team covers up the fact that his team already knew but chose not to act on that knowledge.

Landis, by keeping the focus on a minimum number of players, was doing exactly what the owners (especially Comiskey, who had a large hand in hiring Landis) wanted. Baseball's image would suffer no more than it had already. Management's role, *baseball's* role in covering up the ties between the sport and gambling, was not to be explored, or even mentioned.

Buck Weaver said that he did consider telling Comiskey.

> The only doubt in my mind, was whether I should keep quiet about it or tell Mr. Comiskey. I was not certain just what men, if any, had received propositions or whether they had accepted. I couldn't bring myself to tell on them even had I known for certain. I decided to keep quiet and play my best.[17]

THE LANDIS VERDICT

Landis biographer David Pietrusza observes that banning Weaver "ranks as important as any baseball decision he, or anyone else, ever issued. The game was not 'saved' when Landis banished obvious crooks like Gandil and Risberg and Cicotte. Nor did it become simon-pure because . . . Joe Jackson was bounced."[18] Landis knew exactly what Weaver had done—sat in on meetings with gamblers—and that is one of the activities that he wanted to end with his ban; and he raised having "guilty knowledge" of fixes to the level of the fixing itself. "The Weaver decision had a great chilling effect on dishonest play—and *talk* of dishonest play."

Veeck:

> Landis' great wisdom was in understanding that any attempt to investigate all of the gambling and fixing of the past would not only be impossible from a purely administrative standpoint, but would open a can of worms that would be eating away at baseball for the next decade.[19]

Major League Baseball was sick with gambling in 1920, and the disease might have been fatal, if the scandal of the 1919 Series had been handled differently. The Hal Chase case may have been swept under the rug, but this was bigger. The public amputation of the eight Sox was seen as the only acceptable cure—and the public would see no more dirty linen aired in public, not if baseball could prevent it.

Justice was judged to be less important than the game's image. The focus was kept squarely on the ballplayers and away from the owners with gambling ties. Banning marquee players like Jackson and Weaver also sent the right message: no one was above the new law. Saviors of baseball: Landis and Ruth? Yes, but also, indirectly, Jackson and Weaver.[20]

Landis's verdict has been increasingly questioned as the emotions of 1920 have faded into the past.

Nelson Algren: "The verdict we once applauded as one of Olympian sagacity was nothing more, it has become plain, than a legal mugging by an enraptured Puritan." Weaver is "punished ruthlessly" while "the silence of Comiskey, with equal knowledge of corruption, deserved only praise." Algren asks: "What good would it have done Weaver to inform?" After all, Buck had heard Gleason rant to Comiskey about it; "Jackson, frightened and bewildered, had tried to talk to [Comiskey]; but he had been turned out." Algren adds that a year later, when Eddie Collins told Commy about thrown games at the end of 1920, Comiskey again refused to listen.[21]

Historian Lee Allen liked to refer to Landis's decision as a "ukase"—underlining Landis's image as a Russian emperor, or czar. It was an edict that Landis's successors have never dared to question or touch; they seem to regard his ruling as if it had been chiseled into stone on two tablets and handed to baseball on a biblical mountaintop. But is it immutable?

Fixer Abe Attell always maintained Weaver was "guiltless." And he tried several times to convince reporters to take up Buck's cause and intervene with Landis. To a group of newsmen that included George Barton, "Abe declared Weaver refused to be a party of the fix but was sworn to secrecy by Gandil and Risberg, who threatened him with physical violence if he tipped off the deal to Comiskey or Ban Johnson." Gandil and Risberg "assured" Attell "they had fixed Cicotte, Williams, Jackson, Felsch, and McMullin, but couldn't reach Weaver." Attell was sure Buck had received no cash.[22] Damon Runyon, according to Barton, did intercede with Judge Landis to have Buck "exonerated," but Landis pointed to the "guilty knowledge" Buck had.

Attell told reporter Joe Williams that he later even tried to sway Landis himself. "I even went to Landis and made a personal plea for him [Weaver]. The kid didn't get a dime out of it, and he didn't know what was going on, either."[23] Ironically, the fix became a very poorly kept secret, and sometimes it seems like Jackson and Weaver were the only players *not* talking about it, not letting their friends or relatives in on the big payday.

> George Weaver was the only one of the Sox players under indictment who had the courage to appear [at the end of the 1920 season, after the players were suspended] at Comiskey Park. He came to seek an interview with the owner . . . in the hope of exonerating himself. He was permitted to see Comiskey but at the conclusion of his visit left the ballpark with his head down. . . .
>
> The Old Roman [Comiskey] . . . although stricken with sorrow over the disclosures of crookedness. . . .

Despite what the *Chicago Tribune* reported on September 30, 1920 (above), Comiskey had known about the crookedness for almost a year. He was sorry to see it come to light. And if he went to bat for Buck Weaver, everyone would know that he knew.

No summary of the Buck Weaver story would be complete without a mention of James T. Farrell's memoir.[24]

One Chicago sportswriter remarked to me while Buck was still living: "The two players I have sympathy for are Weaver and Joe Jackson. They were brought up in an environment where you were not supposed to squeal. What could they have done? Jackson once talked to me about it. He said: 'I was just a dope.' And Weaver—I'd like to see him clear himself. If baseball would clear him, it wouldn't hurt baseball."

However, here is some evidence against Buck Weaver to consider. Eddie Collins once said that he "should have recognized the tip-off in the very first game." Collins was on first and Weaver at bat, and Eddie gave Buck the hit and run sign, but Buck missed it and Collins "was out a by yard at second." Collins: "Were you asleep?" Weaver: "Quit trying to alibi and play ball."[25] Collins also recalled a tossed game in 1920 where Weaver made a crucial error. Dickie Kerr was upset: "If you fellows are throwing this one let me in on it." That same day, Collins said, "Schalk beat up Risberg in the dugout."[26] The reporter, Joe Williams, apparently never spoke to Weaver for his side of these stories.

Robert C. Cottrell has observed that these recollections of Eddie Collins, which contain some factual errors, are "virtually the only impressions that Buck Weaver ever did anything on the playing field but play as hard as he was capable of."[27] Kerr's comment, while triggered by an error by Weaver, may have been a sarcastic venting, not really aimed at Weaver.

Buck Weaver earned $6,000 in 1918. He held out in the spring of 1919, and was prepared to leave the White Sox, when Harry Grabiner and Kid Gleason offered him a three-year contract for $7,250 per year— without the ten days clause.[28] Buck signed, and if Weaver was less vulnerable to the promises of gamblers that October, perhaps this unusual (for Buck) security was a factor.

After the 1919 Series, Comiskey knew that as many as eight players had been in on the fix, and he withheld the Series money from precisely those eight men who were eventually indicted and then banned. Yet when contract time came along for the 1920 season, Comiskey was exceedingly generous with Cicotte, Williams, Felsch, and McMullin. Risberg had another year left on his two-year contract. Gandil did not return.

However, when Weaver asked for a raise, he was refused. And Jackson, who wanted $10,000 for 1920, was signed only after a contentious exchange of letters between himself and Comiskey, and finally a personal visit to his winter home by Harry Grabiner. (Jackson settled for $8,000 for three years.) In other words, for Weaver and Jackson, contract time was business as usual, with Buck threatening to hold out again. Of course he changed his mind. All he wanted to do was play baseball.[29]

THE OTHER MEN OUT

The other four players banished by Judge Landis's edict were utility infielder Fred McMullin, shortstop Swede Risberg, center fielder Happy Felsch, and first baseman Chick Gandil.

Apparently **Fred McMullin**, who was close with Risberg and Gandil, eavesdropped his way into the fix, overhearing its mention in the locker room and insisting on a cut. (McMullin may also have heard of the plot from gambler Billy Maharg, who was a drinking buddy of McMullin's.[30]) McMullin scouted the Reds before the Series (Johnny Evers "spied" on the White Sox for the Reds). But McMullin had just two at bats himself; he got one hit, for a .500 average, the highest of any player banned. McMullin, working as a carpenter while awaiting trial, told a *Los Angeles Times* reporter that the prosecution was a "persecution."

McMullin was indicted and posted bond, but when he was re-indicted in the spring of 1921, he declined. A warrant for his arrest was issued, but he never stood trial, as California apparently refused to extradite him, as they did Hal Chase. Landis banned McMullin anyway. But not Chase.

* * * * *

Charles August "Swede" Risberg, a .256 hitter in 1919, claimed to have had a bad cold and played a miserable Series, with just two hits in twenty-five at bats and four errors in the field. (At the 1921 trial, the team trainer testified to having given Swede medicine for a chest cold the evening before Game One.)[31] He was described by Joe Jackson as "a hard guy" when Jackson testified in 1920, and the outfielder requested protection by bailiffs because he feared Risberg would harm him for volunteering what he knew of the fix. In his *Sporting News* obituary is the note that Joe Gedeon, the ninth man out, had learned of the fix from Risberg via a telegram "couching the details in what amounted to a code."

Risberg himself claimed innocence and said little of the fix after he left baseball. "I took no bribe and I did not lay down in that Series. I was not guilty, but I am too old now for reinstatement to do me any good. Milking the cows has made me musclebound."[32]

Bill Burns testified that when the fix was called off, after Game Two, Swede Risberg alone said that he was going through with it and would do his best to lose the rest of the Series. Was Swede more conscious of the risks in double-crossing crooks?

The summer after the Black Sox were banished, a number of them cashed in on their "celebrity" status by playing exhibition games on tour. Risberg managed the "Ex-Major League All Stars" and proved he was indeed a hard guy when he knocked out two of Eddie Cicotte's teeth in a fist fight.[33] Risberg must have forgiven Jackson by then, because he said that he would get Jackson or Lefty Williams to replace Cicotte on the tour.

Risberg broke his silence late in 1926, when he brought to the attention of Commissioner Landis the accusation that virtually the entire White Sox team had pitched in to pay off the Detroit team to toss consecutive doubleheaders to the Sox around Labor Day in 1917. "Landis and the big bosses of baseball don't want to know the facts," Swede told a Chicago reporter. "This is a challenge to the commissioner, let's see what he'll do about it."[34]

The commissioner invited Swede to come to his offices and tell his story. Landis also called in over thirty players and former players from the White Sox and Tigers. Eddie Cicotte refused to come; Joe Jackson also declined. Risberg said that he was not interested in reinstatement, although he would have liked his share of second-place money from 1920. And he was not "squawking to get even with anybody." No, Swede said he was just doing his part in "cleaning up baseball, for the sake of the game." Swede wanted the game to be pure again when his son was old enough to play.

Only Chick Gandil strongly agreed with Risberg's version of the payoff to the Tigers. Buck Weaver tacitly agreed, nodding his head as Risberg told his story to Landis, but Buck would not go on record in support of Risberg, perhaps judging that his case for reinstatement would not be helped by muddying things up for so many others, and for baseball. (The 1927 hearing is covered here later in more detail.)

* * * * *

Oscar "Happy" Felsch became known in the story of the Big Fix for "confessing" to a reporter (but not to the grand jury) and insisting that he himself never did anything crooked. He *might* have, but the opportunities just never came his way. Felsch made several spectacular catches in the series, but also made several awful misplays, and he was charged with two errors in the eight games. A .275 hitter in the 1919 season, Felsch was held to five-for-twenty-six and just three RBIs in the series. However, he socked the ball hard in the series, probably harder than Joe Jackson, hitting into about seven hard outs and being "robbed" of extra-base hits several times by the Reds' outfield.

Felsch's September 29, 1920, interview with Harry Reutlinger was disallowed as evidence in the 1921 trial. The judge stated that there was so little evidence against Felsch and Weaver that he doubted whether he could let a guilty jury verdict stand, and newspapers reported that the two ballplayers were "freed."

Shortly after Felsch's "confession" to Reutlinger appeared in the press, the *Chicago Tribune* reported that the wives of a number of Sox players might be called to talk to the grand jury "as a result of a report said to emanate from the 'square' players still on the Sox team." The report credited Happy Felsch with having placed a $5,000 bet (the amount he told Reutlinger that he received, but had not earned), at 2-to-1 odds, for the Reds to win Game Two. Apparently Felsch's wife was not happy with the $15,000 prize, but they "later made up and Mrs. Felsch deposited the money in a south side savings bank."[35] None of the players' wives testified to the grand jury.

In attempts to make money in 1921, Felsch and the suspended Sox formed barnstorming teams in Chicago, northern Indiana and Wisconsin. Their efforts generally went for naught as ballpark operators and opposing teams were afraid of the consequences of any association with the contaminated Black Sox.

In 1922, Felsch and Risberg sued the White Sox for $100,000 each, declaring that they were ousted from baseball through a conspiracy. Felsch also sought $1,120 in back pay from 1920 and $1,500 for the remainder of a promised 1917 pennant bonus.[36]

Felsch sued for another $100,000 in damages, claiming that his "name and reputation had been permanently impaired and destroyed" and that he had "been barred from playing base ball with any professional base ball team in any of the leagues of organized base ball of the United States." On June 16, Judge John Gregory dismissed the original $100,000 conspiracy complaint. Felsch's case didn't go to trial until 1924, after the trial of Joe Jackson, who, following Felsch and Risberg, had become a client of lawyer Ray Cannon.

> Felsch's civil suit against the Sox was settled out of court. This occurred only minutes before the trial was to have finally begun. All of his claims netted Felsch only $1,166 plus interest and costs for a total of about $1,500. The club, claiming that Comiskey was in poor health, did not want to endure another three-week ordeal.[37]

Happy Felsch was still alive in 1956 when an interview with Chick Gandil appeared in a national magazine. Eddie Cicotte and Happy Felsch were sought out for their reactions, and Happy declared: "The true story is I didn't get a dime from the gamblers, never 'threw' a baseball game, and never intended to 'throw' a game." Chick Gandil's reply: "Felsch is right when he says he never 'threw' a game. We tried to win them."[38]

* * * * *

> From his youth on, [Chick] Gandil combined baseball and gambling. He was a dealer in a gambling house, a prize fighter in winner-take-all bouts. A supplier of information to gamblers, Chick was always looking to make more money any way he could without getting caught. . . . In 1956, Gandil told [Mel] Durslag: "Where a baseball player would run a mile these days to avoid a gambler, we mixed freely. Players often bet. After the games, they would sit in lobbies and bars with gamblers, gabbing away."[39]

Despite the White Sox loss in the Series, the *Chicago Herald and Examiner* had praise for **Charles Arnold "Chick" Gandil**, who was found to have a serious health problem as he left Chicago. He had been game enough to play the Series "with one bum leg, a badly bruised left elbow (which he wore in a bandage) and an attack of appendicitis pending."

In a 1969 interview, the medical problems he had fifty years before were still fresh in Gandil's memory. "I had trouble with my appendix in 1919, during the season. But old Comiskey . . . said to freeze it and go ahead and play, and that they'd operate on me at the end of the season."[40]

When the scandal broke nearly a year after the Series, Gandil was hospitalized in Lufkin, Texas, recovering from an operation that finally removed his appendix. A Houston reporter obtained this reaction from Chick:

> It is impossible for me to believe that Joe Jackson and Williams have said what the newspapers credit them with saying. If Williams has given out such a statement, he has been untruthful and I shall give him a little trouble proving this stuff when I can get out of this hospital.[41]

Gandil said that he planned to go to Chicago just as soon as his doctor would let him. When shown a newspaper account naming him as the go-between of the conspiracy, he is reported to have said, "that is a lie and the perpetrator shall have an opportunity to show his hand. I have never been guilty of anything like this. Furthermore, I am not the one who engineered the frame-up, if there was one."

Chick Gandil was called the "instigator," the "master of ceremonies," and the "ringleader" of the fix. After batting .290 during the season, Chick slumped to .233 in the Series but made just one error in eighty-two fielding chances. It is a tribute to the ultimate uncertainty and murkiness of the Big Fix that a case can still be made for Gandil's innocence. Hardly anybody—not even the very generous Victor Luhrs—anybody, that is, except Gandil himself—has ever tried to make that case.

Gandil first tried convincing Harry A. Williams, a reporter with the *Los Angeles Times*. In an interview that appeared November 18, a little more than a month after the 1919 Series ended, Gandil declared that he was through with the White Sox. Responding to the rumors of crookedness that remained "in circulation with irritable insistence," Gandil said that he wanted to manage in the minors on the West Coast. "He is frankly disgusted with the entire situation created by reports and intimations that certain members of the White Sox 'laid down' to the Cincinnati Reds, and feels that the matter should be cleared up speedily in justice to the players themselves, figuring that talk of the sort places every man on the club under more or less of a cloud."

"My prospects [to manage] in Seattle looked good, until this thing came up." Gandil recalled how he played hurt in the Series. "I was handicapped by a hand, two fingers of which were paralyzed by an injury received in Washington." He noted that the Sox had won the pennant "in the face of heavy odds. Now our world Series checks are being held up." The reporter Williams noted how the fact that the team was holding up some checks was unfortunate, as it "lends color to the reports," and was unfair to the players who are innocent.

> "Comiskey is a strange contradiction," said Gandil. "At times he is the best fellow in the world and at others he is very difficult to please. I think he has been influenced by the talk of bettors who lost on the White Sox. I have given the Chicago club my best at all times."

Gandil also tried making his case to Harry Neily, who spoke with Chick on behalf of Ban Johnson. Neily reported back to Johnson:

> Gandil recites that after the second game of the 1919 Series, Gleason came into the clubhouse and said, "There is something wrong in this Series and the boss knows all about it. You guys better go out there and win with this Series or he will put every one of you guilty guys in jail."
>
> "I [Gandil] spoke up and asked," he said, "if the old man knows so damned much about this, why in hell don't he take out the fellows he thinks ain't on the level? I see where that got me in bad. Commy owns the ball club and if he thought the games were crooked it was up to him to protect himself."[42]

Neily added that the next spring, Gandil said he got a contract offer for $4,000—the same as he had made in 1919, but $2,000 less than what he had asked for. He refused it and got a counteroffer of $5,000. He refused again. (Most of the team was being offered significant raises.) Then "Grabiner sent word that negotiations were off." Gandil denied all crookedness.[43]

When Gandil was sold to the White Sox by the Cleveland team in March 1917, he said, "I will not stand for any cut in pay."[44] Apparently that was still his position in 1920. Or at least it served as a good cover story, whether Gandil had decided not to return for the 1920 season, or whether Comiskey simply would not have him back. "Gandil's wife had been after him for years to return home and play ball on the West Coast. It was too expensive to maintain two places to live."[45]

When Gandil asked Comiskey for his release so he could stay on the Pacific coast, to manage a Seattle club—at one point it was reported that he had signed to manage the St. Anthony, Idaho, team in the Snake River–Yellowstone League—the White Sox owner refused. The *Los Angeles Times* reported in late February that Comiskey thought Gandil would eventually give in and return and that the two were corresponding.

Bibb Falk, a rookie with the White Sox in 1920, had heard rumors about the fix all during the 1920 season. He said that Gandil, who was "supposed to be the ringleader," was not back with the team because "they had so much proof on him gambling."[46]

Gandil also tried making his case with a California newspaper reporter in spring 1921. And he used the argument Joe Jackson would use throughout his life: Look at the record. Gandil went through the Series game by game, recalling his hits, runs driven in, and near-flawless play in the field. He did knock in the winning runs in the first two White Sox victories. The only evidence against him were the words of gamblers and crooked ballplayers.[47]

But in a semi-famous 1956 interview in *Sports Illustrated*, Gandil told Mel Durslag, "I was a ringleader." He went on to describe how the fix was planned, even claiming to have met, in the process, Arnold Rothstein. But the rumors were too thick, he went on to say, so the whole Series was played on the level. The players did receive $10,000 in advance, which they gave to Eddie Cicotte to hold—he put it under his pillow himself (and by some accounts, sewed it into his jacket later). Gandil said the Series was a genuine upset victory earned by the Reds, and he compared the White Sox to the 1954 Cleveland Indians team, which had won 111 games, but then had been swept in the October classic by the New York Giants.[48]

When Gandil's story was published, Eddie Cicotte and Happy Felsch both denied that Gandil told "the real story." Felsch denied getting any money or doing anything to throw a game. Cicotte said, "I took my medicine."[49]

Comiskey's detective John Hunter, on his California road trip in the off-season of 1919–20, said that he was told by Gandil in front of his new house: "I presume people would think I bought this bungalow; and here is a car standing out in front. I presume," he says, "I tell everybody that there is a mortgage of $3500 against this house for fear they might think that I got some money as a result of throwing the World Series."[50]

Gandil told Hunter that he did not receive any money. He repeated that to Durslag in 1956.

Thirteen years after the Durslag interview, and less than two years before he died, Gandil gave a final interview, this time insisting that, "I'll Go to My Grave With a Clear Conscience."

> I have taken an awful beating in this thing. But it's all on record. My hits won two of the games against the Reds. If I'd have been trying to throw the Series, would I have tried to win those games? . . . If I'd have been hooked up with the gamblers, they wouldn't have let me live after I got those base-hits.[51]

Gandil said that wanted to sue for libel when he was scapegoated, "but my mother talked me out of it. She didn't want the publicity, so I went along with her." His wife, Laurel, just wanted to get away from the whole mess, which is why Chick never returned from California when the 1920 season started. "I guess that is why I have been made the goat, because I was the only one who quit after the 1919 season. It was just that I wanted more money from Comiskey. Is that wrong? . . . had to admire about him."

Gandil's "consuming ambition [was] still to have his name cleared somehow by baseball." He said that he wrote Landis three times about clearing his name, but received no replies. Gandil seemed to regret not suing back in the 1920s: "But from now on, I'm gonna sue the hell out of all of them. I'm tired of taking it after all these years." He had spoken to the famous lawyer Melvin Belli, "and he's interested in my case."

Chick Gandil's death on December 13, 1970, went unnoticed for weeks; his wife had him buried quietly, still shunning publicity. His obituary appeared in the *New York Times* on February 26, 1971; in *The Sporting News*, not until March 20. Many of his Calistoga, California, neighbors never knew him as a former ballplayer. In his obituary, Gandil was described as a retired plumber.

* * * * *

McMullin, Risberg, Felsch, and Gandil never appeared before the 1920 grand jury; they were indeed indicted by testimony from gamblers seeking immunity, or from players who may have had incomplete or just plain wrong knowledge of how the fix was pulled off. In the 1921 trial, on the advice of their lawyers, the indicted players never took the stand in their own defense, and all were acquitted of the conspiracy charges. And because few of the banned players ever said much afterward—fearing harm from the gamblers, or just wanting to put it all behind them—the details of the fix seem destined to remain a mystery.

＊ ＊ ＊ ＊ ＊

"There were times when they tried to lose and couldn't, they were so good."—Eddie Collins[52]

Eddie Collins was the White Sox second baseman from 1915 to 1926. He began and finished his twenty-five years in the majors with Connie Mack's Philadelphia team. One of the top players in either league, Collins was the best-paid of the Sox, making $15,000 in 1919. A .319 hitter during the regular season, Collins managed just seven hits, six of them singles, while batting .226 in the 1919 World Series. He also was charged with two errors and stole just one base, after leading the league with thirty-three. Yet Collins was above suspicion in the scandal. Why?

Most historians believe that Collins was never asked about joining the fix conspiracy because the players who were in on it never spoke with Eddie about anything. They respected his play on the diamond, but he otherwise lived in a different world. Some accounts have him ostracized during the infield practice between innings. As the best-paid man on the club, Collins showed the loyalty of a player who aspired to some-day ascend to manager or general manager—which he did.[53]

While catcher Ray Schalk exploded when he sensed that some of his teammates were not giving their best, there is no record of Eddie Collins saying or doing anything in October 1919 related to the fix. Forty years later, Collins recalled Cincinnati "seething with rumors" of the fix before the Series, and the rumors "persisted all during the eight games." But Collins said he and others "shrugged them off as preposterous." He also said, "I want to reiterate I was never suspicious of their [the "crooked" Sox] actions during the Series."[54]

The following season, rumors of meddling by gamblers cropped up again as the pennant race heated up in September. It appeared that some of the players who tossed the 1919 Series, were at it again, this time tilting things so that Cleveland would win the American League flag.[55]

Against this background, Eddie Collins met with team owner Charles Comiskey, on or around September 2.[56] Most sources (but perhaps they are relying on *Eight Men Out*) have Collins complaining about crookedness in his teammates, with Comiskey politely listening and then doing nothing about it. Comiskey denied that Collins talked with him about fixed games in 1920, or about a crooked ballplayer.[57] Collins only said that pitcher Eddie Cicotte "wasn't trying" and if Comiskey talked with him, the Sox could win the pennant. "He [Cicotte] is nervous and coming to a break." Comiskey denied that Collins said Cicotte was crooked.

On September 28, 1920, the White Sox who were *not* indicted gathered in a downtown Chicago restaurant to celebrate over dinner. The *Chicago Tribune* reported that they assembled later at Eddie Collins's south side apartment and partied late into the night. Their hopes for a second straight pennant had been all but dashed, but a "load had been lifted" and they "simply had to explode."

> "No one will ever know what we put up with all this summer," one member of the party said. "I don't know how we ever got along. I know there were many times when things were about to break into a fight but it never got that far. . . . Now the load has been lifted. No wonder we feel like celebrating."

Eddie Collins acknowledged, "We've known something was wrong for a long time, but we felt we had to keep silent because we were fighting for the pennant."[58]

A few days later, the 1920 season over, Eddie Collins was in St. Louis and charged that the Sox failed to repeat as champions because "two players failed to put forth their best efforts."[59] Collins always refused to name the crooks of 1920, but he said they were among the seven who were indicted that September. We can guess that one of them was Eddie Cicotte.

Reporter Frank O. Klein of *Collyer's Eye*, perhaps following up on that comment, wrote under the headline "Collins Charges 1920 Games Fixed" in his October 30 column:

> Probably the one unbroken link that remains to be forged is to "prove up" the fact that Charles A. Comiskey KNEW. If this be necessary, I might add that Eddie Collins, field captain of the White Sox, told me that he KNEW the Series was fixed or at least believed so after two men went to bat in the first game at Cincinnati.

Had this statement appeared in a more reputable magazine, it might have drawn more attention.

An unidentified White Sox player spoke to a writer from *The Sporting News* after the scandal broke, about that 1920 stretch run. "Some of us always had believed we were sold out in the World Series. When the [crooked] players showed they meant to beat us out of getting in on this one we decided to act. Cicotte was told that he would have to win a certain game or he would be mobbed on the field by the honest players on the team—he won it."[60]

Sox shortstop Harvey McClellan and catcher Byrd Lynn told the *Chicago Tribune* that they now recalled seeing teammates toss three games to Boston on a late-season eastern road trip. They claimed the crooked Sox kept one eye on the scoreboard and were apparently trying to keep the pennant race with Cleveland tight. The *New York Times* quoted McClellan and Byrd saying that all season long, the crooked Sox tended to watch the scoreboard "more than even the average player in a pennant race," losing games on purpose to keep the race close.[61] Eddie Collins curiously blamed the absent Chick Gandil for instigating the "corruption."[62]

A POSTSCRIPT ON EDDIE COLLINS

When the late Harold Seymour was researching his classic baseball history Series, he had the opportunity to ask Joe Jackson about his role in the fix. Jackson "denied it to me and said—sarcastically—ask Mr. Edward Collins about it!"[63] Was Jackson suggesting that Collins was in on the fix? That seems unlikely.

Commenting on Jackson's remark to Seymour, Dorothy Jane Mills (Harold's wife and uncredited research partner) wrote, "From this response, Seymour gathered that Collins, one of the 'clean Sox,' had known in advance about the 'fix' but did nothing about it."[64] She may be right, but I think it more likely that Jackson was resenting how Collins came though several scandalous times with an untarnished reputation. And Jackson may have had a 1917 incident in mind.

This interpretation is confirmed by Harold Seymour himself in a 1975 letter to Donald Gropman, in which he comments on Jackson's outburst:

> I never followed this suggestion, but it led me to think at the time, and when I got into the research on the subject many years later his remark reinforced my impression that the so-called

honest players—Ray Schalk, for one—knew what was going on. In fact, it's hard to see how they could not have known.[65]

The 1917 incident took place in the stretch run of the season, when each regular member of the White Sox[66]—and that included manager Pants Rowland and Eddie Collins—contributed $45 or $50 to a pool of $1,100. The pool was either a bribe to pay off Detroit Tiger pitchers to throw four straight games to the Sox, or to reward them for knocking off the rival Red Sox in several vital contests. Eddie Collins said that he contributed to the pool raised by Gandil, but not until the 1917 World Series was in progress, when he first knew that the pool existed.[67]

The incident was brought to public attention by Swede Risberg late in 1926, in the wake of charges that Tris Speaker and Ty Cobb had agreed to tilt the outcome of a meaningless Indians–Tigers game on September 4, 1919, in order to make some extra cash by betting on it. After seeing the evidence—two letters to Dutch Leonard from Cobb and Smoky Joe Wood—Ban Johnson neatly disposed of this case by asking Cobb and Speaker to retire, and the two icons agreed. But when Landis found out, he made the incident public and said he'd look into it. Risberg felt that "They pushed Ty Cobb and Tris Speaker out on a piker bet. I think it only fair that the 'white lilies' get the same treatment."

Risberg took his complaint to Judge Landis, and there were head-line-making public hearings, but nothing much came of it except that the not-so-uncommon practice of "thanking" teams with cash rewards was formally banned. In fact, although it was not widely known at the time, Landis had investigated this incident soon after taking office in January 1921 and had found evidence lacking to make anything more of it.

This was not the first time that Eddie Collins's "clean" image had been threatened. When Collins was interviewed in the months before the 1921 trial, he "made it pretty plain that if any of the cheating White Sox ever got back on Comiskey's ball club, then they could count him off of it."[68]

That gave the opening for a campaign of mud-slinging. At once "rumors were heard" in Chicago that when the cheaters were brought to trial they might spring a big "exposé." It was hinted, so the story ran, that Eddie Collins was mixed up in betting on ball games, too. That back in the fall of 1919 he had proposed that the White Sox players bet their money that the Detroit

Tigers would beat out the New York Yankees [the Tigers finished a half-game behind the Yanks] and the White Sox and
Tigers were just about to open a Series as Collins made the
proposition.[69]

"Quick and vigorous denial" came from Collins, who went on to
add that he had never bet on a ballgame in his life. "Most—not all—of
the Chicago newspaper writers" also sprang to Collins' defense. They
knew that Eddie was not a member of the accused clique. One writer
recalled that the crooked players were also upset with Collins because
they knew he had gone to Comiskey saying that "something had to be
done to straighten out the team or he would leave it." Judge Landis's
reaction was very low-key:

> In my experience on the bench I have noticed that when a
> crook is booked he always will try to drag some clean person
> into the mess if there is a chance. You may have no idea what
> means such people will employ. It generally has been my policy
> to make allowances for such measures.[70]

The Sporting News reported that when Collins's complaints to
Comiskey in September 1920 went unheeded, Collins went to league
president Ban Johnson, "and told him of things." That would suggest
that Collins wanted Comiskey to do more than just have a little calming
chat with Eddie Cicotte.

While Landis's public reaction was calculated to calm the waters,
he privately launched an immediate investigation into the charges that
the White Sox team paid the Detroit team to toss games in early September 1917. Landis questioned Eddie Collins on February 19, 1921; six
days later, he questioned Detroit pitcher George "Hooks" Dauss, and
the next day, pitcher Bill James, who was with Detroit in 1917 but
finished the 1919 season with the White Sox.

Collins insisted that he had done nothing wrong, he had only chipped
in with the whole team and their manager, to reward the Tiger pitchers
who beat Boston later in September. Landis soon was to learn that the
practice was not that rare, but because it could certainly give the appearance of bribery, he ordered it halted in the future. On February 24,
Collins sent Landis a letter stating that he now recalled that Buck Weaver
placed a $40 bet for him (for Collins) that the Sox would sweep Detroit
on Labor Day 1917. The first game was close, and Collins mentioned

the bet to his manager, Kid Gleason, who then assumed half of the bet. Collins insisted that it was the first and last betting on baseball he had ever done. Landis believed him.

The White Sox and Tigers played consecutive doubleheaders on September 2 and 3 in 1917, the latter on Labor Day. The Sox swept all four games. Dauss and James, two of Detroit's top three pitchers, did not start in any of the games—something Dauss recalled as unusual, as odd as the start given to second-year youngster George Cunningham, who had just eight starts all that summer.

The White Sox also stole between eighteen and twenty-one bases (the accounts available at the hearing varied) during the Labor Day doubleheader. When questioned about this, Tiger catcher Oscar Stanage "drew a roar" when he "sheepishly admitted" that this had happened to him before. Landis pointed out later that stealing five or more bases per game was not that uncommon, and the Sox had led their league in that department—although they averaged just over one base per game. Other testimony suggested that the Sox had been able to steal by getting big leads; the Tiger pitchers were not holding them close. This was perhaps the most suspicious fact of the Series, as the accounts of the games described hard play by both teams in several close, seesaw battles.

The Detroit pitchers insisted that the money they received from the White Sox—$200 for each starting pitcher, which included $20 that went to their catcher—was not for laying down in those four games, but for beating Chicago's rival Boston in a doubleheader on September 19, and then again on September 20. James and Dauss *did* pick up wins in that Series, along with Willie Mitchell, who bested Babe Ruth, 1–0, in the finale.

But the rumors about the Chicago–Detroit exchange of money in 1917 would not go away. The very next year, in 1922, lawyer Ray Cannon brought the charges up again, to Comiskey and Landis.

Cannon was working at the time on lawsuits against the White Sox on behalf of Felsch and Jackson, and had asked Comiskey to come to Wisconsin to answer questions about both 1917 and 1919. Comiskey chose not to go.

We offered them evidence about the fixed Series of 1917, which Detroit threw to the White Sox, and the other thrown Series of the American League race of 1919, which the White Sox threw to Detroit. Landis chose not to take advantage of the testimony which we offered him then, with Happy Felsch, Buck Weaver,

Charley Risberg, Joe Jackson and others ready and willing to corroborate everything and tell it all while it was hot.[71]

When the 1917 incident finally became public, thanks to Risberg, in late 1926, Cannon started fanning old flames. He said he knew of two alleged fixes in the National League "which have not come out yet" and predicted Gandil would "tell something sensational. Gandil knows a lot of stuff. Gandil and Swede Risberg have more guts and probably have more stuff to spill than all the rest of them."[72]

Cannon may have read the January 3 report out of El Paso, Texas, where Chick Gandil made headlines supporting Risberg's story.[73] After refusing to talk, Gandil boasted that he would trump Swede's charges. "Risberg knows plenty, but he does not know half as much as I do. Risberg, Weaver and the others know only what's on the surface. I could tell a story that would shake baseball to its very foundations and that would involve many more men than Risberg's story—players that the Swede doesn't know anything about."[74]

The reporter interviewing Gandil predicted that Chick would probably not make his story public through Judge Landis, for whom he "always has felt a bitter antipathy"; nor would Gandil participate in any investigation Landis headed. But the *Chicago Tribune* gave Gandil $500 to cover his expenses to testify at Landis's 1927 hearings. On January 6, he gave a sworn affidavit in the *Tribune* offices, before testifying before Landis, who had requested Gandil's presence.[75] "What Swede has told is true. He couldn't tell all the story because he didn't know it. I can tell it and no one can scare me. . . . I've decided to tell it whether it hurts the hypocrites or not." Gandil said if an attempt was made to "bull him," he'd leave. "Nobody will call me a liar in my hearing," Gandil warned; but he was wrong about that. "Risberg was too easy with those fellows."

Gandil told reporters that he was the one who "sent word to the Detroit players that the Sox would reward them for 'easing up.'"[76] He was also the one who turned over to Bill James between $900 and $1,000. James testified that he had received $850. Gandil also said they did not ask Kid Gleason (a coach then) to participate. The newspaper coverage did not indicate at whom Chick was looking, when he made this comment: "You can't always place your finger on things suspicious."

That observation is similar to one made by Eddie Collins when he was first interrogated by Landis about the 1917 Labor Day weekend games: "Of course, it is hard to say whether anybody on a ball field is doing his best. As you look back on the games they might look peculiar, though at the time they were played there would not seem to be anything peculiar about them."[77] When defending himself, Collins was less sure about "crooked play" than he ever was when he spoke about his teammates' play in the 1919 Series.

Almost all of the thirty-some players and former players, White Sox and Tigers, sided with Eddie Collins in the version of events he gave in the January 1927 hearing. Landis had them testify before about fifty to one hundred reporters, and when humorist and columnist Will Rogers stopped by, he was invited to sit in, too.[78]

Only Risberg and Gandil characterized the exchange of money in 1917 as a bribe and not a reward. (Happy Felsch had made the same charges in 1922 in a lawsuit against the White Sox, and Landis had shrugged them off.[79] Felsch was not invited to the 1927 hearings.) Before one of the sessions, Ty Cobb, under a cloud of scandal himself at the time, greeted Eddie Collins with a handshake and a quip: "Hello, Eddie, I see you are one of us now."

> Collins laughed and said he hoped not. "Isn't it a shame the way these old gossip stories are dragged out?" Cobb said to Weaver. "I was kicked out of baseball on less than that," Weaver said. "I hate to see these things break out as much as anybody. I'm not helping anyone else get kicked out, but Risberg's story is true."[80]

The press reported that while Risberg told his story, Buck Weaver tacitly supported Risberg's charges, nodding his head as Swede spoke. But when called to testify himself, Weaver would not go on record in support of Risberg. This time, Buck chose to "flock together" with the majority of the birds in the room.

But substitute Sox first baseman Bob "Ziggy" Hasbrook mentioned a team meeting in Boston around September 23 that the other Sox had as September 30. The reporters present noted that Judge Landis was surprised by this discrepancy. Nevertheless, Landis took just a few days to mull things over before dismissing Risberg's charges and making it clear that the practice of rewarding teams or individuals with cash or other gifts should cease. Will Rogers said Landis's call was right and fair and called baseball "the least crooked sport ever invented."

Chick Gandil, when he returned to Texas, insisted that he and Risberg had told the truth, "but there were too many witnesses against us. Those other boys had to testify as they did to save their jobs." Gandil added that he understood Landis had to "protect the interests of organized ball. . . . I can't censure him for his verdict." Chick also put in a good word for Ty Cobb: "It would be a joke to clear those players in the 1917 scandal . . . and then blacklist Cobb on the word of Dutch Leonard. Cobb, in my opinion, is more honest and has done more to help the game than any player that was given a clean bill of health by Landis yesterday."[81]

Gandil was, however, disappointed that Buck Weaver had not supported Risberg and himself in the hearings. He said he decided not to sign Weaver to play in the Copper League the next spring after all. "I think I'll let him go. He double-crossed us and didn't tell the truth in Chicago."

Swede Risberg, back on his Minnesota farm, said he, too, was surprised at Buck Weaver's failure to substantiate his statements. He intimated that Landis "may burst another 'bombshell,' after investigating 'mysterious' letters" he had not yet received. Swede added that he and Gandil were ready to go to Washington, if there was to be a federal investigation, as some were calling for. "I told them nothing but the truth and I'll never change my story."[82]

Landis played judge (and jury) in this event, and his actions probably give us a very good idea of how he would have handled the rumors of the Big Fix of 1919, if he had been in charge of baseball then. Keep it as quiet as possible. Bring in the parties involved. Listen, ask questions, think, rule. Keep the press at a safe distance but have them handy at the key moments. Avoid lawyers keep it within baseball and out of the courts. End it as soon as possible. When Landis exonerated the players accused by Risberg, he issued a lengthy press release that gave his reasoning, summarized all he had heard, and included recommendations. These included penalties of ineligibility for a year for betting on ballgames, and permanent ineligibility for betting on games in which the bettor has a duty to perform.[83]

Eddie Collins escaped the events of 1917–27 with his image as clean as his laundered uniform. He would manage the White Sox in 1925 and 1926, finishing fifth both seasons, before turning the team over to Ray Schalk. He was elected as a charter member of baseball's Hall of Fame.

As for Cobb and Speaker, Landis exonerated them, but their teams would not take them back. They wound up playing in 1927 and for one additional season for different American League teams. At the time of the scandal, Cobb admitted that he had written the letter[84] that had gotten them in trouble and that he was involved in betting, but he took the Pete Rose defense: he only bet on his team to win and he himself never played to lose. Later, Cobb seemed to cover up what he could. Speaker was more consistent, he never admitted to anything. Although he was not mentioned in any of the incriminating letters, he still had agreed to leave the Cleveland team after 1926.

Ban Johnson wondered out loud why Landis spent $25,000 on the Risberg hearings without consulting his advisory council, which included the two league presidents. Johnson's ruling that Cobb and Speaker would not play in his league again was overturned by Landis, and in this confrontation Ban Johnson lost the support of enough American League owners that from then on his days in office were numbered.

Was Landis less concerned about the images of Cobb and Speaker than about embarrassing Johnson while maintaining his absolute authority? Perhaps. But certainly, the Cobb–Speaker case is complicated and deserves its own longer treatment elsewhere.

THE QUIET SOX

Once the scandal broke, some of the clean Sox started telling what they knew. They talked more about thrown games in the stretch run of 1920, which was still fresh in mind, than about the World Series of 1919. They were sure that they could have won the pennant again, if everyone had been trying their best to win.

If they had been deaf to the rumors before the Series, their manager Gleason informed them of his and Comiskey's suspicions early on, perhaps before Game Two. Why did they remain silent? Possibly, they were hoping against hope that what they sensed had taken place was just a bad dream. They were as uncertain as everyone else about exactly who was involved, and felt that it was not their place to speak up, not if the team management was aware of what was going on. Their job would be to tell their manager, and he had told *them* about the fix.

Shortly after the scandal broke, a Detroit paper ran an article about one of the clean Sox, Nemo Leibold, "a graduate of Detroit's sand lots."

> Before the start of the last World's Series some of Leibold's former team mates and pals wrote him asking for an inside tip on the Series. Leibold never answered the letters. When Leibold returned to Detroit last winter his friends demanded to know why he ignored their letters. "I was in a spot where I couldn't

advise you either way, so I just didn't answer. That was the only thing I could do," answered Leibold without further information.[85]

No one knows what threats of violence, from their fellow players or from the gamblers, may have been made once the fix was agreed upon. It is not difficult to imagine that the clean Sox may have shared some of the fear that silenced the crooked Sox players, for decades after the fix. The first players to break silence, Cicotte and Jackson, both mentioned threats of physical harm and fears of being shot. The third player, Lefty Williams, never admitted being threatened, but his wife did, years later.

"Thou shalt not squeal" were words to live by—literally. Playing baseball was not supposed to be an occupation hazardous to one's health. But it may have turned out to be just that.

On the night of September 28 after the shameful seven had been indicted and finally dismissed from Comiskey's payroll as a result, the remaining members of the Chicago team celebrated with a dinner. After having to associate with that bunch of cheats and at last being rid of them they felt they just had to take the lid off their suppressed emotions. When all the sympathy is being handed out, these are the boys who really deserve it, for what they had to endure, knowing what they did, and being practically helpless to make a move to remedy things.[86]

The dinner conversation must have been fascinating.

* * * * *

When Swede Risberg passed away on his eighty-first birthday, October 13, 1975, the last of the "eight men out" was gone. For fifty-five years their names had been linked together, and they still are today. Few people can name the five Watergate burglars. They were part of a scandal that toppled a presidency. But many fans can name all eight Black Sox players.

9

THE FIXERS

The idea of taking on seven or eight people in a plot scared me.
I said to [Sport] Sullivan it wouldn't work. He answered, "Don't be silly.
It's been pulled before and it can be again."
—Chick Gandil as told to Mel Durslag in *Sports Illustrated*
September 17, 1956

Rumors of a World Series fix go back to 1905.[1] Fix rumors
flourished about the famous 1908 NL pennant race. There were reports
of teams "lying down" to help friends or foil enemies. The attempt to rig
the 1910 [American League] batting race was no secret.
—Leonard Koppett

O what a tangled web we weave / When we first practice to deceive
—J. R. Pope

When I began researching the 1919 World Series, I had hoped that I could avoid "the gamblers." After all, they were not on the field, not part of baseball. However, to understand the full event and its aftermath, some familiarity with "the gamblers" was needed.

Not one gambler was convicted of any wrongdoing in connection with "the Big Fix"—the throwing of the 1919 World Series. Only a few were brought to trial, along with the ballplayers. One of the gamblers, Abe Attell, described the fix as "cheaters cheating cheaters," and if things were not exactly neatly organized when the fix was on, the confusion only escalated as the gamblers who dared to speak told their stories.

Two things strike one when the gamblers are studied. One has already been mentioned—that the lines between gamblers and ballplayers become blurred. Some of the professional gamblers had been professional athletes, some of them playing major league baseball. Some of the players were big bettors. And not just players, but some

236

major league managers and team owners were heavy gamblers. So were many fans. When attempts were made to rid ballparks of gambling, a common complaint was that the nickel-and-dime folks in the bleachers were arrested, while the highrollers in box seats (they would be in luxury boxes today) were not bothered.

In the 1921 trial, John O. Seys, secretary of the Cubs, admitted that he had acted as stakeholder for several of Abe Attell's bets, as well as for those of the Levi brothers, and he said that Clark Griffith, manager of the Senators, had done the same.

The other thing that is striking is how pervasive gambling was in baseball by 1919. By some accounts, the underworld had players on every team who could be counted on to supply tips or, worse, to tip games the way the gamblers wanted them to go. When the Chicago grand jury convened in 1920 to look at the scope of gambling in baseball, "one of the prosecutor's staff promised that before [long] they would find evidence of the purposeful losing of games in every major-league city."[2]

KEEPING THE SCOPE NARROW

This is one of the reasons why the term "Black Sox scandal" is misleading. Baseball was in the stranglehold of gamblers, and had been for some time. Gambling and cheating in baseball were not isolated, unique, and novel events one can refer to as "scandals"; nor were these activities indulged in only by players. The Black Sox scandal was more like the tip of an iceberg. But Major League Baseball could not let that become widely known, or the sport could collapse. So the fix of 1919 was treated as if it was an awful aberration, a terrible misdeed that was found out and could never be repeated. The paragraph below was written in 1920:

> In Detroit, there has been baseball bookmaking for years. It was done openly season in and season out, with no interference on the part of the authorities. Odds on games in the National and American Leagues and American Association were posted flagrantly and openly. No pains were taken to cover up the betting activities.[3]

Two books that well document the scope of gambling prior to 1919 are Victor Luhrs's *The Great Baseball Mystery* and Daniel E. Ginsburg's *The Fix Is In* (McFarland, 1995).

Sorting out the gamblers is no easy task. Depending on which source you trust, there were two, three, or maybe five different syndicates involved in the fix. Joe Williams, on the sports desk of the *Cleveland News* during the Series, was sure that the players sold out in St. Louis, Detroit, Boston, and Kansas City,[4] as well as in Chicago and even Cincinnati.[5] Williams continued to receive information over the years, some of it from Abe Attell, who also spoke freely with Eliot Asinof, the author of *Eight Men Out*. "They [the players] not only sold it but they sold it wherever they could get a buck," Attell told Williams. "So they got paid in not one but a dozen different places. They peddled it around like a sack of popcorn."

Abe Attell's name was prominent in the 1920 grand jury hearings. Attell denied being a fixer or giving any money to the players—and was probably telling the truth, as he had used Burns and Maharg as go-betweens. He insisted that he was not the "master mind which evolved and operated the whole scheme." Attell said he knew that person's name, as well as the names of ten other gamblers in a syndicate that made at least $250,000. But Attell was never brought to the grand jury and was conveniently out of the country by the time the trial rolled around the next year.

In both the grand jury hearing and the trial, there were references to a group of Pittsburgh gamblers, but no names were identified. "Rumors all season [1919] pointed to a Pittsburgh syndicate . . . as being the main engine for almost daily corruption in both leagues."[6]

In 1920 the *New York Times* interviewed a "prominent gambler" from Pittsburgh, who said,

> The first intimation that we had last year that there was any suspicion in regard to the games between the White Sox and the Reds was the visit here of two Philadelphia men, one by the name of Gilchrist, I believe, who placed bets amounting to $5,000 for the first two games, taking Cincinnati for their end. As the White Sox at that time were the favorites in the betting this aroused suspicion here, and a great many of the betting fraternity placed their money the same way, and of course won out handsomely. However, I am sure, that no one here did any fixing of players or knew anything about it.[7]

But this syndicate may not have been the only one to successfully hide itself through the whole event. After the statements made by Cicotte and Jackson on September 28, 1920, Hartley Replogle announced, "We are going after the gamblers now. There will be indictments in a few days against men in Philadelphia, Indianapolis, Pittsburg, Cincinnati, and other cities." A few days earlier the grand jury foreman had told the *Chicago Tribune* that "Chicago, New York, Cincinnati, and St. Louis gamblers are bleeding baseball and corrupting players. We are going the limit in this inquiry. . . . I am shocked at the rottenness so far revealed."

Leaks from the grand jury that made their way into the *Chicago Tribune* on September 25 had both Abe Attell and Hal Chase "scurrying around, forming a combination to place wagers, intending to have agents in every big city." Chase was reported to have made a deal with "several big gamblers, including one known at New Orleans tracks." (Kid Gleason had received a warning telegram from New Orleans.)

The *Chicago Tribune* had urged the grand jury to call Harry Long, a Chicago broker who handled Sport Sullivan's wagers ("he is supposed to have won at least $60,000 from Chicago fans"). Long told the *Tribune* that Sullivan had made calls to Pittsburg[h], Boston, New York, and Cincinnati during their dealings.[8] In another account, in the *Toronto World*, Replogle's hit list included St. Louis and Des Moines.

In their accounts of the Big Fix, both Eliot Asinof and Nelson Algren have Chick Gandil taking a phone call

> from a brash fellow named Jake Lingle, a newspaper reporter. 'The word is out,' the brash fellow said to Gandil brashly, 'the Series is in the bag.' Gandil hung up on Lingle. He didn't even have Cicotte in the bag and reporters were already beginning to hold their noses.[9]

"Where'd you ever hear that rot!" Gandil replies to Lingle in Asinof's story. In his 1956 interview with Durslag, the probable source for both accounts, Gandil said he replied, "Where did you get that crazy story?" before hanging up on Lingle.

Jake Lingle was indeed a reporter for the *Chicago Tribune*. But after he was gunned down at a subway station in 1930, the public learned that he was also on the payroll of Al Capone (who arrived in Chicago in 1919). Lingle's ties to organized crime in October 1919 are not clear, but Gandil recalled them in 1956.

Attell admitted that his knowledge was limited. The various mobs were not working harmoniously together toward the same end. Some were trying to sabotage the Reds. It is unlikely that any of the gamblers had the big picture, and that is evident in the testimony of those who talked.

Ring Lardner's son John called the Big Fix, "the biggest, sloppiest, crudest fix of a sporting event that ever was known to man. It was a makeshift job, compounded in equal parts of bluff and welsh and cold gall, with no contributor or agent-contributor knowing what the man next to him was up to, and very seldom bothering to find out."[10]

Lardner goes on to write with seeming certainty that one of the keys to the fix was a fake telegram (faked by go-betweens, lower level crooks) that said Arnold Rothstein was backing it. Lardner apparently did not himself believe Rothstein's claim that he was invited in early but passed because it was too risky or too impossible to pull off. In the grand jury hearings and in the trial, those in the hierarchy of gamblers all pointed fingers up and down and sideways, jockeying to shift blame away from themselves. No wonder that judge and jury found little credibility and less hard evidence.

While it is tempting to portray the gamblers as a bungling, almost comical group, it is important to keep in mind that they were also capable of carrying out their real or implied threats. Prohibition had made instant millionaires of any number of gangsters who could keep Americans supplied with alcohol.[11] Once the ballplayers struck a deal to toss the Series, there was no backing out without grave risks. It seems likely that there were indeed threats made, to make sure the players came through with the fix, and then to be sure that they kept quiet about it.[12]

ROTHSTEIN

Watching Rothstein, Sullivan, Burns, Maharg, and Attell and Gandil
making their moves now, half a century later, is like watching a
civilization of beetles in a dusty Mason jar.
—Nelson Algren, *The Last Carousel*

When you shake the gambler's tree, it is not surprising that a lot of ballplayers' names fall out, as well as other athletes. World War I was just over (over there), and the Volstead Act was not going to keep America from partying through the twenties. Big business was making millionaires, even of baseball club owners. So what if there was corruption? Tammany Hall and the Crash were years away. Money was up for grabs, even if the grabbing was on occasion from the hands of "the underworld." *Underworld.* It sounds so sinister, while *subculture* sounds so clean.

In *The Big Bankroll* (see note 11), Leo Katcher paints a vivid picture of life in that underworld, as he traces the life and times of Arnold Rothstein. Katcher points out that without Rothstein, the fixing of the 1919 Series never would have or could have happened—whether "A.R." was backing it or not. The word (from a fake telegram) that Rothstein was in on the fix was a guarantee that it would happen, and it meant that probably no one would be punished. Why? Because Rothstein had great lawyers and the means to pay off any number of law enforcement personnel or judges.

Katcher concludes that Rothstein really *did* judge the Series as too risky to fix—too many players involved, too many others knowing what was going down. Rothstein had lost money betting on the 1917 Series;[13] was that memory still vivid? But Katcher believes that in the end, knowing what he knew, Rothstein made "about $350,000" on the fix, even though A.R. always maintained it was less than $100,000. He carefully made very public bets on the White Sox, too, so he was covered.

Ban Johnson said in 1929 that the information that later came to light indicated Rothstein had won "between $300,000 and $400,000. He won a bet of $90,000 with Sinclair and another with Smathers for $70,000."[14] John Lardner wrote that Rothstein claimed he never made a nickel on the Series, but "people close to him" (and Lardner worked out of New York so he probably knew some of these people) "put the figure at closer to $60,000." In *Tough Jews* (Simon & Schuster, 1998), Rich Cohen disagrees. He has Rothstein telling the White Sox players who approached him, "You'd get lynched if it ever came out." Nevertheless, "popular imagination fastened this piece of corruption to Rothstein's legend." Historian Harold Seymour writes that after Rothstein was shot to death, "affidavits were found in his files testifying to that fact that he paid out $80,000 for the World Series fix."

Years after Arnold Rothstein was gone, his wife of eighteen years, Carolyn Green Rothstein, went on record in a book, *Now I'll Tell.* Regarding A.R. and the fix, Carolyn believes that her husband's record "indicated the soundness of my belief that he never took part in any undertaking outside the law in which other persons were concerned."

If, however, it were charged that Arnold had been sounded out
on the subject of bribing baseball players, that he had declined

to have a part in the transaction, but had used his inside knowledge that they were going to be bribed to make winning bets, I would believe it. As a matter of fact, I do believe it. I might go further than that and say I know it, except that I was not present at any such meetings, of course.[15]

While Rothstein's grand jury testimony vanished—along with anything else said by others that might have incriminated him—Arnold did go on record in another trial that had nothing to do with baseball. In October 1923, he made a "famous appearance" in court, when hearings were being conducted in regard to the bankruptcy of E. M. Fuller Co., in June 1922, which cost the public around four million dollars.

A.R.'s name appeared on the firm's books in many transactions, and so he was called to the witness stand. A partner of Fuller had testified that Fuller lost $331,000 of the firm's money betting with Rothstein. William A. Chadbourne, a lawyer for the creditors, ambushed Rothstein by bombarding him, while he had the chance, with questions about the fixed World Series of 1919.

"This baseball thing has been a sore spot in my career," said A.R., who felt he had been vindicated by the Cook County grand jury when they failed to indict him. Chadbourne asked Rothstein if he knew Abe Attell and Sport Sullivan—he did. Then he asked if Rothstein had spoken to Boston lawyer William J. Kelly about representing Attell and Sullivan and Rothstein himself in Chicago—and Rothstein denied having done this. Rothstein said he had made one bet with Fuller on the fixed Series—"and Fuller won that."

Chadbourne's questioning was relentless.[16] Rothstein dodged questions about Sleepy Bill Burns and about meetings with Attell and Sullivan to plot the Series conspiracy. Charles Stoneham was suspected of being a "dummy" partner with Fuller, and A.R. judged that Chadbourne was out to embarrass both him and Stoneham, who was fully exonerated in the case later.[17]

Chadbourne insisted that the White Sox players had been promised $100,000 ($20,000 after each game they tossed) but had been double-crossed after Game One. Rothstein was accused of having lawyer William Fallon steal the grand jury minutes. (Fallon did not represent Rothstein at the 1920 grand jury hearings; he was there representing Abe Attell and other friends of A.R.[18]) Fallon had denied stealing the minutes of the grand jury proceedings, but admitted having copies of them, "forwarded by his Chicago legal representative, Henry J. Berger."[19]

In Leo Katcher's 1958 version of the fix, Cicotte took the idea to Sport Sullivan, who took it to Rothstein, the only gambler to whom Cicotte's price, $100,000, was ordinary. Cicotte also took the plan to Sleepy Bill Burns, who, like former boxer Bill Maharg, also had "connections" to Rothstein.

Deposed for the Milwaukee trial in December 1922, Maharg said that he had known Bill Burns for about fifteen years. Burns had introduced him to Cicotte and Gandil toward the end of the 1919 season but before the White Sox had clinched the pennant. Maharg said the original deal was $100,000—$20,000 each for Cicotte, Gandil, Williams, Felsch, and Risberg. In Maharg's deposition is the detail that the gamblers had accumulated so much money after the first two games that they packed it up in suitcases for the trip to Chicago.[20]

Ban Johnson had concluded that the money trail led back to Rothstein, and when the scandal broke, he went public with that belief. A.R. threatened to sue for libel, but instead he traveled to Chicago to testify to the grand jury. He basically gave up Attell and Sullivan, who were safely out of reach.

Most books on the fix mention a gambler who was indicted named Rachael (or Rachel, or, in one *New York Times* article, Rafael) Brown. It seems that Mrs. Brown was Rothstein's chief bookkeeper.[21] She, Nat Evans (who in October 1919 went by the name "Brown"), and Attell were in Cincinnati before the Series opened, taking bets and keeping tabs on Burns, their link with the players. Katcher has Evans saying, at this point, "I talked with Burns and some of the players. They're in so deep, they've got to throw the Series, even if it don't mean a dime to them."

After Arnold Rothstein testified to the grand jury, Ban Johnson pronounced him innocent, as did Comiskey's top lawyer, Alfred Austrian. Rothstein and Comiskey had become allies and together (most sources agree), they arranged to have the grand jury paperwork, including the waivers of immunity signed by three players, disappear.[22]

CONNECTIONS

Rothstein at one time was seen regularly in the Polo Grounds box of New York Giant owner Charles Stoneham.[23] Judge Landis, cleaning up baseball's image, eventually leaned on Stoneham to end the practice. Stoneham spent some leisure time at his summer home in Saratoga, where Rothstein operated a casino, The Brook, and a stable. Cicotte's asking price for the Big Fix, $100,000, was do-able for Rothstein because he could clear many times that amount in one good night at The Brook.

George Waller tells the story of how Rothstein became worried one night when multimillionaire contractor Sam Rosoff (the builder of most of New York's subways) got lucky and was ahead $400,000. Rothstein "telephoned Charles Stoneham at his Saratoga cottage and asked for additional funds in case Rosoff cleaned out The Brook's reserves. Stoneham, a gaming proprietor himself, being part owner of casinos in Havana, Cuba . . . took $300,000 from his wall safe and sent it to Rothstein with all possible haste. When the money arrived, Rosoff had lost his winnings and $100,000 more."[24]

On another occasion Waller has Stoneham in Saratoga but unable to visit The Brook because of a wrenched knee. He phoned Rothstein and directed him to place bets at the roulette wheel, taking A.R.'s word for whether the wheel stopped at red or black on each spin. When he hung up, three hours later, he had lost $70,000.

Rothstein's connection with oilmen Harry Sinclair and Joshua Cosden was not fiction, either. Waller has Sinclair dropping $48,000 in one night and writing a check for $50,000, with the extra money going for tips for the croupiers. Waller has Cosden losing $300,000 and $200,000 on consecutive nights, then boasting of his skill on the third night, when he won $20,000. These numbers are mind-boggling to those who imagined that no one would pay ballplayers $20,000 each to toss games.

THE GREAT MOUTHPIECE

Nicknames have always been part of baseball, particularly in the past. I believe that they are a symbol of familiarity between ballplayers and fans and that the scarcity of great nicknames today points to the distance that has grown up between them. The nicknames were not always accurate, and not always politically correct—that is certain— but they added a spice to baseball, made it more fun to follow. After all, it is entertainment, and that calls for stage names that are suitable for headlines, if not marquees.

Plain old Joe Jackson became Shoeless Joe early on, and a case might be made (but not by me) that he is so well remembered to this day partly because of that nickname. No one remembers Oscar Felsch, Claude Williams, Charles Risberg, George Weaver, or Charles Arnold Gandil—but if you are at all acquainted with the White Sox, 1919 vintage, you know all about Happy, Lefty, Swede, Buck, and Chick. It almost seems as if the gamblers went after the players with the great monikers.

Of course, nicknames were common in the underworld, too: Scarface, Baby Face, Bugsy, and so on. The only other place and time that could compete with the first decades of the twentieth century for nicknames might be the Old West: Wild Bill, Bat, Billy the Kid, Doc, the Hole in the Wall Gang, Butch, and Sundance. In the 1919 fix story, we meet Sleepy Bill and Sport; and then there is The Big Bankroll, Arnold Rothstein, always just out of reach.

And if you follow the uncovering of the fix, you run into The Great Mouthpiece: William J. Fallon. Fallon was the attorney hired by Rothstein in 1920 when the scandal broke—not for himself (Hyman Turchin represented A.R., as Rothstein thought Fallon drank too much to be consistently useful), but for his friends. Fallon has been credited with a triple play in the Black Sox story. For Rothstein, the events of 1919–21 were a short chapter in his long biography, and so for Fallon.

William Fallon was a colorful character who would do or try just about anything to keep his clients out of jail. He performed that service for not only Rothstein, but for some of A.R.'s friends as well—Giants owner Charles Stoneham, for example, and his legendary manager John McGraw. When Rothstein's name came up in the grand jury hearing, Rothstein

> consulted his mouthpiece, Mr. Fallon. "I want you to stop this noise." Fallon told him to go "right into the lion's den"—Chicago. At first, Rothstein thought this was a crazy idea, but Fallon persisted. "Go to Chicago and begin brow-beating everyone. Find fault with everything. Be temperamental."[25]

Fallon then arranged for Rothstein's visit to be publicized, and sure enough, he was greeted by a mob of photographers, "enough to have covered World War I." Rothstein complained that such an unruly scene could never have happened in New York, and the press backed right off.

> This was a challenge to their civic pride. So eager were the jurors to match Chicago hospitality with that of New York, that they failed to indict the Master-Mind. For some years later, at least two of the courteous jurors called regularly on Rothstein in New York, receiving from him dinners, baseball and theater tickets.[26]

Ban Johnson's contact with the legal scene in New York, James

R. Price, sent Johnson a letter that included a list of questions that Rothstein might be asked. In the letter, Price wrote that Rothstein had told the Giants' John McGraw that the 1919 Series was "fixed" and had asked McGraw to notify Kid Gleason, but that McGraw had "declined to do so."[27] The *St. Louis Post-Dispatch* had reported that same information after Rothstein testified to the 1920 grand jury, as had the *Chicago Tribune*.

Ban Johnson said that Rothstein told him directly that "he [Rothstein] went to see John McGraw and told him they were going to fix the Series, and that he had better notify Kid Gleason. McGraw, Rothstein related, refused to meddle, saying that he would not bother Gleason just as he was starting into the Series.

"Incidentally, I may say that McGraw, when I gave out Rothstein's statement later, said that Rothstein was several kinds of a liar."[28]

In his *Chicago Tribune* memoir, Johnson added that McGraw's reply to Rothstein's advice had been to say that "Gleason had enough troubles" (preparing his team for the World Series).

Whether any or all of Price's questions were put to Rothstein on the witness stand is not known. But his letter to Johnson suggests that at some point before the Series, Rothstein was testing the rumors of a fix, as well as McGraw's loyalty.

McGraw's loyalty was stronger than Abe Attell's; Attell threatened to tell all after Rothstein blamed him for the fix. Lawyer Fallon finally silenced Abe and made sure he was not extradited to Chicago. When Attell went missing during the grand jury proceedings, Hartley Replogle tried reaching him by telegram; Replogle also wired John McGraw to enlist his help in finding Attell, who was Rothstein's bodyguard.[29]

In 1924, when Fallon took up Cozy Dolan's case after Dolan was banished from baseball by Judge Landis, Ban Johnson said it was "a repetition of 1921," when Fallon had protected Attell.[30]

Fallon probably collaborated with Alfred Austrian, Comiskey's lawyer, to obtain the grand jury testimony and signed confessions and waivers of immunity. Rothstein took no chances, and we know Comiskey was involved because Jackson's confession surfaced again in 1924 from the briefcase of Comiskey's attorney. A few years later, missing affidavits were found in Rothstein's keeping. "In a file marked 'William Kelly' [Sport Sullivan's lawyer] the delving [FBI] authorities found papers showing that [Kelly] had come into possession of four affidavits dealing with the Black Sox affair, and promptly filed a bill with Rothstein for

$53,000. The four affidavits were from Abe Attell . . . Fallon . . . his partner, Eugene McGee, and a Joseph Sullivan." [31]

Kelly received the $53,000 from Rothstein for "legal services rendered"; Rothstein paid him and "got an unconditional release" from Kelly, who later was indicted in Boston for blackmail in a different case. The affidavits told of Rothstein "bribing the 'Black Sox.'" [32]

Henry Chafetz, commenting on the papers that Rothstein left behind: "His innocence was palpably disproved and justice was shown to have been blind when it declared him guiltless in fixing the 1919 World Series." [33] If this evidence was made public at the time, it must have made Ban Johnson very happy indeed.

Finally, Fallon represented Abe Attell, after he was indicted. The New York police swiftly arrested Attell, but Rothstein's $1,000 in bail money had him out in no time. Then Fallon "swore out a writ of *habeas corpus*" and claimed that the man wanted in Chicago "is not the same man as my client, Abe Attell!" [34]

The following May, Fallon "*produced* the man who had made the original complaint [at the Chicago grand jury hearing] against Abe Attell, a citizen named Sam Paas." (Paas had gambled and lost $500 to Attell; he was far from alone.) Under "brief and effective" cross-questioning by Fallon, Paas failed to identify Abe Attell—"I never saw this man before." Remember, some of the gamblers did not use their own names— for example, "Brown" was Nat Evans. And perhaps, for a while, Nat was Abe Attell.

Charges against Attell were dropped, but Abe was rearrested the same afternoon on a warrant calling for his extradition to Chicago. Fallon obtained an immediate release, and Attell went into deep hiding, his skin intact.

Although he gave occasional interviews after Rothstein's death, Attell never did tell the full story, as he once had threatened to do. Damon Runyon wrote that Attell was protecting a friend, who died in the early 1930s; Attell never identified this friend.

Fallon died of a heart attack at age forty-one. That's the end of his story here. But it is interesting that Gene Fowler, writing in 1931, sums up the 1919 fix like this: "Comiskey wrecked his superb team" (no mention of his cover up of nearly a year), and the guilty players were banished from organized baseball. The game was "restored to something of its former prestige" by the hiring of Landis as czar, and by

a pot-bellied, delightful person named Babe Ruth. He began

busting home runs with great swirls of muscle and blows of bat. The magnates seized on the home-run interest of fans and quietly introduced a lively ball into the game. . . . The magnates denied they were using a sensitive type of ball. Only recently have they admitted it in a left-handed manner, by putting another, less lively sphere into play [after the embarrassing offensive outburst in 1930][35]

DAMON RUNYON

The stories surrounding the 1919 Series are so rich that they have attracted the attention of many writers. Most of them research the usual sources, and invariably, if they pursue the topic at all, they find something in their research or interviews, or draw some conclusion from looking at the facts, that has not yet appeared in any work on the subject.

For example, in Jimmy Breslin's book *Damon Runyon* (Ticknor and Fields, 1991), we learn that even the fringe characters in the story have nicknames. Runyon was called "Avisack"—he got the nickname from Arnold Rothstein when a horse that he bet on won big.

Runyon was a fine baseball writer who wound up in the employ of William Randolph Hearst. In one anecdote, Hearst sees a Runyon story from the Giants' spring training camp and asks, "Why is he here?" An aide replies, "Baseball sells the paper." To which Hearst is said to have responded, "War is the number-one newspaper seller of all time. Get Runyon to war." Damon soon found himself in Mexico, looking for Pancho Villa with the U.S. Army. One of his more famous pieces came later, describing Casey Stengel's inside-the-park home run in the first World Series game in Yankee Stadium, October 1923.

His best-known work, *Guys and Dolls*, "... when Rothstein was in his prime. Runyon disguised Rothstein as Nathan Detroit in *Guys*, and as Armand Rosenthal or simply as "The Brain" in his other stories." a collection of stories about gamblers, gangsters, and characters in the sporting world, captures some of the flavor of New York City when Arnold Rothstein was in his prime.

Damon Runyon, writing in the *New York American* on September 27, 1920 (exactly when the scandal was breaking), recalled that his paper had printed an article titled "Rothstein Admits Receiving Offer" the previous October 30, when rumors of the Big Fix were still thick in the air. "What did baseball do about the matter at the time this story was printed nearly one year ago?" Runyon asked. And then he answered.

Not a thing.

Here was something for the league officials to work on. Here was a report that justified the greatest activity and closest investigation on the part of the men supposed to protect the great American game.

What did [National League President John] Heydler and [American League President Ban] Johnson, and all the rest do?

They did nothing. They kept quiet.

Prompt action on their part at the time this story was published might have averted the plague of scandal, which now affects the game.

We believe in the integrity of baseball. We believe that it will be all the better for the cleansing it is now undergoing.

But we believe that the "shush" policy of the league officials has been very damaging to the best interests of the game.[36]

Runyon covered the 1919 Series for Fullerton's paper, the *Chicago Herald & Examiner*. He penned the front-page stories, the ones with the big headlines, that were continued inside, on the sports pages. (Fullerton was the senior writer, at age 46; Runyon was 35, protege Ring Lardner 34. For some perspective, Sox manager Kid Gleason was 54. Comiskey and Garry Herrmann were both 60, Ban Johnson 55. Judge Landis, who always looks 75, was a craggy 53.) After the scandal broke, Runyon observed in the *H & E* pages, "As long as [cleaning up the gambling mess] is out of baseball's hands there is hope that it will eventually be be cleaned up."

HAL CHASE

Bob Hoie believes that "the closest approximation of [Hal Chase's] personality is Paul Newman in *The Sting*." That is, "a rogue, a liar and a cheat, but ultimately an irresistible character."[37] And if a younger Newman had played Chase in a movie, we probably would all think better of Hal today. Instead, Hal Chase is probably the first baseball player who comes to mind when the subject of tossing games comes up.

Martin Donell Kohout's biography of Chase is another book that reminds us how much baseball had been infiltrated by gamblers in the years before 1919. Hugh Fullerton was not shocked to see gamblers at work on the 1919 Series—nothing unusual about that—but was shocked by their brazenness. Baseball truly was on the path toward its destruction, following boxing and horseracing.

Hal Chase was repeatedly mentioned in connection with the fix of October 1919. (Writer Fred Lieb said that a star player of that day told him that Hal Chase was "the evil genius behind" the fix.[38]) Chase's name came up soon after the 1920 grand jury turned its attention to October 1919. An attempt to describe the fix appeared in the *Chicago Tribune* on September 25, 1920; it gave Chase a central role, as the person who first approached Attell with the scheme. This was very different from Maharg's version, which appeared a few days later; Maharg made no mention of Chase. Chase's role, like that of many others, seems destined to remain a mystery.

Donald Dewey and Nicholas Acocella raise the possibility that Chase's name surfaced in connection with the fix because John McGraw wanted it to, for various reasons. "Chase always believed that McGraw had pressured both [Jean] Dubuc and [Fred] Toney into taking the stand against him as the price for their own professional survival." They point out that Bill Burns repeatedly testified that Chase dropped out of the picture after failing in the initial attempt to involve Rothstein.[39]

Recorded in Hal Chase's obituary is the fact that not long before he died, Chase said that his "most costly error" was his failure to notify the league president when he learned about the attempt to fix the 1919 World Series. He insisted that he himself was not involved but that he did know about the conspiracy, having heard of it directly from Bill Burns.[40] Dewey and Acocella's biography includes two interviews Chase gave to *The Sporting News* in the 1940s, in which he gives two different versions of his meetings with Burns. In both interviews, Chase denies being in on the fix.

THE DES MOINES CONNECTION

Ralph J. Christian has explained the Des Moines connection to the fix better than anyone to date.[41] David Zelcer—whose name is nearly always misspelled "Zelser" in works on the subject, because it was misspelled in his indictment—was one of four brothers from Des Moines; he and Abe headed the family gambling activities. Christian notes that David Zelcer's role in the fix is anything but clear. He may have been an assistant to Abe Attell or Hal Chase, posing under the name "Bennett" as a representative of Rothstein; or he may have been a lieutenant of Rothstein. In the investigations after the Series, Zelcer was linked with Carl Zork of St. Louis, and the Levi brothers, Ben and Lou, also of Des Moines, as well as Ben Franklin (Frankel), of Omaha.

A letter from Ban Johnson to Harry Redmon, July 28, 1921, toward the end of the Black Sox trial, indicates that the 1919 World Series was not the first time the Levi brothers had menaced the sport: "That pair of Des Moines crooks have been eating at the vitals of baseball for the last three or four years, and should not go unwhipped of justice."[42]

Redmon had tipped off Ban Johnson about Carl Zork.[43] At the 1921 trial, Redmon testified that he heard Zork openly boasting that he had fixed the Series, "I, the little red-head from St. Louis."[44] Rube Benton fingered Zork "*along with* the red-headed fellow."[45] In any case, Zork denied making the boast.

In spring 1921, Phillie infielder Gene Paulette was suspended by Commissioner Landis for his connection with gamblers. The *New York Times* identified "St. Louis men" Carl Zork and Elmer Farrar as being "responsible for his banishment."[46]

Zork once managed boxer Abe Attell. David Zelcer was a brother-in-law to the Levi brothers and was a longtime friend of Abe Attell. The Des Moines trio were avid White Sox fans. And there was another link between Chicago and Des Moines: the Iowa entry in the Western League was owned by Tom Fairweather, a personal friend of Charles Comiskey. The Des Moines team had a close working relationship with the White Sox (Eddie Cicotte and Red Faber had pitched for them). According to Christian, Fairweather telegraphed Comiskey around New Year's Day 1920 regarding the rumors he heard in Des Moines about the fix. Comiskey had his friend Tip O'Neill reply with a letter asking for specifics. Fairweather put what he knew into a letter to Comiskey a week later.

Initially, five gamblers were indicted: Hal Chase, Sleepy Bill Burns, Abe Attell, "Brown" (Nat Evans), and Sport Sullivan. At the arraignment on February 14, 1921, no gambler showed up in person. The ballplayers were present. On March 26, 1921, a second Cook County grand jury handed up more indictments, this time including Zelcer, Zork, and the rest of the Des Moines Connection.

Among those not indicted was Jean DuBuc, who allegedly received a telegram from Sleepy Bill Burns confirming that the fix was on. He told the grand jury. DuBuc left for Canada before the 1921 trial.[47]

HOW HARD IS IT TO THROW A GAME?

In his weekly column after the fix was uncovered, John B. Sheridan of *The Sporting News* recalled a story told by Edd Roush that showed "how difficult it was for an honest ballplayer to force himself to deliberately do anything on the diamond to injure his team's chances of winning." Years before the fix, it seems, certain Cincinnati Reds habitually bet on their own games—sometimes for the Reds to win, sometimes not, "depending on the odds and other conditions."

Like the other honest players, Roush said he always had his suspicions, but was never certain. One day, he was sure that the suspects were playing hard to win. It was a meaningless game in the standings, and Roush decided that if he got the chance to lose it, he would, to foil the gamblers. Sure enough, late in the game the situation arose where the Reds had a slim lead, but their opponent loaded the bases. Roush decided that on any long hit out his way, he would let it drop, giving away several runs. Sure enough, the batter knocked a long fly to deep center.

> I'll let it go, I said to myself, but while I was saying it I began giving chase after the flying ball. As I neared the ball I again told myself I would let it go, but something within me that had more control over my actions than my mind, caused me to put up my hands. I was still telling myself I would be doing right in missing the catch when I decided I should not deliberately lose a ball game and leaped up and pulled down the ball.[48]

CONCLUSIONS

Millions of dollars changed hands on bets placed in connection with the 1919 World Series. Chicago banks noticed a sharp increase in the number of mortgage foreclosures in the months that followed and concluded that this was due to lost bets. When the fix was uncovered—just days before the World Series of 1920—the two pennant-winning teams, Brooklyn and Cleveland, were thoroughly interrogated to be sure they had not been tampered with. There was not much betting on that Series—it would take a while before fan confidence returned all the way.

Judge Landis hoped that by coming down decisively and hard on the accused White Sox players, he could sever the ties between baseball and gambling. While rumors of later fixes would persist, baseball's image was improved, and the trust of fans restored. The fix of 1919 made gambling a ballplayer's mortal sin. To even discuss the throwing of a game was to risk one's career.

When Pete Rose's gambling became known in the late 1970s,

according to John Helyar, baseball closed its eyes.[49] General managers "wouldn't mess with a gold-plated gate attraction." Commissioner Peter Ueberroth confronted Rose, then "did his part to cover up." If there was one lesson to be learned from the events of 1919–21, it was the dangers of pretending problems will just go away if they are ignored.

Whether Pete Rose bet on baseball, and whether he was treated unfairly by commissioner Bart Giamatti, is the subject of a number of books. Suffice to say here that the banishment of Pete Rose to baseball's ineligible list has linked him in the minds of many fans with Joe Jackson. Both seem to deserve the Hall of Fame, based on their careers played between the lines. Yet both are prevented from appearing on any ballot, until and unless they are reinstated.

Whatever Jackson did happened so long ago, and was so hard to know with certainty even then, that later commissioners have been reluctant to overrule Judge Landis. Similarly, the two commissioners who have followed Giamatti have not been anxious to move on Rose's case. (Giamatti passed away soon after the Rose decision.) Yet both players have loyal supporters who continue to keep their heroes alive, in the media and in baseball conversation. Much of the fun for baseball fans is arguing, whether in the grandstand or over the "hot stove." And the cases of Jackson and Rose certainly provide excellent fuel for this activity, and will continue to do so, whether or not they are ever honored with a bronze Cooperstown plaque.

* * * * *

Sorting out the gamblers in the Big Fix is hardly an easy task. It can be confusing even when the names are familiar enough to be associated with the correct syndicate. Sometimes it has the feel of the famous "Who's on First?" comedy routine, and with that in mind, I now present:

ABBOTT AND COSTELLO MEET THE GAMBLERS

Abbott: You know, strange as it may seem, everybody knows who the eight ballplayers banned by Landis were, but nobody has bothered to make a roster of the gamblers involved.

Costello: Well, somebody must know who they were.

Abbott: I do.

Costello: You do? Then tell me, who's on fir—I mean, who's on top? Arnold Rothstein, "The Big Bankroll"?

Abbott: Said it couldn't be done.

Costello: But he had the money to pull it off, it had to be Rothstein.

Abbott: Said it couldn't be done.

Costello: OK, give me some other names.

Abbott: Well, there was Hal Chase. Chase was working with the Giants' pitcher Rube Benton, and Hal also introduced Sleepy Bill Burns to David Zelcer, and Chase also had links with Jean DuBuc and Fred Toney of the New York Giants . . .

Costello: Fred Toney, the fellow who pitched in baseball's only double-no-hitter, against Hippo Vaughn?

Abbott: That's him, but he was never really linked to the fix. Rube Benton was "cleared" too.

Costello: Benton was cleared?

Abbott: That's correct. The league presidents were upset by Judge Landis' ruling, but he had the final word.

Costello: How about Chase and DuBuc?

Abbott: They were both unofficially bounced out of baseball. It was a long time coming for Chase.

Costello: I thought it was only *eight* men out.

Abbott: No, it was more, and probably could have been a *lot* more. Joe Gedeon of the Browns was bounced because he got a tip from Swede Risberg, one of the crooked Sox players, and bet on it. It's pretty hard to imagine that other players with gambler "friends" didn't do the same.

Costello: Benton and Chase were New York Giants. . . . How does this connect with the White Sox players?

Abbott: Well, Benton, on the grand jury stand in September 1920, implicated Chase, Heinie Zimmermann, and Buck Herzog in a fixed game against the Cubs in September 1919. When he did this, Herzog retaliated with the news that he'd already discussed the bribe attempt with National League President Heydler back in June 1920. Buck produced affidavits from two Boston Braves, Tony Boeckel and Art Wilson, certifying that they won $3,200 on a tip from Chase. Heydler gave Herzog a letter of clearance and told him to keep quiet. But then Herzog forced Benton to admit his knowledge of the 1919 Series fix. Said he saw a telegram from Burns to DuBuc.

Costello: Sounds like Heydler was covering up.

Abbott: You bet! I mean, right! Heydler had let Chase off the hook once, when he had all the goods on him, to the bafflement of all. On the stand, Heydler did mention that Chase and Zimmermann had offered Benny Kauff $500 to toss a game. Kauff refused and went to McGraw, and McGraw finally fired Chase and Zimm.

Costello: Wait a minute—didn't you say before that Benton was cleared?

Abbott: Yes, even though he confessed to have the same "guilty knowledge" that meant the end for Weaver and Gedeon. And Benton also bet based on what he knew, and won. Landis just absolved him, saying, well, it had been a while since it all happened and Rube hadn't corrupted anyone lately so why "deprive him of his livelihood?" Maybe it was Landis's way of thanking Rube for his role in the undoing of the cover-up.

Costello: So Landis wasn't consistent?

Abbott: He didn't need to be, he was the commissioner! Other players may have won several thousand dollars by betting with the advantage of "guilty knowledge," too—Ivy Olson and Johnny Rawlings, for example. Rawlings had played high school ball with Fred McMullin and was said to only bet on sure things.

Costello: Is that about it for crooked players?

Abbott: Well, Claude Hendrix is worth mentioning. Claude was supposed to start for the Cubs in a game against the Phils on August 31, 1920. Before the game there were rumors and lots of betting—just like before the 1919 Series. Veeck, the Cubs' president, yanked Hendrix. (He was never banned, just released the next winter; but no other club signed him. Veeck noted at the time that there was no evidence implicating Hendrix or any other player.) The Cubs started old Pete Alexander instead, to thwart the gamblers.

Costello: There should have been an investigation!

Abbott: There was—a Chicago grand jury was convened to look at the thing. Then they got distracted by the 1919 World Series, and people forgot all about the little Cubs–Phils problem.

Costello: Did that old Hall of Famer Alexander win that game?

Abbott: Are you kidding? Veeck offered him $500 to win. But the Phils won anyway, 3–0. Old Pete, it turned out later, was not above suspicion, but he was an icon, and that definitely counted, as Tris Speaker and Ty Cobb found out later.

Costello: Speaker and Cobb?

Abbott: Yeah, and Joe Wood and—

Costello: OK, let's get back to the gamblers. You mentioned Burns and Zelcer?

Abbott: Sleepy Bill Burns had pitched in the majors, not very well. He was in Cincinnati and heard of the fix. Apparently he made the mistake of betting on the Reds in Game Three and lost all his money. That did make him a willing witness, though.

Costello: And Zelcer?

Abbott: David Zelcer worked out of Des Moines and San Francisco. Zelcer also went by the name Bennett. He was linked by Burns to—guess who?

Costello: Rothstein?

Abbott: Said it couldn't be done.

Costello: So they indicted a guy from Des Moines?

Abbott: No, three. Louis and Ben Levi were gamblers from Des Moines and they were indicted, too. Along with Carl Zork. Ban Johnson is usually given credit for rounding these guys up.

Costello: Was Zork from Des Moines or New York?

Abbott: No, Zork was a St. Louis man. Zork was into blouse-making, but at one time had managed the fixer Abe Attell. Some folks think Zork and another St. Louis fellow, Benjamin Franklin (whose last name was actually Frankel) were the real organizers of the plot.

Costello: Were they?

Abbott: Apparently not. Franklin was not indicted at first, and at the trial, the judge said there was so little evidence against Felsch, Weaver, and Zork, that if they were found guilty, he'd have to overturn the verdict.

Costello: But everyone was found not guilty!

Abbott: Yeah, that was a tough break for Happy and Buck. Landis had this thing about "birds of a feather." . . . If Buck had been dissociated from the others, he might have had a chance.

Abbott: So who gets the credit—I mean, the blame—for the idea to fix the Series?

Costello: Well, Ban Johnson thought a St. Louis gambler named Henry "Kid" Becker tried to fix the 1918 Series, but couldn't come up with the money. Becker was a pal of Zork.

Abbott: So maybe Becker and Zork tried to pull off in 1919 what they couldn't afford the year before?

Costello: No—because Becker was gunned down by "a highwayman," the papers said, in April 1919. Attorney Bill Fallon later claimed that he was shot by a rival for the Kid's girlfriend.[50] Anyway, Becker was gone, but perhaps his idea lived on with Zork, or maybe the 1919 fix was done in memory of the Kid. In the 1921 trial, Harry Redmon said he heard Zork brag that he was the one who started the fix.

Costello: So did Burns approach the players?

Abbott: It's not clear who approached whom first. Some folks said Gandil and Cicotte approached Burns.

Costello: So it was the players' idea first?

Abbott: Well, that's the trouble with great ideas: everybody claims the credit, especially when they work. Some folks thought the big idea came from Benny Kauff, the Ty Cobb of the Federal League. Rothstein told Ban Johnson that Kauff brought a Providence man named Henderson to him; Henderson was a gambler willing to put up $50,000 if Rothstein would do the same,[51] but Rothstein told him—

Costello: It couldn't be done.

Abbott: That's correct.

Costello: Is this the same Kauff that got Chase and Zimmermann fired?

Abbott: Yes, along with Lee Magee, a friend of Chase. When Heydler was investigating Chase, he found a check from Magee for part of a wager. Magee is rated one of the more incompetent of the fixers. Naming Kauff as the mastermind behind the Series fix was probably Chase getting even. Later Kauff was banned from baseball by Landis anyway.

Costello: For fixing games?

Abbott: No, for being in a car theft ring in December 1919. Actually, he was cleared of those charges, but Landis didn't care. Who knows? A New York detective named Val O'Farrell had Benny Kauff in headlines right after the scandal broke, saying that Kauff and a Long Island gambler named Orbie—a friend of Abe Attell—said that his intimate friend Rothstein told *him* that Kauff was the first person to approach him about backing the fix.

Costello: Orbie? Maybe Orbie was Henderson?

Abbott: Maybe. Rothstein told Ban Johnson it was Henderson, but he told O'Farrell, Orbie. By the way, O'Farrell also said he had definite proof that the famous "A.R." telegram of Attell was really sent by Curly Bennett.[52]

Costello: And Bennett was really Zelcer?

Abbott: Apparently. O'Farrell said Attell was sending daily telegrams to Hal Chase, too.

Costello: If this detective O'Farrell knew so much, why didn't the grand jury call him to testify?

Abbott: Well, why didn't they call Hugh Fullerton or Ray Schalk? Maybe they just wanted to keep things simple.

Costello: Simple? Well, is that about it for the gamblers?

Abbott: Oh, no, there are lots more. Like Joseph J. "Sport" Sullivan, from Boston. Sullivan also had Montreal connections. He and Rachael Brown were Rothstein agents and associated with Abe Attell. It's a bit murky here: there is a Brown mentioned by a few gamblers who may be this Brown, or who may really be Nat Evans. Many believe Gandil initially contacted Sullivan in Boston's Buckminster Hotel, three weeks before the Series. "I think we can put it in the bag for you."[53] But many think Gandil contacted Attell first. Chick and Abe had been friends.[54]

Costello: Attell—wasn't he a former boxer?

Abbott: Yes, a former welterweight world champ. Abe would have been a key witness, too, although he thought only five players were in on the fix. Some think Chase had the big idea first and took it to Attell, who took it to Rothstein, who said . . .

Costello: Couldn't be done.

Abbott: Yeah, then later he changed his mind, some say. Well, Attell said so, but then he brought in the Des Moines and St. Louis guys, so maybe Rothstein never told Attell just where he stood.

Costello: Weren't there any *Chicago* gamblers involved?

Abbott: Sure, there was "Nick the Greek" Dandolos, who was said to have "made a killing" on the Series, although he said he lost more betting on the Sox than he won by betting on the Reds. Nick may have won big placing bets for Rothstein.[55]

Costello: Did any other hometown boys make good?

Abbott: Mont Tennes was the most prominent name to come up. Before the Series, Jim O'Leary, whose establishment near the stockyards was the best-known clearinghouse for wagers, said Cincinnati money was more in evidence than White Sox money, so he dropped the odds from 5–4 Sox to win, to 5–6 Reds.

Costello: And how did you dig this up?

Abbott: Not hard. It was reported in the *Chicago Tribune* on October 1. The *Trib* had the odds on October 2, after Game One, shifting to 7–10 Reds. Tennes, incidentally, was a friend of George M. Cohan, the entertainer, who liked to gamble some. Apparently Cohan bet early and had $30,000 down on the Sox before word of the fix made it to him (from Abe Attell). Then he had his partner Sam Harris hedge the bet . . . and put a little extra on Cincinnati. Years later, Cohan told reporter Westbrook Pegler that the Series was "a frame-up."

Costello: Was Tennes indicted?

Abbott: No, but he testified. Tennes was also a friend of Charles

Weeghman, who owned the Federal League Whales . . . built them a park, which happens to be Wrigley Field today.

Costello: Was Weeghman involved?

Abbott: No, but he testified. He thought seven players were in on the fix. That's what his gambler friend Mont Tennes told him, right after the Series. (Mont Tennes said he found out by overhearing two men talking on a train, on their way to the Saratoga race track.[56] Tennes also publicly denied Weeghman's account.) Weeghman said he passed the word to National League President Heydler . . . at least he *thought* he told him . . . he so discounted Tennes's story that he wasn't sure. That was in August of 1919.

Costello: August? I thought the fix was a last-minute deal.

Abbott: No, it just seemed that way. Abe Attell told Joe Williams that "It was painted on the wall in Saratoga Springs in August."[57] Weeghman knew Rothstein, by the way, but when asked if Rothstein was involved, he said he doubted it. After all, Rothstein was once a partner in a pool hall with Giants manager John McGraw. That surely put him above suspicion.

Costello: You mentioned Jim O'Leary—other betting parlors must have had the same experience if this was a national phenomenon.

Abbott: Sure they did, you can look it up in papers across America. Jack Doyle ran the Billiard Academy in New York, which was a big betting center, and he estimated he took in $2 million in bets before Game One. He was widely quoted later as saying, "The thing had an odor."

Costello: How come none of the "clean Sox" who knew about the fix ever spoke up?

Abbott: Well, Ray Schalk tried . . . in a December 19 interview he stated something which Hugh Fullerton had predicted right after the Series, that by the next season, 1920, "seven players will be gone."[58] But by the time *The Sporting News* got to Schalk to verify that, he had changed his story, denied the statement, and said that he saw nothing wrong with the 1919 World Series.

Costello: So the gamblers got to him?

Abbott: No, more than likely it was Comiskey. He owned Schalk, and Commy really wanted all his players back for 1920. There is testimony from the "clean Sox" that games during the 1920 season were tossed and covered up, too. Eddie Collins complained to Comiskey after the Sox seemed to toss a Series in Boston. Commy thanked him, and did nothing.

Costello: So was this Burns guy working alone?

Abbott: Apparently no one worked alone! Attell had a connection with a St. Louis gambler and theater owner named Harry (sometimes Harvey) C. Redmon. Redmon had not been in on it, and lost a bundle betting on the Sox. He tried to recoup some of his losses by going to Comiskey for the reward money.

Costello: Comiskey's offer of $10,000 for hard evidence?

Abbott: Yeah, that St. Louis Browns infielder Joe Gedeon tried for the reward, too. According to Ban Johnson, Gedeon acted as a "betting commissioner" for Carl Zork and won $900 himself. The Browns' owner Phil Ball dropped Gedeon whenever his connection with the fix surfaced. Comiskey listened to their stories, but all they had were *names and places and dates*, no hard evidence!

Costello: So Comiskey turned them away?

Abbott: Yes, but they told Ban Johnson, too. Both Comiskey and Johnson probably learned very little in the 1920 hearings and 1921 trial. After Redmon testified to the grand jury, *The Sporting News* noted that Comiskey had suppressed evidence of his players' "rottenness" because they "cost him a lot of money." They took Commy to task for "protecting his investment at the expense of the public." Oh, then there was Billy Maharg, of Philadelphia.

Costello: Wasn't he a former boxer, too?

Abbott: Yes, and he had baseball connections, too. He roomed with Pete Alexander for a while. Some say Maharg and Burns were the "pioneers" of the fix.

Costello: So Maharg cleaned up big?

Abbott: No, he was in with Burns, and lost everything on Game Three. Maharg's interview with Isaminger in the *Philadelphia North American*, during the grand jury hearing, was one event that got things really rolling. He started naming players, including Cicotte. Of course he only knew what he got from Gandil.

Costello: So did Maharg get Comiskey's reward money?

Abbott: He tried, but Comiskey never responded to his wire. In the 1921 trial, the defense lawyers suggested that Maharg and Bill Burns fabricated their version of the fix in order to collect and split Commy's $10,000 reward. They also accused Burns of making up his story to please Ban Johnson and hurt Comiskey, since it was common knowledge that the two were feuding. Burns denied this, of course.

Costello: So of all the gamblers involved, which ones went to trial?

Abbott: Well, certainly not Rothstein.

Costello: Said it couldn't be done.

Abbott: And, Rothstein knew a great lawyer, William A. Fallon, "The Great Mouthpiece." Ban Johnson met with Rothstein and probably knew that nothing could be traced back to him. However, just to make sure, Fallon had Rothstein go to Chicago to testify to the grand jury. Comiskey's lawyer Austrian said that Rothstein "proved himself guiltless" and Ban Johnson agreed. Rothstein probably only confirmed that his underlings *were* involved, so Attell and Sullivan and Burns were indicted.

Costello: So they were all brought to justice?

Abbott: Not exactly. After Rothstein's testimony, folks started disappearing. Attell went to Montreal, Sullivan left the country, and "Brown" vanished. By the time the trial got under way, the Levi brothers' case was dropped and there was no evidence against Zork. That left David Zelcer the only vulnerable gambler.

Costello: Did they ever figure out who had the big idea first?

Abbott: Not really. Some say Gandil. Some say Cicotte took the idea to Burns, who took it to Maharg and Rothstein . . . Maharg might have found Rothstein at a Giants game, in Charles Stoneham's box, maybe with the big oil guys, Joshua Cosden and Harry Sinclair . . . anyway, Rothstein said it—

Together: Couldn't be done!

Costello: So Rothstein was clear and home free, right?

Abbott: Well, maybe. Rothstein needed to see the rest of the grand jury testimony, to be sure he was not implicated. He also wanted to see what his underlings said about him.

Costello: So he requested a copy of the transcript?

Abbott: No, the papers of the grand jury were sealed. He had to pay for them. Comiskey's lawyer and Fallon may have been behind the theft . . . $10,000 supposedly went to the lame duck District Attorney Hoyne, and his assistant Henry Berger. We know Comiskey was involved, because some of the stolen material—which hindered the trial prosecution, by the way—turned up later in the 1924 Milwaukee trial. Joe Jackson sued for back salary, took Commy to court; then Commy's lawyer produced Jackson's missing 1920 confession.

Costello: That must have gotten Comiskey in real trouble.

Abbott: No one seemed to notice.

Costello: Huh?

Abbott: Just like no one made much of the fact that Comiskey knew almost as much about the conspiracy soon after the Series, as he did after the grand jury hearings and trial.

Costello: Wonder what Rothstein thought about the cover-up?

Abbott: I bet he thought that it *could* be done. And for almost a year, it was done, but then in the end, it came undone.

Costello: So how come this has gone down in history as "the Black Sox scandal" and "eight men out"? I lost count of all the heads that rolled, and that's just players.

Abbott: Because that's the way they wanted it to go down— Comiskey, Johnson, Landis, and Rothstein.

Costello: Said it couldn't be done!

10

DOWN IN HISTORY

Some of the writers whose views or research on the 1919 World Series and its aftermath have shaped the way these events have gone down in history deserve special mention.

RING LARDNER

It is commonly thought that one of the casualties of October 1919 was the loss to baseball of Ring Lardner, who had given the game some of his best writing. Disenchantment with the fixing and/or covering up surely upset Lardner, but there were other reasons for his defection. Lardner blamed his loss of interest in baseball on the way the game changed, from the deadball era of Cobbian strategy, to the lively ball era of Ruthian bombs. "Baseball hasn't meant much to me since the introduction of the TNT ball." (Damon Runyon was disenchanted by the Big Fix, too, and that may have been partly because he had been friends with Arnold Rothstein.[1])

Ring Lardner was a White Sox fan, and he wrote the popular "You Know Me, Al" comic strip from September 1922 until January 1925.[2] Both the comic strip and his earlier book by the same title included real White Sox figures. The strip continued for a while after January 1925 but certainly all Lardner's material was soon exhausted, and his name was removed from the strip after late September 1925.[3]

Ring Lardner had been a kind of protégé of Hugh Fullerton. Ring and Hugh watched the 1919 Series together, then both wrote critically about the fix they saw being covered up after the games. While Fullerton appealed to baseball to investigate, to preserve its reputation as a clean sport, Lardner used humor and heavy sarcasm.

Lardner had been planning to move east when he was assigned to cover the games for the Bell Syndicate. Ring was a good friend of

Eddie Cicotte[4] and an old one of Kid Gleason. So he probably did not mind postponing the move to cover the Series.

In the movie *Eight Men Out*, a memorable scene involving Ring Lardner (played by director John Sayles) takes place on a Pullman car, as the teams travel to Chicago after Game Two.[5] Lardner entertains all who will listen with a song parody. In fact, Ring and three fellow journalists—Tiny Maxwell, Nick Flatley, and James Crusinberry—together wrote new lyrics for "I'm Forever Blowing Bubbles":

> I'm forever blowing ball games/
>> Pretty ball games in the air./
>> I come from Chi.,/
>> I hardly try,/
>> Just go to bat and fade and die./
>> Fortune's coming my way./
>> That's why I don't care./
>> I'm forever blowing ball games,/
>> For the gamblers treat me fair.

Reporter Westbrook Pegler observed: "This song of his [most accounts give Lardner the credit, but it was a collaboration] was very amusing and it spread among the newspaper crowd the next day in Chicago, but still nobody with a reporting job had the intelligence [or] the initiative to take a chance on a story of the brazen operations of the shyster gamblers who were all over the show. It was very, very raw."[6]

Ring Lardner Jr. did not know whether his father sang the song "right in front of the offending team in their Pullman car" or in a Kentucky saloon—"each version has been reliably reported."[7] Ring Jr. adds that the way his father spoke about the event later "gave me the feeling that he was at least as concerned about losing a substantial bet . . . as he was about the moral turpitude of the players."[8]

When Ring Larder was asked to write something about the song he had written for *Collier's* magazine, he said that his collaboration (with Crusinberry, Maxwell, and Flatley) was sung in the roadhouse in Bellevue, Kentucky, but not to taunt the White Sox. "Three of the Cincinnati players were in our party and seemed to enjoy the song."[9]

Reporter Hugh Fullerton recalled just a year later, "That night [after Game Two] a bunch of gamblers and sports, drunk, walked through the crowded lobby of the Sinton [in Cincinnati], singing: 'They are always throwing ball games, Throwing ball games in the air.'"[10]

There is an irony in the lyric—the gamblers were by no means treating the players "fair." Losses in Games One and Two *should* have meant that the players would have had in hand $40,000 to divide. But greed had set in and some of the payoff money was ploughed back into the betting. Lardner's song may have really ticked off the players—especially the last line. It's a memorable scene for John Sayles to play in his film. But if the *Collier's* memoir is correct, then the song's initial audience may have been a less risky one.[11]

In September 1919, Lardner was paid $500 to make a speech at a postseason celebration of the Reds in Cincinnati, and "thought it would be a good gag to bet it vs. the home team."[12]

Ring Lardner did not completely stop writing baseball after the fix. Besides the comic strip noted above, Lardner covered a few more World Series, and his takes are worth looking up. His last Series coverage was in 1927.[13]

ELIOT ASINOF

Unquestionably, the writings of a former minor league ballplayer, Eliot Asinof, have been the greatest influence on current thinking about the fixing of the 1919 Series and its aftermath. Say "Black Sox scandal" and what pops to mind? I would guess *Eight Men Out* would rank high on most people's list of associations. The movie (and video) have reached millions; the book, thousands more. Eliot Asinof's interpretation of the events surrounding the 1919 World Series has become "definitive." Most versions of the story rely on *Eight Men Out* to some degree.

The trouble is, *Eight Men Out* is not history. It certainly is not fiction, either, although it contains some—Asinof was advised to invent a character, so that if anyone stole his material, he could prove it was his. And Eliot Asinof is not primarily a researcher; he does not document everything carefully with footnotes. He was an intelligent writer who tried hard to make sense of the facts and opinions that he collected, and to assemble them into a story told well and worth telling. And he succeeded in doing that.

Asinof's later book, *Bleeding Between the Lines*, tells the story behind *Eight Men Out*. It all began in 1960 when David Susskind, an early television giant who was both a producer and talk show host, approached Asinof to research the Black Sox scandal to see if there was enough material for a ninety-minute television show (the *DuPont Show of the Month*, on CBS). He would be paid $1,000 and was given two weeks.

Enter Ford Frick, baseball's commissioner back then. He convinced the DuPont people that such a production would not be in "the best interests of baseball." Asinof's story was yanked from its slot as the opening *Show of the Month* on September 30, 1960, and put back on the CBS bench.

Susskind later said that the program was pulled out of the CBS lineup because Eddie Cicotte, still alive in 1960, had refused to sign a release to clear the story for television use. Asinof: "So it ended, but not without whetting my appetite, for what became terribly apparent was the extraordinary scope and significance of the incident, infinitely more complex than anyone could even begin to grasp in a week's research."[14]

But David Susskind, a determined maverick, and his business, Talent Associates, had another outlet for the material Asinof had collected so far. The names of Cicotte and any other living person were removed, and sure enough, on January 28, 1961, Shoeless Joe Jackson took the stand on another Susskind-produced show, *Witness*, in a program listing Eliot Asinof as "writer."[15] Asinof's research was apparently used by CBS in the teleplay, although there is nary a reference to the *Witness* episode in *Bleeding*.

A NATIONAL TELEVISION AUDIENCE

Although the narrator notes at the beginning of the *Witness* episode that Joe Jackson and seven other White Sox players were banned for fixing the 1919 World Series, viewers are asked to forget about that and to pretend they are at a hearing just after the Series, to determine whether it was truly fixed or not, and what part had been played by Jackson. No living members of the Black Sox were mentioned by name in *Witness*; there was one casual mention of Weaver by Jackson. Joe was left to take all the heat by himself.

Jackson (played by Biff McGuire—a likeable Andy Griffith type) insists that the Series was played on the up and up. Kid Gleason then takes the stand and insists that the fix was in, as Joe strongly objects. Gleason mentions the gambling going on before the Series. He then accuses Jackson of tossing, and while he admits (under cross-questioning from Jackson!) that Jackson made "no mistakes in the field," Gleason claims that his .375 average was a mirage because in the clutch, Jackson did not deliver.

A slick-looking gambler named Nate Evans is next; speaking for all the gamblers who knew there was no evidence connecting them to the fix, Evans says the fix never got beyond the talking stage. He had only been approached by Bill Maharg, who had been asked about a payoff ($100,000) by some ballplayers. Then the hearing focuses on a September 19, 1919, meeting at the Hotel Clinton (it was the Sinton) in Cincinnati, where Maharg reserved a room for Evans, and brought in eight ballplayers. No explanations are given of why the White Sox were in Cincinnati during the season—a massive scouting party? Never mind. Then Abigail Allison, a chambermaid at the hotel, appears and says that she remembers the meeting well, and she was sure that Jackson was present.

Abigail Allison is fictitious; in most sources, most of the gamblers questioned said that Jackson did not attend the planning meetings, and this is what Jackson insisted all along, too. But in *Witness*, he admits he was there. "But we didn't agree to anything. We turned the money down." Jackson also fingers Rothstein, something the real Jackson never did even when pressured for Rothstein's name before the grand jury.

Asked if he thought of telling Comiskey of the meeting with the gamblers, Jackson replies, "I meant to see him, but never got around to it." (As noted earlier, *The Sporting News*, in a sidebar accompanying its scathing review, was aghast that the television show failed to mention that Jackson "begged" to be benched before the Series "so there could be no doubt."[16])

Charles Comiskey testifies next, and he insists that Jackson "had a hand in the fix." It is not clear where this came from—Comiskey protected his players early on (and even after he knew some of them had sold out), and when he was under oath in 1924 in Milwaukee, Comiskey testified that Jackson never tossed a game in all his seasons as a White Sox player.

The rest of Comiskey's dialog is from the headlines of the day: "Nearly breaks my heart" . . . "My detectives found nothing" . . . "I am going to save baseball" (he was competing with Ban Johnson for the title of Savior, but they both lost to Landis and Ruth) . . . "Baseball is all I live for." When Commy calls Jackson a liar, Jackson tosses back, "I played my heart out for you!"

At this point the show is begging for a climax or perhaps an earthquake, anything to put it all to a stop. Instead, a key witness is introduced, Bill Maharg. (His 1920 interview, when it hit the front pages, had pushed Eddie Cicotte to step forward and confess.)

Maharg says Jackson was in on it "from the top," and Jackson strongly objects. One of the questioners then suggests to Maharg that he is telling them what they want to hear, in order to claim Comiskey's $10,000 reward (which Maharg in fact tried to do; Comiskey ignored him). Then, right on cue, a young boy with a Leave-It-to-Beaver face fights his way to Jackson's side and asks that famous, fictional question. Biff McGuire somehow keeps a straight face.

Unable to keep the truth a secret any longer, Jackson makes a confession. He does get in a few CurtFlood–like shots at the reserve clause, "the system": "They use [ballplayers], and then they dump'em." But the audience does not care about this (the reserve clause was alive and well in 1961)—they have their answers: the Series was fixed, and Joe Jackson was guilty as hell. Television had spoken.[17]

This 1961 video is one of the least useful sources in learning anything factual about the fix and cover-up. But the reaction to it was interesting.[18] Baseball historian Lee Allen calls the *Witness* episode "a production horrible beyond belief."[19]

The *Witness* episode was so thin that it bears no resemblance at all to *Eight Men Out*. Asinof wisely distanced himself from the television show. While it may well have used his research, it did a disservice to the story, which as he knew was quite complex and not, like *Witness*, black and white (no pun intended). And after Asinof wrote *Eight Men Out*, David Susskind wanted *that* script for a television movie, and (because of Asinof's contribution to *Witness*) he felt that he owned it anyway—so much so that he sued Asinof for $1.75 million when Asinof refused.

Interviewed for this book, Biff McGuire, the actor who played Jackson—and who is *still* acting—recalled that the cast in *Witness* had worked without a script. He still has his copy of Warren Brown's 1952 history of the Chicago White Sox, which he was given to read in preparation for his role. He played Jackson the way he read about him, as someone caught up in events, ashamed of what he did, an underpaid ballplayer—and someone who had everyone on the CBS crew on his side and asking him to "Say it ain't so!"[20]

The Susskind lawsuit is the central theme in *Bleeding Between the Lines*. In his battle with Susskind, Asinof wanted to tell just how different his book-writing activity was from the work he did under contract in 1960. *Bleeding* is an interesting book precisely for those passages where Asinof reveals how he went about his research, starting with James T. Farrell. Farrell, in failing health, turned over to Asinof the material he had collected on the subject and advised him to interview the living players.

Here is the connection between Asinof's research for CBS and the book that he wrote later. The publicity stirred up by baseball commissioner Ford Frick over the *Witness* episode had "attracted the eye of a publisher named Howard Cady, then editor at G.P. Putnam's Sons." He contacted Asinof and asked him, "Doesn't it strike you as absolutely incredible that no major work has ever been written about the Black Sox Scandal?"[21]

That was the spark that lit the fuse. Asinof received an advance, and he was off on the trail that resulted in *Eight Men Out*. Asinof thought that he would need a year to research and write the book; it took him three.[22]

Asinof located four of the surviving banned players: Gandil, Risberg, Cicotte, and Felsch; but only Gandil and Felsch would talk with him.[23]

In *Bleeding*, Asinof writes that the question behind *Eight Men Out*, the question that had been driving Farrell before Asinof, was: "Why did they do it?" And that explains why he emphasized Comiskey's tightness, the gamblers' seizing on the vulnerability of underpaid players, and the stubborn "don't squeal" ethic of Buck Weaver.

In a way it is unfortunate that Asinof was forced, in the end, to write a single version of events, instead of exploring the conflicting and complicated stories. And in a way, it is unfortunate that, in the end, the story he tells so well distracts from the story he only sketches—the cover-up. Asinof has noted that the popularity of *Eight Men Out* was given a boost when America learned about Watergate, and investigations that dug beneath cover stories increased. Now Enron and other corporate greed scandals are renewing America's awareness of cover-ups and the "legal shenanigans" of CEOs and others.

A SHORT AND SELECT BIOGRAPHY

Eliot Asinof was born, fittingly, in 1919. He is in my father's generation, *The Greatest Generation* (Brokaw's book makes a strong case). Asinof played baseball, not well enough to make it to the majors, but long enough to gather up many experiences and meet many people who shaped his life and writings. Through everything, Asinof clearly retained his sense of humor, and his sense of wonder about the game. Not the players, not the business—the sport.[24]

The Second World War over, Asinof moved into writing when television knocked out his career with a semi-pro team. (The advent of television is usually credited with the shrinking of the minor leagues.) His new career was thrown a curve when he found out he was on

Senator Joe McCarthy's blacklist. (Much later, Asinof says, he found out the reason: he had once signed a petition outside Yankee Stadium to have the Yanks sign a black ballplayer.)

Asinof finally cracked the literary lineup of baseball with *The Rookie*, based on his own experiences and that of his friend Mickey Rudner. *The Rookie* later was to be the basis for a movie, *Man on Spikes*, and Asinof moved to Hollywood to do its screenplay. But this was scrapped when the movie *Fear Strikes Out* fanned at the box office. Fans of Mel Brooks's *Blazing Saddles* will appreciate this— Asinof lost his next job when he suggested a script in which John Wayne punched out a horse.

Asinof is quick to give James T. Farrell much credit for the project that resulted in *Eight Men Out*—Farrell had been working on a novel about the Black Sox scandal and turned his material over to Asinof when he got the teleplay assignment. That's right, assignment.

Eliot Asinof has said that he felt Joe Jackson was more a victim than anything else and that he should be reconsidered for the Baseball Hall of Fame. He once felt the same way about Pete Rose, "who didn't throw anything." The hall should have no reference to character, except "the honesty with which you play the game." Whether his current opinion of Rose is the same is not known.

Is It History?

Eight Men Out is not a history book, and Sayles's film is not a documentary. The movie simplifies, as most films do, but as long as viewers keep in mind that it is a theory, albeit a well-researched one, it is an enjoyable entertainment. It is well cast and well acted. It may make Eddie Cicotte seem a bit too sympathetic and Comiskey a bit too innocent. It includes "Say it ain't so, Joe" because it simply had to, the audience was waiting for that, and would have doubted the historicity (!) of the film if the detail was missing. For all *Eight Men Out* reveals—for the first time, no doubt, to the majority of its viewers—it also conceals.

"What really happened" before, during, and after the 1919 World Series will never be known with a high degree of certainty. And the possibilities will outweigh the probabilities. There was, in the happy phrase of Chuck Berry, "too much monkey business"—competing syndicates double-crossing each other, stiffing players, players stiffing players, players telling other players who's in and who's out, but lying, perhaps. Then there's the problem of the players who were in on the fix changing their minds—possibly at different times, maybe even during games. Did the Sox win Game Three by accident, or to get even with the gamblers who were not delivering the payoffs?

Sayles's film does a fair job of portraying the ultimate murkiness of the conspiracy, but not as good a job of describing the massive cover-up. So the film, like the edict of Judge Landis, distracts us from baseball's sordid past, focuses on eight men (none of them owners or even management), and gives a sense of unjust treatment of the players—first at the hands of Comiskey and his lawyer, then the grand jury and press, then Landis—without all the details.

John Sayles noted that the story of *Eight Men Out* could easily have been a six-hour mini-Series.[25] But with just two hours to work with, he was not able to "take a side trip" into the 1920 season. Sayles tells an anecdote about Comiskey, "who was asked by a journalist after the second game of the Series if he had 'seen anything,' to which the Old Roman replied 'what do you mean by anything?' I don't doubt that he had bets down on the Series too!"

Is It "Definitive"?

I reread *Eight Men Out*, the "definitive" book, after much of my own research was completed. I expected that I would find a long list of inaccuracies, but it seems that Asinof got most things right. Documentation would have been nice, of course. But I tip my cap to Asinof for telling a very complicated story in an interesting way.

That said, I wish that he had been able to see Jackson's grand jury testimony, and those transcripts from the 1924 trial.[26] Perhaps then Asinof might have resisted lumping the "eight men out" together. He does this right at the beginning, on page five of his book: ". . . eight members of the Chicago White Sox had agreed to throw the World Series." Never mind that Buck Weaver, for one, never agreed to do that. Never mind that other players were also put out of baseball because of their actions regarding the 1919 World Series. It is irksome because Asinof *knows* all about what the labels conceal; he demonstrates this over and over. Yet it is *eight men out*, they plotted to toss the Series, the Series was lost. Down in history.

Asinof has Comiskey and his lawyer Austrian hatching the cover-up even as they launch their investigation, believing "Ban Johnson and the National Commission could be relied on to do absolutely nothing." But later on he describes Ban Johnson's efforts to collect evidence, and to re-collect it after the papers from the grand jury disappear and threaten to cancel the trial. The National Commission was a lame duck in 1919, but Ban Johnson was hardly idle.

Asinof quotes a *New York Times* editorial that appeared in the wake of the breaking news of the fix: "Professional baseball is in a bad way, not so much because of the Chicago scandal as because that scandal has provoked it into bringing up all the rumors and suspicions of years past . . . their general effect is to wrinkle the noses of fans who will quit going to games if they get the impression that this sort of thing has been going on underground for years."

Which it was, and Asinof nicely documents the known history of baseball and gambling. But that editorial indicates why it was so important for baseball authorities to keep the focus on *the 1919 Series* and then, *eight men out*. Hal Chase? Who's he? Better that the public see eight heads lopped off publicly, case closed, than dredge up scandals from the past. They kept popping up, of course, to the dismay of Landis, who finally declared a kind of amnesty.

1919

Eight Men Out is not the final word on the Black Sox scandal. In fact, it is not even *Asinof's* final word.

1919: America's Loss of Innocence is a history book by Asinof that appeared in 1990. In it, Asinof explores four events that reflect America's change in attitude after World War I. One is Woodrow Wilson and his dream of world peace through the League of Nations, eclipsed by the election of Harding on a "return to normalcy" platform. Another is the rise of anti-communism in the wake of the Russian Revolution and the growing labor movement. A third is the Volstead Act (prohibition), which helped make a wealthy underworld. And then there was the Black Sox scandal.

In *1919*, Asinof was more blunt about the cover-up:

> But mostly the secrecy was maintained by the power of the owners themselves. Whatever they knew, or suspected, they concealed, terrified at losing the public faith in the game. At all costs, any suspicious incident would be buried. The probing sportswriter would be warned, or paid off, to stop his digging. Ball players who wanted to blow the whistle would be carefully thanked for their honesty, then disregarded—always in the best interests of baseball. . . . The official, if unspoken policy preferred to let the rottenness grow rather than risk the dangers of exposure, for all the pious phrases about the nobility

of the game and its inspirational value to youth. In fact, that too was part of the business.[27]

Asinof makes this interesting observation: "The cover-up was far better organized than the fix itself. The baseball establishment had years of experience to fall back on." Perhaps taking the cue from *Hustler's Handbook*, Asinof reflects on what Comiskey did *not* do when he learned the fix was in for certain. He went to Heydler. But he "apparently did not see fit to walk into his own locker room, shut the doors to all outsiders, and take the bull by the horns. . . . He did nothing but cover his rear."[28] It appears, however, that Comiskey *did* send a message to his team, via manager Kid Gleason; and that message may have even been effective in ending the fix.

And Asinof commented on Jackson's testimony: "[Jackson] felt that Cicotte's confession of guilt needed to be countered with his own innocence. He had to tell them he was innocent. How else could he protect himself?" He calls Judge McDonald. "Look Judge, you've got to control this thing . . . whatever they're digging up, I can tell you, I'm an honest man." The judge tells him he believes otherwise and hangs up. Jackson then bumps into Swede Risberg, who says, "I swear to you, I'll kill you if you squawk!" Then Jackson "started drinking, too much too quickly." Then he meets with Austrian.

One of the highlights of this later, somewhat more scholarly, Asinof account (which fills sixty pages in *1919*) is his story of interviewing Happy Felsch. It seems Happy's dad was a Socialist from Germany, active in the Carpenter's Union. Happy was satisfied with the "square treatment" he received from Commy. Asinof: "Translation: Comiskey was a club owner whose predictable function was to exploit his ball players." "You hated him, didn't you?" "He was an owner."

The rest of the story is pretty familiar. Of the trial, Asinof observes: "Like all trials, the truth was masked by the need to secure the system. Everything was manipulated by this all-powerful overview." Summing up his book at the very end, Asinof maintains his somewhat cynical, disillusioned tone. "Say it ain't so, Joe" is as believable as the success of prohibition. "Two flights up and ask for Gus." In other words, Asinof believes "Say it ain't so" is a slogan that *conceals*, rather than reveals. At least that is how I read him.

His Most Recent Take

Eliot Asinof contributed to the 2001 ESPN Classic documentary on "The Black Sox Scandal." At the ESPN Classic Web site is a companion article by Eliot Asinof.[29]

"To understand the Black Sox Scandal," Asinof's article at the Web site begins, "the magic word is *cover-up*. And so it was from the day the 1919 World Series fix began." This is not Asinof changing his mind—in *Eight Men Out*, he constantly uses the image of letting the cat out of the bag. After the dust settled, "the cat was quickly returned to the bag and remained there for over forty years." But now, cover-up is his headline.

The rest of his article tells of his almost two years of "crisscrossing the country" doing his research. The old ballplayers he tracked down were mostly still unwilling to talk; the old gamblers "freely spit up their guts." (Maybe this is why in *Eight Men Out* we find so much on the gambling connections.)

20th Century Fox was gung-ho to make the movie of Asinof's book until they were scared off by the threat of a $2 million lawsuit for defaming the character of Dutch Ruether. Asinof had included in his book a Ring Lardner quote revealing that the Reds' pitcher had had a few drinks before Game One—which he won![30]

Eliot Asinof's appearance in ESPN Classic's documentary makes his absence from Ken Burns' baseball epic seem conspicuous. His pioneer effort in bringing the events of October 1919 to public consciousness has earned Asinof a permanent link to the story of the Big Fix and its cover-up.

VICTOR LUHRS

The Great Baseball Mystery, subtitled *The 1919 World Series*, was published in 1966, on the heels of *Eight Men Out*, and that may be one reason why Luhrs takes such a different slant on things. Perhaps because he concludes that the Series was not fixed after all, and the Reds would have won anyway, his book gets little attention today. But *The Great Baseball Mystery* remains a useful source for researchers.

Murray Schumach, reviewing Luhrs's book for the *New York Times*,[31] complained that Luhrs wrote as if his readers were "in the mental age bracket of 8 to 12"; further, his book was "condescending, marked by heavy humor, inadequate original research and slovenly organization." But some readers prefer Luhrs's account to *Eight Men Out*, because Luhrs does not insist on one version of what happened and provokes much thought.

Luhrs (1912–1984) gives his sources up front[32] but does not use footnotes later on, leaving readers to guess which source provided the information. He gives a fairly detailed history of the earlier baseball scandals that involved gambling. His overview reminds readers that the 1919 Series is only the most notorious of such events.

Here is Luhrs' take on Cicotte's and Jackson's grand jury statements: while "fair-size chunks" were printed in the next day's morning papers, not even the *New York Times* carried them in full. Both players were on the stand for "over two hours" but only a few minutes' worth of material found its way into print. Quoted passages varied somewhat from paper to paper.

Luhrs really does believe that the players—all of them—played every game to win, with the exception of Games Two and Eight, the loss of which he blames on Williams. He concludes that Gandil and Risberg "at no point gave their best efforts." He judges that Jackson, Felsch, Weaver, and Cicotte did give their best; he has a long explanation for Cicotte, who confessed in 1920 and in later interviews.

His book tries to make the case that the Reds would have won anyway because the clean Sox players performed, on the whole, worse than those accused of throwing games. *The Great Baseball Mystery* invites readers to look at certain games, players, and events in a variety of ways, then decide which makes most sense. It is less satisfying than *Eight Men Out*, but it remains one of the earliest and most original books on this topic.[33]

DAVID Q. VOIGT

Harold Seymour's *Baseball: The Golden Age* (1971) is one of the first and finest resources on the fix and cover-up. Voigt's competing history, *American Baseball, Volume 2* (1970), is less useful, but Voigt has contributed a significant essay, "The Chicago Black Sox and the Myth of Baseball's Single Sin."[34]

"The myth of baseball's single sin states that the game's promise was thwarted by the 1919 World Series scandal." This is a "myth" because in fact there was a *Four Men Out* (of Louisville) scandal in 1877, and an unknown number of minor scandals swept neatly under the carpet by baseball officialdom prior to 1920, when the Sox scandal broke.

> Certainly a smart baseball man like Comiskey might have known that unpunished corruption breeds more corruption. . . . To save his own investment, Charles Comiskey had stood silent in the

face of corruption. Knowing this, his colleagues isolated him after 1920. His last years were sick and lonely ones; his one consolation was that he kept his franchise.

"By cleverly playing the role of 'puritan in Babylon,' Landis convinced most fans that baseball's 'guilty season' was over." In the end, Voigt credits Landis for the continuing life of the "myth of baseball's single sin." [35]

NELSON ALGREN

Do not be remembering the most natural man ever to wear spiked shoes.
 The canniest fielder and the longest hitter,
 Who squatted on his heels
 In a uniform muddied at the knees,
 Till the bleacher shadows grew long behind him.
 Who went along with Chick and Buck and Happy
 Because they treated him so friendly-like,
 Hardly like Yankees at all.
 With Williams because Lefty was from the South too.
 And with Risberg because the Swede was such a hard guy. Who made an X for his name and couldn't argue with
 Comiskey's sleepers. [Clauses in his contracts]
 But who could pick a line drive out of the air ten feet outside the foul line
 And rifle anything home from anywhere in the park.
 For Shoeless Joe is gone, long gone,
 A long yellow grass-blade between his teeth
 And the bleacher shadows behind him.[36]

The poem above, "A Silver-Colored Yesterday," makes a good warm-up pitch for Nelson Algren's book *The Last Carousel*, which contains "Ballet for Opening Day," subtitled "Swede Is a Hard Guy."[37] Perhaps less well-known than both Asinof's and Luhrs's books, Algren's edgy take on the fix has the merit of coming from someone who lived most of his life in Chicago.

After an excerpt from *Eight Men Out*, Algren opens "Ballet" with this: "Charles A. Comiskey liked being called 'The Grand Old Man of Baseball.' He liked it so much that he hired a little man to see that messages unbefitting his grandeur never reached him."[38]

Algren tries to document Comiskey's cheapness, noting the original meaning of "Black Sox" (his "begrudging of laundry bills"), and the Sox's three dollars *per diem* dining-room budget when on the road. (Four dollars was the standard for most teams.) At the same time, Commy "loaded press-tables with liquor and food." "Had the old man's parsimoniousness not been dangerous, it would have been comical." Algren lists the salaries of the key White Sox players; he repeats the story about Cicotte being denied a bonus for winning thirty, probably relying on Asinof.

After noting how gamblers had invaded baseball, causing scandals followed by investigations in both leagues, but never reaching "the thousand-dollar bettors sitting behind home plate," Algren includes a three-page poem with the title "Gandil." He describes Gandil befriending Sport Sullivan, who introduces Chick to George M. Cohan and Harry Sinclair. (Sinclair was implicated in the Teapot Dome scandal later, but escaped harm.)

In the "Gandil" poem, Algren mentions the mini-scandal from the end of the 1917 season, in which each White Sox player kicked in $45 as a "token of appreciation" for the four Tiger pitchers who beat Boston three straight to give the Sox the pennant. "Gandil" ends with the note that Chick had Swede Risberg collect the cash, starting with Eddie Collins, and everybody chipped in except Buck Weaver. "The Swede was a hard guy. / He wasn't that hard to Buck Weaver."

Algren's poem "Weaver" is just sixteen lines. Here are the last three: "Who guarded the spiked sand around third like his life. / And wound up coaching a girls' softball team / With no heart left in him at all." Then comes "Risberg," but it's not a poem, it's a seven-paragraph biography. Algren portrays him as a dazzling fielder and asks us to imagine how he must have felt making plays beside the equally flashy Collins, but getting paid less than a fifth of Collins's big salary. "Felsch" is next, and he does not rate a poem, either.

"Cicotte" is next: just one paragraph. Eddie worries because one bad season and he's back in the minors, and he's thirty-five. "Williams": "He worked so deliberately, and so methodically, that it was not unusual for him to pitch nine full innings without giving a single walk." (Williams averaged under two walks per nine innings in 1919.)

"Jackson" gets a whole page. Joe was "never so sophisticated that he could play baseball badly for a price." Then there are vignettes on Gleason (who sympathized with his players; he quit baseball for a year because of a salary dispute with Comiskey); Burns (an ex-pitcher and another oil man) and Maharg; McMullin ("Swede's bar-buddy"); and finally The Big Bankroll (Rothstein) and Albert Knoehr (whom we know better as Abe Attell, "The Little Champ").

Algren has Rothstein figuring that if these players throw the Series, they will be hooked for the 1920 season, too. Then Algren tells the story of the fix, with his version of how the gamblers proceeded. He has Rothstein hooking Harry Sinclair for $90,000. Like Asinof, Algren invents a lot of dialog of the sort that may have taken place among the players and gamblers.

Algren has a great deal of detail in his descriptions of the double-crossing that took place before the third game of the Series.[39] Describing the aftermath of the fix, he has "the righteous and churchy pontiff of Comiskey Park" in bed with Rothstein (to purloin material from the grand jury).

At the end of "Ballet for Opening Day" is a final poem. It has no title. Here are its last lines:

The man in deep left field in the uniform muddied at the knees
With the shadows of fifty seasons behind him
Isn't who you think it is.
For Shoeless Joe is gone long gone
With a long yellow grassblade between his teeth
And a lucky hairpin in his hip pocket.
And what a patch of spiked sand around third looks like
Fifty years after
Only a turning wind may remember.

Only a wind that keeps turning, turning
Around an abandoned ball park.
That blows and blows, forever blowing
Away: always away from home.

Algren's version of things is not documented; nary a footnote. But his familiarity with Chicago and the White Sox players makes his account rich and interesting, even if it is not always factually accurate. Algren had a literary reputation for championing underdogs and victims.[40]

DONALD GROPMAN

Say It Ain't So, Joe! is footnote-free, and while it has a respect able list of sources tacked on at the end, the lack of documentation is disappointing. But this Joe Jackson biography is still a good read.

Gropman nicely debunks Ty Cobb's version of the 1911 race for the batting title. (Cobb did *not* psych out Jackson and whiz past him in the final games.) And he provides a detailed account of Jackson's 1918 season and the "slacker" problem.

Gropman has Jackson going to Comiskey before the Series and asking to be benched. "We do not know how much Joe told Comiskey, but at the least he must have mentioned the rumors and his fear of being implicated." A good point—Jackson's name must have been prominent in the pre-Series rumors, along with Cicotte's, to give the fix more credibility. It was unlikely that Jackson would opt out if he was planning to go ahead and participate with the crooked Sox; if he told Gleason and Comiskey before the Series, he was also challenging them to find fault with his performance during the Series.

Gropman's account has Jackson refusing, then grudgingly accepting $5,000 from his pal Lefty Williams, *after* the Series was over. Some accounts—as well as the grand jury testimony of Jackson—have this event after Game Four or Five. In Gropman's version, he took the money with him to Comiskey's office the next morning, but was sent packing by Harry Grabiner.

Gropman writes that when he began his book in the mid-1970s, he believed Jackson was a guilty man. (The revised second edition [1992] is a very different book from the one that was published in 1979. I recommend this later edition, if only for its appendices.[41]) But the evidence "soon led me to the inescapable conclusion that he was literally innocent."

Among those Gropman thanked for help with his book are Eliot Asinof, Furman Bisher, and Judge Robert C. Cannon of Milwaukee, who loaned Gropman the transcripts of the 1924 trial. Gropman worked some of the testimony into his account of things in the book, then tacked onto the appendices what he felt were the key contributions from Jackson.

In the revised edition, Gropman adds to and emphasizes material that underscores the case for Jackson. For example: "Despite the rumors and distortions that have been published ever since, Jackson's grand jury testimony hardly constituted a confession. If there's a more enigmatic and puzzling document in the history of baseball, it has yet to come to light."[42]

As Gropman notes, "Jackson told two completely different stories and nobody ever asked him why." Another good question is why only one of the stories was leaked to the press—the one that, standing alone, might be called a "confession." Was this leak agreed upon by Austrian and Jackson to convince the gamblers that Jackson did what they thought he did?

It is interesting to ponder what might have happened if Jackson's whole testimony had been reprinted for the public the next day. Probably it would have been received much as it is today by people reading it for the first time: they would have believed what they wanted to believe, finding in Jackson's words support for their presumptions of guilt or innocence. A question even more interesting: What if the press had reported only lines like, "I played to win, every game"?

WILLIAM R. HERZOG II

William R. Herzog's 2002 essay "From Scapegoat to Icon"[43] seems to be a well-crafted account of the events of 1919–24, based on research and penned with a conviction that this interpretation is the one that makes the most sense. Herzog "argues that Joe Jackson was wrongfully accused of participating in the fix" but also deals with the scandal, because Jackson's story and that of the 1919 fix are "intricately interwoven."

After a brief biography of Jackson, Herzog retells what he calls "the cover story"—how eight crooked White Sox players conspired with gamblers to toss the Series. He then takes filmmaker Ken Burns to task for telling the cover story "effectively but nowhere more erroneously" than in his epic *Baseball*. Burns' film portrays Jackson as a fallen idol, using the language Hugh Fullerton used after the fall in his "Say it ain't so" piece. Herzog then goes through the Series game by game, concluding that Jackson was playing to win, both in the field and at bat.

Convinced that Jackson informed Comiskey of the fix—or at least of his own "fears and apprehensions"—before the Series, Herzog goes on to conclude that Jackson had been made a scapegoat—at all cost, he had to be prevented from giving his side of the story, because it damned Comiskey; and Comiskey became the architect of the cover-up.

According to Herzog, Jackson never deserved banishment, because he passed each test Landis decreed (in 1921, well after the fix): he did not throw a ballgame; he did not undertake or promise to throw one; he did not sit in conference . . . where the ways and means of throwing games were planned and discussed; and, to boot, he *did* promptly tell his club about it, when he felt the fix was in. Of course, this sidesteps the "fact" that Jackson was approached by Gandil several times prior to the Series and was asked to participate; no one (except Jackson) has suggested that he ever acted on *that* early "guilty knowledge." Jackson may be innocent, by the letter of Landis's law, but not by the spirit. (On the other hand, that spirit can be questioned—it's the Buck Weaver issue: friends do not give up friends.) Herzog:

> If baseball continues to cling to the cover story, it will destroy the faith of a new generation of boys who, with the benefit of hindsight and fuller information, now know that "squareness and honesty" had nothing to do with the banishment of Joe Jackson.

DANIEL A. NATHAN

Saying It's So: A Cultural History of the Black Sox Scandal, is not just another retelling of the story of the 1919 Series. Nor is it slanted to appeal to baseball fans—it might be received with more enthusiasm by history buffs, especially teachers. Because in the end, *Saying It's So* is more the story of the story—examining how the news of the fixed Series was broken to the American public, and then tracing how the story was retold in the decades that followed, right up into the 1990s.

In the first chapter, Nathan explores "history's first draft" in the newspapers of the day—mostly those of Chicago and New York, but there is a nice sampling from at least ten other big cities, too. Nathan quotes so many newspaper accounts and editorials that it starts to feel like he's piling on. It must have felt that way to the eight men who were targeted, too. Looking back from 1932, "the caustic sportswriter-turned-right-wing-crank" Westbrook Pegler wrote,

> The fake Series of 1919 produced some of the worst newspaper reporting that the American press ever has been guilty of and why all of us who were detailed to cover the show were not fired for missing the greatest sports story in twenty years is something I have never understood. We were terrible.

Nathan feels that the reporters did not "miss" the story, although the rumors of the fix went ignored and dismissed for nearly a year. It is not clear that he realizes how close the fix came to being swept under the carpet "forever"—like most of the scandals that preceded the 1919 Series. Once the scandal broke, of course, the papers jumped aboard and "exploited the Black Sox story for everything it was worth."

In the second chapter, Nathan describes the role of Kenesaw Mountain Landis in keeping the Black Sox out of the news, and keeping the version of the fix as eight crooked players lying down for gamblers, intact. The obituaries of Charles Comiskey and Kid Gleason in 1931 and 1933 added some cement. Reporters like Pegler kept the image of traitors alive, and the story became a kind of cautionary tale for America's youth, mostly for boys. Nathan highlights John Lardner's 1938 *Saturday Evening Post* essay and brilliantly puts the writings of Nelson Algren in context. The story was trying to fade away, but supporters of Buck Weaver and Joe Jackson kept agitating for justice. The country had new heroes—Ruth, DiMaggio, Williams, Musial—and "unwittingly, these men induced Black Sox amnesia."

At first, I wondered why Nathan paired Malamud's *The Natural* with Asinof's *Eight Men Out* in chapter 3. It is because, I found out later, he refers to the novel, in which Roy Hobbs takes a bribe and strikes out, and not the movie, where Hobbs hits one of the most memorable home runs ever seen on the silver screen. Nathan makes some points with *The Natural*, but his looks at Boyd's *Blue Ruin* and Stein's *Hoopla* seem more relevant and useful for the subject.

Nathan spends a lot of space on *Eight Men Out*, and this is not unexpected. He is maddened by Asinof's lack of documentation. Instinctively, a book that is "definitive" ought to at least have a hefty bibliography, no?

Nathan covers most, perhaps all, of the key issues. He does an excellent job painting the big picture, the context in which the events took place. His documentation is sometimes overwhelming. He pretty much avoids the gamblers, although he does underline better than most authors the anti-Semitic feelings stirred up by the association of Rothstein, Attell, and others in the fix. Kinsella's novel *Shoeless Joe* and the film *Field of Dreams* lure Nathan into that Iowa cornfield, where he demonstrates the power of movies, which, unlike books, make their way into video stores and onto millions of television screens.

Perhaps the greatest strength of *Saying It's So* is the way Nathan shows and documents how events and sayings go down in history, and why there will never be a final version of things, why some events are revisited over and over, and how the present changes the way we look back. Nathan has looked at the Big Fix through a thousand eyes, scattered over ninety years, and yet he may have something new to write about it tomorrow. Such is the richness of this subject and the way the event has been seen. Satchel Paige advised us, "Don't look back—something may be gaining on you"—but the events of 1919 and their aftermath are irresistible, and to bend Satchel's saying a bit, much is to be gained from looking back, over and over and over.

11

AFTERMATH

"What really matters is the name you succeed in imposing
on the facts—not the facts themselves."
—Cohen's Law

When starting out to right a wrong,
Time has no limitations,
And so the case is passed along
To future generations.

Though evil ways men fall upon
And juries may indict 'em,
Their case goes on and on and on
And so ad infinitum.
—*The Sporting News,* June 23, 1921

This characteristic runs through all baseball affairs:
a simple story, however inaccurate, is preferred to a complicated
explanation, however true. Perhaps it is a general human characteristic.
But it certainly applies to baseball.
—Leonard Koppett

Arguably, if Joe Jackson had not recorded baseball's third-best all-time career batting average, behind Iy Cobb and Rogers Hornsby, few people would care about his membership in Baseball's Hall of Fame. If Pete Rose had not passed Cobb as the all-time hit leader, he would be getting less support for his campaign for Cooperstown from fans outside Cincinnati. It just feels wrong that Joe Jackson is out, given his credentials, while Comiskey (for example) is in. In author Wilfrid Sheed's words "the museum is missing a Rembrandt."

Having a hall that excludes people whose careers *between the lines* really earned them admission is like having a family photo album without all the pictures. So what if Uncle Harry did time and Cousin Al ended up a junkie—they're family. Why pretend they are not? Yes, the criteria for the hall include ability, integrity, sportsmanship, character, and contribution to the game—but in fact, most of the members of the hall are there because of their numbers. And a few would *not* be there if the emphasis on integrity or character was consistent. If Ogden Nash wrote a poem about the Hall of Fame, it might go like this: "It ain'ts / for saints."

If the Rose case demonstrates anything, it is that baseball fans are, after all, a forgiving bunch. As Americans, thanks to the media's focus on things current and "in," their long-term memory is slightly impaired, too; so that helps. Once Pete is in, there will be a shift of pressure on Major League Baseball to deal with Joe Jackson.

Then baseball can take the easy path, forgive Jackson for whatever wrongs he may have done, say he's been punished enough, and let the voters decide. Frankly, I would much prefer baseball to declare that the "justice" meted out in 1921 by Judge Landis may not have been all that just, in certain cases. Let baseball make possible the restoration of the reputations of Jackson, Weaver, and others who were never given a fair chance to clear themselves. Let baseball outline a process for reviewing past injustices, one that does not rely on the views of a "judge and jury" commissioner.

In Jackson's and Weaver's cases, the "not guilty" jury verdict in 1921 is *not* a point in their favor. The 1924 eleven-to-one jury verdict for Jackson is. His performance on the field does not hurt his case, either. The key is Jackson's speaking up to his club before the Series (which at least made them watch him closely), and his repeated attempts to tell Comiskey what he knew, after. Commy knew a lot about the fix, maybe more than anyone else—and he said, under oath, that Jackson played the Series to win.

From all I've read, Ted Williams was a splendid splinter under the nails of the baseball writers of his day. In 1998 Ted was back, lobbying with Bob Feller for the end of Shoeless Joe Jackson's banishment and Jackson's election (by the Baseball Writers) to the Hall of Fame.

Not meeting Joe Jackson was, Williams said in a taped 1987 interview with Pete Williams, "the one great regret about the time I played. Year after year when we headed north after spring training, I never stopped off in Greenville to visit Joe [Jackson]." Perhaps Ted regretted it so much because of what veteran catcher (and occasional United States spy) Moe Berg told Williams in 1940, when Ted was interrogating Moe about the great left-handed hitters of the early days. "If you want to know the type of hitter you most resemble, I'd say it was Shoeless Joe Jackson. He was a little stiffer than you at the plate. You're better than all of them when it comes to wrists."[1]

Ted Williams also was compared to Jackson by Jackson's teammate Eddie Collins, who later was an executive with the Boston Red Sox. "Collins always compared me with Shoeless Joe, and that was such a great compliment. 'Ted, you're the closest thing, I'd say, to Joe Jackson.'" Williams recalled having his swing compared to Jackson's as one of the highest tributes he ever received.[2]

It bothered Ted that one of the game's greatest hitters had no bronze plaque. And he didn't mean Pete Rose. In Ted's keen eyes, Jackson had paid the price, served a lifetime sentence. In his argument for Jackson, Ted went on and on about Jackson's accomplishments on the diamond.

"Of course, there is that matter of the World Series." Ted said he knew all about Jackson and the Black Sox.

> Joe shouldn't have accepted the money . . . and he realized his error. He tried to give the money back. He tried to tell Comiskey . . . about the fix. But they wouldn't listen. Comiskey covered it up as much as Jackson did—maybe more. And there's Charles Albert Comiskey down the aisle from me in Cooperstown— and Shoeless Joe still waits outside.

Oops—Ted implies Jackson covered up. That might not help Jackson get into the hall. What will? I think that the cover-up needs to be clearly demonstrated—it's not that hard. It was hard in 1920 and 1921, because Comiskey was on such a high pedestal then, and all of the others who knew were still in power. And then it needs to be understood that scapegoating Jackson was part of the broader cover-up.

Louis Hegeman, an Illinois attorney, gave a presentation on the case of Joe Jackson at the 1992 Convention of the Society for American Baseball Research (SABR). Much of that presentation is summed up in the seven-page paper "The Big Fix: The 1919 World Series and the Black Sox," dated June 1992. Its opening line: "No two historians have agreed on what occurred in the World Series of 1919 and its aftermath."

The overview presented in "The Big Fix" is familiar. Hegeman placed special emphasis on the pre-Series meeting at the Hotel Sinton in Cincinnati (Room 708); while the fix was discussed, "many historians contend that no specific conclusions, *modus operandi*, or agreement to fix was reached." Perhaps. But by then it was too late to call it off; it was just a matter of agreeing on the size and timing of the payoffs.

As expected, Hegeman spent more time than the average sleuth on the lawyers, particularly Comiskey's, Alfred Austrian, "a shrewd, consummate advocate for Comiskey." He notes that Austrian also had "'free access' to the grand jury rooms, the innermost details of the grand jury proceedings, a fine working relationship with the state's attorney's office, and apparent access to the records."

Noting that all appeals on behalf of Weaver and Jackson had been summarily denied by Major League Baseball, Hegeman concluded thus: "In October 1991, the Chicago Lincoln American Inn of Court filed a petition seeking the restoration of Buck Weaver. Commissioner [Fay] Vincent in responding to the petition enunciated what in effect is a statement of policy on the Black Sox—at least for the Vincent Era: Commissioner Vincent stated that 'we cannot go back in time' . . . that he is 'reluctant to play God with history.'"

Commissioner Landis certainly had no such qualms about playing God, not only with history, but with the lives of real people—people who had the misfortune to turn up in his courtrooms, especially his last one, his czardom, baseball.

The Buck Weaver Petition, filed in Cook County, "respectfully requests" a hearing of the commissioner of Major League Baseball. It seeks to "amend the appellation 'Eight Men Out' to 'Seven Men Out.'"

> The Lincoln Inn tenders this document in the belief that restoring a man's name and reputation, even if [he is] deceased, is a significant and worthy act, consistent with the high standards and integrity of our National Game, and of no less import than [adjusting batting or pitching records for accuracy].

There is not much new in the thirteen dense pages of the petition. Again, it is interesting to see what sticks out to a lawyer—for example, "it would have been a gross dereliction of duty" for the attorneys at the 1921 trial to let the players take the witness stand. (Landis: Buck should have taken the stand to "announce to the public his innocence.")

It is a well-crafted document and a nice summary that might have persuaded a different commissioner to allow a real hearing. Baseball never held a hearing of its own on the 1919 fix, of course, so that would have been a first.

What is most fascinating about the petition, to someone already familiar with the details of the cover-up, are the exhibits attached: two pages of Joe Jackson in the grand jury seat on crudely typewritten pages with hand corrections; the charges, also typed; the jury instructions; several pages of handwritten notes from Buck's lawyer, Thomas Nash; an explanation, for the players, of the indictment; a copy of the 1921 jury's verdict finding Buck Weaver not guilty and signed by all twelve jurors; and a letter, two handwritten pages, from Buck Weaver to a deaf commissioner, asking reinstatement. It was 1953, and Buck was near the end. (Commissioner Ford Frick also refused to listen to others who pleaded Buck's case, such as Hugo Friend, the judge in the 1921 trial.)

The *Wall Street Journal* reported on Louis Hegeman's petition to Major League Baseball.[3]

> Landis later told a newspaper interviewer that, at a meeting in his office after he rendered his decision, Weaver confessed that he attended two sessions with the fixers. [While most sources accept this and move on, Hegeman counters with some interesting points.] Mr. Hegeman replies that 1) there's no record of what was said at any private meetings between Weaver and Landis; 2) Landis might have invented the story to justify his intransigence; and 3) Weaver might have said what he thought Landis wanted to hear in hope he'd be forgiven.

Behind items one and two is the fact that Landis had control of the spin. Of course, item three reminds us that when Weaver wrote to Frick in 1953—saying "I was suspended for doing some thing wrong. Which I new [*sic*] nothing about"—he just might have been using words that he thought Frick wanted to hear. Hegeman: "History tells us things about the fix that weren't apparent then." He feels the fix was a botched mess and no one, player or gambler, was certain of just what was going on.

The *Wall Street Journal* reported that Major League Baseball responded negatively to Hegeman's plea. Stephen Greenberg, deputy commissioner, and Fay Vincent

> believe that "matters such as this are best left to historical analysis and debate" and that no present-day hearing could re-create past events in sufficient depth and detail to permit the overturning of past decisions.[4]

To which Hegemen replied, "Nonsense." Hegeman noted that Mr. Vincent had just erased the asterisk beside Roger Maris's sisty-one seasonal home run record, overturning the 1961 ruling of Ford Frick. (More recently, the all-time seasonal RBI record of Hack Wilson, set in 1930, was adjusted from 190 to 191.)

At the end of the *Wall Street Journal* article, Hegeman says, "I'm a lawyer, so I know how to bother people." Baseball would not give a hearing to Weaver (and Jackson), but that would not prevent a mock hearing in a U.S. district court from taking place.[5] The concept, storyline, and text were credited to Louis Hegeman.

THE TALES OF THE TAPES

Besides *Eight Men Out* and *Field of Dreams*, there are a number of other films available on this subject.

Hegeman's *The Trial of Shoeless Joe Jackson and Buck Weaver,* in which a mock trial is held for the two men, is actually a kind of training video for trial lawyers—complete with commercials for attorneys—and the trial is followed by a discussion among some of the profession of how the defense and prosecution cases were argued. (All get high marks.)

Jackson is defended by a woman from South Carolina, Buck by no less a personage than Clarence Darrow; Teddy Roosevelt comes out of his grave to speak up in praise of baseball. Hegeman does not mention Jackson's request to be benched before the Series. He does have Jackson go to Comiskey, and later Grabiner, with the $5,000 hard evidence of the fix, only to be told by both of them to keep the money and shut up. (That echoes Ted Williams's story; I was told that Ted underwrote at least part of Hegeman's efforts to clear Jackson's name with Major League Baseball.)

In 1997, for The History Channel, Kathleen Earle Killeen produced a documentary called *"World Series Fixed!" The Black Sox Scandal*. It featured a mere four talking heads and gave Eliot Asinof a lot of time, but he was not pressed for his sources. Nor did the program give any sources for its material, not even a bibliography. It contained a few errors (the score of Game Seven was not 5–4—that was Game Six; "most of the players" did not sign away their immunity—only three did). To err is human, but to fail to correct the errors before the videos go on sale seems wrong. And if it was wrong for Ken Burns, it is even more wrong for THC. Would adding a list of errata be so difficult?

In the THC version of things, Joe Jackson tried to inform his club of the fix twice after the Series (the attempts are not specified); and he volunteered to testify (rather than confess) before the grand jury. But Jackson's case is not really important to THC, and Buck Weaver also is given short treatment. Comiskey's lawyer's role in coaching the grand jury testimony and obtaining the signed waivers of immunity is fairly absent.

The THC documentary is best when historians from Cincinnati (Kevin Grace) and Chicago (Richard C. Lindberg) take over. And the film footage of old time baseball is fun to watch, even though it is not really connected to the narration.

ESPN Classic's 2001 *The Black Sox Scandal* airs on that cable network from time to time. One of the talking heads is Eliot Asinof, not just telling the story, but telling us where he got some of his information. For example, he says he heard about the threat to Lefty Williams from Lefty's wife. Gandil was "the man," the ringleader of the fix, according to Happy Felsch. But why did the producers not ask Asinof for more of those missing footnotes? Here was a golden opportunity to put the author of the definitive book on the record.

I am not sure why the ESPNC producers paraded so many different people in front of their cameras. They all have credentials, and that is supposed to give their statements weight, but often they say what anyone who watched *Eight Men Out* might say.

Not that the forty-some minutes are wasted—they are not. The guests talk about the Cicotte bonus for winning thirty in 1919. (Asinof had 1917 in the book, remember; the movie has 1919.) Jim Cicotte, Eddie's grandnephew, is sure that the denied bonus was behind Eddie's decision to throw in with Gandil. But no one points out that in both 1917 and 1919, Cicotte *did* have his shots at that thirtieth win.

Louis Hegeman is very disappointing in his appearance. Hegeman states that Jackson took his $5,000 to Comiskey after the Series and was turned away by Harry Grabiner. He says that story was in Grabiner's diary and not Asinof's book. But that detail is *not* in *The Hustler's Handbook*, in which Bill Veeck prints excerpts from "Harry's Diary," so it cannot be verified. When Hegeman talks about the three players going before the grand jury where "the fear of the Lord" was put into them, he has the order wrong (it was Cicotte, then Jackson, then Williams, on the next day). And there is no evidence that the grand jury intimidated the players as Hegeman suggests.

Jerome Holtzman, dean of Chicago baseball writers and currently baseball's official historian (and thus possibly Jackson's gatekeeper for reinstatement), displays some bias against Jackson. He quotes Jackson's post-testimony statements without noting that just minutes before, Jackson had denied doing anything crooked in any game and claimed that he played to win, at bat and in the field.

When Holtzman trotted out Jackson's batting stats for the first five games (no runs batted in), as if they constitute proof of Jackson's guilt, I was stunned. Someone should have interrupted: "Mr. Holtzman, Joe Jackson's performance in those games was still better than that of both Eddie Collins and Edd Roush. Were they lying down, too?" It was just sloppy. Thank goodness Leonard Koppett followed up by rightly pointing out that we "cannot judge anything by observing the actions of players" . . . that's the nature of fixed games. So much said. So much unsaid. The nature of television documentaries?

THE ONE CONSTANT?

Baseball has enjoyed and even cultivated the *image* of being basically the "same game" since after the Civil War. Timeless, immutable, "the one constant" (Kinsella in *Field of Dreams*), and all that jazz. But is that really baseball?

I am one who thinks the word "purist" is meaningless. Fans are for or against changes in the game, with or without solid reasoning, with or without history on their side. But there is one fact that undermines the idea of "purist" baseball: baseball has never been *one thing*; it has evolved. And if you're looking for constants, Heraclitus had the answer about 2,500 seasons ago: the constant is *flux*—in English, *change*.

Baseball has, however, been a survivor. There was a time when playing games under artificial lights was regarded as a circus stunt. Artificial *grass*? Its seasons have been stretched out, starting in March and ending in November, but the game has survived. Its teams have been divided into haves and have-nots, its two leagues have been shuffled several times, even made to play each other before October, and wild cards have been created—but the game has survived. It is resilient.

When baseball celebrated the fiftieth anniversary of Jackie Robinson's breaking the color barrier, it was fair to ask *why did it take so long!?* Why did integration have to wait until the passing of Judge Landis? Baseball rightly celebrated the achievement, but would it have hurt anyone to answer the other questions, so we could learn from our past mistakes?

TAKE A FRESH LOOK

Here is how former Players Association executive Marvin Miller described the "eureka" experience he had when he first looked at the reserve clause in the Uniform Player's Contract:

> It had obviously been drafted by the owners' lawyers—no docu-ment that had been *negotiated* could ever have been so one-sided. . . . But I did find some interesting provisions, one of which was Paragraph 10a. The first time I read it, I did a double-take. What I had been told—and what the *players believed*—was that once a player signed his first contract, he no longer had control over his career. But the plain words of this section of the contract, as I read it, gave a club a one-year option on a player's services after his contract expired. *Nothing more.*[6]

For about ninety years, the reserve clause had been read a certain way. But a pair of fresh outsider's eyes, read it—as it turns out, cor-rectly. A whole different ballgame, it was.

It has not yet been ninety years since Judge Landis banned eight White Sox players from baseball. Is it possible that fresh eyes, looking back on the documentation, the histories, the anecdotes, and the facts that no one disputes—could reach a new conclusion about the justice of Landis's call? And if that happened, would it signal the destruction of *baseball*?

There can be no doubt that Landis's call was effective. But was it fair? In his anxiety to save baseball and its image, did Landis misjudge any players, simultaneously covering up the role of the owners who had closed their eyes *for years* to the gambling problems baseball suffered?

For more than thirty-five years, I have been in the habit of quot-ing, when the situation arises, T. S. Eliot's line (from *Murder in the Cathedral*), "the greatest treason / is to do the right thing for the wrong reason." After the 2002 season, the Chicago White Sox announced that they were removing Charles A. Comiskey's name from their ballpark. The Sox did it for $68 million. That might have been the wrong reason.

But this illustrates nicely how baseball both changes—the name of the ballpark—and remains the same—by making business decisions to maximize revenues, remain competitive. And it shows how far we have come since 1919, when players could be lured into a conspiracy to toss games for ten or twenty *thousand* dollars.

Using hindsight, it is almost the unanimous opinion within baseball that Judge Landis's decision to ban eight White Sox players and thus close the case on a sorry chapter in the game's history was effective. Never mind what was covered up or who was swept up in his historic call. The game and its image were saved, its integrity restored. Baseball had a czar, someone to watch over the sport and see that it stayed on the straight and narrow path.

But what if events had broken differently after the Series fix, and baseball was fully exposed, like Enron, WorldCom, Tyco International, and other corporations that have been found out in recent years? Like the abuse of stock options, baseball's reserve clause would have come under fire and scrutiny for its role in keeping salaries low and keeping players bound to their teams like slaves to their plantations. Perhaps, once baseball was in court and in the national spotlight, the "color line" might have come under attack, and been identified as a tool of a racist corporate culture.

Would a full-scale investigation of the gambling connection in 1919 have faulted the press for being part of the problem, like Arthur Anderson and accounting firms who really did not do their job properly, because it was too lucrative to just go along?

Would baseball's weak National Commission have taken much of the blame for failing to act, as government regulatory agencies failed to act eight decades later? And for failing to change an environment of "greed supported by quiet tolerance"?[7]

If Enron and the others are seen today as corrupt, with greedy CEOs getting rich "legally" at the expense of shareholders—if they are the tip of a crooked iceberg and not "a few bad apples"—is it not better to know it, for the sake of a healthy future economy? Is it ever better to cover up? I don't think so. Someone once said "the truth shall set you free—but first it will really piss you off."

Just after the cover-up was ended, in October 1920, the editors of the magazine *Outlook* agreed with the dictum of the *Sun* and *New York Herald*—that "if the public should ever come to the conclusion that professional baseball is crooked, then the ownership of the best club in the country would not be worth a lead quarter." Oddly enough, it seemed to be in the best interests of baseball—the best *financial* interests, that is—that the tampering with games by gamblers be covered up—and if discovered, should be quickly portrayed as the rare exception to the rule of honest play.

Perhaps, in 1920, the country was not ready to handle the truth about the business of baseball. I'm not certain that it is today, either.

> Officially, then, the MLB narrative emerges as a kind of "felix culpa" comedy, a fortunate fall reconciling honest players, fans, and owners. This comic construction of events was, of course, necessary to restore the fans' faith in the game and keep them coming through the turnstiles, and it was exactly what the press fed the public of the day, thus perpetuating the mythology of the national pastime as representing, in American League [President] Ban Johnson's words, "the sinew and gut of the American spirit."[8]

A MINOR MYSTERY

It is always good practice in doing research to be wary of "facts" that show up in just one source. They should automatically raise suspicions. Even if they show up in two sources, it is best to check and see if the later source is just quoting the earlier.

Yet, I found one orphaned item in the Black Sox file in Cooperstown's library that had about it the ring of truth—even though I have seen it cited nowhere else. Sportswriter Tom Swope, writing a memoir for *The Sporting News* in 1935,[9] told a story that explained the poor attendance for the 1919 World Series' Game Seven in a way that no one else has, before or since. Solving the mystery of the low turnout for Game Seven has nothing to do with the fix. But it illustrates something about how things in baseball, and especially in that Series, got covered up.

To refresh memories: the Sox, down 4–1 in the best-of-nine showdown, won Game Six, preventing the Reds from clinching the championship at home. Game Seven was also in Cincinnati. More than 32,000 fans had turned out for Game Six, paying the first World Series gate of more than $100,000 (a then-record $101,968). The first two games in Cincinnati drew around 30,000, too. Yet Game Seven's attendance was only 13,923. How come?

Most sources skip over the question of the low turnout. The weather was perfect—warm and sunny. There had been traffic problems the day before. There were also rumors flying that the Reds were tossing games, so the Series would go nine and bring in more money. Asinof mentioned both of these explanations in *Eight Men Out*. Harvey Frommer guessed that the Reds' fans were so disappointed with their team's showing in Game Six that they decided to stay home.[10] But think about it: this was the *first time* the Reds were in a World Series, and their fans were rabid.

Victor Luhrs concluded that so few fans showed up for Game Seven because "the fix rumors had taken place and fans had become disgusted."[11] Luhrs was referring, by the way, to the rumors that the *Reds* were now coughing up the Series. Joseph Krueger agrees that the Reds fans were "thoroughly displeased" with the way Game Six had gone and stayed away from Game Seven to punish the Reds.[12]

The Reds had sold their 1919 Series tickets in an unusual way. Fans could purchase three-game strips for the games that were guaranteed (barring a sweep) to be played in Cincinnati—Games One, Two, and Six.[13] Demand for tickets ran high; the *New York Times* reported that scalpers received as much as $140 for a seat for Game One. Perhaps there was a nice discount for those who bought the strips, but maybe the single-ticket price for Games Seven was set too high?

Before the Series, headlines like "Mad Scramble for Tickets—Many Left Out in the Cold"[14] showed how fans in both Chicago and Cincinnati were "fighting for pasteboards." Reds fans had lined up at the ballpark gates at midnight, fourteen hours before game time, to get the best seats in the bleachers and pavilion. Fans spilled onto the field, creating the "ground rule triple" for balls that disappeared into the ring of fans around the warning track. The Sox had been world champs just two Octobers earlier, but the Reds had not been on top in fifty years, and the fever must have been several degrees higher in Cincinnati.

The *Spalding Guide* explains the falloff in attendance for the fourth game in Cincinnati (Game Seven) as "due to a misunderstanding concerning the sale of tickets." It also chides the Cincinnati fans for being too depressed after the Reds lost Game Six, thus failing to clinch the championship.

In *The Sporting News* was speculation that the Reds' management was so sure that the Reds would win the Series in Game Six that it "evidently didn't make the arrangements that should have been made for the tickets for the seventh game in Cincinnati." Seats at the ballpark went on sale at noon, causing a "sudden jam" that discouraged fans. But *The Sporting News* had no good explanation for the "blocks and blocks of empty seats" and noted that it was "hardly a good showing" by the hometown fans.

Baseball Magazine in its December 1919 issue suggested that Cincinnati was a small city, and there were just not enough people in the city and its surrounding area to furnish crowds of over 30,000 on consecutive weekdays. "Furthermore there was hopeless confusion in the distribution of the tickets which kept thousands from the game. The newspapermen were aware of these facts. Why did they attempt to read from the modest attendance at that seventh game a meaning that could not properly be drawn?"

The meaning, namely, that nine games was too long for a World Series. The *Baseball Magazine* editors liked the nine-game format and said it was "a fairer test of club ability than seven."

In his *New York Times* column, Christy Mathewson wrote:

> When the seventh game of the last world's Series was played in Cincinnati about one-half of the seats were unoccupied. At previous games, the stands had been packed, so naturally this lack of attendance was the cause of comment.
>
> It is now evident that the reason for the empty seats at Redland Field was the sending out of rumors that seats were hard to get. Out-of-town fans instead of rushing to buy them up stayed away because they thought they couldn't get good ones, and they were not willing to make the trip to Cincinnati and then be left out in the cold.[15]

There were plenty of cover stories, but no good explanation.

But then there is Tom Swope's *Sporting News* column. It begins with a nice description of the Reds' owner (and swing vote on the National Commission) Garry Herrmann. Garry was a party animal, it seems, and he was having one fine Oktoberfest. Herrmann had been influential in reviving the World Series after the Giants just said no in 1904, and it was Herrmann's idea to try the best-of-nine format in 1919.

More than 32,000 fans had turned out for Game Six at Redland Field, paying over $100,000 for a new record in receipts. With his team still up four games to two, Herrmann partied well into the night on October 7, feasting on "sausages and conversation" at Cincinnati's Sinton Hotel.

And the next day, he slept in. Game Seven would not start till 2:00 p.m. Why rise before noon? According to Swope, Herrmann not only slept later, but bathed and had a manicure, as well. Meanwhile, prospective ticket buyers and team officials were searching for the pasteboards to purchase and sell. Why? Because in his suitcase, Herrmann had *all* of the reserved seat tickets for Game Seven. "Garry, a man who loved to attend to all sorts of little details himself, had planned to open the ticket sale himself down town on the evening of the sixth game and then had forgotten it, while playing host." Herrmann may have had the tickets in his possession, not because he was the owner of the team in the host city, but because of his position as head of the National Commission. He was keeping the tickets safe from the hands of scalpers.[16]

At just about the same time that Herrmann realized that he had the tickets, he was found by his son-in-law, Karl Finke. There was less than two hours left before game time, and practically all of the 13,923 tickets were sold in a frantic effort in that short span. Presumably, the game may have been delayed a little, but no one reported that.

Again, Tom Swope's version is not corroborated. But it seems believable. It is clear to anyone rooting around in the 1919 scene that there was a lot of drinking going on. It is not much of a strain to imagine Herrmann and Ban Johnson emptying pitchers of Cincinnati suds, and while they may not have had a victory to celebrate, they both must have been very much relieved that the White Sox had not laid down again in Game Six, as they may have earlier. It is also pretty clear that *everyone* had by then heard the rumors of the Big Fix being in, and those four losses served up by the Sox aces, Cicotte and Williams, made the rumors believable. So yes, Garry and Ban were old friends on top of the world—Garry's team was still in a good position, Ban was chortling over Comiskey's problems—they had a lot to celebrate.[17]

In 1919, reporters were not out to embarrass club owners. More likely, they drank along with the magnates and would no more report an owner drunk and disorderly (for example—I'm not talking about Garry Herrmann here), as they would write about their own peccadilloes. And if they tried, there were editors to remove anything potentially libelous—or scandalous. "The media" had not yet developed its shark-like interest in blood, the kind that flows from celebrities when they are caught with their pants down—sometimes literally.

So even if reporters knew that Garry Herrmann had slept while his suitcase full of tickets went unsold, no one would want to embarrass him by putting that in print. Unfortunately there was no good cover story, either. Which left historians to wonder: What was wrong with those Reds' fans? Why did they practically boycott Game Seven? Here is a day-after account from a Cincinnati paper:

> Some few were informed that they could purchase tickets in the evening at the Hotel Sinton but there was no general sale.

Then it was announced that all tickets would be at the ball park at 8 o'clock yesterday morning, but most of the reserve seats were held out and kept up town and thousands were turned away at the yard, unable to attain what they wanted in the way of reservations.

Joe Sweeney and his assistants handled the downtown sale as well as they could, but it was impossible for them to take care of the crowds that thronged the office, and hundreds of willing fans turned back when they found that they would have to stand in line for a couple of hours in order to secure tickets.[18]

The *Chicago Herald and Examiner* commented the next day on the long lines of men, women, and children that stretched for blocks at every ticket outlet in the city, lines that could be seen by those on their way to work on the morning of the game. But they had no ideas about the reason for them.

Another newspaper reported that Garry Herrmann had issued a statement about 1:00 p.m., an hour before game time, that he was sorry, but he had doubts that the crowd that day would be very large. "It is impossible to handle such a large sale of tickets overnight. I do not think the attendance will be more than 15,000." It was not.

Prohibition was phasing in, so reporting that Herrmann slept in after partying the night before might have been a real problem.[19] Speakeasies had sprung up everywhere. Cincinnati had been a dry town since July 1919. Garry Herrmann died in 1931. Prohibition was repealed in December 1933. The article by Tom Swope appeared in October 1935. He hoped that his account would "refute the 16-year old canard that Cincinnati had quit on its team" by "setting forth the facts."

How credible a source is reporter Tom Swope?[20] Not long after his column on Herrmann and Game Seven, Swope was elected president of the Baseball Writers Association. Baseball historian Cliff Kachline told me, "So far as I'm aware, Tom Swope always had a reputation as a reliable baseball writer. Swope had his idiosyncrasies, one of which involved carrying a light bulb with him on trips with the Reds because some press boxes provided insufficient light." How fitting, that the fellow who finally shed some light on the mystery of Game Seven's attendance should be remembered for his light bulb.

But Kevin Grace, who has researched Herrmann for over twenty years and has heard this story several times, dissents, as he told me.

Frankly, not much basis in fact. Swope was a good reporter but sometimes was more intent on telling a good story and got a little carried away. Many years ago, I interviewed an elderly lady by the name of Fairweather who had been a secretary to Finke off and on from 1918 until the late '20s. She had also heard this story, and according to her, Herrmann only had the tickets for his personal guests and other dignitaries.

Everyday sales of tickets were typically handled by the Strauss Tobacco Shop and at the ballpark. Herrmann was indeed someone who enjoyed a good party and that evening was no different. And, he was so meticulous about his personal appearance, that he would have bathed and had a manicure before the game. However, his whereabouts and tardiness had nothing to do with Prohibition—it hadn't happened yet. Prohibition didn't go into effect until January 16, 1920. Herrmann had to rush off to the ballpark to make sure his guests could go in.

The general attendance may have been low for a couple of reasons: although Herrmann managed to have the Series go nine games instead of seven in order to recoup some of the lost income due to the changes effected by the war, fan attention was wavering by game seven. This could have been due to the length of the Series, but it also could have been that a fix of some sort was becoming more and more of an open secret. Certainly there were enough journalists and team hangers-on who had suspicions, so this suspicion could have filtered down to the everyday fan and diminished interest.

Also, when Swope wrote this article, Herrmann was dead, and the stories that people told about how colorful and gregarious he was just improved and expanded with the telling. He was a great favorite with fans and reporters during his life, well before his baseball career and certainly during it, and people liked to talk about the "Herrmann days."[21]

Those who thought a nine-game Series was a bad idea in the first place, seized on the low turnout for Game Seven as proof that fan interest could not be sustained. But a sellout crowd of 32,930 showed up for Game Eight in Chicago. Presumably these fans heard the same rumors about fixes that the Cincinnati fans heard.

As with so many things about the 1919 World Series, there is no unanimity about just what happened. And what we do not know for sure seems to outweigh what we do know.

GAME NINE

The site of the ninth game of the 1919 World Series, if it were necessary, would have been Cincinnati. And that is because the Reds won a coin toss after Game Seven. National League President John Heydler did the honors in Garry Herrmann's office. He flipped a quarter, Charles Comiskey called heads. This was the second coin toss the White Sox lost to Herrmann; after the first one, with son Louis and team secretary Harry Grabiner representing the Sox, Herrmann won the right for the Reds to play at home for the first two games.

The Cincinnati newspapers after Game Seven said tickets for Game Nine, if there were to be one, would go on sale at 4:00 p.m. the day before and the offices would stay open until 10:00 p.m.; they would reopen at 8:00 a.m. on the day of the game. The papers also carried an ad from the Baltimore Formula Company. For one dollar, they would mail customers the "formulas and instructions for making at home, rye whiskey, real beer and choice wines," prepared by men who were formerly in the brewing and distilling business.

CONCLUSION

I remember an old Charles Schultz *Peanuts* cartoon. My recollection of the details may be a little off. Linus kneels on the sidewalk as his sister Lucy approaches. "Come look at this butterfly—he flew all the way up here from Brazil!" Lucy, always quick to contradict Linus with the cold water of her logic, checks it out. "That's not a butterfly—that's a potato chip!" Linus takes another look. "Hmm. You're right. Now how do you suppose a potato chip flew all the way up here from Brazil?" As Winston Churchill once put it, "Man will occasionally stumble over the truth, but most of the time he will pick himself up and continue on."

Many people have formed their opinions about the Black Sox scandal believing that they were looking at a butterfly. What is amazing is that even after historians and researchers and writers, starting with Asinof, have pointed out that there is no butterfly, only a potato chip—so many have continued to believe that the thing flew up here from Brazil.

Possibly, we have all become skeptical of revisionists and prefer our old way of seeing things. We really do not want to have to dig things out ourselves and make up our own minds—and who has the time? *Eight men out*, that's *all* we need to know.

I know this: that I have lived for many years with mistaken ideas about the Big Fix. Now I know that the more I learn about it, the more there seems to be to be learned. Certainty about things related to the fix and the cover-up is elusive. And perhaps that is not such a bad thing. It keeps our minds open and searching.

EPILOG

The Chicago White Sox won the World Series in 1917. When the Fix of October 1919 came to light, with three games left in the 1920 season, the suspension of the suspected players ruined the team's shot at a third pennant in four years. The club that might have continued for some time as a dynasty was shattered.

It would be forty years before the White Sox won its next American League pennant. And forty-six more seasons before they would once again reign as champions of baseball, in 2005.

This author does not happen to believe in curses. But I vividly recalls the joy of a pennant that is won after decades of drought, from my hometown Pittsburgh's triumph in 1960. And then from Boston's exhilarating achievement in 2004.

Curses and jinxes may haunt baseball. But the fact is that baseball is a sport with a long memory. Its seasons are connected, and its fans travel back in forth in time using those seasons like steps in a ladder.

So naturally, as the White Sox of 2005 inched closer to the grand prize that every season offers, the seasons of the past came to mind. *Would this be another 1920 or 1955 or 1964, seasons of coming close?* Once the team clinched a spot on the post-season playoffs, the question became, *Can the Sox make it to the Series?* And once there, *will they go all the way, like the 1906 Hitless Wonders, or the 1917 Sox? Or will they disappoint their fans, like the Go-Go Sox of 1959?*

The 1919 Series may not have been the only one influenced by gamblers "fixing" players, but it is the only one that has gone down in baseball history that way. The Big Fix embarrassed baseball, to say the least, and certainly damaged its "clean" image among American sports. But the so-called Black Sox — the eight players who were expelled

302

from the game after the Fix — were not the only ones suspected of "tossing" games, or of having "guilty knowledge" of the strangling influence of gamblers. That baseball committed "a single sin" is indeed a myth.

The White Sox triumph in 2005 will not bury the Black Sox — they will only rest in peace when their story is finally told. They can no longer speak for themselves. But taking the journey back to 1919, using baseball's magic ladder, can, to borrow a phrase from W. P. Kinsella, ease their pain. It is never too late to understand, to forgive, and then to never forget the lessons their story holds.

APPENDIX

TRIPLES IN THE 1919 WORLD SERIES

I thank Jim Sandoval for sharing part of his collection of play-by-plays from the 1919 World Series. Here are the descriptions of the seven triples hit by the Reds:

The accounts are from these sources (see abbreviations):

Neft and Cohen World Series (N&C); *The Sporting News* (TSN); *Cincinnati Enquirer* (CE); *Reach Guide 1920* (RG); *Spalding Guide 1920* (SG); and *New York Tribune* (NYT).

GAME ONE AT CINCINNATI

Ruether 4th inning: Triple to fence in left center (N&C); Ruether tripled to center (TSN); Ruether's mighty blows caromed off the short, temporary fence in left center and the centerfield fence (CE); Ruether's tremendous drive to left center that bounced back off the temporary wire fence into Felsch's hands (CE); Ruether hit over short into the crowd in left center for three bases (SG); his long left-handed swing met the ball solidly and sent it out to centre [*sic*] field. The pellet rolled to the edge of the crowd for three bases (NYT).

Daubert 7th inning: Ground rule triple into crowd in right (N&C); tripled to right field (TSN); Daubert hit into crowd (CE); Daubert opened up with a powerful smash into the right field seats (bounded into seats) for a triple (CE); Daubert caught one on the end of his bat and hit it so far to right field that it hopped into the crowd on the first bound. This was a ground rule triple (SG); Jake picked on Wilkinson and drove the ball into loving hands in the right field bleachers. This, according to ground rules, went for a three-bagger (NYT).

Ruether 8th inning: Tripled to deep center (N&C); triple to left center (TSN); Ruether slugged a wonderful drive far over Felsch's head, which rolled clear to the concrete wall in deepest center (CE); Ruether smashed to the center field fence for another triple (SG); His concluding performance was another three-bagger right through centre field, a long hit in any ballpark (NYT).

Game Two at Cincinnati

Kopf 4th inning: Tripled to fence in left (N&C); Kopf tripled into the crowd in left center (TSN); Kopf to left center, bounded back from wire fence for three bases (CE); Kopf hammered the first ball for a clean three-bagger to left center (SG); Kopf—the hit was a triple that rolled to the temporary inside fence at centre field (NYT).

Game Five at Chicago

Roush 6th inning: Tripled to deep center (N&C); Roush followed with a high fly that Felsch could not hold, though he touched it on the run and it went for a three base hit (TSN); Roush whaled the ball over Felsch's head for three bases. Hap misjudged the ball, then let the ball trickle off his left hand (CE); Felsch played Roush's fly badly and finally muffed it, but the scorers were liberal and called it a three-base hit (SG).

Game Six at Cincinnati

Neale 4th inning: Tripled to deep right (N&C); Neale tripled to right, a tremendous blow to right center (TSN); Neale tripled mightily to right field. John Collins dashed over and came near blocking it down but the ball took a band [*sic*] bound away from him (CE); Neale sent one to right, which took an eccentric bound (RG); J. Collins overran Neale's safe hit to right field and the ball rolled far enough to give the batter a triple (SG).

Game Eight at Chicago

Kopf 5th inning: Tripled to right center field fence (N&C); Kopf tripled along the right field foul line (TSN); Kopf smashed a triple to right field, the ball eluding Gandil (CE); Kopf bounced one past Gandil and way down on the safe side of the foul line for a triple (RG); Kopf hit along the right field line for three bases (SG); Kopf tripled to right, the ball going over first base and reaching the extreme right field corner before Felsch retrieved it (NYT).

NOTES

Introduction

1. Veeck, Bill, with Ed Linn. *The Hustler's Handbook* (G. P. Putnam's Sons, 1965).

2. Holtzman, Jerome. *Baseball, Chicago Style* (Bonus Books, 2001).

3. Personal email and conversation with author.

4. Gardner, Paul. *Nice Guys Finish Last: Sport and American Life* (Universe Books, 1974).

Chapter 1

1. *Joe Jackson vs. Chicago White Sox,* Trial Transcripts and Related Documents, Milwaukee, WI, January/February 1924, 912.

2. Personal email and conversation with Mr. Cannon.

3. *Milwaukee Journal*, February 15, 1924.

4. bid.

5. bid.

6. Nitz, James. "Happy Felsch," at the website of the Society for American Baseball Research, Bioproject 2003. http://bioproj.sabr.orgbioproj.cfm?a=v&v=1&bid=707&pid=4328

7. Vaughan, Irving. "A Case of Cheaters Cheating Cheaters," *The Sporting News*, February 21, 1924. Vaughan's conclusions did not even rate a *Sporting News* headline. They appeared in an editorial, under the heading, "A Case of Cheaters Cheating Cheaters"—a phrase that one of the fixers, Abe Attell, would repeat for years after. For the ten questions, see Appendix G in Donald Gropman's *Say It Ain't So, Joe!*, revised second edition (Carol Publishing Group, 1992).

8. *Washington Post*, February 16, 1924.

9. Black Sox Scandal (American League). A. Bartlett Giamatti Research Center, National Baseball Hall of Fame and Museum, Cooperstown, NY.

10. Comiskey had hired John R. Hunter, of Hunter's Secret Services in Illinois. Alfred Austrian, Comiskey's lawyer, had used them many times before, but not for this sort of job.

11. For example, in his "white paper" to the *New York Times* November 5, 1920.

12. When Menke's articles were introduced to readers of *The Sporting*

News in the April 10, 1924, issue, they were to be a four-part Series. However, only two more articles appeared, on April 17 and April 24.

13. On page 338, in the 2001 paperback revised second edition.

14. Experts from Harry Grabiner's diary are reproduced in a chapter in Veeck and Linn, *The Hustler's Handbook*.

15. Holtzman relies on Tennessee lawyer James Kirby, whose article on the fix appeared in the *American Bar Association Journal,* February 1, 1988. It is worth looking up, for the legal aspects of the subject.

Chapter 2

1. Lane, F. C. Editorial in *Baseball Magazine*, November 1915.

2. Bass, Mike. "Baseball," *The Sporting News*, October 17, 1994.

3. *Lake County (IL) Times*, October 2, 1917.

4. Asinof, Eliot. "Baseball's Endless Cycle of Scandal," *New York Times*, March 9, 1986.

5. *Washington Post*, September 22, 1919.

6. *The Sporting News*, October 30, 1919. The Chicago publication referred to is probably *Collyer's Eye*.

7. "The Advantages of Being a Port-Sider," *Baseball Magazine*, February 1920.

8. Algren, Nelson. "The Swede Was a Hard Guy," *Southern Review*, Spring 1942.

9. *Washington Post*, October 1, 1920.

10. Ibid.

11. Meany, Tom. *Baseball's Greatest Teams* (A. S. Barnes, 1949).

12. *Washington Post*, October 1, 1920.

13. "Greasy Neale Offers Proof 1919 Series Wasn't Fixed," *Zanesville (OH) Times Recorder*, September 24, 1961.

14. *New York Times*, October 1, 1920.

15. Ibid.

16. Ritter, Lawrence S. *The Glory of Their Times* (William Morrow, 1966).

17. *New York Times*, October 1, 1920.

18. *New York Times*, September 30, 1920.

19. Frommer, Harvey. *Shoeless Joe and Ragtime Baseball* (Taylor Publishing, 1992). Ernie Quigley's quote is from *The Sporting News*, October 7, 1920.

Chapter 3

1. Axelson, Gustav W. *"Commy": The Life Story of Charles A. Comiskey* (Reilly & Lee, 1919).

2. Kirby, James. "The Year They Fixed the World Series," *American Bar Association Journal*, February 1, 1988.

3. *Toronto World*, December 21, 1918.

4. The *New York Times* reported on September 17, 1919, that they had learned that Judge Landis would be offered the top job the next day, as the "neutral chief" that was needed to replace Garry Herrmann. But it would be another year of struggling for power before Landis was finally offered the post.

5. *New York Times*, September 17, 1919.

6. There is no agreement about just what the odds were, but the consensus among researchers is that they favored the White Sox until the day or two before the Series began on October 1. See Joseph Reichler, "The Black Sox Scandal," in *The World Series: A 75th Anniversary* (Simon & Schuster, 1978); Joseph J. Krueger, *Baseball's Greatest Drama* (Classic Publishing, 1942); and Bob Broeg and Bob Burrill, *Don't Bring That Up!* (A. S. Barnes, 1946). However, one syndicated column had the odds favoring White Sox going into Game One, then swinging to 10–7 Reds after the Sox lost the opener. See the *Syracuse Herald*, October 2, 1919.

7. Sugar, Burt Randolph. *Baseball's Fifty Greatest Games* (JG Press, 1986).

8. From Tennes's *New York Times* obituary, August 7, 1941.

9. Veeck and Linn, *The Hustler's Handbook*.

10. G. W. Axelson's short 1919 biography of Charles Comiskey, published in Chicago, has some vivid descriptions of the Woodland Bards. It is a flattering portrait of Comiskey, with a number of quotations from the Old Roman himself, who was a great storyteller.

11. Vaughan, Irving . *Chicago Tribune*, November 4, 1931.

12. Weir, Hugh C. "The Real Comiskey," *Baseball Magazine*, February 1914.

13. Ibid.

14. "'Woodland Barflies' might have been a more appropriate name," quipped Victor Luhrs in *The Great Baseball Mystery* (A. S. Barnes, 1966), a highly original and worthwhile study.

15. Seymour, Harold. *Baseball: The Golden Age* (Oxford University Press, 1971). Seymour's historian's treatment of the 1919 World Series is excellent and puts the event in context.

16. Also on strike was George Cohan, who produced and wrote, in addition to his acting. It was more complicated than that, of course; Cohan ended up lending support to one of the competing unions. So labor relations was surely a log on the Bards' 1919 hot stove. There are various stories about Cohan's betting on the 1919 World Series. For an example, see Fullerton's column in the *Atlanta Constitution*, October 29, 1921.

17. During the Cook County grand jury hearings in September 1920, Milwaukee attorney Ray Cannon unsuccessfully tried to call attention to stock ticker services as aids to the gambling syndicates. Brokers' news services had been used, Cannon claimed, to pass along fake reports of player injuries and other distorted information. Cannon suggested to the grand jury that a full investigation of the gambling syndicates' work should not end with "crooked ballplayers." *New York Times*, September 26, 1920.

18. Axelson, *"Commy."* A program for the January 19, 1917, Woodland Bards Trophy Room Dedication at Comiskey Park once sold on the Internet for $288.

19. Victor Luhrs notes that boxer Jack Dempsey and his manager Jack Kearns were Bards. If Judge Landis and Babe Ruth are credited with taking the minds of baseball fans off the Big Fix, someone else also deserves an assist: Jack Dempsey. James Elfers, while researching his book on the 1913–14 World

Tour, made a partial list of Bards. It included Chicago brewery owner William Buhl; Dick Bunnel ("Commy's jack of all trades"); sheet music salesman Joe Farrell; Tip O'Neill, the tour treasurer; Commy's best friend, Ted Sullivan; and many more. The group included businessmen, construction magnates, politicians, sportswriters (Ring Lardner was a "quasi-member"), doctors, judges, athletes, and entertainers.

20. Mullin, John. "Comiskey Rewarded Pals With Sox-Giants World Tours," *Chicago Tribune*, March 30, 1998.

21. Lindberg, Richard C. *Stealing First in a Two-Team Town* (Sagamore, 1994).

22. Miller, William D. *Pretty Bubbles in the Air: America in 1919* (University of Illinois Press, 1991).

23. Considine, Robert. "On the Line", *Washington Post*, October 1, 1939.

24. The *Chicago Tribune* reported July 16, 1919, that the postseason trips to the Jerome Club in Wisconsin were over. Comiskey and Ban Johnson both withdrew their $250 membership fees, and Commy dropped his lawsuit to take control of the club, "after difficulties had risen between the original members and the 'new members' who were mostly Woodland Bards."

25. Kieran, John. "Charley Comiskey, The Old Roman," *New York Times*, October 27, 1931. The column appeared just after Comiskey's death.

26. Weir, Hugh C. "The Real Comiskey," *Baseball Magazine*, February 1914.

27. Pegler, Westbrook. " Fair Enough Those Black Sox," *Washington Post*, October 4, 1939.

28. Pegler, Westbrook. " Fair Enough World Series Memoirs," *Washington Post*, September 30, 1941.

29. Cottrell, Robert C. *Blackball, the Black Sox and the Babe* (McFarland, 2002).

30. Farrell, James T. "Freedom From Scandal," *New York Times*, August 18, 1974.

31. Kieran, "Charley Comiskey."

32. Wray, and John E. Stockton. "Ban Johnson's Own Story," St. Louis Post-Dispatch, February 10–March 3, 1929.

33. Fullerton, Hugh. "Charles Comiskey Plays a Prank on Ban Johnson," *The Sporting News*, October 18, 1902.

34. Wray and Stockton, "Ban Johnson's Own Story."

35. Creel, George, quoting Ban Johnson. "Making the American League," *Saturday Evening Post*, March 22, 1930.

36. If Quinn had been signed by Chicago, he might have prevented the conspiracy to fix the Series simply by giving the White Sox manager another healthy arm that October. With his fourth starter Red Faber ailing, Gleason had to rely solely on his trio of starters, making the Sox more vulnerable to the fix.

37. Comiskey, Charles A. "Comiskey Tells His Story of Black Sox and Feud With Ban," letter to *Cleveland Plain Dealer*, January 13, 1929.

38. Obenshain, Earl. "Famous Baseball Feud Between Ban and Comiskey Arose Over Jack Quinn Deal," *Cleveland Plain Dealer*, January 7, 1929. This was the sixth article. The Series started on December 3, 1928.

39. Comiskey, "His Story."

40. Wray and Stockton. "Ban Johnson's Own Story."

41. Seymour, *Baseball: The Golden Age.*

42. Wray and Stockton "Ban Johnson's Own Story."

43. Fullerton, Hugh S., Sr., "I Recall," *The Sporting News*, October 17, 1935. "Hugh Fullerton recalls the old days," went the innocent front-page *The Sporting News* teaser. For an earlier version of his story about his arrival in Cincinnati before Game One, see "Hugh S. Fullerton Vividly Describes the Full Details of Great Baseball Scandal," *Atlanta Constitution*, October 3, 1920.

44. *The Sporting News*, October 7, 1920.

45. Seymour, *Baseball: The Golden Age.*

46. *Chicago Tribune*, October 2, 1919.

47. Ibid.

48. I was surprised to see the phrase "whitewashing bastards" in *The Sporting News* in 1935. Using the Internet search engine Paper of Record to do a search, it appears that it was the first use of the word "bastard" since *The Sporting News* started up in 1886. And the word did not appear in that publication again until forty years later, in a quotation from Ty Cobb.

49. Runyon, Damon. "Attell Keeps Secret of Big Sport Scandal," *Washington Post*, October 4, 1939.

50. Fullerton "The Full Details ".

51. Fullerton, Hugh S., Sr. "Are Baseball Games Framed? The Inside Story of What Led Up to the Major League Scandals," *Liberty*, March 19 and 26 and April 2, 1927. Steve Klein wrote a master's thesis on "Hugh S. Fullerton, the Black Sox Scandal, and the Ethical Impulse in Sports Writing" in 1997 at Michigan State University.

52. *New York Times*, October 1, 1920.

53. *New York Times*, September 27, 1920.

54. Wray and Stockton, "Ban Johnson's Own Story."

55. Murdock, Eugene C. *Ban Johnson, Czar of Baseball* (Greenwood Press, 1982).

56. Wray and Stockton, "Ban Johnson's Own Story."

57. In a letter dated May 16, 1921, to D. T. Green, a Pinkerton representative in Boston, Ban Johnson recalled how three or four years earlier the Pinkerton Agency had given him a list of sixty gamblers. Johnson had forwarded the names to the team presidents in both leagues, telling them to bar the men named from the parks. "No action was taken by them." Johnson recalled later for Wray and Stockton that he himself had had thirty-three of them arrested and prosecuted, and obtained thirty-three convictions, all of them gamblers who had operated in American League parks. He recalled receiving no cooperation, especially from Frazee and Haughton (the two Boston presidents). See the records under "Black Sox Scandal (American League)" at the A. Bartlett Giamatti Research Center, National Baseball Hall of Fame and Museum, Cooperstown, NY.

58. Fleitz, David L. *Shoeless: The Life and Times of Joe Jackson* (McFarland, 2001).

59. Pietrusza, David. *Rothstein: The Life, Times and Murder of the Criminal*

Genius Who Fixed the 1919 World Series (Carroll & Graf, 2003).

60. Wray and Stockton. "Ban Johnson's Own Story."

61. Becker used the occupational designation "capitalist," according to a story that appeared in the *St. Louis Post-Dispatch* the day after his death. Becker had been friends with powerful politicians and had made his fortune directing a network so large that it required "an office with bookkeepers, stenographers, cost accountants, adding machines, filing cabinets and card indexes." A model of organized crime who operated "without serious police interference," it does not seem to be implausible that he left behind a blueprint for others to follow.

62. Kirby, "The Year They Fixed the World Series."

63. This final version appeared when Charles Comiskey wrote about the event in a letter to the *Cleveland Plain Dealer*, September 13, 1929.

64. Murdock, *Ban Johnson, Czar of Baseball*. But Murdock feels that the evidence from Allen and Spink on how Johnson was notified is credible.

65. Vaughan, Irving, quoting Ban Johnson. "Thirty-Four Years in Baseball—The Story of Ban Johnson's Life," *Chicago Tribune*, February 24, March 3, and March 10, 1929.

66. Allen, Lee. *The American League Story* (Hill and Wang, 1962). J. G. Taylor Spink had been the editor of *The Sporting News*, which was founded by his uncle Alfred, since 1914. Spink was close to Ban Johnson. He was also one of the official scorers in the 1919 Series. Like Fullerton and others, he saw the odds drop before the Series and smelled the fix. In *Judge Landis and 25 Years of Baseball* (Thomas Y. Crowell, 1947), Spink confirms Lee Allen's account.

67. Lieb, Fred. *The Story of the World Series* (G. P. Putnam's Sons, 1949).

68. Veeck and Linn. *The Hustler's Handbook*.

69. *Los Angeles Times*, November 18, 1919.

70. *New York Times*, January 2, 1927. Apparently Judge Landis believed Risberg. Replying to Buck Weaver's plea for reinstatement during the January 1927 Risberg hearings, Landis stated that Gleason had a meeting with his players during the Series at which he (Gleason) stated that something was wrong. See the *Chicago Tribune*, March 13, 1927.

71. Feldman, Chic. Interview with Eddie Murphy in *The Scrantonian* (Scranton, PA), September 13, 1959.

72. *Chicago Tribune*, November 5, 1931.

73. *Pietrusze, David, Matt Silvermann, and Michael Gershman. Baseball: The Biographical Encyclopedia*, (Tota Sports).

74. Brown, Warren. *The Chicago White Sox* (G. P. Putnam's Sons, 1952).

75. *Joe Jackson vs. Chicago White Sox.*

76. *Chicago Times*, October 11, 1919.

77. When Comiskey was charged with conspiring against some of the accused players in a 1922 lawsuit announced by Ray Cannon, one of the questions Comiskey and the White Sox were called on to answer was why the $10,000 reward was offered, when they had in their "possession all the facts concerning the fixing of . . . games and were indirectly participants in the fixing of the games." See the *New York Times*, May 12, 1922. The conspiracy charges were later dropped from the suit.

78. Fullerton, "The Full Details."

79. *Joe Jackson vs. Chicago White Sox,* 1541.

80. Considine, "On the Line."

81. *Joe Jackson vs. Chicago White Sox*, 1548.

82. Cottrel, *Blackball,* 118.

83. Seymour. *Baseball: The Golden Age.* But not that much later. In his syndicated column that appeared just after the scandal broke in late September 1920, Fullerton said Comiskey was his authority for saying "seven will not return."

84. Allen, *American League Story.*

85. *New York Times*, September 26, 1920.

86. *Joe Jackson vs. Chicago White Sox*, 374.

87. *Los Angeles Evening Express,* March 14, 1921.

88. Veeck and Linn, *The Hustler's Handbook.* The figures come from Dan Daniel, "Black Sox Story Butchered in TV Show," *The Sporting News*, February 8, 1961.

89. Clyde Elliot was also the president of the Greater Stars Production Company (and longtime cohort of the notorious big-game hunter Frank "Bring 'Em Back Alive" Buck, whose African adventures made a small fortune for RKO Radio and Fox films).

90. Wray and Stockton, "Ban Johnson's Own Story."

91. *Washington Post*, October 27, 1920. The *St. Louis Post-Dispatch* had Gedeon meeting with gamblers Abe Attell, Bill Burns, Ben Franklin, and Joe Pesch. A grand jury leak to the *Chicago Tribune* on September 26, 1920, had Gedeon sleeping at Fred McMullin's apartment in Chicago during the 1919 Series, and traveling back and forth between Chicago and Cincinnati that October.

92. Fullerton, "The Full Details."

93. Veeck and Linn, *The Hustler's Handbook.*

94. *Chicago Tribune*, October 27, 1920.

95. Comiskey, "His Story."

96. Wray and Stockton, "Ban Johnson's Own Story."

97. Nationally known betting commissioner Thomas M. Kearney "had reports that an attempt was being made to fix the Series several days before it was due to begin," and he concluded from the betting he handled for Game One that the fix was in. "Men who ordinarily would only bet a small sum were wagering thousands, because it was a sure thing." He met beer baron Otto Stifel, a Browns' stockholder, on the street. "Get Ban Johnson on the phone in Cincinnati at once," Kearney told him. "Tell him the first game was thrown and the players have sold out the entire Series." But Stifel just laughed. "Tom, if I did not know you so well I would think that you are crazy."

(Otto Stifel had been a co-owner of the St. Louis Federal League Terriers, before becoming a partner in the Browns's ownership. He also owned race horses, including one named Otto Stifel. He sold his Browns stock two months after the 1919 Series and left baseball forever. In June 1920 he announced his candidacy for the Republican nomination for Congress. Angry over prohibition, in debt to gamblers, and saddled with other problems, Stifel committed suicide in August 1920. Enough brewery owners did the same, that the phrase "the Dutch Act" was coined to describe the event.)

98. Wray and Stockton. "Ban Johnson's Own Story."

99. Daniel, "Black Sox Story Butchered in TV Show."

100. *New York Times*, October 2, 1920.

101. Taylor, C. B. "Ray Schalk Talks Himself Into Trouble About Seven Members of the White Sox," *Savannah Morning News*, January 10, 1920.

102. *Toronto World*, November 2, 1920.

103. Fullerton, "The Full Details."

104. Tygiel, Jules. *Past Time: Baseball as History* (Oxford University Press, 2000).

105. *Washington Post*, March 25, 1923. At the 1924 Milwaukee trial, Comiskey's lawyer said that he advised the owner to sign his players, despite the fix rumors, because "you can't blacken a man and throw him out of a job on a suspicion." See also the *Chicago Tribune* trial coverage, February 7, 1924.

106. Veeck and Linn. *The Hustler's Handbook.*

107. Murdock, *Ban Johnson, Czar of Baseball.* The Spink quote is from *The Sporting News*, December 3, 1942.

108. Burk, Robert F. *Never Just a Game: Players, Owners and American Baseball to 1920* (University of North Carolina Press, 1994).

109. *New York Evening World*, March 6, 1920.

110. *Chicago Tribune*, June 24, 1920.

111. Gambling was plaguing the minor leagues, too, and some of them (the Pacific Coast League, for example) were taking strong measures to correct the situation—stronger than the majors.

Chapter 4

1. It appears that Carmichael interviewed Jackson in Greenville, while preparing the team history.

2. Email correspondence from Richard C. Lindberg.

3. Rich Thurston characterizes Carmichael as "a flashy and opinionated sports writer, who became sports editor for the *Chicago Daily News*. He was a skilled writer whose annuals often gave blunt evaluations of a team's prospects for the coming year."

4. Some books state that Jackson had "the strongest arm" in baseball, and the *Sporting News* commentary clears that up. At the Tim Murnane benefit game at Fenway Park in 1917, Jackson won a trophy for throwing a baseball 396'8". (Babe Ruth threw that day, too, for Boston, on the mound, defeating a team of AL All Stars.)

5. Fullerton's testimony ultimately did help Jackson's case, however, as it indicated that Fullerton, who communicated with Comiskey about his investigation, had what turned out to be valuable knowledge of whom to interrogate to dig out the truth. That Comiskey's detectives failed to follow up those leads, with the result that they found nothing of use, underlined the likelihood that Comiskey's search was for show.

6. Fullerton may have done just that (evaded editors) in a memoir that appeared in *The Sporting News*, October 17, 1935. Too loyal to embarrass his

friend Charles Comiskey when the team owner was alive, Fullerton admitted after Comiskey's death that Comiskey knew about the fix before Game One but refused to take Fullerton's advice to postpone the Series to investigate.

7. Jackson recalls as the cause of Johnson's public feud with Comiskey, the Old Roman's sending Johnson some trout he caught in Wisconsin, which spoiled along the way. But he makes no mention of the Jack Quinn or the Carl Mays cases.

8. According to a Joe Williams *World-Telegram* column from January 28, 1961, Ford Frick's primary concern with the program was with its "outrageous abuse of truth in the name of dramatic license." *The Sporting News* suggested that pressure exerted on the sponsors by Major League Baseball had caused the postponement, but Joe Williams wrote that it had been moved because CBS was negotiating a television deal with Major League Baseball.

9. "Why Can't TV Let Well Enough Alone?" October 12, 1960.

10. *Witness* was a thirty-minute crime drama that aired weekly between September 29, 1960, and February 2, 1961. *The Complete Encyclopedia of Television Programs, 1947–1976* describes it this way: "People who have witnessed or become innocently involved in crimes appear and through the questioning of a panel of defense attorneys relate their experiences. The program attempts to expose rackets and criminals by making people aware of confidence games." And the show was effective, too, as there have been no rumors of a fixed World Series since *Witness* featured Shoeless Joe Jackson.

11. The regular panel of lawyers on the show was played by William Geoghan, Richard Steele, Benedict Ginsberg, and Charles Hayden. Biff McGuire played Jackson; Royal Beal played Comiskey; Warren Finnerty and Frank Sutton played gamblers Evans and Maharg; and Bill Zuckert played Kid Gleason.

12. Daniels: "After forty years, the script writers figured they could get away with anything. The script plays up the purely apocryphal 'Say it ain't so.' . . . No boy asked Jackson that question. The dramatic bit was written into the baseball drama by a Chicago writer named McNamara—and a good writer he was." In his 1966 *The Great Baseball Mystery*, Victor Luhrs called the program "atrociously inaccurate." Asinof himself wrote to me, "For [anyone] to take a TV show like this seriously as a historian is like blaming the loss of the Vietnam war on a peace march. . . . TV dramas such as *Witness* are, at best, 25 percent truth."

13. *The Sporting News* even protested to an ad agency to try to keep the *Witness* episode off the air.

14. This is as astonishing as Comiskey—testifying under oath in Milwaukee in 1924 and standing to forfeit more than $16,000 if he loses the case— saying that Joe Jackson did nothing crooked on the ballfield in all his days in a White Sox uniform. If Jackson's lawyer had said the same thing, not an eyebrow would have been raised.

15. *Joe Jackson vs. Chicago White Sox,* 69.

16. *Joe Jackson vs. Chicago White Sox,* 1378.

17. Deposition by Jackson, September 4, 1923.

18. One of the most colorful versions of the post-Series confrontation between Jackson and Comiskey comes from a most unlikely source. See Elden

Auker, with Tom Keegan, *Sleeper Cars and Flannel Uniforms* (Triumph, 2001). Mr. Auker is a member of SABR. When I asked him, "Where did you get this information?" he promptly wrote back: "Yes, Ted Williams had done a lot of research on Jackson because he felt Jackson should be in Baseball's Hall of Fame. Ted had a lot of detailed information and some of it was the Comiskey story." Just where Ted Williams heard the story is one more unsolved mystery.

19. *Joe Jackson vs. Chicago White Sox,* 1374.

20. *Joe Jackson vs. Chicago White Sox,* 1380.

21. Paul Galloway. "It Ain't So 68 Years Later, Fans Seek Pardon for Shoeless Joe," *Chicago Tribune*, North Sports Final Edition, October 20, 1988.

22. The correspondence is a gem in the appendices that Donald Gropman added to his revised editions of *Say It Ain't So, Joe!*

23. These conjectures are from fragments of an article that appeared on the sports page of an unknown newspaper in 1989 and which are kept in Joe Jackson's Cooperstown file.

24. *Joe Jackson vs. Chicago White Sox,* 1155.

25. Ibid., 1157.

26. Ibid., 1374.

27. Ibid., 1379.

28. *The Sporting News*, February 11, 1915.

Chapter 5

1. Steve Klein: "Fullerton's faith in the game may not have separated him from his peers, but the disillusionment that resulted from the impact gambling was having on the game made him a unique player in the Black Sox Scandal." Another Fullerton researcher, Tom Nawrocki, notes that the reporter had "a workaholic's thirst for further knowledge of the game." See Richard Orodenker, ed., *20th Century American Sportswriters*, vol. 171 in *The Dictionary of Literary Biography* (Gale Research, 1996).

2. Alexander, Charles C. *Our Game: An American Baseball History* (Henry Holt, 1991).

3. Aylesworth and Minks (Aylesworth, Thomas, and Benton Minks, *The Encyclopedia of Baseball Managers* [Crescent, 1990]) have the odds swinging before Game One from 3–1 Sox to 8–5 Reds. They quote one New York gambler saying, "You couldn't miss it. The thing had a rot. I saw smart guys take even money on the Sox who should have been asking five to one." The shift may not have been as great as Aylesworth and Minks have it, but it was definitely noticeable, and it drew the attention of betting commissioners across the country.

4. The black Prince of Baseball: Hal Chase and the Mythology of the Game (Sport Classics Books, 2004).

5. *The Sporting News*, October 17, 1935. Rube Benton was suspended but later reinstated by Landis, a ruling that many, including J. G. Taylor Spink, saw as a "complete refutal of his own decision in the cases of Joe Gedeon, Benny Kauff, Gene Paulette, and . . . Buck Weaver." (See Spink's biography, *Judge Landis and 25 Years of Baseball*.) Spink believed the reason for Landis's decision about Benton was to establish and emphasize (especially to Ban

Johnson) his authority over the league presidents. The second Fullerton quote is from Sugar, *Baseball's Fifty Greatest Games* .

6. *The Sporting News,* October 17, 1935..

7. *Los Angeles Times*, October 21, 1924.

8. Fullerton, "The Full Details."

9. There was practically a phobia of libel in the press of that day, and it no doubt was a factor in the reluctance of newspapers to report specific charges and names. Writing after the fix was made public, John B. Sheridan of *The Sporting News* chided the Chicago papers for their timidity after the crooked Series.

10. Voigt, David Q. *American Baseball, Volume 2* (University of Oklahoma Press, 1970).

11. Cohen, Richard M, and David S. Neft. *The World Series* (Dial Press, 1979).

12. Wray and Stockton. "Ban Johnson's Own Story."

13. *Atlanta Constitution*, October 3, 1920.

14. *Atlanta Constitution*, October 21, 1919.

15. Ibid.

16. Ibid.

17. *Atlanta Constitution*, November 6, 1919.

18. *Atlanta Constitution*, November 9, 1919.

19. *New York Times*, January 11, 1920.

20. *The Sporting News*, January 8, 1920.

21. In his novel *Blue Ruin* (W. W. Norton, 1991), Brendan Boyd describes Fullerton locking himself up in a storage closet and banging out his indictment, then being told a few days later, "We can't use this," without further explanation, by his *Herald and Examiner* editor.

22. Lieb, *The World Series.*

23. Fullerton, "The Full Details."

24. Although Fullerton wrote in December 1919 that he did not believe the rumors until he saw suspicious play in the Series, in a 1935 memoir he wrote that he was convinced enough even before Game One started to try to persuade Comiskey, Ban Johnson, and other baseball authorities to investigate at once, and not wait until the rumors proved to be true.

25. This plan for investigation appeared in the *Evening World* of December 17. It was an exhibit at the 1924 Milwaukee trial. Hugh Fullerton was questioned about the article at some length, as well as the others he wrote about the same time for the *World*.

26. Cottrell, *Blackball.*

27. Fullerton's integrity was questioned not only by the national baseball publications, but also by those in his own city. Studs Terkel, who portrayed Fullerton in the film *Eight Men Out*, described Fullerton's ordeal as "the slings and arrows of an enraged Chicagodom." (Linfield, Susan. "Studs Terkel: World Serious," *American Film*, July/August 1988).

28. Email correspondence from Eddie Frierson.

29. *New York Times*, January 8, 1920.

30. Lardner, John. "Remember the Black Sox?" *The Saturday Evening*

Post, April 30, 1938.

31. For more on Fullerton, see Carney, Gene. "Uncovering the Fix of the 1919 World Series: Hugh Fullerton's Role," *NINE,* vol. 13, no. 1 (September 2004).

32. Vaughan, "Thirty-Four Years."

33. Joe Williams, "By Joe Williams," *New York World-Telegram*, October 3, 1939.

34. Ibid.

35. Joe Williams, "By Joe Williams," newspaper unknown, May 25, 1944.

36. Yardley, Jonathan. *Ring: A Biography of Ring Lardner* (Athenum, 1984).

37. The *Chicago Tribune* on October 23, 1920, reported that Gleason told the story of the July 17 café meeting to the grand jury. The *Trib* account had former Phillies manager Billy Murray with Gleason at the table with Attell.

38. Gutman, Dan. *Baseball Babylon* (Penguin, 1992).

39. Alexander may not have been the best substitute for a game with lots of money riding on it. Old Pete had some ties to gamblers himself, according to Harry Grabiner's diary (see *The Hustler's Handbook*). Maybe Veeck should have offered Pete more than $500 to win. Alexander was also familiar with Billy Maharg, one of the go-betweens, with Bill Burns, in the Black Sox fix.

40. Black Sox Scandal (American League). A. Bartlett Giamatti Research Center, National Baseball Hall of Fame and Museum, Cooperstown, NY.

41. Murdock, *Czar of Baseball.*

42. Linn, *The Hustler's Handbook.* See the chapter, "Harry's Diary."

43. A. Bartlett Giamatti Research Center.

44. Platt, George M. "Claude Hendrix: Scapegoat or the Ninth Man Out?" in William M. Simons, ed., *The Cooperstown Symposium on Baseball and American Culture, 2001* (McFarland, 2002).

45. Cottrell, *Blackball.* Cottrell cites the *New York Times* of September 6, 1920.

46. Platt. "Claude Hendrix."

47. This account is from Eugene C. Murdock's biography of Johnson.

48. Wray and Stockton, "Ban Johnson's Own Story" Judge McDonald's name, incidentally, is on a plaque commemorating the Woodland Bards at the White Sox's current ballpark.

49. Untitled editorial, *The Sporting News*, February 10, 1921. See also the *Chicago Tribune*, February 4, 1921.

50. A. Bartlett Giamatti Research Center.

51. Otto Floto was a Johnson supporter, and he just happened to be working on a two-year hitch in Kansas City. Most of his storied and colorful career was spent in Denver, with that city's *Post.*

52. Platt, "Claude Hendrix."

53. Vila's column and the younger Comiskey's telegram were exhibits at the 1924 Milwaukee trial.

54. Fleitz, *Shoeless.*

55. Condon, Dave. *The Go Go White Sox* (American Sports Publishing, 1960).

56. Platt, "Claude Hendrix."

57. A. Bartlett Giamatti Research Center.

58. Platt, "Claude Hendrix."

59. *Los Angeles Times* and *Chicago Tribune*, September 5, 1920.

60. Crusinberry, James. "A Newsman's Biggest Story," *Sports Illustrated*, September 17, 1956. Crusinberry's boast is supported by a story told by James L. Kilgallen in the *Atlanta Constitution*, October 31, 1920 ("Here's the Inside Story of the Baseball Scandal"). Kilgallen quotes assistant state's attorney Replogle admitting that Crusinberry (and witness Sam Pass) were the two men who "started the ball a-rolling" for the grand jury.

Crusinberry had told the grand jury about the July 17 meeting with Attell in New York, and then recommended that the grand jury talk with Sam Pass—who had been best man at Ray Schalk's wedding, and who was the godfather of Schalk's baby. Pass had known all the players personally, entertaining them on many occasions. He traveled with the team. According to Kilgallen, it was Pass who first told the grand jury about a conference between players and gamblers in the Warner Hotel, and about how "former friendships on the team had been severed."

61. Comiskey had complained about Johnson's Cleveland ties before, in August 1919, when Johnson tried to block the Yankees' acquisition of Boston pitcher Carl Mays.

62. A. Bartlett Giamatti Research Center.

63. At least that is the way Benton was quoted in the *Washington Post*, December 28, 1922.

64. Vaughan, "Thirty-Four Years."

65. Seymour, *Baseball: The Golden Age.*

66. *New York Times*, October 5, 1920.

67. A. Bartlett Giamatti Research Center.

68. The *Chicago Tribune* reported on September 26 that "Pittsburgh gamblers . . . won hundreds of thousands of dollars," betting on instructions wired before each game by Abe Attell. District attorney Harry H. Rowand of Pittsburgh was investigating.

69. A. Bartlett Giamatti Research Center.

70. *New York Times*, September 25, 1920.

71. *The Sporting News*, September 30, 1920.

72. Cottrell *Blackball.*

73. Burns, Ed. Untitled, interview with Ray Schalk in *The Sporting News*, November 28, 1940.

74. *Washington Post*, September 26, 1920.

75. *Chicago Tribune*, September 27, 1920.

76. H. Walter Schlichter's role in bringing Maharg's tale to light is rarely noted, although in his story, Isaminger states that "a *North American* man visited [Maharg] yesterday." That credit is found in Isaminger's obituary in the *Philadelphia Inquirer*, for whom Isaminger later worked. Izzy Meyer was named by Maharg in the 1921 trial as the first person to whom he told his story. In all probability, Maharg was not actually "Graham" (Maharg spelled backward) as some sources have suggested.

77. Norman L. Macht in *The Ballplayers,* Shatzkin, Mike, ed. (William Morrow, 1990).

78. Wray and Stockton, "Ban Johnson's Own Story."

79. Brown, Warren. *The Chicago White Sox* (G. P. Putnam's Sons, 1952).

80. Mel Durslag of the *Los Angeles Herald-Examiner*, writing in *The Sporting News*, May 24, 1969.

81. *Los Angeles Times*, September 29, 1920.

82. *Joe Jackson vs. Chicago White Sox*, 964.

83. Ibid., 898.

84. *Joe Jackson vs. Chicago White Sox.*

85. *New York Times*, July 26, 1921.

86. *Joe Jackson vs. Chicago White Sox*, 896.

87. This is the view of James Kirby, a law professor who took a look at the legal aspects of this episode in sports history in "The Year They Fixed the World Series."

88. Durslag, Mel. "This Is My Story of the Black Sox Series," *Sports Illustrated*, September 17, 1956. As told to Durslag by Arnold "Chick" Gandil.

89. *Los Angeles Evening Express*, March 14, 1921.

90. *Chicago Tribune*, November 17, 1920.

91. *Joe Jackson vs. Chicago White Sox*, 945.

92. Ibid., 952.

93. *New York Times*, July 26. 1921.

94. From accounts in the *New York Times* and the *Savannah Morning News*, July 26, 1921.

95. *New York Times*, July 26, 1921.

96. Ibid.

97. *Savannah Morning News*, July 26, 1921.

98. *Savannah Morning News*, July 27, 1921.

99. *New York Times*, July 26, 1921.

100. *New York Times*, September 29, 1920.

101. *New York Times*, July 26, 1921.

102. The indictments that followed Cicotte's testimony caused Charles Comiskey to suspend those named immediately. It seems likely that if Comiskey had not suspended his players, the league president Ban Johnson would have, and Comiskey was not going to let that happen. Public anger with the "crooked" players had been building and whoever dealt with them first would seem to be a champion of justice. That Comiskey's decision was correct is seen, for example, in this commentary from the December 4, 1920, *National Police Gazette*:

> No man in the history of the sport has done as much for baseball as Charles Comiskey. The measure of his honesty was found in his quick decision to disrupt his club when it had another pennant within its grasp. Some criticism was cast his way because he had not taken action when the first suspicion of crookedness . . . was conveyed to him. This criticism was unjust and unmanly, for neither Comiskey nor any other person has a right to condemn his fellows and deprive them of their chief means of livelihood until positive proof of wrongdoing

is produced. When Comiskey obtained that proof he took action in a way that will cause his name to be linked with the greatest figures in baseball as long as the sport endures.

103. Gutman, Dan. *Baseball Babylon* (Penguin, 1992).

104. *Savannah Morning News*, quoting the *New York Herald*.

105. *Savannah Morning News*, July 27, 1921.

106. Kirby, "The Year They Fixed the World Series." What the players "confessed" to the grand jury has been reported many different ways. For example, reporting on the confessions when they were read into the trial record, the *New York Times* on July 27, 1921, had both Cicotte and Jackson declaring that even after taking money, they had played to win—Cicotte "after the first game" and Jackson "all the way." Williams "admitted that he could have played harder in two of his games."

107. *Detroit Free Press*, March 15, 1921.

108. Povich, Shirley. "This Morning/Say It Ain't So, Joe," *Washington Post*, April 11, 1941. Jackson complained to Povich that Landis had not let him play after he was acquitted, but he was not bitter toward baseball.

109. *New York Times*, September 29, 1920.

110. "Did Jackson have reason to believe that Austrian was his lawyer? Did Austrian clarify the matter? Did he tell Jackson that he was *not* his lawyer, that he was Comiskey's lawyer, and therefore a conflict of interest prevented him from even discussing the matter with Jackson, and advise Jackson to retain his own counsel? Austrian, of course, did none of these things. Instead, he used the situation to entrap Jackson and to direct his actions for the sole benefit of his only client in the matter, Charles Comiskey." Gropman, *Say It Ain't So, Joe!*

Chapter 6

1. Nitz, "Happy Felsch."

2. Ibid.

3. Swede Risberg denied that he ever threatened Jackson, according to his obituary in *The Sporting News*, November 1, 1975.

4. Dewey, Donald, and Nicholas Acocella. *The Black Prince of Baseball: Hal Chase and the Mythology of the Game* (Sport Classic Books, 2004).

5. Luhrs, Victor T. *The Great Baseball Mystery* (A. S. Barnes, 1966).

6. In Fullerton's *Sporting News* obituary (January 3, 1946) is this anecdote: New York writer Bill Hanna once admonished Fullerton, "Hughie, you would sacrifice accuracy for the sake of a good story." Fullerton replied, "Bill, you would sacrifice a good story for the sake of accuracy." In other words, a little embellishing by Fullerton would not have been out of character.

7. Nelson Algren, "The Silver-Colored Yesterday," in the first volume of *The Fireside Book of Baseball,* ed. Charles Einstein, (Simon & Schuster, 1956). Charles Einstein comments, "There are many viewpoints that deal with the infamous Chicago Black Sox scandal. Here is one. There can be none more vivid. Mr. Algren's piece was done in 1951." Also see Algren's *Chicago: City on the Make* (Doubleday, 1951).

8. Algren, "The Swede." A story that is equally as moving as Algren's,

describing how a youth who was rooting for his Reds in October 1919 was stunned by the news of the fix, can be found in James A. Maxwell's "Shine Ball" in *The New Yorker*, October 7, 1950, and reprinted in Dawidoff's *Baseball: A Literary Anthology* (The Library of America, 2002). The disenchantment is strikingly similar, and so it must have been for a generation of young American boys—and many fathers.

9. John Lardner, "Remember the Black Sox?" *The Saturday Evening Post*, April 30, 1938. Give Lardner points for originality—"Shoeless Joseph" is not seen anywhere else.

10. Schaap, Dick. "Say It Ain't So, Joe," *Coronet*, September 1960.

11. Lindberg, Richard C. *The White Sox Encyclopedia* (Temple University Press, 1997).

12. Al Kermisch of SABR wrote in *The Baseball Research Journal* in 1997 that "Say it ain't so, Joe" never reached Jackson's ears. "It started out as an AP story out of Chicago" (he cites Fullerton's version) and was questioned, if not debunked, as early as 1921—for example, in an August 4 column by Gordon McKay in the *Philadelphia Inquirer.* Kermisch seems to place more weight on Joe Jackson's own denial in a September 24, 1942, *Sporting News* interview, "declaring by oath that no such words" had been spoken.

13. *Washington Post*, September 4, 1978.

14. Schaap, Dick. "Say It Ain't So, Joe."

15. Columnists over the years have had some fun with the saying, as today's late-night comedians would if the story was in the news today. For example, Westbook Pegler, tongue firmly planted in cheek: "I have always considered the possibility that this kid [who said 'Say it ain't so, Joe; say it ain't true'] was misquoted or that he was a boy with leanings toward the law and was merely advising Jackson to plead not guilty." *Chicago Tribune*, December 26, 1926.

16. Farrell, James T. *My Baseball Diary* (A. S. Barnes, 1957).

17. Kavanagh, Jack. *Shoeless Joe Jackson* (Chelsea House, 1995).

18. Camp, Walter. "The Truth About Baseball," *The North American Review*, April 1921.

19. *Washington Post*, September 29, 1920.

20. *Washington Post*, October 1, 1920.

21. Kuenster, John. "Warm Up Tosses," *Baseball Digest*, September 1970.

22. Gardner, Paul. *Nice Guys Finish Last: Sport and American Life* (Universe Books, 1974).

23. *New York Times*, October 1, 1920.

24. For more details about the selection of Landis as commissioner, see David Pietrusza, *Judge and Jury* (Diamond Communications, 1998).

25. *New York Times*, November 5, 1920.

26. *Los Angeles Times*, October 28, 1920.

27. Harry Grabiner's diary refers to a list of twenty-seven names, turned over by the White Sox to Landis in 1921. Johnson probably informed team owners that the grand jury might have indicted only a fraction of players involved with gamblers, and asked them to patrol their players carefully in the wake of the scandal.

28. *Collyer's Eye*, October 2, 1920. The *Eye* also took National League President John Heydler to task for covering up the crookedness of Hal Chase in 1918. Apparently the *Eye* had seen the affidavits produced by Greasy Neale, Christy Mathewson, W. D. (Pol) Perritt, Jimmy Ring, and John McGraw in August 1918, along with a letter by M. J. Regan. This was damning evidence, and the *Eye* asked why Chase had *not* been banned? Why did Heydler whitewash him? And why did McGraw let him keep playing?

29. Some historians believe Chase would not have been permitted to continue playing if Mathewson had been able to testify against him; but Matty was serving in the military overseas at the time. Ban Johnson believed that there would have been no fix in October 1919 if Chase had been properly dealt with; Joe Gedeon had apparently told Johnson that Chases's dismissal would have sent a strong warning to all ballplayers, and he (Gedeon), for one, "would not have fallen into evil ways" if that warning had been given. After he was barred from baseball by Landis for having knowledge of the fix, Ban Johnson employed Gedeon the following year as an investigator. Gedeon's obituary in his hometown *Sacramento Bee* noted that Johnson considered Gedeon "entirely innocent." Gedeon was never called to testify in the 1921 trial as a witness for the prosecution.

30. Fullerton, Hugh S., Sr., "Baseball on Trial," *New Republic*, October 1920.

31. *Chicago Tribune*, October 23, 1920.

32. *Chicago Tribune*, March 10, 1929.

33. Murdock, *Czar of Baseball.*

34. Ibid.

35. Vaughan, "Thirty-Four Years."

36. *New York Times*, January 18, 1927.

37. *The Sporting News*, February 10, 1921.

38. Murdock, *Czar of Baseball.*

39. Lieb, Fred. *The Baseball Story* (G. P. Putnam's Sons, 1950).

40. Letter from Ban Johnson to Garry Herrmann, July 28, 1921 (during the trial). The Harold and Dorothy Seymour papers, No. 4809. Division of Rare and Manuscript Collections, Cornell University.

41. *Washington Post*, February 22, 1921.

42. *Washington Post*, March 10, 1921.

43. *Washington Post*, March 21, 1921.

44. *Chicago Tribune*, February 24, 1929.

45. Wray and Stockton, "Ban Johnson's Own Story."

46. A. Bartlett Giamatti Research Center.

47. Ibid.

48. Wray and Stockton. "Ban Johnson's Own Story."

49. *New York Times*, July 21, 1921.

50. A. Bartlett Giamatti Research Center.

51. *Chicago Tribune*, May 7, 1921.

52. A. Bartlett Giamatti Research Center. In the 1921 trial, Burns stated that Johnson's secretary had registered him as "Williams" at the Great Northern Hotel "to avoid publicity."

53. *The Sporting News* and J. G. Taylor Spink, playing up Judge McDonald's role, seemed displeased that Landis had been selected over Ban Johnson's nominee for commissioner, Judge McDonald. While heaping credit on McDonald, they also began challenging Landis to "find time to lay down a few principles on American freedom as a platform on which an organization could stand to combat bigotry." They chided Landis for calling baseball a national institution but doing nothing to integrate the sport.

54. A. Bartlett Giamatti Research Center.

55. Wray and Stockton, "Ban Johnson's Own Story." In the version of this abduction plot that Johnson gave to the *Chicago Tribune* on February 24, March 3, and March 10, 1929, he noted that the agent who had taken the $5,000, "presumably of Rothstein's money," had been offered only $500 by Johnson, to "rustle [Attell] out of the state without legal formality.... We saw we were up against a powerful combination."

56. *Chicago Tribune*, September 27, 1920.

57. Johnson had become persuaded about Rothstein's involvement partly by James R. Price, a New York City attorney whose numerous handwritten letters kept Johnson informed on the legal maneuvering to arrest or extradite Abe Attell, who could bring down Rothstein. Price told Johnson that Eugene McGee (the famous lawyer William Fallon's partner) took $10,000 to Chicago, and gave it to Henry Berger in exchange for grand jury material; McGee was promised $10,000 for his part, but never received it. Berger apparently got the material from a man named Kenney (Price was not sure of that), and delivered the "minutes of the grand jury" to Fallon in Washington. Fallon took them to Rothstein. Rothstein had all references to himself removed, then gave the documents to a friend, who offered them for sale. That the papers were offered for publication was reported by the *New York Times* on February 3, 1921, just a month or so after they went missing. Price advised Johnson to keep the name of the friend confidential: "Do not breathe his name to anyone" or Rothstein will make him disappear. See the records at the A. Bartlett Giamatti Research Center. (See also Pietrusza's *Rothstein* and the Wray and Stockton Series, "Ban Johnson's Own Story.")

58. A letter dated May 16 from William A. Lange, a San Francisco Real Estate and Insurance broker, informed Johnson that entertainer Al Jolson had won a big bet and bought stock in the St. Louis Browns. Lange said that according to Jolson, there is "about one player in each club that should be expelled for crookedness." A letter from W. G. Evan dated May 26 indicated that Evan had spoken with Eddie Collins and Ray Schalk. All they had noted of a fix was Cicotte's "steady refusal to pitch spit balls." Black Sox Scandal (American League, A. Bartlett Giamatti Research Center, National Baseball Hall of Fame ans Museum, Cooperstown, NY.

59. Kirby, "The Year They Fixed the World Series." After the jury was agreed upon, the opposing teams of lawyers sorted through six hundred veniremen. The chief prosecutor, George Gorman, was assisted by two special prosecutors employed by Ban Johnson for the American League (interested third parties could hire lawyers to assist in the prosecution of certain cases).

60. *Chicago Tribune*, July 7, 1921.

61. *New York Times*, July 12, 1921.

62. Kirby, "The Year They Fixed the World Series."

63. Ibid.

64. *St. Louis Post-Dispatch*, February 18, 1929.

65. Ibid.

66. *Washington Post*, August 2, 1921.

67. Lindberg, Richard C. *Who's on Third, The Chicago White Sox Story* (Icarus Press, 1983).

68. Seymour, *Baseball: The Golden Age.*

69. Fullerton Hugh , Sr. "On the Screen of Sport," *Atlanta Constitution*, July 30, 1921.

70. Voigt, David Q. *America Through Baseball* (Nelson Hall, 1976). *Literary Digest* noted that with the lone exception of the *Buffalo Times*, newspapers across America applauded Judge Landis for doing the right thing. The editor of the *Boston Globe* found his verdict "reassuring." The acquittal showed, in the words of the *Washington Evening Star*, "a dangerous lesion in the American moral sense." And the *Pittsburgh Dispatch* pointed out the "astonishing feature of the situation": the scandal did not hurt baseball.

71. Fleit, *Shoeless.*

72. Tygiel, *Past Time.*

73. Pietrusza, *Judge and Jury* .

74. James, Bill. *The New Bill James Historical Abstract* (Free Press, 2001).

75. Helyar, John. *The Lords of the Realm* (Villard, 1994).

76. Faith in baseball was restored by the installation of a commissioner with unlimited powers. Maybe faith in the stock market can only be restored by something similar—an effective watchdog that keeps corporate greed from pillaging stockholders, workers, and consumers. See Lerach, William S. "Plundering America: How Wall Street, the Big Accounting Firms, and Corporate Interests Chloroformed Congress and Cost America's Investors Trillions," speech of May 22, 2003.

77. Ron Story wrote of the 1919 World Series fix: "To peel off its many layers is to uncover connections among wielders of urban influence and power in the early twentieth century." Joe Jackson learned that in taking on Comiskey, he was up against the establishment: "politicians (aldermen, public prosecutors, judges), press (publishers, editors, reporters), and the proprietors of pool halls or saloons on whose police-protected turf bets could be laid on ballgames." See Story's course book prepared for the University of Massachusetts History Department, Course 185A, Spring 1977.

78. The picture that comes to mind is another Chicagoan, Mayor Richard Daley, losing it on national television, defending himself and his city in 1968 at the Democratic National Convention.

79. Dickson, Paul, ed. *The Dickson Baseball Dictionary* (Avon, 1989).

80. Veeck and Lin, *The Hustler's Handbook.*

81. Creel, George. "Making the American League," *The Saturday Evening Post*, March 22, 1930.

82. Sheridan, John B. "Back of the Home Plate," *The Sporting News*, October 7, 1920.

83. Gillespie, Ray. "St. Louis Policeman Recalls Details of Black Sox Case," *The Sporting News*, October 9, 1957. See also "The Scandalous Black Sox" by Harold Rosenthal in *Sport* magazine, October 1959. Hoagland is given credit for discovering, quite by accident, the evidence that was "the start of the whole thing." Rosenthal bases his story on a feature by Ray Gillespie that appeared in *The Sporting News*, October 9, 1957.

Exactly when this incident took place is not clear. Rosenthal's article suggests that it was late winter or spring of 1920, before the fix was revealed. But an article in the *New York Times* on April 2, 1921, "Four New Yorkers Held," probably refers to the arrests at the Jefferson Hotel made by Hoagland and Vasey. Gambler Nate Evans, "the missing link in the 1920 big league baseball scandal," was arrested, along with Sydney Stajer, Hyman Cohen, and Elias Fink.

84. See Robert Smith, *Baseball in the Afternoon* (Simon & Schuster, 1933), for an interesting treatment of the 1923 "mini-scandal," as well as a detailed treatment of the Cobb-Speaker scandal. "Had Landis not put a lid on it [when it broke seven years later], it would have, or should have, put the Black Sox in the shade."

85. This was the view of J. G. Taylor Spink. See his *Judge Landis.*

86. *New York Times*, August 24, 1923.

87. Ibid.

88. Baxter, N.W. In the Press Box, *Washington Post*, August 31, 1923.

89. Commenting on the case in his *Sporting News* column, August 30, 1923, W. A. Phelon recalled, "It is true that *Collyer's Eye* dug up the Black Sox Scandal," but this was one of the few places that the *Eye*'s earlier credibility was noted. The *Eye* "stubbed its toe" this time, Phelon added.

90. *New York Times,* August 31, 1923.

91. *Washington Post*, September 8, 1923. The lawsuit cost the National League $3,313.84, according to Pietrusza in *Judge and Jury.*

92. *Washington Post*, March 23, 1924.

93. Spink, *Judge Landis and 25 Years of Baseball.* As Bert Collyer was making his peace with baseball, his publication "ran yet another inflammatory piece," before the February 28, 1928, settlement. See Pietrusza, *Judge and Jury.*

94. Letter from Hugh Fullerton to Captain Joseph Medill Patterson, January 10, 1923.

95. Klein, Steve. "Hugh S. Fullerton, the Black Sox Scandal, and the Ethical Impulse in Sports Writing." Masters Thesis, Michigan State University, 1997.

96. The missing articles with Fullerton's own version of "the crooked world Series" may yet turn up someday. Steve Klein found letters that have Fullerton giving to *Tribune* sports editor Frank Smith, a "typewritten copy of Comiskey's dictated account of his connection with the Series," which Smith took for safe-keeping. "I won't let it out of my hands." He may have kept the sixty-four articles of Fullerton, too. Finding these documents would be as exciting to baseball historians as Bill Veeck's discovery of Harry Grabiner's diary in the early sixties, or the 1920 grand jury transcripts turning up in 1988.

Chapter 7

1. Not only was Jackson famous; so was his trademark bat, forty-some–

ounce, 34-inch-long Black Betsy. He apparently named other bats, too—Old Ginril, Dixie, Big Jim, Blond Betsy, and Caroliny—and according to Burt Sugar in *Rain Delays* (St. Martin's Press, 1990), Jackson attributed virtues and shortcomings to each one of them. He took his bats south with him for the winter, saying, "Bats are like ballplayers—they hate cold weather." In 2001, a collector agreed to give Black Betsy a warm, year-round home for $577,610, and in May 2002, the transaction was completed.

2. *The Sporting News*, October 7, 1920.

3. Dickie Kerr, the Sox starting and winning pitcher in Games Three and Six, spoke many years later to reporter Joe Williams about Game Two. Williams's column, "Dickie Kerr Discusses the Black Sox," is in the *New York World Telegram,* June 25, 1949. Kerr recalled Gleason sending in Fred McMullin to pinch-hit, only to learn later that McMullin was in on the conspiracy.

4. Krueger, Joseph J. *Baseball's Greatest Drama* (Classic Publishing, 1942).

5. *New York Times*, October 5, 1919.

6. *Zanesville (OH) Times Recorder*, September 24, 1961.

7. First by Carter "Scoop" Latimer, the sports editor of the *Greenville News*, and then by W. P. Kinsella in his fiction, *Shoeless Joe* (Ballantine, 1982).

8. Barra, Allen. *Clearing the Bases* (St. Martin's Press, 2002).

9. The "five assists" legend seems to have started in July 1922, when that error appeared in a petition that was circulated nationally by promoter Eddie Phelan, in an effort to clear Jackson's name. See the *New York Times*, July 16, 1922, for the full petition and a description of Phelan's plans.

10. Robert Smith notes that when he was in the minors, Jackson "stole" an occupied base on three different occasions. See *Baseball* (Simon & Schuster, 1947). William Herzog II, in *The Faith of Fifty Million,* eds.Christopher H. Evans and William R. Herzog II (John Knox Press, 2002), addresses the lone criticism of Jackson's base-running in the 1919 Series: that he failed to score from third on a ground ball hit to short. An account in the *New York Times* has the Reds' shortstop Kopf "playing in on the grass" to prevent the runner on third from scoring. Herzog notes that "Jackson held at third because he was an alert base runner, not because he is playing to lose." But again, it is impossible to judge from such a distance and be sure.

11. "Baseball Is Honest," *Collier's,* October 1920.

12. Meany, Tom. *Baseball's Greatest Teams* (A. S. Barnes, Inc., 1949).

13. Greenberg, Eric Rolfe. *The Celebrant* (Everest House, 1983), a historical novel.

14. *Joe Jackson vs. Chicago White Sox.* Hamilton testified on January 28, 1924.

15. Farrell, *My Baseball Diary.*

16. To illustrate again how different eyes see different things, see J. C. Kofoed in *Baseball Magazine*, November 1919. He wrote that Jackson's peg home should have gone to second base, and he assigned Jackson a mental error. See Cottrell's *Blackball,* and other descriptions of Jackson's play in the Series.

17. Robinson, Ray. *Matty: An American Hero* (Oxford University Press, 1993).

18. Ibid.

19. Fleitz, *Shoeless.*

20. Team owners who saw their players opt for the "shipyard leagues" after the government issued its "work or fight" order, must have had mixed feelings. Their personnel were at a safe distance from the front lines, and playing ball, and some were probably earning more in the shipyards than in their major league jobs. The shipyards were under some scrutiny, so the men working there had to do actual work; they could not just pretend to work between ballgames. The shipyards boasted of their recruits, and if the war had not ended when it did, the shipyard leagues might have eventually rivaled the majors for talent.

21. Gropman, *Say It Ain't So, Joe!*

22. According to Gropman, baseball's first commissioner, Judge Kenesaw Mountain Landis, was a big fan of military conscription, and when the United States entered World War I, "he went after pacifists and anti-war defendants with a vengeance." Landis, never accused of being impartial or objective as judge or commissioner, may well have recalled Joe Jackson as the poster boy for "slackers" in World War I, when he had the duty of ruling on Jackson in 1921 and deciding the punishment.

23. *Joe Jackson vs. Chicago White Sox.*

24. Gropman, *Say It Ain't So, Joe!*, appendix I.

25. This is according to Watergate figure John Dean, appearing in February 2003 on C-Span, on a panel concerned with presidential tapes.

26. *Joe Jackson vs. Chicago White Sox*, 652.

27. Ibid., 655.

28. Another hit was taken away from Jackson and ruled an error—if the ruling had stood, his Series average would have been .406, instead of .375. Of course, .406 makes us think of Ted Williams, and that would be fitting, given Ted's interest in clearing Jackson's name.

29. Algren, Nelson. *The Last Carousel* (G. P. Putnam's Sons, 1973). Algren describes Jackson's condition in the Series as "pitiful."

30. *The Spalding Guide* is a refreshing read, written immediately after the 1919 Series. The authors enjoyed the "whirlwind" Series, and found the overall quality satisfying. In fact, they were relieved that the Series featured no "strike" like the year before, when the players almost sat out a game in protest of their diminished pay (the game started late). There was a rainy Sunday, but the rest of the 1919 Series was played in Indian summer warmth in both cities, and the *Guide* writers were relieved, because in 1917, "the cold winds of Lake Michigan swept across the playing field and spectators huddled in their thick overgarments while the players vigorously swung their arms enveloped in their heavy sweaters to keep up circulation."

31. Evans and Herzog, The Faith of Fifty Million. William R. II., eds. *The Faith of Fifty Million.* In his analysis of Jackson's play in the Series, Herzog notes: "In addition, Jackson advanced runners by hitting the ball to the right side of the infield. . . . Jackson was a model of consistency, batting .500 (4 for 8) when leading off an inning and .250 (2 for 8) when hitting with the bases empty but not leading off. He hit .375 (6-for-16) with runners on base and [exactly the

same] with nobody on."

32. For those who might be swayed by the supposedly cold logic of mathematical arguments, Jay Bennett's analysis of Jackson's play in the Series is worth looking up. The math is beyond me, but Bennett reports that his test "provides substantial support to Jackson's subsequent claims of innocence." See Jay Bennett, "Did Shoeless Joe Jackson Throw the 1919 World Series?" *The American Statistician*, vol. 47, no. 4, (November 1993).

33. Williams, "Dickie Kerr Discusses the Black Sox."

34. Seymour, *Baseball: The Golden Age*. Williams repeated the story in his *World-Telegram* column, September 24, 1959.

35. Asinof, *Eight Men Out,* 76. Asinof wrote his take before the grand jury statement of Jackson was available.

36. Asinof was speaking at the annual Symposium on Baseball and American Culture in Cooperstown in 1999.

37. Luhrs, *The Great Baseball Mystery*. Luhrs also wrote, "Jackson was no more able to play dishonest baseball than he was able to teach advanced Greek."

38. Voigt, *American Baseball, Volume 2.*

39. Seymour, *Baseball: The Golden Age*. Dorothy Mills Seymour has an opposite view, "based on Jackson's confession." Neither the Seymours nor David Voigt had access to Jackson's 1924 trial material.

40. Algren, *The Last Carousel.*

41. Gropman, *Say It Ain't So, Joe!*

42. Alexander, *Our Game.*

43. Frommer, *Shoeless Joe.*

44. Kavanagh, Jack. *Shoeless Joe Jackson* (Chelsea House, 1995). Kavanagh seems to side with those who think Jackson did not give his best effort in every game.

45. Fleitz, *Shoeless.*

46. Evans and Herzog, *The Faith of Fifty Million.*

47. Nathan, Daniel A. *Saying It's So: A Cultural History of the Black Sox Scandal* (University of Illinois Press, 2003).

48. Bak, Richard. *Cobb Would Have Caught It* (Great Lakes Books, 1961, and Wayne State University Press, 1991).

49. Green, Paul. *Sports Collectors Digest*, circa 1983–84.

50. Gambler Abe Attell went into detail in a 1934 interview with Joe Williams, about the decision to make the first batter the signal to bettors all over the country. See Peter Williams, ed. *The Joe Williams Baseball Reader* (Algonquin Books of Chapel Hill, 1989).

51. *Joe Jackson vs. Chicago White Sox*, 1288.

52. *Chicago Tribune*, September 29, 1920.

53. Ibid.

54. *Joe Jackson vs. Chicago White Sox,* 360 and 1363.

55. *New York Times*, July 26, 1921.

56. Fullerton, "I Recall." See image in photo section.

57. "The Basis of a Pitcher's Success," an interview with Eddie Cicotte, *Baseball Magazine*, December 1919/January 1920.

58. *Los Angeles Times*, July 27, 1921.

59. *Washington Post*, July 21, 1921. The other evidence that Cicotte had been threatened with physical harm if he did not keep his part of the bargain is examined later.

60. Asinof, Eliot. *1919: America's Loss of Innocence* (Donald I. Fine, 1990).

61. *The Sporting News*, May 15, 1919.

62. *Joe Jackson vs. Chicago White Sox*, 1287.

63. "The Basis of a Pitcher's Success." Cicotte had gone on record long before 1919 with his belief that a pitcher should not be charged with a loss when the score is 1–0; he argued that a pitcher cannot possibly win if his team gives him no run support at all, and felt that he should not be "penalized in the records with a defeat" when that occurs.

64. Wray and Stockton, "Ban Johnson's Own Story."

65. Leonard, Jim. "Dissension Plagued ' 19 Flag Team," *The Sporting News*, November 1, 1950. This is the fourth installment of Collins's life story.

66. Fleitz, *Shoeless.*

67. Harry "the Cat" Brecheen, regarded as one of the top-fielding pitchers ever, committed just eight errors in twelve seasons, for a .983 fielding average. In fact, only seven pitchers (since 1900) have made more errors than Eddie Cicotte. According to Sean Lahman, going into the 2004 season, Cicotte ranked as the thirty-sixth worst fielder among 1,415 pitchers with a minimum of 200 games since 1900.

68. Fullerton, "The Full Details."

69. Robinson, Ray. "No Glory in Winning What Others Lost," *New York Times*, October 7, 1984.

70. Fullerton, "The Full Details."

71. Ritter, *The Glory of Their Times*. The transcripts can be found in the A. Bartlett Giamatti Research Center, National Baseball Hall of Fame and Museum Coopertown, NY.

72. Roush seldom mentioned his source by name in other interviews that he gave after the scandal broke. In a few, the source was transcribed "Jimmy Wigmore." Not until research by Susan Dellinger, Edd Roush's granddaughter, was published in July 2004 has the exact identity of his source been made known. See "A Shadow in the Night . . . The Graying of the White," in *Baseball in the Buckeye State*, a publication for the National Convention of the Society for American Baseball Research, Cincinnati, OH, July 2004 (Sports Publishing LLC).

73. *The Sporting News*, October 7, 1920.

74. Murdock, Eugene C. *Baseball Between the Wars: Memories of the Game by the Men Who Played It* (Meckler, 1992).

75. Transcripts for Ritter, *The Glory of Their Times*. See note 67.

76. Widmeyer, recalled by Roush as a newsman, was called "The Million Dollar Newsboy." The *Washington Post* called him "King of Newsboys" in an October 25, 1925 profile; Widmeyer's connections with politicians and boxers were noted.

77. Murdock, *Between the Wars.*

78. Reichler, Joseph. "The Black Sox Scandal," *The World Series: A 75th*

Anniversary (Simon & Schuster, 1978).

79. Ibid.

80. Werber, Bill, and C. Paul Rogers III. *Memories of a Ballplayer* (Society for American Baseball Research, 2001), 9. See also Pete Rose with Rick Hill, *My Prison Without Bars* (Rodale, 2004).

81. Algren, "The Swede."

82. This does not call everything in *Eight Men Out* into question. But it underscores the need to check the record, whenever possible, especially when trying to verify stories heard from old ballplayers, one of whom apparently was Asinof's source for the bonus story. A number of stories told by old-timers in Lawrence Ritter's *The Glory of Their Times* have been debunked, but the book is still a classic worth reading.

83. James, Bill. *The Baseball Book 1990* (Villard, 1990).

84. Comiskey did offer bonuses, but rarely big ones. In 1920 Lefty Williams's contract contained a $500 bonus for winning fifteen games and $1,000 for winning twenty, and he received both before he was suspended.

85. The league ace Walter Johnson was nearly lured to the short-lived Federal League five years earlier with a promise of $18,000–$20,000 a year. The Federal League rose up to challenge the major leagues and attracted enough major league players so that it is today regarded as having been a major league. The Senators, on a tight budget, still paid "The Big Train" $12,500 and gave him a multi-year contract.

86. It is worth underlining that the owners had just recently broken the Federal League (credit an assist to World War I), and then attendance *really* sagged in 1918, making tight operations even worse. The 1919 player salaries reflected the owners' caution about baseball's ability to rebound after the war.

87. Kermisch, Al. "From a Researcher's Notebook," *The Baseball Research Journal*, No. 23, 1994.

88. *Chicago Tribune*, October 1, 1919.

89. James, Bill. *The Baseball Book 1991* (Villard, 1991).

90. See David Marasco's article on Cicotte at the website of *The Diamond Angle*. www.thediamondangle.com/marasco/hist.html.

91. *Thorn, John, ed. Total Baseball*, seventh Edition (Total Sports Publishing, 2001).

92. Blaisdell, Lowell. "Legends as an Expression of Baseball Memory," *Journal of Sport History*, Vol. 19, No. 3 (Winter 1992).

93. Lefty Williams's contract card, for example. Claude had a bonus clause in one of his last seasons. Lefty earned a cool $375 because he won more than fifteen games in 1919.

94. See www.deadball.com/cicotte.htm: "If you recall the movie, *Eight Men Out*, where the gambler threatens Lefty Williams' wife—it was actually both pitchers' wives who were threatened. The depiction of the conversation between Comiskey and Cicotte, i.e., '29 is not 30,' is highly accurate, as is the fact that Eddie's career, despite his performance in 1917–1920, was about over due to the increasing pain he suffered in his pitching arm. He continued through sheer force of will and the fact is that under Comiskey he wasn't making enough to just quit."

95. Eliot Asinof has suggested that Cicotte was motivated not just by his low salary, but also by the denial of a chance to earn a $10,000 bonus in 1917 by winning thirty games. Yet he did have his shot at thirty wins. But maybe Eddie was motivated partly by recalling a different bonus that he and others were denied in 1917. At the Milwaukee trial, there was testimony by players that Comiskey promised his team that they would see at least $5,000 if they won the 1917 World Series. They did win, but their shares were only around $3,600 or so. So some of them claimed they were owed $1,500 by the team. Even though Eddie Collins, Ray Schalk, and Red Faber sent depositions denying that this bonus had been promised, the jury in their special verdict voted eleven to one on the evidence they had heard that there was a promise made. (But because there was nothing in writing, they awarded Jackson no $1,500 bonus, only his back pay—before their verdict was set aside.)

96. *Washington Post*, January 3, 1927.

97. Falls, Joe. "Cicotte, 46 Years Later," *Detroit Free Press*, 1965.

98. "Where Jackson Goes Williams Follows," *The Sporting News*, March 13, 1919. A Web site reported that Joe Jackson sold his Chicago pool hall to Lefty Williams for a dollar, October 6, 1921. The contract sold at auction over eighty years later for $36,098.

99. Excerpts from Williams's statement are at the Famous Trials website of Douglas O. Linder. http://www.law.umkc.edu/faculty/projects/ftrials/blacksox/inquotes.html.

100. *Joe Jackson vs. Chicago White Sox,* 64.

101. Gropman, *Say It Ain't So, Joe!*

102. *Joe Jackson vs. Chicago White Sox*, 768.

103. Ibid., 857.

104. Ibid., 844.

105. Ibid., 850.

106. Or "Lyra," which is how Lefty spelled his wife's name, when asked to do so in the deposition filed on May 5, 1923.

107. Isaminger, James. "Gamblers Promised White Sox $100,000 to Lose," *Philadelphia North American*, September 27, 1920.

According to William A. Cook's *The 1919 World Series: What Really Happened* Williams would have been shot while on the mound if he didn't comply. But the source of this information is not made clear.

108. Ward, Geoffrey C., and Ken Burns. *Baseball, An Illustrated History* (Knopf, 1994).

109. Algren, *The Last Carousel*. Algren also says the fee for the hit was $500.

110. Koppett, Leonard. *Koppett's Concise History of Major League Baseball* (Temple University Press, 1998).

111. Boyd, *Blue Ruin*.

112. For examples, in the 1994 book that accompanies the Ken Burns marathon classic video "documentary" *Baseball* (BMG Video), "Harry F." is referred to as a real person; Asinof's book is not credited as the source. In his 2003 book *Rothstein*, David Pietrusza also gives "Harry F." credit, but not Asinof.

Chapter 8

1. According to *The Dickson Baseball Dictionary*, "Lowdermilk" became a noun, "an eponymous term for a pitcher given to wildness." In case you're wondering *"how wild was he,"* he walked 376 in 590 innings—just under 6 per 9 innings.

2. Algren, "The Swede."

3. See Smith, Leverett T., Jr. *The American Dream and the National Game* (Bowling Green University Popular Press, 1970).

4. *The Sporting News*, August 12, 1920, cited in Smith, *The American Dream.*

5. Will, George F. *Bunts: Curt Flood, Camden Yards, Pete Rose and Other Reflections on Baseball* (Scribner, 1998).

6. Smith, Red. "Black Sox, Orioles: Different Outlooks," *Washington Post*, September 29, 1971.

7. Fullerton, Hugh. "Clean-Up of Game Coming," *Atlanta Constitution*, November 3, 1920.

8. Buck could *not* have argued team chemistry—the Sox were not at all close-knit. See the Chicago Historical Society website: www.chicagohs.org/history/blacksox.html.

9. Fullerton, "On the Screen, *Atlanta Constitution*, July 16, 1921."

10. Ibid. Fullerton: "There were a few [players] with honor enough and courage enough to force the facts out. It is to be hoped that while this nasty mess is being stirred up again in the courts the public will be told plainly just which players had the guts and the honesty to denounce the crooks. Let the entire story of the White Sox team be told, and the fans will root hard for at least four fellows who were on that ill-fated team."

11. *Washington Post*, January 29, 1921.

12. Fred batted just twice in October 1919—a useless pinch single in a 9–1 loss; and he made the final out with two on, in a 4–2 Reds win. He did, however, scout the Reds before the Series. According to *The Sporting News* Conlon Collection, card 1039, McMullin took Gandil's spot as chief liaison with gamblers in 1920; "the conspirators were forced to throw key games under threat of being exposed." The source of this information is not known, and the threat of exposure assumes that (a) the gamblers could and would somehow produce evidence, which would be self-incriminating; and (b) baseball officials did not already know that the fix was in. In 1920 the threat of physical harm was more likely to be used in any altercation between gamblers and players than it would be today.

13. Weaver may have received money but refused to keep it. In his column of October 3, 1939, in the *New York World-Telegram*, Joe Williams wrote that Buck found a thousand dollars under his pillow in a Cincinnati hotel, presumably before or after one of the first two games of the Series. But he didn't keep a dime. Did he turn the bribe over to his manager? Some think so.

14. Fullerton, "The Full Details."

15. Buck did admit, however, that he later gave Tiger infielder Oscar Vitt a handbag for Christmas. But was this his share of the contribution, as the *Los Angeles Times* had it on January 2, 1927? Or was Weaver correct when he

testified that Vitt hosted him on mountain hunting trips, and Buck had thanked him annually with presents such as shirts, socks, and once with a gold knife?

16. *Chicago Tribune*, March 13, 1927; *New York Times*, March 14, 1927. Buck did take the opportunity, while speaking with Landis face to face for the first time during the Risberg hearings, to ask the commissioner for reinstatement. Landis said he would get back to him. Two months later, he sent Buck a letter turning him down. Buck had testified that when Cicotte invited him into the plot, he turned him down, saying that Cicotte was crazy and fixing a Series could not be done. "The world's Series was then played and so played that even during the Series your manager, at a meeting of the players, stated that something was wrong. You knew your club officials were seeking to ascertain the facts, but you kept still."

17. *New York Times*, January 14, 1922. Buck Weaver may not have justice, but he does have his own website: www.gingerkid.com. Mike Nola, a strong advocate for both Weaver and Joe Jackson: "I have never subscribed to the Saint Joe or Saint Buck theory. These men surely knew about the Fix, but they lived by the code of the day, and that was, you didn't rat on your friends, no matter what. I believe Jackson and Weaver should have been punished for their 'guilty knowledge,' but not to the extent they were and continue to be punished."

18. Pietrusza, *Judge and Jury.*

19. Veeck and Linn, *The Hustler's Handbook.*

20. Or did Landis try to salvage one of the game's superstars? See the interview of Ray French by Dick Dobbins and Jon Twichell for their history of San Francisco Bay-area baseball, *Nuggets on the Diamond* (Woodford Press, 1994). Ray French believed that Landis practically pleaded with Shoeless Joe Jackson of the White Sox to deny knowledge of the World Series scandal.

21. Algren, *The Last Carousel.*

22. Barton, George. "Weaver's Role in Fixed Series," *Baseball Digest*, April 1956. Barton has Attell, Bill Burns, and Billy Maharg as the "three men assigned by Rothstein" to "lay the groundwork" with Gandil and Swede Risberg, "ringleaders in the plot," and to prepare them to persuade Cicotte, Williams, and the others to throw the Series. Barton claims he got his story directly from Attell (along with Damon Runyon, Westbrook Pegler, W. O. McGeehan, Warren Brown, Tom Laird, and Hype Igoe), in Atlantic City in 1926. "Jack Dempsey was training for his first fight with Gene Tunney."

23. Williams, Peter, ed. *The Joe Williams Baseball Reader* (Algonquin Books of Chapel Hill, 1989). A column from April 10, 1934, of the *New York World-Telegram* is cited. Attell stated in that interview that Buck Weaver "didn't have any more to do with throwing that Series than Greta Garbo"—an actress known for her silence.

24. Farrell, *My Baseball Diary.* Farrell grew up in Chicago, a Sox fan, and is known for his Studs Lonigan trilogy. Farrell provided Eliot Asinof with material (and a lot of encouragement) that helped make *Eight Men Out* a reality. Farrell interviewed Weaver in the fall of 1954, and "Buck Weaver's Last Interview" is also in Farrell's *Diary.*

25. *New York World-Telegram*, July 10, 1943, quoted in Williams, *The Joe*

Williams Baseball Reader.

26. Ibid.

27. Cottrell, *Blackball.* Cottrell cites a front-page story that ran in *Collyer's Eye*, October 30, 1920, in which Collins charges certain teammates, including Weaver, of tossing the 1919 Series and a number of games during the 1920 season.

28. Ibid.

29. For more on Buck Weaver, see *The Ginger Kid* by Irving Stein (Elysian Field Press, 1992), and *Hoopla* by Harry Stein (Dell, 1983).

30. Algren, "The Swede."

31. Perhaps Swede just was not cut out to be a Mr. October. In 1917, rookie Risberg slumped badly at the end of the season and was benched for the Series, getting only two pinch-hit appearances.

32. *Los Angeles Times*, January 2, 1927. In 1931, Risberg told a reporter from the Sioux Falls *Argus-Leader* that the banishment by Landis cost him $150,000 to $200,000 and "What did they have on me? Nothing. The records show I made a new mark for shortstops in the World Series, accepting 53 chances and making 31 assists [the Macmillan Encyclopedia has 30]. They said I hit into double plays. They were all line drives, and it was just tough luck that they didn't go safe." See "Gandil and Risberg: Last of the Black Sox," by Paul Walsh, *Minneapolis Star Tribune*, September 25, 1994.

33. *Chicago Tribune*, June 25, 1922. It sounds like a line from a late-night television comedian, but the *Trib* said the rumpus started when Eddie asked for his pay in advance.

34. *Los Angeles Times*, December 31, 1926.

35. *Chicago Tribune*, October 1, 1920.

36. Nitz, "Happy Felsch."

37. Ibid.

38. *Chicago Daily Tribune*, September 14, 1956.

39. Schuld, Fred. "Chick Gandil: Before the Black Sox Scandal," paper presented at the Seymour Medal Conference of the Society for American Baseball Research, Cleveland, OH, April 17, 1999.

40. Chapin, Dwight. "Gandil: 'I'll Go to My Grave With a Clear Conscience,'" *The Sporting News*, September 6, 1969.

41. *Los Angeles Times*, October 1, 1920.

42. Letter from Neily to Johnson, January 22, 1921. A. Bartlett Giamatti Research Center, National Baseball Hall of Fame and Museum, Coopertown, NY.

43. Ibid.

44. Schuld, "Chick Gandil."

45. Ibid.

46. 1974 audiocassette interview with Bibb Falk. In the Eugene C. Murdock Baseball Collection, Cleveland Public Library, Cleveland, OH.

47. Los Angeles Evening Express, March 14, 1921.

48. Durslag, "This Is My Story."

49. *Chicago Daily Tribune Los Angeles*, September 14, 1956.

50. *Joe Jackson vs. Chicago White Sox*, page 1347.

51. Chapin, "Gandil."

52. Quoted in a column by Joe Williams, *New York World-Telegram*, October 3, 1939.

53. In a memoir, Collins said, "I always hoped and dreamed and maybe even prayed that someday I'd get my chance to prove my ability as a manager." Collins, Eddie, as told to Jim Leonard, "Dissension Plagued ' 19 Flag Team."

54. Ibid.

55. Lindberg, *The White Sox Encyclopedia*. "The available evidence suggests that the gamblers pressured the corrupted ballplayers to throw games down the stretch." But if the gamblers lost control of those players during the 1919 World Series, how much control could they exert nearly a year later? Of course, there may have been a new group of gamblers at work in 1920, using new bribes or threats.

56. Ibid.

57. *Joe Jackson vs. Chicago White Sox,* 1545.

58. Seymour, *Baseball: The Golden Age.* In his notes, Seymour wondered if Collins and the others expressing their relief had "guilty knowledge" of the events of October 1919. See The Harold and Dorothy Seymour papers, #4809. Division of Rare and Manuscript Collections, Cornell University.

59. *New York Times*, October 3, 1920.

60. "When Baseball Gets Before the Grand Jury," *The Sporting News*, October 7, 1920.

61. *New York Times*, October 4, 1920.

62. *Williamsport (PA) Grit*, October 3, 1920.

63. Seymour, *Baseball: The Golden Age,* 333. Seymour has the remarkable paragraph reproduced below. Notice the omission of Eddie Collins' name:

> And the so-called Clean Sox were not quite so pure as some have made them out to be. . . . They knew that something was wrong, and more than once admitted as much, but they did nothing about it. In a sense they are accessories to the fact. It may even be that some who were considered honest were implicated. I once asked Joe Jackson about the scandal, and he named one of the "honest" players and suggested that I see him. For that matter, the entire team, as well as Comiskey and his manager, had participated in a highly dubious project in 1917 which some interpreted as bribery.

64. Mills, Dorothy Jane. *A Woman's Work: Writing Baseball History With Harold Seymour* (McFarland, 2004).

65. The Harold and Dorothy Seymour papers, No. 4809. Division of Rare and Manuscript Collections, Cornell University.

66. In Nelson Algren's version of the 1917 incident in *The Last Carousel*, only Buck Weaver refused to participate. Eddie Collins's recollection was that Tex Russell was the only one not to chip in. But the Risberg hearings in January 1927 made clear that Weaver was definitely the one (regular) man out. Russell said, "I gave $45," while part-timer Eddie Murphy testified that he was not asked to give and did not.

67. Meany, *Baseball's Greatest Teams*.

68. *The Sporting News*, February 10, 1921. Untitled, uncredited report on a Philadelphia interview with Eddie Collins and reactions.

69. Ibid.

70. Ibid.

71. *Chicago Tribune*, January 5, 1927.

72. Ibid.

73. *New York Times*, January 3, 1927.

74. Ibid.

75. The entire affidavit appeared in the *Chicago Tribune*, January 7, 1927, 19–20. Gandil remembered getting "promises or cash" from all the regular players, including Eddie Collins, Eddie Murphy, and Tex (Reb) Russell. He did not mention Buck Weaver.

76. *Los Angeles Times*, January 7, 1927.

77. Transcripts of the 1921 hearing are among the items found in the material donated to the National Baseball Library in 1995 by the American League. They can be found under Black Sox scandal (American League in the A. Bartlett Giamatti Research Center, National Baseball Hall of Fame and Museum, Cooperstown, NY.

78. Will Rogers's original account of the Risberg hearings can be read in his January 23, 1927, column in the *Washington Post*. Rogers had met Landis on several occasions and knew most of the Tiger and White Sox players. He personally knew Risberg and Gandil for years. "Now I know that I am supposed to report some comedy with things that come along under my observation. Well, I dident [sic] see any."

79. Seymour, *Baseball: The Golden Age*.

80. *Washington Post*, January 6, 1927.

81. *Los Angeles Times*, January 14, 1927.

82. *Washington Post*, January 10, 1927.

83. The *New York Times* printed the entire text on January 13, 1927.

84. Seymour. *Baseball: The Golden Age*.

85. *The Sporting News*, October 7, 1920.

86. Ibid.

Chapter 9

1. Actually there is some evidence that a gambler tried to tamper with the very first Series game in 1903 by offering Boston catcher Lou Criger a bribe of $12,000.

2. Smith, *Baseball*.

3. Salsinger, H. G. "Ed Cicotte Crossed His Detroit Friends," *The Sporting News*, October 7, 1920.

4. "By Joe Williams," *New York World-Telegram*, October 3, 1939.

5. "By Joe Williams," *New York World-Telegram*, May 25, 1944. For a more detailed and well-researched look at the Cincinnati connection to the gambling side of the fix, see *Red Legs and Black Sox,* by Susan Dellinger (Emmis Books, 2006).

6. Dewey and Acocella, *The Black Prince*. In 1908, 1909, and 1910,

according to Hugh Fullerton, "a certain clique of Pittsburgh gamblers was extremely active. They formed the friendship of a number of the Chicago Cubs." But their aim was to find out pitching rotations, and when Frank Chance, the Cub manager, found out, he "purposely misled them at every opportunity until they grew tired of betting on false information." See Fullerton, Hugh S., Sr. "Judge Landis Asked to Take Charge of Investigation," *New York Evening World*, December 20, 1919.

7. *New York Times*, September 30, 1920.

8. *Chicago Tribune*, October 22, 1920.

9. Algren, *The Last Carousel*.

10. Lardner, John "Remember the Black Sox?" *The Saturday Evening Post*, April 30, 1938.

11. Leo Katcher recalls in *The Big Bankroll* (Harper, 1958), which is not at all a baseball book, how prohibition meant fortunes for the underworld, and also how in that underworld of the twenties, knocking off enemies was hardly uncommon, and rule number one was "thou shalt not squeal." Arnold Rothstein followed the rule to the end, refusing in the hours before he passed away to identify the person who had fatally shot him. When Eliot Asinof tried to interview the living Black Sox players, over forty years after the fix, they still would not talk about it.

12. This vignette from Mike Nola illustrates the point: "The famous crime boss Frank Costello was asked in the 1950s 'What would have happened to Joe Jackson had he told what was going on?' Costello asked, 'Before or after the bets were placed?' The reply was 'After.' Costello simply showed how serious these guys were with his answer: 'Jackson wouldn't have made it home that day.'" www.gingerkid.com.

13. Lindberg, *The White Sox Encyclopedia*.

14. Vaughan, "Thirty-Four Years."

15. Rothstein, Carolyn. *Now I'll Tell* (Vanguard Press, 1934). This is Mrs. Arnold Rothstein.

16. Carolyn Rothstein's account of Chadbourne's interrogation of her husband reads as if she had a copy of the transcript handy, and it takes up fourteen pages in her book. A very similar account appears in Donald Henderson Clarke's *In the Reign of Rothstein*, published five years before Mrs. Rothstein's book by the Vanguard Press, 1929. Clarke adds a detail that illustrates how insulated from the fix of October 1919 Rothstein portrayed himself, just a few years after the scandal. Asked who won the World Series in baseball from 1919 through 1921, Rothstein replied that he didn't know. "But he had heard that the White Sox had gotten into difficulties one of those years."

17. David Pietrusza, in his biography of Rothstein, has A.R. being the "middleman" for Charles A. Stoneham when he purchased the New York Giants in January 1919.

18. Rothstein, *Now I'll Tell*. Rothstein's wife made it very clear that Fallon had not represented her husband.

19. *New York Times*, July 27, 1921.

20. *Joe Jackson vs. Chicago White Sox*.

21. Katcher, *The Big Bankroll*.

22. Asinof, Eliot. *Bleeding Between the Lines* (Holt, Rinehart, and Winston, 1979).

23. Abe Attell also frequented the Polo Grounds. Hugh Fullerton, after the scandal broke, railed against the magnates of all sports to bar from their clubs all persons who had been banned from other sports. He mentioned Rothstein's presence at the Polo Grounds as well as at exclusive clubhouses at racetracks, and at boxing matches. See Fullerton's column in the *Atlanta Constitution*, July 30, 1921.

24. Waller, George. *Saratoga: Saga of an Impious Era* (Prentice-Hall, 1966). According to Waller, Rothstein put The Brook up for sale after the end of the 1922 racing season. Reformers in Saratoga had removed the politicians who had become too friendly with the gamblers and bookmakers. And Rothstein had too many other sure things going, which required his attention.

25. Fowler, Gene. *The Great Mouthpiece* (Covici, 1931).

26. Ibid.

27. The *Chicago Daily Journal*, October 26, 1920, had reported that Rothstein gave that same story to the grand jury when he testified before them (see Pietrusza's *Rothstein*).

28. Wray and Stockton, "Ban Johnson's Own Story."

29. *Los Angeles Times*, October 14, 1920.

30. *Washington Post*, October 22, 1924.

31. Thompson, Craig, and Allen Raymond. *Gang Rule in New York: The Story of a Lawless Era* (Dial Press, 1940).

32. Ibid.

33. Chafetz, Henry. *Play the Devil* (Clarkson N. Potter, 1960).

34. Fowler, *The Great Mouthpiece*. The emphasis is Fowler's.

35. Ibid. Is the "lively ball" yet another example of the maxim that I bent to describe the events following the big fix? Power covers up, and absolute power covers up absolutely—but not permanently.

36. Reisler, Jim, ed. *Guys, Dolls, and Curveballs: Damon Runyon on Baseball* (Carroll & Graf, 2005).

38. Kohout, Martin Donell. *Hal Chase: The Defiant Life and Times of Baseball's Biggest Crook* (McFarland, 2001).

39. Lieb, *The Baseball Story.*

40. Dewey and Acocella, *The Black Prince.*

41. *Washington Post*, May 19, 1947.

42. Christian, Ralph J. "Beyond Eight Men Out: The Des Moines Connection to the Black Sox Scandal," presented at the 2003 National Convention of the Society for American Baseball Research, Denver, CO, July 2003.

43. Harry Redmon owned the Majestic Theater in St. Louis, and may have lost up to $14,000 on the fix, although most sources have his losses at $5,500—his asking price for the information he had. See Daniel, "Story Butchered."

44. Ibid.

45. *Washington Post*, July 23, 1921. The account of Redmon calling Zork "the little red-head who started it all" is detailed by James L. Kilgallen in "Zork Fixed Black Sox," *Atlanta Constitution*, July 23, 1921. Redmon claimed that in a meeting at Chicago's Hotel Morrison after Game Three, Zork talked for three

hours about raising money to fix (or re-fix) the Series, claiming that he was the one who had "started it all" in the first place.

46. *New York Times*, July 27, 1921.

47. This is pure speculation, but if there was a plan to fix the 1918 World Series, originating in St. Louis (see Pietrusza's Kid Becker theory in *Rothstein: The Life, Times and Murder of the Criminal Genius Who Fixed the 1919 World Series* [Carroll & Graf, 2003]), perhaps Zork had somehow involved Gene Paulette, then a St. Louis Cardinal; and perhaps it was Gene *Paulette* and not Gene *Packard* beside whose name Harry Grabiner jotted in his famous diary, "1918 Series fixer." It would be an easy enough mistake to make. See the chapter on "Harry's Diary" in Veeck's *The Hustler's Handbook*.

48. As a scout, DuBuc has been credited with signing Hank Greenberg.

49. Sheridan, "Back of the Home Plate.

50. Helyar, *The Lords of the Realm.*

51. Pietrusza, *Rothstein.* For a lengthy account of Arnold Rothstein's involvement, and some fascinating theories about all of the fixers, David Pietrusza's book is must reading.

52. Wray and Stockton, "Ban Johnson's Own Story."

53. *New York Times*, September 30, 1920.

54. Twombly, Wells. "The Last Days of Chick Gandil," *The Sporting News*, March 20, 1971.

55. Lindberg, *The White Sox Encyclopedia.*

56. *New York Times*, October 6, 1920.

57. Hynd, Alan. *True Detective*, November 1938. Victor Luhrs, in *The Great Baseball Mystery*, has Weeghman, who owned the old Chicago Whales and then (1914–18) the Cubs, testifying at the grand jury in 1920 that he first heard rumors of the fix in August 1919, from Mont Tennes, who in turn had gotten it from Rothstein, at "Rothstein's showplace, The Brook, at Saratoga" (which was brand new in 1919). According to Luhrs's sources, Weeghman went on to name Abe Attell, Nate (or Nat) Evans, and Nicky Arnstein—the latter's name shows up so rarely in books about the fix, that you would guess Rothstein had it sanitized out of the record along with his own.

58. Williams, Joe. "By Joe Williams," *New York World-Telegram*, May 25, 1944.

59. Seymour, *Baseball: The Golden Age.*

Chapter 10

1. Orodenker, Richard, ed. *20th Century American Sportswriters*, Volume 171 in *The Dictionary of Literary Biography* (Gale Research, 1996).

2. Peel, Mark, of the Society for American Baseball Research. Email correspondence.

3. According to Peel, the strip was originally drawn by Will B. Johnstone and later by Dick Dorgan; Dorgan continued the strip with his brother Tad after Lardner moved on. The setting of the strip is the early 1920s, and one of the characters is the old White Sox ace Big Ed Walsh, who was an American League umpire in 1922 before returning to the Sox as a coach. Comiskey and Kid Gleason appear, too. Harcourt Brace issued a collection, *Ring Lardner's*

You Know Me, Al, in the early 1980s.

    4. Lardner had written a semi-famous poem in July 1912 to introduce Cicotte to the Chicago fans (Ring and Eddie had been together in Boston). The poem struggles for the correct pronunciation of Eddie's last name, suggesting at least four variations.

    5. The actual event may have taken place across the river from Cincinnati, "at a roadhouse in Bellevue, Kentucky," according to Jonathan Yardley, who says that's the way Lardner told the story. See Yardley's *Ring.*

    6. *Washington Post*, November 16, 1932.

    7. Lardner, Ring, Jr. *The Lardners, My Family Remembered* (Harper and Row, 1976). Lardner had four gifted sons. One of them, John, wrote about the Black Sox for the *Saturday Evening Post* in 1938. Ring, Jr., won two Oscars and a spot on the roster of the "Hollywood Ten" blacklisted in the 1950s; he was quizzed before the House Committee on Un-American Activities by Richard Nixon.

    8. Ring Lardner was among those who lost by betting on the July 4, 1919, Dempsey–Willard fight, something he admitted in his newspaper column; so the Sox defeat a few months later was even harder to take, both emotionally and financially.

    9. Wheeler, John N. "Ring Lardner," *Collier's*, March 17, 1928.

    10. Fullerton, "The Full Details."

    11. Forever Blowing Bubbles was a new and popular song in 1919—the band at Redland Park played it during the White Sox' pre-game practice before Game One, according to the *New York Times*, perhaps trying to psych the visitors. The original lyrics were written by John/Jean/Jaan Kenbrovin (or Ken Brovin)—Kenbrovin being a pseudonym for James Kendris, James Brockman, and Nat Vincent. Incidentally, the lyrics are very reminiscent of the 1918 popular song by Joseph McCarthy and Harry Carroll, that begins, "I'm always chasing rainbows / Watching clouds drifting by / My dreams are just like all my schemes / Ending in the sky." The music of "Bubbles," most sources agree, belonged to John William Kellette. One source has it John Kenbrovin Kellette. Is nothing about the 1919 Series plain and simple? Another popular song in Cincinnati in October 1919 was "If the Ocean Was Whiskey and I Was a Duck, I'd Dive to the Bottom and Never Come Up." See the *Syracuse Herald* "Series Notes," October 2, 1919.

    12. *Washington Post*, October 4, 1925.

    13. In his coverage of the 1925 World Series for Bell Syndicate, Lardner, just back from Spain, compared the Series to a bullfight and recalled his lost wagers in October 1919.

    Ring Lardner, an American original, died in 1933 at age forty-eight. He had been a prolific writer, nineteen books before his death and a number after, in collections and readers. Some of his titles are wonderful: *Gullible's Travels*; *The Young Immigrunts*; *Say It With Oil*; *Treat 'Em Rough*; and *The Real Dope*. For an overview, I recommend either *Ring*, by Jonathan Yardley, or *The Lardners, My Family Remembered* by Ring, Jr.

    14. Asinof, *Bleeding Between the Lines.*

    15. The television program episode of *Witness*, "The Trial of Joe Jackson,"

aired Thursday, January 28, 1961, 9 p.m. eastern time, on CBS-TV. A copy of the video, donated to the author by Jim Mallinson of Mt. Sinai, New York, is now in the National Baseball Library in Cooperstown, NY.

16. *The Sporting News*, February 8, 1961.

17. All but a few of the commercials were edited out of the video. Those that survived plugged Woolite, which is still alive and well, and AeroWax, both Johnson and Johnson products. So there was no massive consumer revolt stirred up by this program. *Witness* was soon off the air, coast-to-coast.

18. I reported *The Sporting News* response in chapter 4. Daniel Nathan reports sportswriter Joe Williams's reaction in *Saying It's So*. In the *New York World-Telegram*, Williams described the episode as "squalid and spurious" and suggested it was "slanderous." Williams was especially upset with the portrayal of Comiskey, whom he recalls as "a man of courage and fairness" who "wrecked his team." But Comiskey was simply a businessman who only suspended his suspicious players when he absolutely had to—not a day sooner, and not eleven months sooner when he could have—and should have, if he was truly courageous and fair.

19. Allen. *American League Story,* 94.

20. Warren Brown told Dick Schaap in a September 1960 interview for *Coronet* that while he "dutifully reported the standard version" of the "Say it ain't so, Joe" story in his book, he himself did not think it ever happened. But it is what readers—and later, television and film audiences—expected. Asinof doubted the historicity of "Say it ain't so, Joe," too. Despite the views of the writers behind *Witness*, American television viewers were fed "Say it ain't so, Joe" in the *Witness* episode.

21. Asinof, *Bleeding Between the Lines.*

22. James, *The Baseball Book 1990.*

23. Although Asinof's access to surviving figures from the events of 1919 makes *Eight Men Out* a unique resource, the book was published before some significant material became available. A few years after *Eight Men Out*, Bill Veeck's *The Hustler's Handbook* appeared, which revealed the infamous "Harry's Diary." I was curious to know whether Asinof found anything in Veeck's book to be surprising or in any way striking. Asinof: "Veeck told me how impressed he was that E.M.O. was so like the Diary (which he discovered when he was with the White Sox)." Joe Jackson's grand jury statement was not published until almost thirty years after *Eight Men Out*. The transcripts and affidavits from the 1924 Milwaukee trial are still not generally available.

24. A 1999 speech by Eliot Asinof in Cooperstown is the source for the short biography in this chapter.

25. Johnson, Dick. "Interview with John Sayles," *The SABR Review of Books*, Vol. IV, 1989, published by the Society for American Baseball Research.

26. Anyone who thinks that knowledge of the 1924 trial transcripts makes little difference needs to compare Donald Gropman's 1979 *Say It Ain't So, Joe!* with the revised edition.

27. Asinof, *1919,* 301–2.

28. Ibid.

29. See http://espn.go.com/classic/s/black_sox_moments.html for

information on the ESPN Classic documentary and an article by Eliot Asinof, one by Rob Neyer (who plays a kind of devil's advocate for fans of Shoeless Joe Jackson), a link to collectibles, and a link to a short rundown of "baseball scandals."

30. This essay is really a good read for fans of movies who want lots of tidbits about how directors work with books, go for realism (or not), work with the author on the set, and so on. *Eight Men Out* may not portray Joe Jackson in all the complexity he deserves—but at least it shows him batting left-handed.

31. *New York Times*, August 9, 1966.

32. Luhrs relies on three New York papers, the *Times*, *American*, and *Tribune*; and contemporary issues of *Baseball*, *The Sporting News*, and *Spalding's Baseball Guides*.

33. I recommend Luhrs's hard-to-find book because of its detailed treatment of other events both before and after the 1919 Series; its information from the grand jury hearing; and its treatment of Judge Landis. The book also includes a play-by-play of the Series, from the 1920 *Spalding Baseball Guide*.

34. This essay was first published in the *Journal of the Illinois State Historical Society* (Autumn 1969), and it appears in a "slightly revised" version in Voigt's *America Through Baseball*.

35. Because of his article's title, I asked Voigt if he found it hard to place or if he had gotten any negative feedback from Major League Baseball. "No trouble placing the article. Over the years, no negative feedback from MLB— I don't think they read all that much."

36. *A Silver-Colored Yesterday* is not from Nelson Algren's book *The Last Carousel*—but you can find it at Douglas Linder's "Chicago Black Sox Trial," at the Famous Trial website. (http://www.law.umkc.edu/faculty/projects/ftrials/blacksox/inquotes.html) It is not to be confused with the essay of the same title by Algren in the first volume of *The Fireside Book of Baseball*.

37. Most of the items in *The Last Carousel* were previously published in various magazines; but not "Ballet," and that strikes me as very strange, because it is such a good read and so highly original.

38. Harry Grabiner was Comiskey's team's secretary—in effect, the general manager. Although Grabiner may have been stingier than Comiskey in negotiating contracts and running the club, it is Comiskey who has been portrayed by some as a Scrooge.

39. Algren has a theory about why the Sox won Game Three that I have not seen elsewhere. Algren has catcher Ray Schalk calling Kerr's pitches in such a way that Risberg doesn't handle a ball all day. But that theory does not hold up. Risberg fielded a grounder from the lead-off batters in the first two innings, en route to a four put-out, six-assist, no-errors day in the field. He did fumble a possible double-play ball in the second inning, but recovered and got the runner at first. Later, he started a 6-4-3 double-play. Three singles and not a man past second for the Reds. Gandil, who had assured his gambler contacts that game three was in the bag, drove in two early runs and became a hero— perhaps an unwilling one.

40. For more on Algren, see Nathan, *Saying It's So*.

41. The appendices include Jackson's grand jury testimony; Comiskey–

Jackson correspondence written from October 27, 1919 through February 18, 1920; correspondence between Jackson, Ban Johnson, and Landis; six pages of excerpts from Jackson's testimony in Milwaukee, 1924; "Recent Support for Jackson" (including that of Ted Williams) and the Ted Williams–Bob Feller Petitions, prepared by Louis Hegeman.

42. Gropman forgets that one has come to light—Casey Stengel's testimony before a congressional subcommittee in 1958. But "Jackson-to-grand jury" is right up there, too.

43. Evans and Herzog, *The Faith of Fify Million.*

Chapter 11

1. Seidel, Michael. *Ted Williams, A Baseball Life* (Contemporary Books, 1991).

2. Ceresi, Frank J. "Shoeless Joe Jackson: An Interview With Joe Anders," *The Vintage and Classic Baseball Collector*, July/August 1997.

3. "Amnesty for Black Sox Third Baseman?" *Wall Street Journal*, January 17, 1992. The Chicago Lincoln American Inn of Court is a "group of lawyers and jurists who meet periodically to discuss issues of import to their profession." Louis Hegeman was with the Chicago law firm of Gould and Ratner at the time.

4. "Amnesty for Black Sox Third Baseman?" quoting a letter dated December 12, 1991.

5. *The Trial of Buck Weaver and Joe Jackson*, Chicago Lincoln and Chicago American Inns of Court, "performed" on June 18, 1992, is preserved on video. At the end of the trial, ninety-some spectator-jurors voted. Regarding Joe Jackson, the verdict was "It ain't so"—forty-five to twenty for immediate restoration, twenty-three for a time-limited ban. Buck Weaver fared even better: sixty-eight to nine for immediate restoration, ten for a ban of a fixed period.

6. Miller, Marvin. *A Whole Different Ball Game* (Birch Land Press, 1991).

7. Martinez, David H. *The Book of Baseball Literacy* (Plume, 1996).

8. Carino, Peter. "Novels of the Black Sox Scandal: History/Fiction/Myth," *Nine: A Journal of Baseball History and Social Policy Perspectives*, Spring 1995. For an in-depth analysis of the way the Black Sox scandal can be seen as an example of a "foreign menace"—(gamblers) undermining and disrupting a "clean" American institution (baseball)—and not as an issue of unfair labor practices and an exploited workforce—see Robin Bachin's "At the Nexus of Labor and Leisure" in the Summer 2003 *Journal of Social History.*

9. Swope, "I Recall."

10. Frommer, *Shoeless Joe.*

11. Luhrs, *The Great Baseball Mystery.*

12. Krueger, *Baseball's Greatest Drama.*

13. Lieb, *The Story of the World Series.*

14. This headline was in the *Toronto World*, but similar stories appeared across the continent.

15. *New York Times*, January 8, 1920.

16. There had been mini-scandals involving the sale of World Series tickets in the past. In October 1911, Ban Johnson called for the expulsion of the New York Giants from the National League if proof could be found that the team had

colluded with "speculators" who sold Series tickets at inflated prices. A dozen men were arrested at the Polo Grounds, but the National Commission, headed by Herrmann, refused to investigate further. Herrmann did suggest, however, that the National Commission would have "full jurisdiction" over tickets to October's game in the future. There was a similar ticket-scalping scandal in 1908, and while Herrmann denied any "skullduggery," he went on record saying it was not fair to the fans who turned out during the regular season, to be "soaked" by having to pay big prices for the Series. Ban Johnson suggested cutting the price in half for the next Series.

17. As Doug Pappas has noted, Johnson (whose career started in Cincinnati) and Herrmann had a friendship that "had been cemented in saloons across the Queen City." In 1909 Pittsburgh owner Barney Dreyfuss had complained to *The Sporting News*, "The Commission is a joke, just as anybody in baseball knows. Its members do too much drinking." See "The Centennial of Modern Organized Baseball," *Outside the Lines*, Business of Baseball Committee Newsletter of the Society for American Baseball Research, vol. 9, no. 3, Summer 2003.

18. *Cincinnati Enquirer*, October 9, 1919.

19. *World Book Encyclopedia*: "No whiskey was manufactured after September 8, 1917. No beer was manufactured after May 1, 1919. On July 1, 1919, under the wartime act, no more intoxicants were sold. No saloon in America could operate legally after that date."

20. Baseball historian Norman Macht on Tom Swope (1888–1969): "Writer. After brief stints with the Dayton *Herald* in 1908 and Cleveland *Press* in 1914, Swope was named sports editor and baseball writer of the Cincinnati *Post* in 1915 and stayed for forty-one years." Shatzkin, Mike, ed. *The Ballplayers* (William Morrow, 1990).

21. Email to the author.

BIBLIOGRAPHY

BOOKS

Alexander, Charles C. *Our Game: An American Baseball History* (Holt , 1991).

———. Algren , Nelson *Chicago: City on the Make* (Doubleday, 1951) .

———. *The Last Carousel* (G. P. Putnam's Sons, 1973).

Allen, Lee. *100 Years of Baseball* (Bartholomew House, 1950).

———. *The American League Story* (Hill and Wang, 1962).

———. *The Cincinnati Reds* (G. P. Putnam's Sons, 1948).

Asbury, Herbert. *Gem of the Prairie* (Knopf, 1940).

Asinof, Eliot. *1919: America's Loss of Innocence* (Donald I. Fine, 1990).

———. *Bleeding Between the Lines* (Holt, Rinehart, and Winston, 1979).

———. *Eight Men Out* (Holt, Rinehart, and Winston, 1963).

Auker, Elden, with Tom Keegan. *Sleeper Cars and Flannel Uniforms* (Triumph, 2001).

Aylesworth, Thomas, and Benton Minks. *The Encyclopedia of Baseball Managers* (Crescent, 1990).

Axelson, Gustav W. *"Commy": The Life Story of Charles A. Comiskey* (Reilly and Lee, 1919). Reprinted by McFarland, 2003.

Bak, Richard. *Cobb Would Have Caught It* (Great Lakes Books, 1961, and Wayne State University Press, 1991).

Barra, Allen. *Clearing the Bases* (St. Martin's Press, 2002).

The Baseball Encyclopedia: The Complete and Official Record of Major League Baseball (Eighth Edition) (Macmillan, 1990).

Bisher, Furman. *The Furman Bisher Collection* (Taylor, 1989).

Bloch, Arthur. *Murphy's Law* (Price/Stern/Sloan, 1977).

Boyd, Brendan. *Blue Ruin* (W. W. Norton, 1991).

Breslin, Jimmy. *Damon Runyon* (Ticknor and Fields, 1991).

Broeg, Bob, and , Bob Burrill. *Don't Bring That Up!* (A. S. Barnes, 1946).

Brown, Warren. *The Chicago White Sox* (G. P. Putnam's Sons, 1952).

Burk, Robert F. *Never Just a Game: Players, Owners and American Baseball to 1920* (University of North Carolina Press, 1994).

Chafetz, Henry. *Play the Devil* (Clarkson N. Potter, 1960).

Clarke, Donald Henderson. *In the Reign of Rothstein* (Vanguard, 1929).

Cohen, Rich. *Tough Jews* (Simon & Schuster, 1998).

Cohen, Richard M., and David S. Neft. *The World Series* (Dial Press, 1979).

Cook, William A. *The 1919 World Series: What Really Happened* (McFarland, 2001).

Condon, Dave. *The Go Go White Sox* (American Sports Publishing, 1960).

Cottrell, Robert C. *Blackball, the Black Sox and the Babe* (McFarland, 2002).

Dawidoff, Nicholas, ed. *Baseball: A Literary Anthology* (Library of America, 2002).

Dellinger, Susan. *Red Legs and Black Sox* (Emmis Books, 2006).

Dewey, Donald, and Nicholas Acocella. *The Black Prince of Baseball: Hal Chase and the Mythology of the Game* (Sport Classic Books, 2004).

Baseball's Greatest Quotations (HarperCollins, 1991).

———. *The Dickson Baseball Dictionary* (Avon, 1989).

Dobbins, Dick, Dikson, Paul, ed. and Jon Twichell. *Nuggets on the Diamond* (Woodford Press, 1994).

Evans, Christopher H., and William R. Herzog, eds. *The Faith of Fifty Million* (John Knox Press, 2002).

Farrell, James T. *My Baseball Diary* (A. S. Barnes, 1957).

Fitzgerald, Ed, ed. *The American League* (Grosset and Dunlap, 1963). Includes White Sox team history by John Carmichael.

Fleitz, David L. *Shoeless: The Life and Times of Joe Jackson* (McFarland, 2001).

Fowler, Gene. *The Great Mouthpiece* (Covici, 1931).

Frommer, Harvey. *Shoeless Joe and Ragtime Baseball* (Taylor Publishing, 1992).

Fullerton, Hugh S. *Jimmy Kirkland and the Plot for a Pennant* (Winston Co., 1915).

Gardner, Paul. *Nice Guys Finish Last: Sport and American Life* (Universe Books, 1974).

Ginsburg, Daniel E. *The Fix Is In: A History of Baseball Gambling and Game Fixing Scandals* (McFarland, 1995).

Greenberg, Eric Rolfe. *The Celebrant* (Everest House, 1983).

Gropman, Donald. *Say It Ain't So, Joe!* Revised second edition (Carol Publishing Group, 1992); (also Lynx Books, 1979, 1988).

Gutman, Dan. *Baseball Babylon* (Penguin, 1992).

Helyar, John. *The Lords of the Realm* (Villard, 1994).

Holtzman, Jerome. *Baseball, Chicago Style* (Bonus Books, 2001).

———. *The Commissioners* (Total Sports, 1998).

———. *The Jerome Holtzman Baseball Reader* (Triumph, 2003).

Honig, Donald. *A Donald Honig Reader* (Simon & Schuster, 1988).

James, Bill. *The Baseball Book 1990* (Villard, 1990).

———. *The Baseball Book 1991* (Villard, 1991).

———. *The New Bill James Historical Abstract* (Free Press, 2001).

Kahn, Roger. *A Flame of Pure Fire* (Harcourt, Brace, 1999).

Katcher, Leo. *The Big Bankroll* (Harper, 1958).

Kavanagh, Jack. *Shoeless Joe Jackson* (Chelsea House, 1995).

Kinsella, W.P. *Shoeless Joe* (Ballantine, 1983).

Klingaman, William. *1919: The Year Our World Began* (St. Martin's Press, 1987).

Kohout, Martin Donell. *Hal Chase: The Defiant Life and Times of Baseball's Biggest Crook* (McFarland, 2001).

Koppett, Leonard. *Koppett's Concise History of Major League Baseball* (Temple University Press, 1998).

Krueger, Joseph J. *Baseball's Greatest Drama* (Classic Publishing, 1942).

Lardner, Ring, Jr. *The Lardners, My Family Remembered* (Harper and Row, 1976).

Leventhal, Josh. *Take Me Out to the Ballpark* (Black Dog/Leventhal, 2000).

Lieb, Fred. *The Baseball Story* (G. P. Putnam's Sons, 1950).

———. *The Story of the World Series* (G. P. Putnam's Sons, 1949).

Lindberg, Richard C. *Stealing First in a Two-Team Town* (Sagamore, 1994).

———. *The White Sox Encyclopedia* (Temple University Press, 1997).

———. *Who's on Third, The Chicago White Sox Story* (Icarus, 1983).

Lovinger, Jay, and Hunter S. Thompson. *The Gospel According to ESPN: Saints, Saviors and Sinners* (ESPN, 2002).

Luhrs, Victor T. *The Great Baseball Mystery* (A. S. Barnes, 1966).

Martinez, David H. *The Book of Baseball Literacy* (Plume, 1996).

Meany, Tom. *Baseball's Greatest Teams* (A. S. Barnes, 1949).

Miller, Marvin. *A Whole Different Ball Game* (Birch Land press, 1991).

Miller, William D. *Pretty Bubbles in the Air: America in 1919* (University of Illinois Press, 1991).

Mills, Dorothy Jane. *A Woman's Work: Writing Baseball History With Harold Seymour* (McFarland, 2004).

Murdock, Eugene C. *Ban Johnson, Czar of Baseball* (Greenwood Press, 1982).

———. *Baseball Between the Wars: Memories of the Game by the Men Who Played It* (Meckler, 1992).

———. *Baseball Players and Their Times, Oral Histories of the Game, 1920–1940* (Meckler, 1991).

Nardinelli, Clark. *Baseball History*, "Judge Kenesaw Mountain Landis and the Art of Cartel Management," (Meckler, 1989).

Nathan, Daniel A. *Saying It's So: A Cultural History of the Black Sox Scandal* (University of Illinois Press, 2003).

Neft, David, Roland T. Johnson, Richard M. Cohen, and Jordan A. Deutsch. *The Sports Encyclopedia: Baseball* (Grosset and Dunlap, 1974).

Orodenker, Richard, ed. *20th Century American Sportswriters*, Vol. 171 in *The Dictionary of Literary Biography* (Gale Research, 1996). See Tom Nawrocki on Hugh Fullerton, Paul J. Sandin on Damon Runyon, and Peter Cava on Ring Lardner.

Pietrusza, David. *Judge and Jury* (Diamond Communications, 1998).

———. *Rothstein: The Life, Times and Murder of the Criminal Genius Who Fixed the 1919 World Series* (Carroll & Graf, 2003).

Platt, George M. "Claude Hendrix: Scapegoat or the Ninth Man Out?" in *Cooperstown Symposium on Baseball and American Culture, 2001*, William M. Simons, ed. (McFarland, 2002).

Ritter, Lawrence S. *The Glory of Their Times* (William Morrow, 1966).

———. Transcript, interview with Edd Roush, January 29, 1964. National Baseball Library, Cooperstown, NY.

Robinson, Ray. *Matty: An American Hero* (Oxford University Press, 1993).

Rothstein, Carolyn (Mrs. Arnold). *Now I'll Tell* (Vanguard, 1934).

Rose, Pete, with Rick Hill, *My Prison Without Bars* (Rodale, 2004).

Seidel, Michael. *Ted Williams, A Baseball Life* (Contemporary Books, 1991).

Seymour, Harold. *Baseball: The Golden Age* (Oxford University Press, 1971).

Shannon, Mike, ed. *The Best of Spitball* (Simon & Schuster, 1988).

Shatzkin, Mike, ed. *The Ballplayers* (William Morrow, 1990).

Silverman, Jeff, ed. *Lardner on Baseball* (Lyons, 2002).

Skipper, James K. *Baseball Nicknames* (McFarland, 1992).

Smith, Leverett T. *The American Dream and the National Game* (Bowling Green University Popular Press, 1970).

Smith, Robert. *Baseball* (Simon & Schuster, 1947).

———. *Baseball in the Afternoon* (Simon & Schuster, 1933).

Spink, J. G. Taylor. *Judge Landis and 25 Years of Baseball* (Thomas Y. Crowell press, 1947).

Stein, Harry. *Hoopla* (Dell, 1983).

Stein, Irving M. *The Ginger Kid* (Elysian Fields, 1992).

Story, Ron. Course book prepared for University of Massachusetts History Department, Course 185A, Spring 1977.

Sugar, Burt Randolph. *Baseball's Fifty Greatest Games* (JG Press, 1986).

———. *Rain Delays* (St. Martin's Press, 1990).

Sullivan, Dean, ed. *Middle Innings: A Documentary History of Baseball, 1900–1948* (University of Nebraska Press, 1998).

Terracem, Vincent. *The Complete Encyclopedia of Television Programs, 1947–1976* (A. S. Barnes., 1976).

Thompson, Craig, and Allen Raymond. *Gang Rule in New York: The Story of a Lawless Era* (Dial press, 1940).

Thorn, John, ed. *Total Baseball*, Seventh Edition (Total Sports, 2001).

Thorn, John, Pete Palmer, and Joseph M. Wayman. "The History of Major League Baseball Statistics," *Total Baseball*, seventh edition (Total Sports Publishing, 2001).

Tygiel, Jules. *Past Time: Baseball as History* (Oxford University Press, 2000).

Veeck, Bill, with Ed Linn. *The Hustler's Handbook* (G. P. Putnam's Sons, 1965).

Voigt, David Q. *American Baseball, Volume 2* (University of Oklahoma Press, 1970).

———. *America Through Baseball* (Nelson Hall, 1976).

Waller, George. *Saratoga: Saga of an Impious Era* (Prentice-Hall, 1966).

Wallop, Douglass. *Baseball: An Informal History* (W. W. Norton, 1969).

Ward, Arch, ed. *The Greatest Sports Stories From the Chicago Tribune* (A. S. Barnes 1953).

Ward, Geoffrey C., and Ken Burns. *Baseball, An Illustrated History* (Knopf, 1994).

Werber, Bill, and C. Paul Rogers III. *Memories of a Ballplayer* (Society for American Baseball Research, 2001).

Will, George F. *Bunts: Curt Flood, Camden Yards, Pete Rose and Other Reflections on Baseball* (Scribner, 1998).

Williams, Peter, ed. *The Joe Williams Baseball Reader* (Algonquin Books of Chapel Hill, 1989).

Yardley, Jonathan. *Ring: A Biography of Ring Lardner* (Athenum, 1984).

ARTICLES

Algren, Nelson. "The Swede Was a Hard Guy," *Southern Review*, Spring 1942.

"Amnesty for Black Sox Third Baseman?" *Wall Street Journal*, January 17, 1992.

Anderson, William B. "Saving the National Pastime's Image: Crisis Management During the 1919 Black Sox Scandal," *Journalism History*, Fall 2001. (The year after Landis' ban, Major League Baseball developed a "press office to respond to media requests.")

Asinof, Eliot. "Baseball's Endless Cycle of Scandal," *New York Times*, March 9, 1986.

Bachin, Robin F. "At the Nexus of Labor and Leisure: Baseball, Nativism, and the 1919 Black Sox Scandal," *Journal of Social History*, Summer 2003, Vol. 36, Issue 4.

Barton, George. "Weaver's Role in Fixed Series," *Baseball Digest*, April 1956.

"Baseball Is Honest," *Collier's*, October 1920.

"The Baseball Scandal," editorial, *Nation*, October 13, 1920.

"The Basis of a Pitcher's Success," *Baseball Magazine*, December 1919/January 1920, an interview with Eddie Cicotte.

Bass, Mike. "Baseball," *Sporting News*, October 17, 1994.

Baxter, N. W. "In the Press Box," *Washington Post*, August 31, 1923.

Bennett, Jay. "Did Shoeless Joe Jackson Throw the 1919 World Series?" *American Statistician*, Vol. 47, No. 4, November 1993.

Bevill, Lynn. "Outlaw Baseball," *Cochise Quarterly*, Summer 1991. Cochise County Historical and Archeological Society, Douglas, AZ.

Bevis, Charlie. "The Evolution of World Series Scheduling," *Baseball Research Journal*, No. 31, Society for American Baseball Research, 2003.

Bisher, Furman. "This Is the Truth," *Sport*, October 1949.

Blaisdell, Lowell. "Legends as an Expression of Baseball Memory," *Journal of Sport History*, Vol. 19, No. 3, Winter 1992.

Bloom, David. "Dick Kerr, Breaking 17-Year Silence, Tells of '9 Series," *Sporting News*, February 25, 1935.

Boren, Steve. "The Bizarre Career of Rube Benton," *Baseball Research Journal*, Society for American Baseball Research, 1983.

Brenner, Marie. "The Enron Wars," *Vanity Fair*, April 2002.

Brown, J. L. "The Big Baseball Scandal," *American Mercury,* Vol. 47, No. 185, May 1939.

Burns, Ed. Untitled, *Sporting News*, November 28, 1940.

Camp, Walter. "The Truth About Baseball," *North American Review*, April 1921.

Carino, Peter. "Novels of the Black Sox Scandal: History/Fiction/Myth," *Nine: A Journal of Baseball History and Social Policy Perspectives*, Spring 1995.

Carmichael, John. "Chicago White Sox," No.10 in a *Major League Club History* series; this also appeared in *Sport*, June 1951.

Ceresi, Frank J. "Shoeless Joe Jackson: An Interview With Joe Anders," *The Vintage and Classic Baseball Collector*, July/August 1997.

Chapin, Dwight. "Gandil: 'I'll Go to My Grave With a Clear Conscience,'" *Sporting News*, September 6, 1969.

Comiskey, Charles A. "Comiskey Tells His Story of Black Sox and Feud With Ban," letter to *Cleveland Plain Dealer*, January 13, 1929.

Considine, Bob. "On the Line," *Washington Post*, October 1, 1939.

Creel, George. "Making the American League," *Saturday Evening Post*, March 22, 1930. As told to Creel by Ban Johnson.

Crusinberry, James. "A Newsman's Biggest Story," *Sports Illustrated*, September 17, 1956.

Daniel, Dan. "Black Sox Story Butchered in TV Show," *Sporting News*, February 8, 1961.

Dellinger, Susan. "A Shadow in the Night . . . The Graying of the White," in *Baseball in the Buckeye State*, a publication for the National Convention of the Society for American Baseball Research, Cincinnati, OH, July 2004 (Sports Publishing LLC).

Durslag, Mel. "This Is My Story of the Black Sox Series," *Sports Illustrated*, September 17, 1956. The experiences of Arnold "Chick" Gandil as told to Mel Durslag.

Falls, Joe. "Cicotte, 46 Years Later," *Detroit Free Press*, 1965. (Reprinted in *Baseball Digest*, February 1966).

Farrell, James T. "Freedom from Scandal," *New York Times*, August 18, 1974.

Feldman, Chic. Interview with Eddie Murphy in *Scrantonian* (Scranton, PA), September 13, 1959.

Flagler, J. M. "Requiem for a Southpaw," *New Yorker*, December 5, 1959.

"The Flaw in the Diamond," *Literary Digest*, October 9, 1920.

"Are Baseball Games Framed? The Inside Story of What Led Up to the Major League Scandals," *Liberty*, March 19, March 26, and April 2, 1927.

————. "Baseball on Trial," *New Republic*, October 1920.

"Comiskey Told Me in 1919 7 Players Were Crooked," *Chicago Journal*, September 29, 1920.

————. "Hugh S. Fullerton Vividly Describes the Full Details Of Great Baseball Scandal," *Atlanta Constitution*, October 3, 1920. (This is the same article that appeared days before in the Chicago *Journal*—with twelve paragraphs removed.)

————. "I Recall," *Sporting News*, October 17, 1935.

————. "Is Big League Baseball Being Run for Gamblers, With Players in the Deal?" December 15, 1919; "Scandal of World's Series Will Not Down; Here Is a Way to Settle It," December 17; "Comiskey Has Been On Point of Dropping Several Men," December 18; "Judge Landis Asked to Take Charge of Investigation," December 20; and "Wishes Baseball a Scandal-Less New Year," January 2, 1920, *New York Evening World*.

Galloway, Paul. "It Ain't So 68 Years Later, Fans Seek Pardon for Shoeless Joe," *Chicago Tribune*, North Sports Final Edition, October 20, 1988.

Gaughran, Richard. "Saying it Ain't So: The Black Sox Scandal in Baseball Fiction," *Cooperstown Symposium on Baseball and the American Culture* (1990), Alvin Hall, ed. (Meckler, 1991).

Gillespie, Ray. "St. Louis Policeman Recalls Details of Black Sox Case," *The Sporting News*, October 9, 1957.

Green, Paul. Interview with Happy Chandler, *Sports Collectors Digest*, circa 1983–84.

Hamilton, Jim. "Time to Set the Story Straight on Claude Hendrix," *Oneonta (NY) Daily Star*, June 1, 2002.

"Herrmann Ready to Act," *New York Times*, August 24, 1923.

Hynd, Alan. *True Detective*, November 1938.

Isaminger, James. "Gamblers Promised White Sox $100,000 to Lose," in *Philadelphia North American*, September 27, 1920. (Reprinted in *Baseball Digest*, October–November 1959.)

"James C. Isaminger Dies at Age 65," *Philadelphia Inquirer*, June 17, 1946.

Johnson, Dick. "Interview With John Sayles," *SABR Review of Books*, Vol. IV, 1989, Society for American Baseball Research.

Kermisch, Al. "From a Researcher's Notebook," *Baseball Research Journal* of the Society for American Baseball Research, No. 23, 1994, and No. 26, 1997.

Kieran, John. "Charley Comiskey, The Old Roman," *New York Times*, October 27, 1931.

Kilgallen, James L. "Here's the Inside Story of the Baseball Scandal," *Atlanta Constitution*, October 31, 1920.

————. "Zork Fixed Black Sox," *Atlanta Constitution*, July 23, 1921.

Klein, Frank O. "Collins Charges 1920 Games 'Fixed,'" *Collyer's Eye*, Vol. 6, No. 31, October 30, 1920.

Kirby, James. "The Year They Fixed the World Series," *American Bar Association Journal*, February 1, 1988.

Kuenster, John. "Warm Up Tosses," *Baseball Digest*, September 1970. (Interview with Ray Schalk.)

"Landis Is Asked to Sift Charges. Collyer Urges Investigation of His Story That Gamblers Approached Players," *New York Times*, August 25, 1923.

Lardner, John. "Reinstatement Plea Echoes Ball Scandal," *Los Angeles Times*, January 28, 1934.

———. "Remember the Black Sox?" *Saturday Evening Post*, April 30, 1938.

———. "The Riddle of Buck Weaver," *Newsweek*, February 27, 1956.

Lardner, Ring, Jr. "Foul Ball: John Sayles's *Eight Men Out*—Or, How My Father Watched the White Sox Throw the 1919 World Series," *American Film*, July/August 1988.

Latimer, Carter (Scoop). Interview with Joe Jackson. *Sporting News*, September 24, 1942.

Leonard, Jim. "Dissension Plagued '19 Flag Team," *Sporting News*, November 1, 1950. This is the fourth installment of Collins's life story as told to Jim Leonard.

Lieb, Fred. "Fullerton, Famed Forecaster, Named Spink Award Winner," *Sporting News*, November 7, 1964.

Linfield, Susan. "Studs Terkel: World Serious," *American Film*, July/August 1988.

Lord, Timothy C. "Hegel, Marx and Shoeless Joe: Religious Ideology in Kinsella's Baseball Fantasy," *Aethlon*, Fall 1992.

"Making the 'Black Sox' White Again," *Literary Digest*, August 1921.

Menke, Frank G. "Elevated Upon the Shoulders of Wrong and Rebellion." *Sporting News*, January 31, 1924

———. "Judge Gregory Mourned; Funeral to Be Saturday," November 30, 1939.

———. "Menke Details Startling Revelations at Jackson's Suit Against White Sox," *Sporting News*, April 24, 1924.

———. "Menke Writes Another Chapter in White Sox Scandal Investigation." *Sporting News*, April 17, 1924.

———. "What Became of $10,000 Reward Comiskey Offered for Discovery of World Series Crookedness?" *Sporting News*, April 10, 1924.

Miles, Bruce. "Black Sox Scandal: Misunderstood Chapter in Baseball History," *Chicago Daily Herald*, October 27, 1994.

Mullin, John. "Comiskey Rewarded Pals With Sox-Giants World Tours," *Chicago Tribune*, March 30, 1998.

"Mystery Man in Sox Case Tells Hunt for Burns," *Chicago Times*, July 24, 1921.

Nathan, Daniel A. "Anti-Semitism and the Black Sox Scandal," *Nine*, Vol. 4, No. 1, Fall 1995.

Obenshain, Earl. "Famous Baseball Feud Between Ban and Comiskey Arose Over Jack Quinn Deal," *Cleveland Plain Dealer*, January 7, 1929. This was the sixth article in a series that appeared weekly, starting on December

3, 1928. Obenshain wrote ten articles in the series in 1928-1929.

Outlook, "For Honest Baseball," editorial, October 1920.

Pappas, Doug. "The Centennial of Modern Organized Baseball," *Outside the Lines*, Business of Baseball Committee Newsletter of the Society of American Baseball Research, Vol. IX, No. 3, Summer 2003.

Pegler, Westbrook. "Fair Enough/ Those Black Sox," *Washington Post*, October 4, 1939.

———. "Fair Enough/World Series Memoirs," *Washington Post*, September 30, 1941.

Povich, Shirley. "This Morning/Say It Ain't So, Joe," *Washington Post*, April 11, 1941.

"Record Betting Cause of Alarm, Starts Scandal," *Chicago Times*, October 5, 1919.

Reichler, Joseph. "The Black Sox Scandal," *The World Series: A 75th Anniversary* (Simon & Schuster, 1978).

Robinson, Ray. "No Glory in Winning What Others Lost," *New York Times*, October 7, 1984.

Rosenthal, Harold. "The Scandalous Black Sox," *Sport*, October 1959.

Runyon, Damon. "Attell Keeps Secret of Big Sport Scandal," *Washington Post*, October 4, 1939.

Salsinger, H. G. "Ed Cicotte Crossed His Detroit Friends," *Sporting News*, October 7, 1920.

Sanborn, Irving E. "The Slimy Trail of the Baseball Pool," *Baseball Magazine*, July 1925.

Schaap, Dick. "Say It Ain't So, Joe," *Coronet*, September 1960.

Sheed, Wilfrid. "One Man Out . . . Too Long," *GQ*, August 1990.

Sheridan, John B. "Back of the Home Plate," *The Sporting News*, October 7, 1920.

Simons, Herbert. "How the 1919 Series Was Thrown," *Baseball Digest*, October/November 1959.

"Sleepy Bill Burns Caught Napping in Series Sell-Out," *The Sporting News*, October 21, 1920.

Smith, Red. "Black Sox, Orioles: Different Outlooks," *Washington Post*, September 29, 1971.

February 10, 1921. Untitled, uncredited report on Philadelphia interview with Eddie Collins and reactions. Same issue, untitled editorial on Judge Charles A. MacDonald.

———. February 21, 1924. Untitled editorial.

St. Louis *Post-Dispatch*, "Gambling World Mourns Henry Becker, Capitalist," April 16, 1919.

Stein, Irving. "Buck Weaver: An Innocent Victim of 1919 Scandal," *Baseball Digest*, March 1990.

Swope, Tom. "I Recall," *Sporting News*, October 24, 1935.

Taylor, C. B. "Ray Schalk Talks Himself Into Trouble About Seven Members of the White Sox," *Savannah Morning News*, January 10, 1920.

Thompson, Lewis, and Charles Boswell. "Say It Ain't So, Joe!" *American Heritage*, June 1960.

Twombly, Wells. "The Last Days of Chick Gandil," *The Sporting News*, March 20, 1971.

Vaughan, Irving. "Little New Shown in Jackson's Suit," *The Sporting News*, February 7, 1924.

———. "Thirty-Four Years in Baseball—The Story of Ban Johnson's Life," *Chicago Tribune*, February 24, March 3, and March 10, 1929.

———. Untitled column, *The Sporting News*, February 21, 1921.

Vintage and Classic Baseball Collector, March 1995. Reprint of the play-by-play of the 1919 World Series from *Spalding Guide*.

Walsh, Paul. "Gandil and Risberg: The Last of the Black Sox," *Minneapolis Star Tribune*, September 25, 1994.

Weir, Hugh C. "The Real Comiskey," *Baseball Magazine*, February 1914.

Wheeler, John N. "Ring Lardner," *Collier's*, March 17, 1928.

"When Baseball Gets Before the Grand Jury," *The Sporting News*, October 7, 1920.

"Where Jackson Goes Williams Follows," *The Sporting News,* March 13, 1919.

Williams, Joe "By Joe Williams," *New York World-Telegram*, October 3, 1939.

———. "By Joe Williams," newspaper unknown, May 25, 1944.

———. Column title unknown. *New York World-Telegram*, September 24, 1959.

———. "Dickie Kerr Discusses the Black Sox," *New York World-Telegram*, June 25, 1949.

Williams, Ted. "It's Time to Open the Door," *National Pastime No. 18*, Society for American Baseball Research, 1998.

Wray, John E., and J. Roy Stockton. "Ban Johnson's Own Story," *St. Louis Post-Dispatch*, February 10 through March 3, 1929.

NEWSPAPERS

Besides the articles noted above, the *New York Times*, *Chicago Times*, *Los Angeles Times*, *Chicago Herald and Examiner*, *St. Louis Post-Dispatch*, *Washington Post*, *Atlanta Constitution*, *Toronto World*, and the *Savannah Morning News* were consulted, as well as *The Sporting News* and *Baseball Magazine*. The *Milwaukee Journal* coverage of the trial of Joe Jackson vs. Chicago White Sox, January and February, 1924, was very useful. The coverage of the scandal in the *National Police Gazette* was not.

PAPERS

Black Sox Scandal (American League). A. Bartlett Giamatti Research Center, National Baseball Hall of Fame and Museum, Cooperstown, NY.

Christian, Ralph J. "Beyond Eight Men Out: The Des Moines Connection to the Black Sox Scandal," presentation at the 2003 National Convention of the Society for American Baseball Research, Denver, CO, July 2003.

The Harold and Dorothy Seymour papers, #4809. Division of Rare and Manuscript Collections, Cornell (NY) University.

Joe Jackson vs. Chicago White Sox, Milwaukee, WI, January/February 1924. Trial transcript and related documents, Courtesy of Thomas G. Cannon, Attorney at Law.

Klein, Steve. "Hugh S. Fullerton, the Black Sox Scandal, and the Ethical Impulse in Sports Writing." Masters Thesis, Michigan State University, 1997.

Legal briefs from the 1923 libel lawsuit brought by the Cincinnati Reds against the Chicago-based newspaper *Collyer's Eye.* National Baseball Library, Cooperstown, NY.

Lerach, William S. "Plundering America: How Wall Street, the Big Accounting Firms, and Corporate Interests Chloroformed Congress and Cost America's Investors Trillions," commencement speech delivered May 22, 2003, at the University of Pittsburgh Law School.

Schuld, Fred. "Chick Gandil: Before the Black Sox Scandal," presented at the Seymour Medal Conference of the Society for American Baseball Research, Cleveland, OH, April 17, 1999.

WEBSITES

NOTE: Some of these sites may no longer be available.

http://1919blacksox.com/memorabilia.htm Eddie Cicotte's 1919 contract sold for $6,750 in August 2002; a year earlier, Jackson's "Black Betsy" bat fetched $577,610.

www.thediamondangle.com/marasco/hist.html "Cicotte's 29 Wins in 1919" by David Marasco.

www.deadball.com/cicotte.htm Relative of Cicotte says wife was threatened, too.

http://bioproj.sabr.org/bioproj.cfm?a=v&v=1&bid=707&pid=4328Nitz, James. "Happy Felsch," Web site of the Society for American Baseball Research, Bioproject 2003.

http://www.law.umkc.edu/faculty/projects/ftrials/blacksox/inquotes.html Famous Trials website, Douglas O. Linder. Its "findagrave" link leads to biographies, including Abe Attell's.

www.gingerkid.com Devoted to Buck Weaver, "The Ginger Kid."

www.rootsweb.com/~argreene/dickkidkerr.htm More on Dickie Kerr.

BaseballLibrary.com Baseball biographies, including Tom Swope's. Also, see Harvey Frommer's book *Shoeless Joe Remains a Scapegoat.*

www.pubdim.net/baseballlibrary/excerpts/elden_auker4.stm Review of *Sleeper Cars and Flannel Uniforms* by Elden Auker.

www.wikpedia.org/wiki/Black+Sox+scandal A handy summary.

www.nelsonalgren.com If you enjoy *The Last Carousel*, here's more on Nelson Algren. His take on the scandal is highly original.

www.haroldseymour.com Baseball history kept alive by Dorothy Mills Seymour. Dorothy also edits several e-newsletters.

www.blackbetsy.com A treasure trove of facts and opinions. The site also has numerous links, including *The Shoeless Joe Jackson Times*. This site is one place you can look up Joe's testimony.

www.baseballreliquary.org Joe Jackson is in The Shrine of the Eternals.

www.amazon.com/exec/obidos/ for link to *Baseball: The Biographical Encyclopedia*, by David Pietrusza, Matt Silvermann, Michael Gershman (TotalSports).

www.baseball-almanac.com/ws/vrl1919ws.shtml Sean Holtz's The Baseball Almanac is one of the sites where Jackson's grand jury testimony appears in full.

www.baseball1.com Sean Lahman's The Baseball Archive is the home of "Notes from the Shadows of Cooperstown."

www.mc.cc.md.us/Departments/hpolscrv/blacksox.htm This site is run maintained by Montgomery College in Maryland. Be sure to have your audio on.

http://caselaw.lp.findlaw.com/scripts/getcase.pl?court=US&vol=259&invol=200 For 1922 ruling on baseball's antitrust exemption.

www.memory.loc.gov/ammem/ndlpcoop/ichihtml/cdnhome.html Thousands of photos from the archives of the *Chicago Daily News*.

http://espn.go.com/classic/s/black_sox_moments.html Information on the ESPN Classic documentary and an article by Eliot Asinof.

http://www.reallegends.com/auctions/joe_history/page4.html Has a detailed description of Jackson's bats, including Black Betsy.

http://thedeadballera.crosswinds.net/JacksonJoesGrave.html Pictures of Joe Jackson's gravesite and *New York Times* obituary.

www.baseballimmortals.net/Jackson_Joe/jackson—innocent.shtml "Joe Jackson—Innocent of Any Wrongdoing in the 1919 World Series."

www.h-net.msu.edu/~arete/ See Trey Strecker's review of Daniel A. Nathan's *Saying It's So*.

www.davidpietrusza.com/Rothstein-Chronology.html An Arnold Rothstein chronology, including his role in the Big Fix.

www.blueear.com/library.cfm "The Lone Horseman of Baseball's Apocalypse" [Hugh Fullerton] by Steve Klein.

www.historicbaseball.com/scplayers/jacksonmedia.html "Hugh Fullerton and the Press' Revealing Coverage of the Black Sox Scandal, 1919–1921," by Shaun Payne.

VIDEOS

The Black Sox Scandal, documentary, ESPN Classic, 2001.

The Chicago White Sox: A Visual History, produced by Major League Baseball via Phoenix Community Group, 1987.

Eight Men Out, Orion Home Video, 1988.

"The Faith of Fifty Million People," *Baseball, Inning 3,* Ken Burns. BMG Video, 1994.

The Trial of Buck Weaver and Joe Jackson, Chicago Lincoln and Chicago American Inns of Court, 1992.

Witness, "The Trial of Joe Jackson," episode aired January 28, 1961, CBS-TV.

"World Series Fixed!" The Black Sox Scandal, documentary, The History Channel, 1997.

OTHER

The Eugene C. Murdock Baseball Collection, Cleveland Public Library, Cleveland, OH. Audiocassettes of interviews taped from 1973 to 1976 with Red Faber, Larry Kopf, Bibb Falk, and Edd Roush.

Major League Baseball transaction card collection, donated to the National Baseball Library, Cooperstown, NY. Each player has a card with a record of team, salary, and bonuses; any exceptions to the standard player contracts are noted.

INDEX

ABOUT THE AUTHOR

GENE CARNEY has written about baseball since 1989. He is the author of *Romancing the Horsehide: Baseball Poems on Players and the Game* and numerous articles, reviews, poems, essays, and short fiction in publications ranging from *USA Today's Baseball Weekly* to academic journals and small magazines. Since 1993 he has edited the newsletter "Notes from the Shadows of Cooperstown," which moved to the Internet in 1999.

A member of SABR since 1991, Carney headed a panel on the 1919 World Series at the 2004 national SABR convention, appeared on ESPN programming regarding the Black Sox in May 2005, and presented his baseball play "Mornings After" at the 2005 national SABR convention. A native of Pittsburgh, he lives in Utica, New York.